WORSHIP IN THE EARLY CHURCH

WORSHIP IN THE EARLY CHURCH

An Anthology of Historical Sources

Volume Four

Lawrence J. Johnson

A PUEBLO BOOK

Liturgical Press Collegeville, Minnesota

www.litpress.org

A Pueblo Book published by Liturgical Press

Cover design by David Manahan, OSB

Library of Congress Cataloging-in-Publication Data

Johnson, Lawrence J., 1933–
    Worship in the early church : an anthology of historical sources / Lawrence J. Johnson.
        p.   cm.
    "A Pueblo book."
    Includes index.
    ISBN 978-0-8146-6197-0 (v. 1) — ISBN 978-0-8146-6198-7 (v. 2) — ISBN 978-0-8146-6199-4 (v. 3) — ISBN 978-0-8146-6226-7 (v. 4)
    1. Worship—History—Early church, ca. 30–600.   2. Church history—Primitive and early church, ca. 30–600.   I. Title.
    BV6.J64   2009
    264.00937—dc22

                                       2009035344

Contents

Chapter XII. Sixth Century. East   197

Abbreviations

Prov	Proverbs	2 Thess	2 Thessalonians
Ps/Pss	Psalms	1 Tim	1 Timothy
Rev	Revelation	2 Tim	2 Timothy
Rom	Romans	Titus	Titus
Ruth	Ruth	Tob	Tobit
1 Sam	1 Samuel	Wis	Wisdom
2 Sam	2 Samuel	Zech	Zechariah
Sir	Sirach	Zeph	Zephaniah
1 Thess	1 Thessalonians		

PERIODICALS AND BOOKS MOST FREQUENTLY CITED

AB	*Analecta Bollandiana* (Brussels, 1882ff.).
ABR	*American Benedictine Review* (Atchison, KS, 1950ff.).
AC	*Antike und Christentum* (Münster, 1929–50).
AER	*American Ecclesiastical Review* (Washington, D.C., 1889–1975).
Altaner (1961)	B. Altaner, *Patrology*, trans. H.C. Graef, 2nd ed. (New York, 1961).
Altaner (1966)	B. Altaner, *Patrologie. Leben, Schriften und Lehre der Kirchenväter*, 6th ed., rev. A. Stüber (Freiburg/Basel/ Vienna, 1966).
Altaner (1978)	B. Altaner, *Patrologie. Leben, Schriften und Lehre der Kirchenväter*, 8th ed., rev. A. Stüber (Freiburg/Basel/ Vienna, 1978).
ALW	*Archiv für Liturgiewissenschaft* (Regensburg, 1950ff.).
Amb	*Ambrosius* (Milan, 1925–60).
ANF	A. Roberts and J. Donaldson, eds., *The Ante-Nicene Fathers: Translations of the Writings of the Fathers down to* A.D. *325* (New York, 1885, 1926).
Ant	*Antonianum* (Rome, 1926ff.).
APB	*Acta Patristica et Byzantina* (Praetoria, 1990ff.).
ApT	*Apostolic Tradition.*
Assem	*Assembly* (Notre Dame, 1974ff.).
AThR	*Anglican Theological Review* (New York, 1918ff.).
Aug	*Augustinianum* (Rome, 1961ff.).
AugMag	*Augustus Magister*, Congrès international augustinien (Paris, Sept. 21–24, 1954). Vols. I and II: *Communications*; vol. III: *Acts.*
BALAC	*Bulletin d'ancienne littérature et d'archéologie chrétienne* (Paris, 1911–14).

Bardenhewer (1908)	O. Bardenhewer, *Patrology: The Lives and Works of the Fathers of the Church*, trans. T.J. Shahan (Freiburg i. B./ St. Louis, 1908).
Bardenhewer (1910)	O. Bardenhewer, *Patrologie* (Freiburg i. B., 1910).
Bardenhewer (1913)	O. Bardenhewer, *Geschichte der altkirchlichen Literatur*, 5 vols. (Freiburg i. B./St. Louis, 1913–32).
Bardy (1929)	G. Bardy, *The Greek Literature of the Early Christian Church*, trans. Mother Mary Reginald, Catholic Library of Religious Knowledge 2 (St. Louis, 1929).
Bardy (1930)	G. Bardy, *The Christian Latin Literature of the First Six Centuries*, trans. Mother Mary Reginald, Catholic Library of Religious Knowledge 12 (St. Louis, 1930).
Bautz	F.W. Bautz, ed., *Biographisch-bibliographisches Kirchenlexikon* (Hamm Westf., 1970ff.).
BCE	*Bulletin du comité des études* (Paris, 1953–70).
Bib	*Biblica* (Rome, 1920ff.).
BLE	*Bulletin de littérature ecclésiastique* (Toulouse, 1899ff.).
Bouyer	L. Bouyer, *Eucharist: Theology and Spirituality of the Eucharistic Prayer* (Notre Dame, 1968).
BT	*The Bible Today* (Collegeville, 1962ff.).
BVC	*Bible et vie chrétienne* (Brussels/Paris, 1953–68).
CA	*Cahiers archéologiques* (Paris, 1945ff.).
Campbell	J.M. Campbell, *The Greek Fathers*, Our Debt to Greece and Rome series (New York, 1929).
CATH	G. Jacquemet, ed., *Catholicisme*, 9 vols. (Paris, 1947ff.).
CB	*Collationes Brugenses* (Bruges, 1896–1954).
CC	*La Civiltà Cattolica* (Rome, 1850ff.).
CCL	*Corpus Christianorum, Series Latina* (Turnhout, 1954ff.).
CE	*Catholic Encyclopedia*, 13 vols. + index (New York, 1907–14).
CH	*Church History* (Chicago and Tallahassee, 1932ff.).
CHECL	F. Young, L. Ayres, and A. Louth, eds., *The Cambridge History of Early Christian Literature* (Cambridge, 2004).
ChQ	*Church Quarterly Review* (London, 1875–1968).
Chr	*Christus* (Paris, 1954ff.).
CollMech	*Collectanea Mechliniensia* (Mechlin, 1927–70).
ComL	*Communautés et liturgies* (Ottignies, 1975ff.).
Con	*Concilium* (Glen Rock, NJ, etc., 1965ff.).
Courtonne	Y. Courtonne, ed., *Saint Basile: Lettres*, 3 vols. (Paris, 1957, 1961, 1966).
CPG	M. Geerard and F. Glorie, eds., *Clavis Patrum Graecorum*, 5 vols. (Turnhout, 1974–87).

CPGS	M. Geerard and others, eds., *Clavis Patrum Graecorum Supplementum* (Turnhout, 1998).
Cph	*Classical Philology* (Chicago, 1906ff.).
CPL	E. Dekkers and A. Gaar, eds., *Clavis Patrum Latinorum*, 3rd ed. (Turnhout/Steebrugge, 1995).
CR	*The Clergy Review* (London, 1931–87).
CRI	*Comptes-rendus de l'Académie des Inscriptions et Belles Lettres* (Paris, 1857ff.).
Cross	F.L. Cross, *The Early Christian Fathers* (London, 1960).
CS	*Chicago Studies* (Mundelein, IL, 1962ff.).
CSEL	Corpus Scriptorum Ecclesiasticorum Latinorum (Vienna, 1866ff.).
CV	G.M. Diez, *Concilios visigóticos e hispano-romanos* (Barcelona/Madrid, 1963).
DACL	F. Cabrol and H. Leclercq, eds., *Dictionnaire d'archéologie chrétienne et de liturgie*, 15 vols. (Paris, 1913–53).
DCA	W. Smith, ed., *A Dictionary of Christian Antiquities*, 2 vols. (London, 1876–80).
DCB	W. Smith and H. Wace, eds., *A Dictionary of Christian Biography, Literature, Sects and Doctrines*, 4 vols. (London, 1877–87).
DDC	R. Naz and others, eds., *Dictionnaire de droit canonique*, 7 vols. (Paris, 1935–65).
DDCon	P. Palazzini, ed., *Dizionario dei Concili*, 6 vols. (Rome, 1963–67).
DEC	N.P. Tanner, ed., *Decrees of the Ecumenical Councils* (London/Washington, D.C., 1990).
Deiss	L. Deiss, *Springtime of the Liturgy: Liturgical Texts of the First Four Centuries* (Collegeville, 1979).
DGA	P.-P. Joannou, ed., *Disciplina Generale Antique* (Rome, 1962).
DHGE	A. Baudrillart, ed., *Dictionnaire d'histoire et de géographie ecclésiastiques* (Paris, 1912ff.).
DictSp	M. Viller and others, eds., *Dictionnaire de spiritualité ascétique et mystique* (Paris, 1937ff.).
Did	*Didache.*
Didas	*Didascalia Apostolorum.*
Di Sante	C. di Sante, *Jewish Prayer: The Origins of the Christian Liturgy*, trans. M.J. O'Connell (New York, 1991).
Div	*Divinitas* (Vatican City, 1957ff.).
Dix	G. Dix, *The Shape of the Liturgy*, 4th ed. (Westminster, 1949).
DLW	J.G. Davies, ed., *A Dictionary of Liturgy and Worship* (New York, 1972).
Dolbeau	F. Dolbeau, ed., *Vingt-six sermons au peuple d'Afrique / Augustin d'Hippone; retrouvés à Mayence*, Collection des études augustiniennes, Série Antiquité 147 (Paris, 1996).
DPAC	A. di Berardino, ed., *Dizionario Patristico e di Antichità Cristiane*, 3 vols. (Marietti, 1983–88).

DR	*Downside Review* (Bath, England, 1880ff.).
DT	*Divus Thomas* (Fribourg i. S., 1871–1953).
DTC	A. Vacant, E. Mangenot, and E. Amann, eds., *Dictionnaire de théologie catholique*, 15 vols. (Paris, 1903–50).
DV	*Dieu vivant* (Paris, 1945–55).
EC	P. Paschini and others, eds., *Enciclopedia Cattolica*, 12 vols. (Vatican City, 1949–54).
ED	*Euntes Docete* (Rome, 1948ff.).
EEC	A. di Berardino, ed., *Encyclopedia of the Early Church*, trans. A. Walford, with a foreword and bibliographic amendments by W.H.C. Frend, 2 vols. (New York, 1992).
EEChr	E. Ferguson, ed., *Encyclopedia of Early Christianity*, 2 vols., 2nd ed. (New York, 1997).
EgT	*Eglise et théologie* (Ottawa, 1970–99).
Elbogen (1962)	I. Elbogen, *Der jüdische Gottesdienst in seiner geschichtlichen Entwicklung*, 4th ed. (Hildesheim, 1962).
Elbogen (1993)	I. Elbogen, *Jewish Liturgy: A Comprehensive History*, trans. R.P. Scheindlin (Philadelphia/New York, 1993).
EO	*Echos d'Orient* (Paris, 1897–1942).
EOr	*Ecclesia Orans* (Rome, 1984ff.).
EphL	*Ephemerides Liturgicae* (Rome, 1887ff.).
ERP	*Etudes religieuses, philosophiques, historiques, et litteraires* (Paris, 1888–1940).
EstAg	*Estudio Teologico Augustiniano* (Valladolid, Spain, 1973ff.).
Et	*Etudes* (Paris, 1897ff.).
ETL	*Ephemerides Theologicae Lovanienses* (Louvain, 1924ff.).
ETR	*Etudes théologiques et religieuses* (Montpellier, 1926ff.).
ExpT	*The Expository Times* (Edinburgh, 1889ff.).
FF	*France franciscaine* (Lille, 1912–29).
FLDG	Forschungen zur christliche Literatur- und Dogmengeschichte (Mainz/Paderborn, 1910–38).
Folia	*Folia. Studies in the Christian Perpetuation of the Classics* (Worcester, MA, 1959–79).
FThSt	Freiburger theologische Studien (Freiburg i. B., 1910ff.).
FZPT	*Freiburger Zeitschrift für Philosophie und Theologie* (Fribourg i. S., 1954ff.).
GCS	Die griechischen christlichen Schriftsteller der ersten (drei) Jahrhunderte (Berlin, 1897ff.).
Goodspeed	E. J. Goodspeed, *A History of Early Christian Literature*, rev. and enl. R. Grant (Chicago, 1966).
GOTR	*Greek Orthodox Theological Review* (Brookline, MA, 1954ff.).
Greg	*Gregorianum* (Rome, 1920ff.).

Hamell	P.J. Hamell, *Handbook of Patrology* (New York, 1968).
Hänggi	A. Hänggi and I. Pahl, *Prex Eucharistica: Textus e Variis Liturgicis Antiquioribus Selecti* (Fribourg i. S., 1968).
Harp	*Harp: A Review of Syriac and Oriental Studies* (Kerala, India, 1987–2000).
Hefele (1905)	C.J. Hefele, *Histoire des conciles d'après les documents originaux*, trans. H. Leclercq, 11 vols. (Paris, 1905–52).
Hefele (1871)	C.J. Hefele, *A History of the Councils of the Church: From the Original Documents*, trans. W.R. Clark and H.N. Oxenham, 5 vols. (Edinburgh, 1871–96).
HS	*Hispania sacra* (Madrid, 1948ff.).
HThR	*Harvard Theological Review* (New York, 1908–9; Cambridge, MA, 1910ff.).
Idelsohn	A.Z. Idelsohn, *Jewish Liturgy and Its Development* (New York, 1967).
IER	*Irish Ecclesiastical Record* (Dublin, 1864–1968).
Imp	*Impacts: Revue de l'Université catholique de l'Ouest* (Angers, 1967ff.).
Ire	*Irénikon* (Amay, 1926ff.).
Ist	*Istina* (Paris, 1954ff.).
ITQ	*Irish Theological Quarterly* (Dublin, 1906–22; Maynooth, 1951ff.).
Jasper	R.C.D. Jasper and G.J. Cuming, *Prayers of the Eucharist: Early and Reformed*, 3rd rev. ed. (Collegeville, 1992).
JBL	*Journal of Biblical Literature* (Boston/New Haven, 1890ff.).
JECS	*Journal of Early Christian Studies* (Baltimore, 1993ff.).
JEH	*The Journal of Ecclesiastical History* (London, 1950ff.).
Jeremias (1960)	J. Jeremias, *Die Abendmahlsworte Jesu*, 3rd. ed. (Göttingen, 1960).
Jeremias (1966)	J. Jeremias, *The Eucharistic Words of Jesus*, trans. N. Perrin (London, 1966).
JL	*Jahrbuch für Liturgiewissenschaft* (Münster, 1921–41).
JLH	*Jahrbuch für Liturgie und Hymnologie* (Kassel, 1955ff.).
JQR	*The Jewish Quarterly Review* (London, 1889–94; New York, 1896–1908).
JR	*The Journal of Religion* (Chicago, 1921ff.).
JThSt	*The Journal of Theological Studies* (London, 1900–1905; Oxford, 1906–49; n.s. 1950ff.).
JucL	*Jucunda Laudatio* (Milan, 1963ff.).
Jurgens	W.A. Jurgens, *The Faith of the Early Fathers*, 3 vols. (Collegeville, 1970–79).
Kat	*Katholik: Zeitschrift für katholische Wissenschaft und kirchliches Leben* (Mainz, 1821–89).

Labriolle (1947)	P.C. de Labriolle, *Histoire de la littérature latine chrétienne*, 3rd rev. ed. (Paris, 1947).
Labriolle (1968)	P.C. de Labriolle, *History and Literature of Christianity from Tertullian to Boethius*, trans. H. Wilson, History of Civilization (New York, 1968).
LAC	*L'Ami du clergé* (Langres, France, 1888–1968).
Latomus	*Latomus. Revue d'études latines* (Brussels, 1937ff.).
Lau	*Laurentianum* (Rome, 1960ff.).
Leigh-Bennett	E. Leigh-Bennett, *Handbook of the Early Christian Fathers* (London, 1920).
LJ	*Liturgisches Jahrbuch* (Münster, 1951ff.).
LMD	*La Maison-Dieu* (Paris, 1945ff.).
LMF	*Le messager des fidèles* (Mardesous, 1884–89).
LNPF	P. Schaff and H. Wace, eds., *A Select Library of Nicene and Post-Nicene Fathers of the Christian Church* (repr. Grand Rapids, 1951ff.).
LO	Lex Orandi (Paris, 1944–71).
LQF	Liturgiegeschichtliche Quellen und Forschungen (Münster i. W., 1918–39).
LThPh	*Laval théologique et philosophique* (Quebec, 1970–82).
LTK	W. Kasper and others, eds., *Lexikon für Theologie und Kirche*, 11 vols., 3rd ed. (Freiburg i. B., 1993–2001).
LV	*Lumière et vie* (Bruges, 1951–60).
LWP	*Liturgical Week Proceedings, North American*
LwQF	Liturgiewissenschaftliche Quellen und Forschungen (Münster i. W., 1919–2005).
LXX	Septuagint.
Mansi	J.D. Mansi, ed., *Sacrorum Conciliorum Nova et Amplissima Collectio*, 31 vols. (Florence, 1759–98).
Mel	*Melto. Melta. Recherches orientales* (Kaslik, Liban, 1965–69).
Millgram	A.E. Millgram, *Jewish Worship* (Philadelphia, 1971).
MilS	*Milltown Studies* (Dublin, 1978ff.).
Mnem	*Mnemosyne: Bibliotheca classica Batava* (Leyden, 1852ff.).
MRR-1	J. Jungmann, *The Mass of the Roman Rite: Its Origins and Development (Missarum Sollemnia)*, trans. F.A. Brunner, 2 vols. (New York, 1951).
MRR-2	J. Jungmann, *The Mass of the Roman Rite: Its Origins and Development (Missarum Sollemnia)*, trans. F.A. Brunner, rev. C.K. Riepe (New York, 1959).
MS	*Mediaeval Studies* (Toronto, 1939ff.).
MSR	*Mélanges de science religieuse* (Lille, 1944ff.).
Mus	*Le Muséon* (Louvain, 1882–1916, 1921ff.).

NCE	*New Catholic Encyclopedia*, 14 vols. + index (New York, 1967) + 3 supplementary vols. 16–18 (1974–89).
NCES	*New Catholic Encyclopedia, Second Edition*, 15 vols. (Detroit/ Washington, D.C., 2003).
NDSW	P.E. Fink, ed., *The New Dictionary of Sacramental Worship* (Collegeville, 1990).
Not	*Notitiae* (Rome, 1965ff.).
NRTh	*Nouvelle revue théologique* (Tournai, 1869–1913, 1920–39, 1945ff.).
NTes	Novum Testamentum (Leiden, 1956ff.).
NTS	New Testament Studies (London, 1954ff.).
NWDLW	J.G. Davies, ed., *The New Westminster Dictionary of Liturgy and Worship* (Philadelphia, 1986).

OC	Oriens Christianus (Wiesbaden, 1931–39, 1953ff.).
OCA	Orientalia Christiana Analecta (Rome, 1935ff.).
OCP	*Orientalia Christiana Periodica* (Rome, 1935ff.).
ODCC	F.L. Cross, *The Oxford Dictionary of the Christian Church*, 3rd ed., ed. E.A. Livingstone (New York, 1997).
Oesterley (1911)	W.O.E. Oesterley, *The Religion and Worship of the Synagogue*, 2nd ed. (London, 1911).
Oesterley (1925)	W.O.E. Oesterley, *The Jewish Background of the Christian Liturgy* (Oxford, 1925).
OLZ	*Orientalische Literaturzeitung* (Berlin, 1909ff.).
OrSyr	*L'Orient syrien* (Paris, 1956ff.).
OstkSt	*Ostkirchliche Studien* (Würzburg, 1952ff.).

ParL	*Paroisse et liturgie* (Bruges, 1946–74).
PB	*Pastor Bonus* (Trier, 1889–1943).
PEA (1894)	A.F. von Pauly, *Paulys Real-encyclopädie der classischen Altertumswissenschaft* (Stuttgart, 1894–1919).
PEA (1991)	H. Cancik and H. Schneider, eds., *Der neue Pauly. Enzyklopädie der Antike* (Stuttgart, 1991ff.).
PG	J.P. Migne, *Patrologia Graeca*, 162 vols. (Paris, 1857–66).
PhW	*Philologische Wockenschrift* (Leipzig, 1881–1940).
PL	J.P. Migne, *Patrologia Latina*, 221 vols. (Paris, 1844–64).
PLS	J.P. Migne, *Patrologiae Cursus Completus. Series Latina Supplementum*, ed. A. Hamman (Paris, 1958ff.).
PO	*Parole de l'Orient. Melto dmadnho* (Kaslik, Lebanon, 1970ff.).
PP	*Parole et pain* (Paris, 1964–73).
PrO	*Présence orthodox* (Paris, 1967–81).
PrOChr	*Proche-orient chrétien* (Jerusalem, 1951ff.).

QL	*Questions liturgiques* (Louvain, 1970ff.).
QLP	*Questions liturgiques et paroissiales* (Louvain, 1919–69).

Quasten | J. Quasten, *Patrology*, 4 vols. (Westminster, MD, 1962ff.). (Vol. 4, 1986, is a translation of vol. 3 of *Patrologia*, ed. A. di Berardino.)

RAC | *Rivista di Archeologia Cristiana* (Rome, 1924ff.).
RACh | *Reallexikon für Antike und Christentum*, ed. T. Klauser (Leipzig, 1950ff.).
RAM | *Revue d'ascétique et de mystique* (Toulouse, 1920–71).
RAp | *Revue pratique d'apologétique* (Paris, 1905–21).
RAug | *Recherches augustiniennes* (Paris, 1958ff.).
RB | *Revue bénédictine* (Maredsous, 1890ff.).
RBibl | *Revue biblique internationale* (Paris, 1891ff.; n.s. 1904ff.).
RBPh | *Revue belge de philologie et d'histoire* (Brussels, 1922ff.).
RCF | *Revue du clergé francais* (Paris, 1894–1920).
RCT | *Revista catalana de teología* (Barcelona, 1976–88, 1990ff.).
RDC | *Revue de droit canonique* (Strasbourg, 1951ff.).
REAug | *Revue des études augustiniennes* (Paris, 1955ff.).
REF | *Revue d'histoire de l'Eglise de France* (Paris, 1910ff.).
REG | *Revue des études grecques* (Paris, 1888ff.).
REJ | *Revue des études juives* (Paris, 1880ff.).
REL | *Revue ecclésiastique de Liège* (Liège, 1905–67).
RELA | *Revue des études latines* (Paris, 1923ff.).
Res | *Résurrection* (Paris, 1956–63).
ResQ | *Restoration Quarterly* (Abilene, TX, 1957ff.).
RET | *Revista española de teología* (Madrid, 1940ff.).
RevAgusEsp | *Revista augustiniana de Espiritualidad* (Calahorra, Spain, 1960–79).
RevAug | *Revue augustinienne* (Louvain, 1901–10).
RevSR | *Revue des sciences religieuses* (Strasbourg, 1921ff.).
RHE | *Revue d'histoire ecclésiastique* (Louvain, 1900ff.).
RHL | *Revue d'histoire et de littérature religieuse* (Paris, 1896–1922).
RHPR | *Revue d'histoire et de philosophie religieuses* (Strasbourg, 1921ff.).
RIT | *Revue internationale de théologie* (Berne, 1893–1910).
RivAM | *Rivista di Ascetica et Mistica* (Florence, 1956ff.).
RL | *Rivista Liturgica* (Turin, 1914ff.).
Rocz | *Rocznik theologico-kanoninczne* (Lublin, Poland, 1949–90).
RPLH | *Revue de philologie, de littérature et d'histoire anciennes* (Paris, 1845–47; n.s. 1877–1926; 3. s. 1927ff.).
RQ | *Römische Quartelschrift für christliche Altertumskunde* (Freiburg i. B., 1887ff.).
RQH | *Revue des questions historiques* (Paris, 1866–1939).
RR | *Revue réformé* (Saint-Germaine-en-Laye, France, 1950ff.).
RRel | *Review for Religious* (St. Louis, 1942ff.).

RSPT	*Revue des sciences philosophiques et théologiques* (Paris, 1907ff.).
RSR	*Recherches de science religieuse* (Paris, 1910ff.).
RT	*Revue thomiste* (Paris, 1924–65).
RTAM	*Recherches de théologie ancienne et médiévale* (Louvain, 1969ff.).
RTL	*Revue théologique de Louvain* (Louvain, 1970ff.).
RTP	*Revue de théologie et de philosophie* (Lausanne, 1921ff.).
RUO	*La revue de l'Université d'Ottawa* (Ottawa, 1931–87).

Sal	*Salesianum* (Turin, 1939ff.).
SC	*Scuola Cattolica* (Milan, 1902ff.).
SCA	Studies in Christian Antiquity (Washington, D.C., 1941–85).
ScE	*Science et esprit* (Montreal, 1928ff.).
SChr	Sources chrétiennes (Paris, 1941ff.).
SCJ	*Second Century: Journal of Early Christian Studies* (Abilene, TX, 1981–92).
Scr	*Scripture* (London, 1969–75).
SE	*Sacris Erudiri* (Bruges, 1948ff.).
SJT	*Scottish Journal of Theology* (Edinburgh, etc., 1948ff.).
SM	*Studia Monastica* (Barcelona, 1959ff.).
SP	*Studia Patristica: Acts of the International Conventions of Oxford* (TU) (Berlin, 1957ff.).
SPMed	Studia Patristica Mediolanensia (Milan, 1974ff.).
ST	*Studi e Testi* (Rome, 1900ff.).
StC	*Studia Catholica* (Nijmegen, 1924–60).
Steidle	B. Steidle, *Patrologia: seu Historia Antiquae Litteraturae Ecclesiasticae, Scholarum Usui Accommodata* (Freiburg i. B., 1937).
StGKA	Studien zur Geschichte und Kultur des Altertums (Paderborn, 1907ff.).
STh	*Studia Theologica* (Lund, 1947ff.).
StLit	C. Jones and others, eds., *The Study of Liturgy*, rev. ed. (New York, 1992).
StP	*Studia Patavina* (Padua, 1954ff.).
Strack	H.L. Strack and P. Billerbeck, *Kommentar zum Neuen Testament aus Talmud und Midrasch*, vol. iv/i, 2nd ed. (Munich, 1956).
StudEnc	*Study Encounter* (Geneva, 1965–76).
StudLit	*Studia Liturgica* (Rotterdam, 1962ff.).

TD	*Theology Digest* (St. Louis, 1953ff.).
Theol	*Theology* (Norwich, England, 1976ff.).
ThGl	*Theologie und Glaube* (Paderborn, 1909ff.).
ThQ	*Theologische Quartalschrift* (Stuttgart/Tübingen, 1831–1928; various places, 1929ff.).
ThStKr	*Theologische Studien und Kritiken* (Gotha, 1828–42).
Tixeront	J. Tixeront, *A Handbook of Patrology*, trans. S.A. Raemers (London/St. Louis, 1947).

Tra	*Traditio: Studies in Ancient and Medieval History, Thought, and Religion* (New York, 1943ff.).
TRE	G. Krause and G. Müller, eds., *Theologische Realenzyklopädie* (Berlin, 1976ff.).
TS	*Theological Studies* (Baltimore/Woodstock, 1940ff.).
TU	Texte und Untersuchungen zur Geschichte de altchristlichen Literatur (Berlin, 1882ff.).
TV	*Theologia Viatorum: Jahrbuch der kirchlichen Hochschule Berlin* (Berlin, 1948/49–1979/80).
TZ	*Theologische Zeitschrift* (Basel, 1945ff.).
VC	*Vigiliae Christianae* (Amsterdam, 1947ff.).
VerC	*Verbum Caro* (Taizé, France, 1947–69).
VetChr	*Vetera Christianorum* (Bari, 1964ff.).
VS	*La Vie Spirituelle* (Paris, 1919ff.).
WEC	L. Johnson, ed., *Worship in the Early Church: An Anthology of Historical Sources*, 4 vols. (Collegeville, 2009).
Werner	E. Werner, *The Sacred Bridge: The Interdependence of Liturgy and Music in Synagogue and Church during the First Millennium* (London/New York, 1959).
Wor	*Worship* (Collegeville, 1952ff.; formerly *Orate Fratres*, 1926–51).
Wright (1928)	F.A. Wright, ed., *Fathers of the Church: Tertullian, Cyprian, Arnobius, Lactanius, Ambrose, Jerome, Augustine: A Selection from the Writings of the Latin Fathers* (London, 1928).
Wright (1932)	F.A. Wright, *A History of Later Greek Literature from the Death of Alexander in 323 B.C. to the Death of Justinian in 545 A.D.* (London, 1932).
WSt	*Wiener Studien: Zeitschrift für klassische Philologie* (Vienna, 1879ff.).
ZAW	*Zeitschrift für die alttestamentliche Wissenschaft* (Berlin/New York, 1881ff.).
ZKG	*Zeitschrift für Kirchengeschichte* (Gotha, 1877–1930; Stuttgart, 1931ff.).
ZkTh	*Zeitschrift für katholische Theologie* (Innsbruck, 1877–1940; Vienna, 1947ff.).
ZNeW	*Zeitschrift für die neutestamentliche Wissenschaft und die Kunde der älteren Kirche* (Giessen/Berlin/New York, 1900ff.).
ZNW	*Zeitschrift für Missionswissenschaft* (Münster, 1911–37).
ZTK	*Zeitschrift für Theologie und Kirche* (Tübingen, 1891ff.).
/	= "or," e.g., 543/554
[ ]	Textual material supplied by translator of the original source or by the present editor/translator

Introduction

Recent decades have witnessed numerous Christian denominations reforming and renewing their communal worship structures. Well before such a venture occurred, there took place, mainly though not exclusively in Europe, a scientific study of the early development of the Church's common prayer, a study that continues today. Both professional and amateur historians have applied and are applying their expertise to this important task, for understanding the past is not merely an intellectual exercise but offers one of the all-important keys for understanding the present.

Yet many students of worship have but little direct contact with the great literary heritage that witnesses the way Christians lived their liturgical life during the early ages of Christianity. Often a person's acquaintance with the primitive Church's written documentation is only by way of citations in end- or footnotes. Frequently access to the excellent English language collections of early source material is limited, since these are for the most part found only in the libraries of theological schools and major universities. The same is true of texts related to particular subjects, e.g., initiation. Furthermore, a large amount of pertinent material has simply not appeared in English. Texts in Latin, Greek, and other languages—apart from their inherent problems for many students of the liturgy—are no less difficult to obtain.

The four volumes of the present series aim to present a selection or thesaurus (representative, to be sure) of a wide selection of source material illustrating the growth of the Church's common prayer, in both East and West, from its Jewish roots down to the end of the sixth century. Included are texts from homilies, dogmatic and spiritual treatises, letters, monastic rules, church orders, prayer formulas, conciliar and synodal legislation, inscriptions, and the like. The subject matter is not only sacramental celebration but also the liturgical year, the times of the day for personal or group prayer, music and song, the physical arrangement of the church building, times for fasting (considered to be so closely allied with prayer), veneration of the martyrs, liturgical roles, decorum within and without the church, etc.

The user of these volumes fortunate enough to have access to a major theological library may well profit from the references to patristic and other manuals, as well as from the bibliography of pertinent periodical articles and treatises.

In a few cases the most recent edition of a text was, for various reasons, unavailable to me. Also, several texts initially intended to appear in this work are in fact not included since a particular volume could not be obtained.

It should be noted that, unless otherwise indicated, the enumeration of the psalms follows the Hebrew.

All cited texts have been translated by the present editor from the source indicated ("Translated from . . .") or are taken from a preexisting translation ("Translation from . . .").

A note on format

Each subhead (author, anonymous document, synods, etc.) is assigned an identification number, which is usually followed by a letter indicating a particular work of an author or a particular synod.

The internal enumeration of paragraphs usually corresponds to that of the edition from which the text was translated. Marginal numbers, running sequentially, are assigned to paragraphs of the text.

Cross-references are indicated by the abbreviation for *Worship in the Early Church*, i.e., WEC, followed by the volume number and then either the subhead number in bold text (e.g., WEC 4:**151** or WEC 4:**180-G**) or else the marginal paragraph number (e.g., WEC 4:4234).

There are three types of footnotes: daggers, letters, and numbers. Daggered notes indicate the sources from which translations have been made, lettered notes contain explanations for words and phrases used in the text, and numbered notes indicate scriptural references.

* * *

No work of this kind can reach completion without the encouragement and assistance of many people. And thus I must express my gratitude to Mr. Peter Kearney for sharing his expertise in Latin and Hebrew. To the Rev. James Challancin, a priest of the diocese of Marquette, Michigan, and a former professor of liturgy, for his many words of encouragement. To the staff (especially Jessica) of the Escanaba, Michigan, Public Library for such gracious assistance in procuring by means of interlibrary loans ever so many volumes from libraries throughout the country. To the whole publishing team at Liturgical Press and especially to Stephanie Lancour, my copy editor, whose careful reading of the text has saved me from any number of embarrassing moments. And especially to my wife, Marlene Winter-Johnson, not only for her patience throughout this endeavor but especially for the numerous hours in researching materials found in the library of The Catholic University of America and in that of the University of Notre Dame, as well as for helping to prepare the work's manuscript for publication.

Chapter XI

Sixth Century. West

AFRICA

150. FULGENCE OF RUSPE

Fulgence (468–533 or perhaps ca. 462–527), son of a prominent family, was a native of Telepte in the African province of Byzacena. He eventually embraced monastic life and was (ca. 502/507) ordained bishop of Ruspe, a small seaport in northwest Africa. The times were violent since the Vandal kings, who were Arian, did not hesitate to persecute, or encourage the persecution of, orthodox Christians, with books being burned, churches being destroyed, the clergy being harassed. With sixty other bishops Fulgence was exiled to Sardinia. He returned ca. 510/515, only to be banished again, and then came back in 523. A chronicle of Fulgence's life has been written by Ferrandus of Carthage (WEC 4:**151**).

Though not an original theologian, Fulgence was a strong adversary of Arianism and Pelagianism. Strongly influenced by Augustine (WEC 3:**98**), he left several treatises, letters, and sermons.

CPL 814ff. * Altaner (1961) 587–90 * Altaner (1966) 489–90 * Bardenhewer (1908) 616–18 * Bardenhewer (1910) 532–34 * Bardenhewer (1913) 5:303–16 * Jurgens 3:285–300 * Labriolle (1947) 2:769–70 * Labriolle (1968) 496–97 * Steidle 240–41 * Tixeront 346–48 * CATH 4:1669–71 * CE 6:316–17 * DCB 2:576–83 * DictSp 5:1612–15 * DPAC 1:1407–9 * DTC 6.1:968–72 * EC 5:1802–5 * EEC 1:331–32 * EEChr 1:442–43 * LTK 4:220–21 * NCE 6:220 * NCES 6:23–24 * ODCC 646 * PEA (1894) 7.1:214–15 * PEA (1991) 4:699–700 * RACh 8:632–61 * TRE 11:723–27

J. Stiglmayr, "Das Quicumque und Fulgentius von Ruspe," ZkTh 49 (1925) 341–57. * M. Jugie, "Considérations générales sur la question de l'épiclèse," EO (1936) 324–30. * S. Salaville, "L'épiclèse africaine," EO 39 (1941–42) 268–82. * J.J. Gavigan, "Fulgentius of Ruspe on Baptism," Tra 5 (1947) 313–22.

150-A. The Forgiveness of Sins[†]

The Forgiveness of Sins (Ad Euthymium de Remissione Peccatorum), in two books, was written for an otherwise unknown Euthymius. The treatise is dated not before 512 and not after 523.

[†] Translated from *Sancti Fulgentii Episcopi Ruspensis Opera*, vol. 2, ed. J. Fraipont, CCL 91 A (Paris, 1968) 667ff.

3998   I.XIX.1. Only in the Catholic Church is the forgiveness of sins given and received. To this Church—which the Spouse has called his only dove, his chosen one, the Church he built on a rock—he gave the keys of the kingdom of heaven. He granted it the power to loose or to bind as Truth itself promised to blessed Peter, "You are Peter and upon this rock I will build my Church, and the gates of hell will not prevail against it; I will give you the keys of the kingdom of heaven, and whatever you bind on earth will be bound in heaven; and whatever you loose upon earth will be loosed in heaven."[1]

3999   I.XIX.2. Those outside this Church, which has received the keys of the kingdom of heaven, will not walk the path to heaven but to hell. Nor will they go on to the abode of eternal life but will hasten to the punishment of eternal death. This is true not only for unbaptized pagans but also for those who have been baptized in the name of the Father and of the Son and of the Holy Spirit and remain heretics. Nor does baptism merit true life if those who have been baptized, whether within or without the Church, do not end their lives within the Catholic Church. Nor will those who do not share the Church's faith and love find life through the sacrament of the Church's baptism. Saved by this baptism are those whom the unity of love will have kept within the Catholic Church till the end of our present life.

4000   I.XXII.1. [. . .] Outside the Catholic Church there is no forgiveness of sins. Just as within the Catholic Church "one believes with the heart and so is justified and one confesses with the mouth and is thereby saved,"[2] so outside this same Church belief in what is evil cannot be turned into righteousness but into punishment, and an evil confession does not save the person confessing but carries death. Outside this Church the name "Christian" assists no one; neither does baptism save nor is a pure sacrifice offered to God; neither is the forgiveness of sins received nor is the joy of eternal life found.

4001   I.XXIV.2. Our Lord and Savior did not say that sins not forgiven in this world will be forgiven in the world to come. What he points out is that in the future world only sins already forgiven in the one and true Catholic Church will be forgiven. Only to the Church has the Lord given the power to bind and loose, saying, "I will give you the keys of the kingdom of heaven; whatever you bind upon earth will be bound in heaven; whatever you loose upon earth will be loosed in heaven."[3] Therefore what the holy Church does not remit in this world remains unremitted so that not even in the future world is anything remitted. Bound is every person whom the Church has not loosed. Nor does a person obtain beneficial forgiveness unless he or she returns to penance in the Church and hopes that his or her sins will be forgiven. [. . .]

4002   II.XVII.3. So we recognize that sins are not forgiven unless penance is performed in this life. Nor will penance in this life profit anyone who

---

1. Matt 16:18–19.   2. Rom 10:10.   3. Matt 16:19.

despairs of the forgiveness of sins. The wicked will not be converted in the future, their sorrow being continuous yet useless. Just as no forgiveness will be granted them, so their remorse will never end. They fail to recognize the time during which penance is fruitfully done by sinners and during which God's goodness pardons sins. [. . .]

II.xxii.3. Whoever does not wish to endure unending misery only has to seek the Lord's mercy. Whoever does not wish to suffer eternal death only has to seek out eternal life. Whoever does not wish to be condemned by eternal punishment should now confess before God. It is now that penance is fruitfully carried out, now that forgiveness is granted to those who do penance. [. . .]   4003

150-B. Rule of Faith[†]

The *Rule of Faith* (*De Fide ad Petrum seu de Regula Fidei*) was written between 523 and 526 for an otherwise unknown Peter, who needed a theological tool wherewith to combat any heretics he might encounter during his journey to Jerusalem.

43. [. . .] From the time when our Savior said, "Those who are not reborn of water and the Spirit cannot enter the kingdom of God,"[1] those lacking the sacrament of baptism cannot enter the kingdom of heaven and receive eternal life, the exception being those in the Catholic Church who shed their blood for Christ. Whoever is baptized, whether in the Catholic Church or in any heretical or schismatic sect, receives the whole sacrament. However, salvation, being the very essence of the sacrament, will not be attained if this individual was baptized outside the Catholic Church. Such a person must return to the Church and is not to be baptized a second time since baptism is not to be repeated for any baptized person who has already been baptized. One must return in order to receive eternal life within the Catholic community. As to eternal life no one is fitting, not even with the sacrament of baptism, if he or she remains estranged from the Catholic Church.   4004

62. Hold firmly and never doubt that God's only begotten Word was made flesh and offered himself for us as a fragrant sacrifice[2] and victim to God. To the Word together with the Father and the Holy Spirit animals were sacrificed at the time of the old covenant by the patriarchs, prophets, and priests. Now—namely at the time of the new covenant—it is to him and to the Father and the Holy Spirit with whom he is one in divinity that the holy Catholic Church does not cease to offer the sacrifice of bread and wine throughout the whole world, doing so in faith and love. [. . .]   4005

70. Hold firmly and never doubt that not only people having the use of reason but also infants—whether they died in the wombs of their mothers   4006

[†] Translated from CCL 91 A:740ff.

1. John 3:5.   2. See Eph 5:2.

or whether they were in fact born—who leave this world lacking the holy sacrament of baptism which is conferred in the name of the Father and of the Son and of the Holy Spirit, are punished with the everlasting torment of eternal fire. Even though they committed no personal sin, nonetheless, they assume the damnation of original sin through bodily conception and birth.

4007   79. Hold firmly and never doubt that the sacrament of baptism can be found not only within the Catholic Church but also among heretics who baptize in the name of the Father and of the Son and of the Holy Spirit. Yet outside the Church such a baptism profits nothing. Indeed, just as salvation within the Church is conferred through the sacrament of baptism upon those who correctly believe, so outside the Church, unless they return to it, those baptized by the same baptism come to naught. It is the unity as such of the Church's society that avails unto salvation, so that one is not saved by a baptism given in a place where it should not be given. [. . .]

4008   80. Hold firmly and never doubt that a person baptized outside the Catholic Church cannot share eternal life unless prior to the end of life he or she has returned to the Church and has been incorporated into it.

150-C. Against Fabian[†]

Only thirty-nine large fragments of a treatise against Fabian, an Arian bishop, remain.

4009   XXVIII.17. The sacrifice is offered so that the death of the Lord, who died for us, may be proclaimed and commemorated. He said, "No one has more love than to lay down one's life for one's friends."[1] So it was out of love that Christ died for us. When we commemorate his death during the sacrifice, we ask that love be granted us through the coming of the Holy Spirit. We ask that through the very love by which Christ deigned to be crucified for us that we, having received the grace of the Holy Spirit, may consider the world as being crucified to us and we as being crucified to the world.[2] Imitating the death of our Lord—in that Christ "died to sin, dying once but that he lives, living for God"[3]— may we also walk in newness of life. Having accepted the gift of love, may we die to sin and live for God. "God's love has been poured into our hearts through the Holy Spirit who is given to us."[4]

4010   XXVIII.18. When we eat the Lord's Bread and drink from his cup we share in the Lord's Body and Blood. This indeed encourages us to die to the world and to lead a life hidden with Christ in God. It prompts us to crucify our own bodies with its sins and impure desires. So may it be that all the faithful who love God and neighbor drink the cup of the Lord's love even if they do not drink the cup of his bodily passion. [. . .]

[†] Translated from CCL 91 A:183ff.

1. John 15:13.   2. See Gal 6:14.   3. See Rom 6:10.   4. Rom 5:5.

xxviii.19. The gift of love allows us to truly be what we celebrate in the 4011
mystical sacrifice. As the apostle said, "Because there is one bread we,
though many, are one body." He adds, "May all of us share in the one
bread."[5] This is what we request at the time of the sacrifice. We have the
most salutary example of our Savior. Being our high priest, he desired that
we petition this when we commemorate his death. Being close to death, he
asked this for us when he said, "Holy Father, protect in your name those
whom you have given us."[6] And somewhat later, "Not for them only do
I pray but for them also who through their word will believe in me. That
they all may be one as you, Father, in me and I in you; that they may also
be one in us; that the world may believe that you have sent me. And the
glory that you have given me I have given to them, that they may be one
as we are one: I in them and you in me."[7]

xxviii.23. [. . .] When the holy Church, while offering the sacrifice of 4012
Christ's Body and Blood, asks that the Holy Spirit be sent upon it, the
Church thereby requests the gift of love whereby it may safeguard the
unity of the Spirit in the bond of peace. It is written, "Love is as strong as
death."[8] It was through love that the Redeemer was moved to freely die
for the Church, which requests love for its members on earth. Thus the
Holy Spirit sanctifies the sacrifice of the Catholic Church; and so the faithful remain Christian in faith and love while through the gift of the Holy
Spirit they worthily eat and drink the Lord's Body and Blood. They do so
because each has a correct belief regarding God, and since by living justly
they are not separated from the unity of the body of the Church.

150-D. Letters

The corpus of Fulgence's letters contains eighteen letters, including five
sent to him by others.

150-D-1. LETTER 12. TO FERRANDUS, A DEACON[†]

26. I believe, my holy brother, that what we have talked about and 4013
what has been confirmed by the writing of such an excellent teacher as
Augustine[a] should leave no room for any doubt, namely, that the faithful
share in Christ's Body and Blood when by baptism they have been made
members of Christ's body. United in this body they are not to be considered
as separated from the assembly of the Bread and the Cup even if they depart this world before eating that Bread and drinking from that Cup.[b] [. . .]

---

5. 1 Cor 10:17.   6. John 17:11.   7. John 17:20–23.   8. Cant 8:6.

† Translated from *Sancti Fulgentii Episcopi Ruspensis Opera*, vol. 1, ed. J. Fraipont,
CCL 91 (Paris, 1968) 380–81.

a. WEC 3:98.

b. This concerns a person who, while unconscious, was baptized but did not receive the Eucharist.

150-D-2. LETTER 14. TO FERRANDUS, A DEACON[†]

4014   10. [. . .] Just as there can be individual persons in the Trinity, so there can be separate works of the Trinity. May we heed what Holy Scripture says concerning Wisdom: "She is the splendor of eternal light."[1] Just as we see splendor inseparably united to light, so we must admit that the Son cannot be separated from the Father. As stated by apostolic authority, "He is the splendor of God's glory and the imprint of God's substance."[2] Then there is blessed Ambrose's morning hymn which declares that the Son is the splendor of the Father's glory.[a]

4015   44. [. . .] Therefore in the very sacrifice of Christ's body we begin by giving thanks so that we might demonstrate that Christ is *not to be given* us but that he has in truth *already been given* us. By giving thanks to God when offering Christ's Body and Blood we acknowledge that Christ *has been slain* and not that he *will be slain* for our sins; that we *have been redeemed* by his blood, not that we *will be redeemed* by his blood. [. . .]

151. FERRANDUS OF CARTHAGE

As a layman Ferrandus (d. before 546) accompanied Fulgence of Ruspe (WEC 4:**150**) into exile during the time of Vandal-Arian persecution. Upon returning, he went to Carthage, where he was ordained a deacon. Though few of his writings survive, Ferrandus has gained the reputation of being a trustworthy theologian.

CPL nos. 847ff. * Altaner (1961) 588 * Altaner (1966) 489 * Bardenhewer (1913) 5:316–20 * Bautz 2:19 * Steidle 240–41 * Tixeront 349–50 * CATH 4:1196–97 * CE 6:317–18 * DCB 2:583–84 * DDC 5:831 * DictSp 5:181–83 * DPAC 1:1352–53 * DTC 5:2174–75 * EEC 1:322 * LTK 3:1243 * NCE 5:892 * NCES 5:691–92 * ODCC 606–7 * PEA (1894) 6.2:2219–21 * PEA (1991) 4:482

151-A. Life of Fulgence of Ruspe[††]

Unlike many biographies of the time, Ferrandus's work is highly factual, missing the miracles and legendary elements found in genres of this type dating from this period.

4016   LIX. Fulgence was most diligent in seeing that no cleric wears ostentatious garb or is remiss in his ecclesiastical duties due to secular concerns. He prescribed that no cleric should reside far distant from the church and that each personally attend to his own garden. Also that the psalms be sung in an agreeable manner and that the greatest attention be given to

---

[†] Translated from CCL 91:397, 440.

a. See WEC 2:**53-T**. However, the text for *Splendor paternae gloriae* is not given in WEC.

1. Wis 7:26.   2. Heb 1:3.

[††] Translated from PL 65:147.

their words. He commanded that each week on Wednesday and Friday all clerics, widows, and those among the laity who were able, should fast and ordered that one be present for the daily vigils, observe the fasts, and attend morning and evening prayer. [. . .]

ITALY

152. MAGNUS FELIX ENNODIUS

Born of a noble family in Arles in 473/474, Ennodius was raised in Pavia, south of Milan in northern Italy. Perhaps married, he was ordained to the diaconate. About 496 he moved to Milan, where he taught rhetoric. In 514 Ennodius was ordained bishop of Pavia. Twice he led missions (both unsuccessful) on behalf of the pope to the East in order to effect some type of reconciliation with Rome. His death occurred in 521.

Ennodius is especially noted for his attempt to fuse classical pagan literature with Catholic doctrine. Among his abundant writings are 297 letters, numerous speeches, poems, and hymns. Scholars often refer to his Latin as "turgid."

CPL nos. 1487ff. * Altaner (1961) 572–74 * Altaner (1966) 478–79 * Bardenhewer (1908) 622–25 * Bardenhewer (1910) 536–38 * Bardenhewer (1913) 5:236–49 * Bardy (1930) 177–78 * Bautz 1:1516–17 * Labriolle (1947) 2:752–54 * Labriolle (1968) 489–91 * Steidle 235–36 * Tixeront 352–53 * CATH 4:206–7 * CE 5:478–79 * DCB 2:123–24 * DPAC 1:1155–56 * DTC 5.1:126–29 * EC 5:364–65 * EEC 1:272–73 * EEChr 1:371 * LTK 3:677–78 * NCE 5:444 * NCES 5:264–65 * ODCC 547 * PEA (1894) 5.2:2629–33 * PEA (1991) 3:1046–47 * RACh 5:398–421

152-A. Libellus de Synodo†

The papal election in 498 was disputed: Laurentius, a Roman deacon, was selected by his partisans, Symmachus by others. The proponents of Laurentius attacked the character of Symmachus. Consequently, a Roman synod was called (in 501). Although not addressing the particulars of the case, the delegates declared Symmachus to be the rightful pope. Ennodius, present at the synod, wrote this book in defense of the papal office.

[. . .] Was there any occasion when they were celebrating Mass that his (the pope's) name was not commemorated? Did these bishops ever at your bidding offer incomplete sacrifices, those contrary to the Catholic rite and the ancient manner? [. . .]

4017

152-B. Life of Epiphanius††

Epiphanius was ordained bishop of Pavia in 466 and was succeeded by Ennodius.

---

† Translated from CSEL 6, ed. W. Hartel (Vienna, 1882) 311.
†† Translated from CSEL 6:332.

4018   [. . .] When he was hardly eight years old, Epiphanius began serving in the heavenly army. As previously indicated by a sign that came from heaven, he became an ecclesiastical reader. [. . .]

153. HORMISDAS, POPE

An Italian with a Persian name, Hormisdas, archdeacon at Rome, was elected pope in 514. He is especially noted for ending in 519 the Acacian schism between Rome and Constantinople. This division, lasting for thirty-five years and occasioned by the Monophysite position espousing only one nature in Christ, began during the patriarchate of Acacius (471–89). Hormisdas died on August 6 in 523.

CPL nos. 1683ff. * Altaner (1961) 554 * Altaner (1966) 464 * Bardenhewer (1913) 5:279–80 * Bautz 2:1057–58 * Steidle 228 * CATH 5:942–43 * CE 7:470–71 * DACL 13.1:1215 * DCB 3:155–61 * DHGE 24:1123–24 * DPAC 2:2538–39 * DTC 7.1:161–76 * EC 9:360–61 * EEC 1:399–400 * EEChr 1:545 * LTK 5:279–80 * NCE 7:148 * NCES 6:110–12 * ODCC 790–91 * PEA (1991) 5:729

S.M. Meo, "La formula mariana 'Gloriosa semper Virgo . . .' nel canone romano e presso due pontefici del VI secolo," in *De primordiis cultus mariani*, vol. 2 (Rome, 1970) 439–58.

153-A. Letters

Some ninety letters and other related documents, mostly concerning the Acacian schism, are generally counted as authentic. However, the corpus of this pope's letters, as is sometimes the case, also contains correspondence sent to Hormisdas by others.

153-A-1. LETTER 59. FROM BISHOPS GERMANUS AND JOHN, DEACONS FELIX AND DIOSCORUS, AND BLANDUS, A PRESBYTER[†]

4019   2. Before we entered the city of Scampina,[a] Trojan, the venerable bishop, came out to meet us with his clergy and people. How God was praised on that day! What festivity ensued! [. . .] A gathering took place in the Basilica of Saint Peter. We confess to Your Holiness: we saw such devotion, such great praise of God, so many tears, such joy as hardly can be found among other people. Almost all the men and women with candles as well as the soldiers with crosses received us into the city. Mass was celebrated. Only your name was recited, not that of just anyone connected to religion. Germanus, our venerable bishop, celebrated Mass. They promised that hereafter only the names of those recognized by the Apostolic See would be commemorated. [. . .]

[†] Translated from CSEL 35, ed. O. Guenther (Vienna, 1895) 850.
a. Scampina: located in northwest Greece.

153-A-2. LETTER 146. FROM JOHN OF CONSTANTINOPLE[ta]

4. We have written only to give assurance that the venerable name of   4020
Leo, once archbishop of Rome, is affixed to the diptychs said at the time of
the consecration and that your holy name likewise is proclaimed in them.
This is due to the agreement we made. [. . .]

154. RULE OF THE MASTER[++]

The Rule of the Master (*Regula Magistri*), dating from the first quarter of
the sixth century, is an anonymous treatise originating in south-central
Italy and is probably the result of various redactions. The writer gives co-
pious details regarding monastic life, yet at times his liturgical directives
lack completeness. It is generally agreed that Saint Benedict of Nursia
(WEC 4:**155**) borrowed from this rule.

CPL no. 1858 * Altaner (1961) 579 * Altaner (1966) 482–83 * CATH 8:211–12 * DPAC
2:2980 * EC 10:664–65 * EEC 2:746–47 * LTK 8:977–78 * NCE 12:208 * ODCC 1377 *
PEA (1991) 10:838–43

F. Masai, "Le 'Regula Magistri' et l'histoire du bréviaire," in *Miscellanea Liturgica in
Honorem L. Cuniberti Mohlberg*, vol. 2 (Rome, 1949) 423–39. * C. Gindele, "Die Satisfaktionsordung von Caesarius und Benedikt bis Donatus," RB 69 (1959) 216–36.
* C. Gindele, "Das Alleluia im 'Ordo Officii' der 'Regula Magistri,'" RB 70 (1960)
504–25. * V. Janeras, "Notulae liturgicae in 'Regula Magistri,'" SM 2 (1960) 359–64.
* A. de Vogüé, "Lacunes et erreurs dans la section liturgique de la 'Regula Magistri,'" RB 70 (1960) 410–13. * A. de Vogüé, "Le rituel monastique chez s. Benoît et
chez le Maître," RB 71 (1961) 233–64. * A. de Vogüé, "Le sens d'antifana' et la lon-
geur de l'office dans la 'Regula Magistri,'" RB 71 (1961) 119–24. * A.M. Mundó, "A
propos des rituels du Maître et de s. Benoît: la 'Provolutio,'" SM 4 (1962) 177–91.
* C. Gindele, "Ansatzpunkte für die Rekonstruktion der werktäglichen Vigilien
der Magisterregel," RB 75 (1965) 329–35. * A. de Vogüé, "La Règle du Maître et la
lettre apocryphe de s. Jérôme sur le chant des psaumes," SM 7 (1965) 357–67. * A.
de Vogüé, "'Orationi frequenter incumbere': une invitation à la prière continuelle,"
RAM 41 (1965) 467–72. * C. Gindele, "Zum grossen Rekonziliationsritus nach der
Magister- und Benediktusregel," RB 80 (1970) 153–56. * C. Gindele, "Die Magis-
terregal und ihre altmonastische Alleluia-Psalmodie," RB 84 (1974) 176–81. * E.
de Bhaldraithe, "The Morning Office of the Rule of the Master," *Regulae Benedicti
Studia. Annuarium Internationale* 5 (1976) 201–23. * C. Gindele, "Verspätung, Ver-
zügerung und Krürzung im Gottesdienst der Magister- und Benediktusregel," RB
86 (1976) 306–21. * A. Verheul, "La prière monastique chorale avant Benoît: son influence sur le culte en occident: la prière des heures avant la Règle et dans la Règle

---

[+] Translated from CSEL 35:592.

a. John II (d. 520): patriarch of Constantinople.

[++] Translated from *La Règle du Maître*, vol. 2, ed. A. de Vogüé, SChr 106 (Paris,
1964) 48ff. An excellent commentary on the monastery's liturgical life appears in
SChr 105:65–86. An English translation of the rule's text and the SChr commentary
is *The Rule of the Master*, trans. L. Eberle (Kalamazoo, MI, 1977).

de s. Benoît," QL 62 (1981) 227–42. * A. Wathen,"The Rites of Holy Week according to the Regula Magistri," EOr 3 (1986) 289–305. * R. Taft, *The Liturgy of the Hours in East and West: The Origins of the Divine Office and Its Meaning for Today* (Collegeville, 1986) 122–30. * A. Verheul, "Les psaumes dans la prière des heures: hier et aujourd'hui," QL 71 (1990) 261–95. * A. Wathen, "Rituals of Admission in the Rule of the Master," in *Monastic Profession* (Petersham, MA, 1998). * J.H. Dyer, "Observations on the Divine Office in the Rule of the Master," in *The Divine Office in the Latin Middle Ages: Methodology and Source Studies, Regional Developments, Hagiography*, ed. M.E. Fassler and R.A. Baltzer (New York, 2000).

Question of the disciples
xiv. How is an excommunicated monk to do penance?
The Lord has replied through the Master:

4021   When an hour of the divine office is celebrated in the oratory, namely, when at the end of a psalm all prostrate for prayer, the excommunicated monk will prostrate himself before the oratory's entrance and cry out while weeping, "I have sinned and I acknowledge my sin."[1] I have strayed; I promise to amend my ways; I will sin no more.[2] Intercede for me, holy communities, from which I—by my negligence and at the urging of the devil—am separated. Intercede for me, you my former deans.[a] Pardon me, "O good shepherd" and kind abbot, "who leaves the ninety-nine for the one."[3] [. . .]

4022   The guilty one, stretched out on the floor, will address the brothers in this way when they conclude the psalms, doing so at each prayer. At the completion of the Holy Work [*Opus Dei*] in the oratory, while the guilty one continues to lie before the entrance and at the moment the abbot is departing, the whole brotherhood, including the deans, will humbly kneel on behalf of the sinner. When this has been done and if the fault is not serious, the abbot, agreeing to grant immediate pardon, will without delay order the guilty monk's deans to lift him to his feet. Once again the abbot will reproach him for his failing. When the sinner has responded that he will henceforth amend his ways, the abbot will immediately say to the whole community: "Come, brothers, together with tears let us pray in the oratory for this sheep of your flock who, recognizing his sin,[4] promises to henceforth correct himself. May we reconcile him before the Lord who was provoked by his disobedience."

4023   Then the abbot will enter the oratory with the brothers. Before they begin to pray, the guilty monk's deans, still outside, will lead him by the hand, one on the right and the other on the left, and will accompany him into the oratory while both deans say this verse, "Praise the Lord, for he is

---

a. The monastery, at least normatively, was to consist of two sections, each section having ten monks and two deans [*praepositi*]. The function of the deans was to impart instruction as well as to oversee various aspects of the section's life of prayer and work.

1. Ps 51:3.   2. See Ps 119:176.   3. John 10:11.   4. See Ps 51:3.

good," and the rest of the community will respond, "Because his goodness is forever."[5] Thus, when the deans from the outside press for confession on the part of the penitent by this verse, immediately from within the oratory, and by means of the mouth of the brothers who respond, the good God promises mercy.

Once the deans have led the guilty one back into the oratory, they will have him prostrate at the foot of the altar. Immediately all do likewise and together with the abbot they pray on his behalf. Then, prostrate, the guilty monk prays to the Lord for his fault, with tears, saying, "Lord, 'I have sinned' and 'I acknowledge my iniquity.'[6] I pray to you, I beseech you, pardon me, O Lord, pardon me.[7] 'Do not drag me along with my sins'[8] nor condemn me[9] into the nether regions[10] nor forever charge me with my evil deeds, for you are a God of repentance."[11] [. . .]   4024

When he has said all this with tears, the abbot will immediately lift him up by the hand, saying: "Take care, my brother, take care that you sin no more. Should you do so, you will be obliged to do penance a second time, and this second penance will cast you among the heretics." Then the repentant monk will say, "I have strayed like the sheep that was lost. Lord, receive your servant," and all will respond. Then the abbot will call his deans and hand the monk over to them, saying: "Receive your sheep, make your group complete. Once again allow him to eat at the table. 'For he who was dead is now living; he who was lost is now found.'"[12] [. . .]   4025

On this day, as a sign of a return to humility, he will wash the hands of the brothers when they enter for Communion.[b] While so doing he will kiss their hands, first those of the abbot, then those of all the brothers. While pouring the water, he will ask each to pray for him. Furthermore, once having entered the oratory, he will again and in a loud voice remind all to pray for him; upon exiting with the brothers he will assume his customary place at meals.   4026

As to children under fifteen years old, we prescribe punishment, not excommunication but rather corporal punishment. After fifteen years of age they receive not bodily punishment but excommunication, for from this age on they understand how they should do penance and correct evil deeds committed in adulthood. [. . .]   4027

Question of the disciples

XXI. How are the kitchen servers and the cellarer to receive Communion? The Lord has replied through the Master:

When the brothers are standing before the abbot in the oratory to receive Communion, after all have shared the sign of peace and the abbot has received, no one is to receive after him, but the deans of the weekly   4028

---

b. Entering for a canonical hour that precedes the Mass?

5. Ps 106:1.   6. Ps 51:5–6.   7. See Matt 6:12.   8. Ps 28:3.   9. See Job 10:2.
10. See Ps 63:9.   11. See Jer 18:8–10.   12. Luke 15:32.

servers immediately request permission to leave in order to summon their servers for Communion. [. . .]

Question of the disciples
XXII. After all the kitchen servers have left, in which order are those remaining in the oratory to receive Communion after the abbot?
The Lord has replied through the Master:

4029   After the abbot's Communion the dean whose turn has placed him next to the abbot will receive Communion, and his deanery, each member in turn, follows him. Once they have finished, the other dean will receive Communion. Then his deanery, each member in turn, follows him. But if, with the Lord's help, the community is more numerous, the others will do likewise. They should stand in the oratory, as commanded, and receive Communion.

4030   Should a brother become proud in regard to Communion and refuse to receive, let him abstain. But when he desires to receive Communion, this is denied him for the same period of time as he refused to receive. For as long as he was proud without reason, for such a length of time let the abbot or the dean be rightly displeased with him. [. . .]

4031   The place next to the abbot in the oratory will be occupied a day at a time by the deans and the other brothers so that the second place is always flexible. In this way no one, assured and proud of his status, will cause others to despair. [. . .]

4032   Furthermore, after the abbot and at his direction it will be the deans who will always lead the antiphonal psalms from each choir. When they have finished, and always at the abbot's directive, the brothers who are lower in rank do so from the two choirs—one after another, as they have been directed by name—namely, first from one choir and then from the other choir.

Question of the disciples
XXXIII. The divine offices throughout the night
The Lord has replied through the Master:

4033   At the night office during winter, the nocturns are sung[c] before cockcrow since the prophet says, "During the middle of the night I will rise to praise you."[13] As to summer, he also says, "At night my spirit watches for you, O God,"[14] namely, in one part of the night, after cockcrow, the signal to rise is given.

4034   In winter those keeping vigil should take care that the cockcrow neither precedes nor surprises the nocturns, for during winter the nights are long. In fact, cockcrow signals the end of the night since it is night that brings

---

c. Ancient liturgical documents use the words "say," "sing," "recite," etc. interchangeably. See R. Taft, *The Liturgy of the Hours in East and West: The Origins of the Divine Office and Its Meaning for Today* (Collegeville, 1986) 50, 138.

13. Ps 119:62.   14. Isa 26:9, LXX.

forth the day. [. . .] In winter the cockcrow must come after the nocturns since the nights are long. Thus the brothers, refreshed by sleep, will have their spirits enlivened and made fit for understanding the Work of God which they perform. If an interval is allowed, it is so that the lengthening of the night might put an end to the drowsiness of sleep.

On the other hand, during spring and summer, namely, from Easter till 24 September, which is the winter equinox, the shortness of the night causes the brothers to begin the nocturns at cockcrow. When they have completed the number of psalms, they immediately link them to Matins with its appointed number of psalms. We have enjoined that during these short nights the nocturns are to begin after cockcrow and are to be joined to Matins, so as to avoid having the brothers return to bed after the nocturns, fall back to a deep sleep, and—overburdened by a most welcome sleep of the morning—not only miss Matins but even be so disordered as to be late for Prime. 4035

If we have said that the nocturns are to be joined to Matins after cockcrow, it is also so that the brothers, rendered fit by prolonged sleep, may celebrate both offices with full understanding. Once the divine debt of Matins has been paid, the brothers can, should they so desire, rest till Prime. In this way during these hours they put off all lethargy of sleep and are disposed to work with a refreshed body after Prime. We have an historical example of this in Saint Helenus of whom it was said: "He was accustomed to rest after Matins."ᵈ [. . .] 4036

As to the psalms at the winter nocturns—namely, from the winter equinox to the spring equinox, that is, from 24 September to 25 March or better till Easter—since the nights are long, it is necessary to say <thirteen>ᵉ antiphonal psalms,ᶠ always according to their order in the psalter, and then three responsorial psalms so as to obtain sixteen *inpositiones*,ᵍ matching the number of prophets, but not counting the lessons, the verse, and the *rogus Dei*.ʰ Thus these sixteen *inpositiones* of the nocturns with the eight *inpositiones* at Matins have us prostrate before God twenty-four times while we praise him, doing so in imitation of the twenty-four elders.[15] The reason for singing more psalms during the long winter nights is this: since God 4037

---

d. Eugenia: a martyr during the third century who was baptized by Helenus, bishop of Heliopolis; see *Passio s. Eugeniae*, ed. B. Mombritius, *Sanctuarium 2*, under the title *Passio ss. Prothi et Hiacynthi martyrum* (Paris, 1910) 392.

e. Angle brackets indicate text material inserted by A. de Vogüé, editor of SChr 106.

f. For various methods of rendering the psalms, e.g., antiphonally, responsorially, directly, see, at least in regard to Benedict's Rule, R. Taft, *The Liturgy of the Hours*, 139.

g. *Inpositio*: a liturgical unit consisting of a psalm, the "Glory be," a prostration, and a prayer; see R. Taft, *The Liturgy of the Hours*, 123–24.

h. *Rogus Dei*: probably a litany; see R. Taft, *The Liturgy of the Hours*, 125–26.

15. See Rev 4:4; 5:8–9; 7:11–12.

has added to the night a time for further rest, so we also should add acts of thanksgiving to his praise.

4038   But during the summer, namely, from Easter to 24 September, <nine> antiphonal psalms are said, always following the sequence given in the psalter as said earlier, together with three responsories, in addition to the lessons, the verse, and the *rogus Dei.* Thus these twelve night *inpositiones* with the eight morning *inpositiones* to which they are joined will have us prostrate before God twenty times only. We are bound to do this because of the shortness of the night, for sleep, when it is brief, appears pleasing to the body when the human body, tired by the day's labor, has less repose during a short night. Therefore throughout the summer, as we indicated above, since the nights are short, there are nine antiphonal psalms and three responsories so as to obtain twelve *inpositiones,* this number corresponding to the list of the apostles. For during the summer these nocturns, as we said earlier, begin and end after cockcrow; when they are finished, Matins is immediately added due to the shortness of the night.

4039   At all times, however, both in winter and in summer, during the day as well as during the night, and also at vigils, when chanting the psalms care is to be taken not to couple them since this is forbidden. On the contrary, each is to end with the "Glory be" so as not to lose the prayers that are to occur between them and so as not to give the impression that we are withholding the "Glory be" from the praise of God when the psalms are crowded together, for the prophet who imposed a beginning on each psalm also assigned it an end.

4040   If some type of necessity should befall those chanting the psalms, they will not join together every two psalms but will link every three, each three with its own "Glory be" so as to finish more quickly and yet not reduce the number of psalms. The reason we say the psalms one by one or in groups of three is that just as we confess unity in the Trinity and the Trinity in unity, so we should believe that it is necessary to say the psalms one by one or when necessary in groups of three and yet with their doxologies. It is, in fact, absolutely forbidden to join two psalms together since Christians cannot adapt themselves to what is more or less than one and three and since our faith is not perfect unless we acknowledge the Trinity in unity and unity in the Trinity.

4041   But if some more urgent necessity, no matter what the hour, afflicts those chanting the psalms, they will say one section of each of the psalms that are to be said and conclude with a single doxology; they will then exit the oratory. Thus, whatever the necessity, the impression will not be given that the Work of God has been left undone.

Question of the disciples
xxxiv. The divine offices throughout the day
The Lord has replied through the Master:

It is especially and preeminently in the arrangement of the divine office   4042
that the rule of holy service should be established; following ancient custom and the rule established by the institutions of our elders, the correct
hours to be observed are Matins, Prime, Terce, Sext, None, Vespers, and
Compline so that we may carry out the decree of the prophet who says to
the Lord, "Seven times a day have I praised you."[16]

But Prime, said in the same manner as the twelfth hour which is called   4043
Vespers, should occur when the rays of the sun are already giving light;
Vespers when these rays are fading, for just as the Work of God begins the
day, so the day is concluded in similar fashion. In this way is fulfilled the
Scripture: "From the rising of the sun to its setting"—it does not say "after
its setting"—"praise the name of the Lord,"[17] for the Lord "takes delight
in what comes from the morning and the evening."[18] It is at such moments that the Lord, thanks to our angels, takes delight in telling the good
deeds accomplished by the just throughout the day, as Saint Paul says in
his revelation: "Sons of men, bless the Lord without cease, but especially
when the sun is setting."[i] But an exact indication of the day's beginning
and end is given us by the sun, which as it sets introduces the darkness of
the night.

Because of summer's short nights the *lucernarium* [Vespers] is begun   4044
when the sun is still somewhat high. In this way, when the brothers are
fatigued by working in the heat and by fasting, their insufficient rest may
receive additional sleep, taken at a time when it is still daylight, to make
up for the brevity of the night.

Question of the disciples
xxxv. The manner and number of the psalms during the day
The Lord has replied through the Master:

As to the psalms at Matins, in every season there are to be six; also one   4045
responsory, the verse, the reading from the Apostle, and the reading from
the Gospel which is always done by the abbot, and the *rogus Dei*.

As to the psalms at the hours designated above, namely, at Prime,   4046
Terce, Sext, and None, there are always three psalms and according to the
sequence given by the psalter; also the responsory, the reading from the
Apostle, the reading from the Gospel which is always done by the abbot
or, in his absence, by the deans in turn, and then the *rogus Dei*.

Question of the disciples
xxxvi. The psalms at the *lucernarium*
The Lord replies through the Master:

---

i. *Visio Pauli* 7, ed. M.R. James, *Apocrypha Anecdota*, Texts and Studies 2.3 (Cam-
bridge, 1893). Also known as the *Apocalypse of Paul*, this is an apocryphal work
originally written in Greek during the latter half of the fourth century.
16. Ps 119:164.   17. Ps 113:3.   18. Ps 65:8.

4047   At the *lucernarium* in winter there should be six psalms, always in the sequence given in the psalter; also one responsory, the verse, the lesson from the Apostle, the Gospel[j] which is always said by the abbot, and then the *rogus Dei*. Thus there are [eight] psalm *inpositiones* when we include the responsory but not the verse and the lessons. Then there are the four *inpositiones* at each hour of the day, that is, the three antiphonal psalms and the responsory at each of these hours, namely, Prime, Terce, Sext, and None. So altogether there are sixteen *inpositiones*, not counting the verses and the lessons. As a result we prostrate twenty-four times when chanting the psalms, doing so in imitation of the twenty-four elders who, adoring God without ceasing in heaven, throw down their crowns and lie prostrate, praising the Lord day and night as they glorify God.

4048   Likewise during summer at the *lucernarium* there are to be eight *inpositiones* with the responsory and the Gospel but not including the verse and the lessons. Thus these eight *inpositiones*, as we said above, result in our having twenty-four *inpositiones* in accord with the twenty-four elders in heaven,[19] and so they cause those of us on earth to prostrate before God in praise twenty-four times a day in every season.

4049   During summer the *lucernarium* is begun earlier because of the short nights during this season.

Question of the disciples
XXXVII. The psalms at Compline
The Lord has replied through the Master:

4050   At Compline there are three psalms, the responsory, the lesson from the Apostle, the lesson from the Gospel which is always said by the abbot when he is present, the *rogus Dei*, and the closing verse.

Question of the disciples
XXXIX. How the psalms are to be chanted at Matins
The Lord has replied through the Master:

4051   At Matins the psalms are always sung antiphonally, namely, four without the Alleluia; then two with the Alleluia; subsequently the responsory, the verse, the lessons, the Gospel[k] which is read by the abbot without the Alleluia but with the Alleluia on Sunday till the Epiphany. Thus with the Gospel there are eight *inpositiones*, excluding the verse and the lessons. Matins, however, consists of canticles except for Psalm 50 and the praises.[l] Yet on Sundays and other feasts, and on the anniversaries of the saints, the *Benedictiones*[m] are said. After these, on Sundays there is no prostrating till

---

j. The "Gospel" here would seem to mean a Gospel canticle; see R. Taft, *The Liturgy of the Hours*, 126–27.

k. See note j above.

l. Namely, Psalms 148, 149, and 150.

m. Namely, Dan 3. See R. Taft, *The Liturgy of the Hours*, 128–29.

19. See Rev 4:4; 5:8–9; 7:11–12.

the nocturns, and once the *Benedictiones* have been said, all the antiphonal psalms and the responsories are said with the Alleluia up to the nocturns of Monday.

Question of the disciples
XL. How are the psalms at the hours to be chanted?
The Lord has replied through the Master:
    The psalms sung at Prime, Terce, Sext, and None are always antiphonal   4052
psalms. Except from the Epiphany on, the third psalm is always sung with the Alleluia and always follows the sequence given in the psalter. There is always the responsory, the lesson from the Apostle, the lesson from the Gospel which is always read by the abbot or in his absence by the deans in turn, the verse, and the *rogus Dei.*

Question of the disciples
XLI. How are the psalms at the *lucernarium* to be chanted?
The Lord has replied through the Master:
    The psalms at the *lucernarium* are to be sung with antiphons, the last   4053
two with the Alleluia and always following the sequence of the Psalter. There is always the responsory, the verse, the lesson from the Apostle, and the Gospel[n] which is always given by the abbot without the Alleluia but on Sunday with the Alleluia. On Sunday after the *Benedictiones* the antiphonal psalms are all chanted with the Alleluia; on this day there is no prostrating till Monday's nocturns.

Question of the disciples
XLII. How are the psalms at Compline to be chanted?
The Lord has replied through the Master:
    In every season the psalms at Compline are sung with their antiphons.   4054
However, the third psalm begins with an Alleluia. According to the prophet we are to praise God seven times during the day.[20] And so all the psalms are sung in the same fashion because of the sevenfold Spirit who in no way can be divided.[21]

Question [of the disciples]
XLIV. How are the psalms at night to be sung?
The Lord has replied through the Master:
    At the nocturns the opening verse and the exhortatory response are   4055
said by the abbot. In winter there are [nine] antiphonal psalms without the Alleluia, a responsory without the Alleluia, [four antiphonal psalms with the Alleluia] and always according to the sequence in the psalter, another responsory, this time with the Alleluia to make sixteen *inpositiones*, the lesson from the Apostle, the lesson from the Gospel which is always read by

---

n. See note j above.
20. See Ps 119:164.   21. See Isa 11:2–3.

the abbot or if he is absent by the deans in turn, the verse, and the *rogus Dei.*

4056   In summer, however, from the Pasch to winter's equinox, which is September 24, six antiphons without the Alleluia are sung after the opening verse and the abbot's responsory. Then follows a responsory, likewise without the Alleluia. Next there are three antiphons with an Alleluia, always following the sequence of the psalter as we have said above. Then another responsory, this time with the Alleluia, all of which make twelve *inpositiones.* There are two readings, one from the apostle, the other from the Gospels and which is read by the abbot or in his absence by the deans in turn. Finally there is a verse followed by the prayer to God.

4057   As to the lesson, the person appointed to read should do so by heart and not use a book; vigils are the only exception here. We prescribe this so that the brothers may more often meditate on and retain the Scriptures in their memories. And so whenever there is no book, no matter where, the text of the lesson or of the page is, if necessary, recited by memory.

4058   When the nights are long, a candle or a lamp will be lit in the dormitory, and the abbot, if he so pleases, will do the reading, or indeed each brother of his own accord will obtain permission to read, to listen, to study something, or to work for the benefit of the monastery. [. . .]

Question of the disciples
xlv. How are the psalms to be sung on feasts?
The Lord has replied through the Master:

4059   From Easter to Pentecost all the antiphonal psalms and the responsories, both during the day and during the night, are chanted with the Alleluia. During this time there is no prostrating.

4060   Furthermore, from the Lord's Nativity to the Epiphany all the antiphonal psalms and the responsories, both during the day and the night, are chanted with the Alleluia; during this time no one prostrates, fasts, or abstains. But during the eight days preceding the Lord's Nativity the brothers fast and abstain as they do during Lent; the orations are prayed as one customarily prays them during Lent. May we, imitating the sadness of Lent, be like servants who go beyond their daily duties in giving service in order to obtain pardon. In so doing we will rejoice that the Lord's Nativity has arrived with its rewards and gifts.

4061   As to the Epiphany, it is only during the night of the vigil and the day itself that all the antiphonal psalms and the responsories are sung with the Alleluia. Starting from this day the Alleluia is locked up and the festal decorations are immediately removed from the oratory. On Epiphany itself there is no prostration. As we have said, the Alleluia is sung only on Epiphany itself with its vigil and not till its octave; the reason for this is that the hundred days of fast and abstinence before Easter begin from this day.

4062   Furthermore, on all Sundays after the *Benedictiones*, all the antiphonal psalms and the responsories are said with the Alleluia up to the nocturns of Monday, and there is no prostrating because Sunday is devoted to the paschal resurrection. On the other hand, on every Sunday, from the *Benedictiones* up to the end of the Mass in the church, the following verse is always said at the Work of God: "The saints will exalt in glory; they will rejoice in their chambers,"[22] namely, that wherever there are chambers of the saints—in other words, churches—there Mass is joyfully celebrated.

Furthermore, when there is a feast of a saint, no matter on which day, once the *Benedictiones* are said there is no prostrating till Prime. But if it is the feast of a saint in whose oratory the psalms are being sung, then once the *Benedictiones* have been said, there is no prostrating till the procession at the Mass celebrated there on this day by a priest; and as a sign of joy for the oratory's own feast, throughout the whole day up to the nocturns that follow, everything will be sung with the Alleluia as is the practice on Sunday.

4063

Question of the disciples
XLVI. Intoning the psalms in the oratory, whatever the season
The Lord has replied through the Master:

After the abbot, it is the deans who intone the antiphonal psalms. They do so at the directive of the abbot and, as we have said, according to the sequence found in the psalter. When the deans have finished, each of the brothers from all the deaneries will intone, each in turn, when directed to do so by the abbot when he is present.

4064

The lessons from the Apostle will always be read by the deans who take turns doing so. The lessons from the Gospel will always be read by the abbot when he is present; but if he is not present, then by the deans who take turns doing this. At Matins as well as at the *lucernarium*, after the lesson from the Apostle has been read, the abbot, when present, always follows with a reading from the Gospel. In his absence the deans take turns doing this. Thus, according to the order in which the clerics do the readings at Mass—namely, when a lower cleric finishes reading the Apostle, it is a deacon, his superior, who proceeds to read the holy Gospel—so in the monastery one preserves the hierarchy of the Lord by following the order of dignity.

4065

During the nocturns, Matins, and the *lucernarium*, the responsories are sung integrally. But at Prime, Terce, Sext, and None two sections of the responsory are said each time, and immediately the "Glory be" is said so that the brothers may more quickly depart the oratory and go back to their assigned manual labor.

4066

Question of the disciples
XLVII. The manner of chanting the psalms
The Lord has replied through the Master:

We are to chant the psalms with such great reverence and seriousness that it is evident that the Lord is ever more pleased to hear what we have

4067

---

22. Ps 149:5.

to say, as Scripture says, "You take delight in the coming of the morning and evening."[23] Also, "Sing for him in jubilation because the word of the Lord is good."[24] Also, "Rejoice before him with fear."[25] Also, "Sing praises with wisdom."[26] If then he enjoins us to sing wisely and with fear, it is necessary that whoever chants the psalms stands with a motionless body, with head bowed, and that he sing praises to the Lord with reserve since he is fulfilling his service before the divinity, as the prophet teaches when he says, "In the presence of angels I will sing to you."[27]

4068   Whoever sings the psalms should unceasingly take care not to allow his spirit to roam elsewhere lest, should our spirit yield to distractions, God may say regarding us, "This people honors me with its lips, but its heart is far from me."[28] May he also not say of us, "Their mouth blesses, but their heart curses."[29] When we praise God only with our tongue, then we allow God to enter only the door of our mouth while we introduce and install the devil within, in the dwelling of our heart. In fact, whoever goes inside is more greatly esteemed by the person bringing him in than is he who is left waiting without. And so for such a great and important task the heart should agree with the tongue in order to render with fear what is due to the Lord each day. Those who chant the psalms are to concentrate in their hearts on each and every text spoken, for if one thus concentrates on each verse, the soul will draw profit for salvation and will there find all that is sought, "for the psalm says all that contributes to edify"[30] since the prophet says, "I will sing and understand in the unspotted way when you will come to me."[31] May he whose name resounds in the voice be also in the mind of those who sing. Therefore may we sing with both voice and understanding, as the apostle says, "I will sing in the spirit, I will sing with the mind."[32] We should cry out to God not only with our voices but also with our hearts.

4069   On the other hand, when singing the psalms we should also take care to avoid frequent coughing, prolonged panting, or continually spitting out saliva. Whoever is chanting the psalms will also take care not to discard in front of him the filth found in his nose; it is behind him that the brother is to dispose of such, for we learn that the angels stand in front of those who sing the psalms, as the prophet says, "In the presence of the angels I will sing to you."[33] And so when the devil presents all these obstacles to those who sing the psalms, the person singing will immediately make the sign of the cross on his mouth.

Question of the disciples
XLIX. Vigils in the monastery
The Lord has replied through the Master:

---

23. Ps 65:8.   24. Ps 33:3–4.   25. Ps 2:11.   26. Ps 47:7.   27. Ps 138:1.   28. Matt 15:8; see Isa 29:13.   29. Ps 62:4.   30. 1 Cor 14:3, 26.   31. Ps 101:1–2.   32. 1 Cor 14:15.   33. Ps 138:1.

Every Saturday a vigil is to be celebrated in the monastery from evening 4070
till the second cockcrow; this is followed by Matins. The reason it is called
a vigil is that the brothers rouse themselves from sleep, chant the psalms,
and hear the lessons. After Matins they return to their beds.

Question of the disciples
Here begins the Rule for Lent
LI. The prayers of Lent during the day
The Lord has replied through the Master:
    All are to say a simple prayer between Matins and Prime. Likewise be- 4071
tween Prime and Terce, between Terce and Sext, between Sext and None,
between None and Vespers; also between Vespers and Compline. This
must be done each day during Lent.

Question of the disciples
LII. The prayers without psalms during the night
The Lord has replied through the Master:
    After the first period of sleep, all rise and say a prayer at their beds. 4072
After the abbot concludes the prayer, all return to bed. Once again after
the nocturns, all go back to sleep; when the cock has crowed, all rise and
pray at their beds; the abbot concludes the prayer and all lie down again.
And so it is necessary that the "watchful cocks" [*vigigallos*] be especially
vigilant during the nights of Lent and very attentive throughout the day
so as to alert the brothers that the hour for prayer has arrived. For this reason all should sleep in the same room; in this way these prayers may be
said by all in common at their beds and all may be able to hear the abbot
conclude them. Once again one rises and celebrates Matins, for before Easter Matins is still said separately from the nocturns. And again between
Matins and Prime a simple prayer is said.

Question of the disciples
LIII. Abstinence from food and drink during Lent
The Lord has replied through the Master:
    [. . .] These [monks who during Lent do more than is required by the 4073
Rule] in fact merit to rejoice with Christ at his resurrection on Easter.
They have crucified their bodies with him by abstaining during Lent as
Scripture says when it speaks of sadness: "Those who sow with tears
will reap with joy,"[34] and "Afflicted in little things, in many they shall be
rewarded."[35] For this reason Lent is a type of the present world, whereas
for those who are good Easter signifies the eternal joy of the life to come
insofar as the food that we are permitted to eat during the rest of the year
is not taken during these forty days. Likewise, the soul of the brother who
in the present life of this world curbs his desires and body is in the other
world allowed to grow abundantly fat and always has more abundant

---

34. Ps 126:5.   35. Wis 3:5.

divine delights. For having wished to be sad for the sake of the Lord during this very brief season, he will also merit to rejoice with him in the future.

4074　　On Holy Thursday they will cut the hair on their heads, wash themselves, and take everything they abstained from other than the flesh and blood of land animals.[36] [. . .]

4075　　During these forty days the weekly servers will not wash the feet of the brothers in the monastery, but they will be content to remove their footwear. The feet of all visitors from afar will be washed because of the scriptural passage of the woman who washed the Savior's feet when he was at supper and who, using an alabaster jar, anointed them.[37] On Holy Thursday, however, in place of the blessing, they will wash the feet of the abbot, and then the abbot will wash the feet of all the deans, assisted by the brothers, but the abbot himself begins this. Furthermore, the superior will personally wash the feet of the porters. Thus, having proved himself humble by serving them in this fashion, the abbot will be judged worthy of the honor that places him above all. Afterwards, each dean will wash and dry the feet of the brothers who belong to his deanery.

4076　　At dawn on the Friday before Holy Saturday, only the nocturns are celebrated—these are said before cockcrow and thus still belong to Thursday—and henceforth <neither> Matins nor the other hours nor the usual divine offices are said till Mass on Saturday when the new Alleluia of the joyous Resurrection will end the long silence of the psalms in the mouths of those who chant them. Then, although they chant no psalms from the nocturns on Thursday till the Mass on Saturday, they will, however, pray the simple prayers of Lent; and all day on Friday they will quietly meditate on the Lord's suffering, not even greeting each other when they meet.

4077　　[. . .] The sacrament of the altar, kept in a large glass vessel, will be entirely consumed. In this way when the Jews on Friday seek out Christ in order to have him suffer, he will on this day be enclosed in our hearts; in this way Saturday might appear to us as a new sacrament because of his resurrection. Henceforth, those who wish to have a meal on Friday will do so without receiving Communion to show that it is not right to take a meal without Christ.

4078　　On the same day various objects are washed, and preparations are made for Easter. Also on this day the altar veil is removed; additionally all decorations are removed from the oratory. Furthermore, all lights and lamps within the monastery are to be removed so that everything among us be sorrowful on this day—a day when the true light of the Lord left the world due to his passion,[38] and because all is joyfully restored at dawn on the following Saturday when the light of joy will return to us because of Christ's resurrection. At all times the monastery is to be well-arranged and uncluttered; when viewed from the entrance all the places are to be clean

---

36. See Gen 9:4; Acts 15:29.　　37. See Luke 7:36–46; John 12:2–8.　　38. See John 1:9.

and adorned with hangings. Throughout it is to be the image of a church. Thus wherever the brothers gather is to be fitting, pleasing, and conducive to prayer.

End of the Rule for Lent
LIV. When the hour for the divine office arrives, the brothers should immediately hasten to the oratory

When the signal given in the oratory announces that the time for the 4079 Work of God has arrived, the workers immediately put aside their chores, the artisans leave their tools; the copyists do not complete the letters they are drawing; the hand of each brother will leave what it is doing; the feet must immediately and with all purpose hasten to the oratory; their thoughts are to be directed toward God so that all may immediately gather for the first prayer. Like bees seeking honey, the brothers will swarm toward the oratory's entrance so that the holy oratory, till then silent, is immediately filled with the clamor of the psalms, and that the silence of the holy place will spread toward the deserted workshops and unfinished tasks.

Meanwhile, each time that the signal is sounded in the oratory, all who 4080 hear it, before hastening off, trace the sign of the cross on their foreheads and reply, "Thanks be to God."

Question of the disciples
LV. The distance required for a brother to abandon his work and hurry to the oratory
The Lord has replied through the Master:

When the signal given by the abbot in the oratory is heard, the brother 4081 who is working, whether alone or with others, immediately is to put down his tool and by means of a quick glance determine whether he should or should not hasten to the oratory. If he is fifty steps from the monastery's entrance, he should hurry there with all speed. But if the distance is greater than this, he does not go. But remaining where he is, putting aside the tool he has in his hand, and bending the neck as the brothers bend the knees in the oratory, he too will carry out the Work of God, doing so quietly and apart.

If a brother has some urgent task to do, he will say the psalms in groups 4082 of three with the "Glory be" because the doxologies that are said between the psalms replace the prayers. The person saying the psalms always says these doxologies with bowed head. The psalms are said directly because, as we said earlier, the work to be done is pressing. After these psalms with the verse and the oration have been concluded, he himself will conclude and immediately resume what he was doing. [. . .]

As to those within the monastery who are detained by tasks that are 4083 immediately necessary for the life of the community, they will ask aloud— once the psalm is concluded and all stand for the prayer—that they be remembered by those within the oratory. Nevertheless, in the very place where they are detained they are to carry out the Work of God, doing so silently by following the words said in the oratory. In addition, each time that they complete a psalm, in the very place where they are standing or sitting they are to prostrate themselves for the prayer.

LXXIII. Brothers who arrive late for the Work of God

4084   As to the brother who is tardy for the first prayer or psalm at the nocturns, Matins, and the *lucernaria*, the abbot shakes his head at him in the oratory in order to inspire fear and then, outside, privately warns him to correct his ways. If the brother misses the second prayer or psalm, he will be severely reprimanded in the oratory itself, in the presence of the community and after the psalm. But if he enters after the third prayer or psalm, he and his deans will be immediately excommunicated and evicted from the oratory. They will not be forgiven till they have all completed a humble satisfaction before the oratory's entrance. Yet this is to be understood in accordance with what we already said about being less than fifty steps distant.

4085   After the signal has been given for Prime, Terce, Sext, and None, whoever does not arrive on time for the first prayer and the first psalm will be severely reprimanded in the oratory itself and in the presence of all. The brother who arrives after the second prayer or the second psalm will first be excommunicated, and he with his deans must leave. [. . .]

4086   Yet these reprimands and excommunications are directed only at those who come late by reason of willful negligence and are not detained by any task necessary for the community. Even if they cry out with their own voices requesting that they be remembered in the oratory as absent ones in the prayers, the brothers will not mention them. They should know that they are excommunicated since it was not an affair of the monastery that delayed them but their own lack of concern. As to those detained by urgent affairs of the monastery, those in the oratory rightly recall these absent ones who in the very place where they are detained perform the Work of God.

4087   As to the brother who has been reprimanded in the oratory, even if he has not been ordered to leave the oratory, he will not pray or read a psalm, a responsory, a lesson, a verse, till he has done satisfaction for his fault within the oratory by prostrating himself and by humbly requesting that others pray for him.

4088   A brother who is detained because of urgent community business is to be remembered in the oratory as someone who is absent. Those detained by negligence or laziness are passed over in silence since they sin by refusing to remember God in prayer.

LXXV. Rest on Sunday

4089   Starting from the ninth hour on Saturday, after the meal, in summer there is no more reading. In winter, beginning with None on Saturday, as prescribed above, there is no work. In addition, on the following day, Sunday, all manual work ceases as well as the daily memorizing that normally occurs for three hours each day during each season, both winter and summer. But after Mass in the church, each will read as much as he wishes, and permission is granted to return to bed. In this way all are happy that Sunday has been assigned as a day of rest.

155. BENEDICT OF NURSIA

Almost all the information we have regarding Benedict's life comes to us from Book II of Gregory I's *Dialogues* (WEC 4:**165-B**).

Born ca. 480 in Nursia (Norcia) in Tuscany, Benedict was sent as a boy to Rome for his education. However, he fled the city because of its immoral lifestyle and ca. 500 took refuge in a cave near the town of Subiaco, where he lived as a hermit. Gradually disciples came to him, and Benedict established small monasteries for them in the locality. Leaving Subiaco because of local rivalries, Benedict ca. 530 went to Monte Cassino, where he established a monastery on the site of an abandoned pagan temple. It was from here that monks were sent out to various places in the West, where they brought about a revival of the monastic life. And it was at Monte Cassino that Benedict wrote his famous Rule.

Although he preached, Benedict does not seem to have been ordained. Nor does it appear that he intended to establish a religious order. His sister, Scholastica (ca. 480–ca. 543), is said to have established a convent at Plombariola, a short distance from Monte Cassino. Benedict died on March 21, 543.

CPL no. 1852 * Altaner (1961) 559, 576–78 * Altaner (1966) 481–82 * Bardenhewer (1908) 627 * Bardenhewer (1910) 540 * Bardenhewer (1913) 5:228–36 * Bautz 1:494–96 * Labriolle (1947) 2:799–801 * Steidle 233–34 * Tixeront 353 * CATH 1:1446–52 * CE 2:467–72, 436–41 * DCB 1:309–11 * DDC 2:297–349 * DHGE 8:225–41 * DictSp 1:1371–1409 * DPAC 1:521–22 * DTC 2:1709–17 * EC 2:1251–62 * EEC 1:119 * EEChr 1:179–81 * LTK 2:203–4 * NCE 2:271–73 * NCES 2:236–38 * ODCC 182–83 * PEA (1991) 2:559–61 * RACh 2:130–36 * TRE 5:538–49

"Saint Benoît et le signe de la croix," LMF 1 (1884–85) 315–17. * "Saint Benoît et l'esprit de prière," LMF 1 (1884–85) 411–12. * "L'évangile dans la liturgie," LMF 1 (1884–85) 318–26, 363–68, 460–64, 506–13, 557–63. * F. Cabrol, "Le 'Book of Cerne': les liturgies celtiques et gallicanes et la liturgie romaine," RQH 76, n.s., 32 (1904) 210–22. * U. Berlière, "Les hymnes dans le 'cursus' de s. Benoît," RB 25 (1908) 367–74. * F. Cavallera, "Ascétisme et liturgie," BLE 5, 6th ser., 6 (1914) 49–68, 97–107. * C. Callewaert, "Tu autem Domine miserere nobis," CB 28 (1928) 471–75. * C. Callewaert, "De Parvis Horis Romanis ante Regulam s. Benedicti," CB 29 (1929) 481–92. * C. Callewaert, "De Completorio ante s. Benedictum," CB 30 (1930) 225–30. * C. Callewaert, "De Capitulis in Officio Romano ante s. Benedictum," CB 30 (1930) 318–21. * C. Callewaert, "Les étapes de l'histoire du 'Kyrie': s. Gélase, s. Benoît, s. Grégoire," RHE 38 (1942) 20–45. * A. Strittmatter,

"The Monastic Blessing of the Weekly Reader in Missal W. 11 of the Walters
Art Gallery," Tra 3 (1945) 392–94. * J. Gaillard, "Le dimanche dans la Règle de s.
Benoît," VS Supplement (1947) 469–88. * I. Hausherr, "Opus Dei," OCP 13 (1947)
195–218. * G. Le Maître, "L'oraison dans l'Ordre Bénédictin," Chr 2 (1955) 238–42.
* E. von Severus, "Monastische Liturgie," ALW 4 (1955–56) 506–65. * C. Gindele,
"Die Satisfaktionsordung von Caesarius und Benedikt bis Donatus," RB 69 (1959)
216–36. * E. von Severus, "Monastische Liturgie," ALW 6 (1959–60) 520–80. * P.
Rouillard, "Temps et rythmes de la prière dans le monachisme ancien," LMD, no.
64 (1960) 32–52. * P. Bellet, "'Data benedictione': nota sobre el capítulo XI de la
Regla de san Benito," SM 4 (1962) 365–67. * A. de Vogüé, "Le rituel monastique
chez s. Benoît et chez le Maître," RB 71 (1961) 233–64. * A.M. Mundó, "A propos
des rituels du Maître et de s. Benoît: la 'Provolutio,'" SM 4 (1962) 177–91. * A. de
Vogüé, "'Orationi frequenter incumbere': une invitation à la prière continuelle,"
RAM 41 (1965) 467–72. * A. de Vogüé, "Le sens de l'office divin d'après la Règle
de s. Benoît," RAM 42 (1966) 389–404. * R.E. Sommerville, "'Ordinatio Abbatis'
in the Rule of St. Benedict," RB 77 (1967) 246–63. * A. de Vogüé, "Le sens de
l'office divin d'après la Règle de s. Benoit II: psalmodie et oraison (RB 19–20),"
RAM 43 (1967) 21–33. * G. Morin, "Une demi-heure d'oraison chaque jour dans
le monastères de s. Benoît?" SM 11 (1969) 99–103. * C. Gindele, "Zum grossen Rekonziliationsritus nach der Magister- and Benediktusregel," RB 80 (1970) 153–56.
* J. Gribomont, "Rome et les moines: le principal document sur l'office divine au
VIe siècle remis en question," LMD, no. 114 (1973) 135–40. * B. de la Héraudière,
"Le repas monastique," Chr 21 (1974) 474–85. * C. Gindele, "Verspätung, Ver-
zügerung und Krürzung im Gottesdienst der Magister- und Benediktusregel," RB
86 (1976) 306–21. * F. Débuyst, "La personalisme communautaire dans la Règle
de s. Benoit," ComL 61:5 (1979) 407–19. * M. van Parys, "La prière brève et pure
selon s. Benoît," Ire 52 (1979) 507–12. * B. Fischer, "Prière commune institution-
nelle et prière personnelle libre dans la Règle de s. Benoît," LMD, no. 143 (1980)
153–73. * A. Louf, "La prière dans la Règle de s. Benoît," VS 134 (1980) 511–29. *
Ph. Rouillard, "Prière et communauté dans la Règle de s. Benoît," Not 16 (1980)
309–18. * M. Marrion, "God the Father as Foundation for Constant Prayer in the
'Regula Benedicti,'" SM 23 (1981) 263–305. * N. Mitchell, "The Liturgical Code in
the Rule of Benedict," in *RB 1980: The Rule of St. Benedict in Latin and English with
Notes*, ed. T. Fry (Collegeville, 1981) 379–414. * A. Verheul, "La prière monastique
chorale avant Benoît: son influence sur le culte en Occident: la prière des heures
avant la Règle et dans la Règle de s. Benoît," QL 62 (1981) 227–42. * A. de Vogüé,
"Les chapitres de la Règle bénédictine sur l'office: leur authenticité," SM 23 (1981)
7–10. * A. de Vogüé, "Vie monastique et temps de prière commune," Con (F) 162
(1981) 125–32. * A. Verheul, "La prière chorale dans la Règle de s. Benoît," QL 63
(1982) 25–36. * A. Verheul, "Les valeurs permanentes de la prière des heures selon
s. Benoît," QL 63 (1982) 217–22. * O. Raquez, *Offices byzantines en l'honneur de s.
Benoît de Nursie* (Cureglia, Switzerland, 1983). * R. Taft, *The Liturgy of the Hours in
East and West: The Origins of the Divine Office and Its Meaning for Today* (Collegeville, 1986) 134–40. * A. Verheul, "Les psaumes dans la prière des heures: hier et
aujourd'hui," QL 71 (1990) 261–95. * A. Borias, "Etude sur les chapitres 27 et 28
de la Règle bénédictine," RB 104 (1994) 284–94. * C. Stewart, *Prayer and Community: The Benedictine Tradition* (Maryknoll, NY, 1998).

155-A. Rule[†]

Written between 535 and 540 at Monte Cassino, Benedict's Rule, consist-
ing of a prologue and seventy-three chapters, employed, in addition to
Scripture, various other sources: e.g., the Rule of Basil (WEC **2:67-B**), John
Cassian (WEC **3:118**), Augustine (WEC **3:98-V**), and Caesarius of Arles
(WEC **4:168-A-1**). There is also a close relationship between Benedict's
Rule and the Rule of the Master (WEC **4:154**), although not all scholars
agree as to which document came first. For Benedict the primary focus of
the community's life is the *Opus Dei*, the "Work of God," the Divine Office,
and this observance is supported by private prayer and reading as well as
by labor. The document has been characterized as a work of wisdom, bal-
ance, and mildness.

VIII. The divine offices during the night

As circumstances allow during the season of winter, namely, from the   4090
calends of November till Easter, the brethren rise at the eighth hour of the
night so that having rested after midnight they might be refreshed. The
time remaining after the vigil[a] will be used for study by those brothers
who still have parts of the psalter or the lessons to learn.

From Easter to the above-mentioned calends of November the hour for   4091
the vigil will be arranged so that, after a very short period of time when
the brothers can tend to the needs of nature, Morning Prayer,[b] said at daybreak, may immediately follow.

IX. How many psalms are to be said during the night hours

During the season of winter mentioned above, having first said the   4092
verse *Deus in adiutorium meum intende*, the brothers then say the *Domine,
labia mea aperies, et os meum adnuntiabit laudem tuam*,[1] repeating it three
times. Then Psalm 3[c] with the *Gloria* follows. Afterwards Psalm 94 with
its antiphon[d] is said or chanted.[e] A hymn[f] follows; then six psalms with

---

[†] Translated from *La Règle de s. Benoît*, vol. 2, trans. and ed. A. de Vogüé and
J. Neufville, SChr 182 (Paris, 1972).

a. *Vigilia* or *nocturnus*: terms used by Benedict for the office celebrated at night.
In this translation the term "night office" is used.

b. *Matutinus*: a term used by Benedict for the celebration of the office at daybreak. In this translation the term "Morning Prayer" is used. He uses the word
laudes to refer to Psalms 148–50, in this translation rendered as "psalms of praise."

c. Benedict follows the numbering of the psalms according to the LXX, an enumeration retained in this translation.

d. For antiphonal singing, see R. Taft, *The Liturgy of the Hours in East and West:
The Origins of the Divine Office and Its Meaning for Today* (Collegeville, 1986) 139.

e. Benedict uses interchangeably various terms for rendering the psalmody, e.g.,
to "sing," to "psalm," to "say."

f. Benedict at times, as here, employs the term *ambrosianum* for "hymn."

1. Ps 51:15.

antiphons. When these and the verses have been said, the abbot gives the blessing; all are seated on benches, and the brothers read alternately three lessons from a book located on a reading stand; a responsory is sung after each of them. Two of the responsories are said without the *Gloria*, but after the third lesson the brother who is chanting says the *Gloria*. When he begins it, all immediately rise from their benches as a sign of honor and reverence for the Holy Trinity. At vigils are read the books of divine authority, both the Old and the New Testaments as well as the explanations given by the eminent and orthodox Catholic fathers.

4093   After these three lessons with their responsories, six other psalms follow and they are sung with the Alleluia. The reading from the Apostle follows, being recited from memory; then the verse and the invocation of the litany, namely, the *Kyrie eleison*. In this way the night offices end.

x. How the night office is to be celebrated during the summer season

4094   On the other hand, from Easter to the calends of November all the psalmody indicated above is retained. However, no lessons are read from the book due to the shortness of the night; replacing these three lessons is one lesson, memorized and from the Old Testament; this is followed by a short responsory. Everything else is done as we said, namely, at the night vigils there are no fewer than twelve psalms, not including Psalms 3 and 94.

xi. How to celebrate the Sunday vigils

4095   On Sunday the brothers rise earlier for the vigils where the following regulation is to be observed, namely, once the six psalms and the verse have been sung as arranged above, and once all according to order and rank are properly sitting on their benches, four lessons with responsories are read from the book. It is only at the fourth responsory that the cantors sing the *Gloria*. When they intone it, all immediately stand, doing so with reverence.

4096   After these lessons there are six other psalms, following in order as previously, with antiphons and verse. Then four other lessons with their responsories are read according to the order given above.

4097   After these come three canticles, selected by the abbot, from the Prophets; these are sung with the Alleluia. Once the verse has been said and the abbot has given the blessing, four other lessons are read from the New Testament according to the order indicated above, but after the fourth responsory the abbot intones the hymn *Te Deum laudamus*. When this has been completed, the abbot reads the lesson from the Gospel while all stand with reverence and awe. At the end of the Gospel reading all respond *Amen*, and immediately the abbot follows up with the hymn *Te decet laus*, and once the blessing has been given, Morning Prayer begins.

4098   This order for the vigil is to be observed on Sunday at each season, during the summer as well as during the winter except if—God forbid—the brothers should arise late and the readings or responsories have to be somewhat shortened, and yet every care is to be taken that this does not occur. But if it should happen, the brother whose neglect caused this to happen is to make in the oratory a fitting satisfaction to God.

xii. How to celebrate the solemnity of Morning Prayer

On Sunday, Morning Prayer begins with Psalm 66 without an antiphon, directly.ᵍ Afterwards Psalm 50 with the Alleluia is said. Then Psalm 117 and Psalm 62. Next, the blessings and the songs of praise [*laudes*], one lesson from Revelation said by heart, the responsory, the hymn, the verse, the canticle from the Gospel, the litany with which the office concludes.

4099

xiii. How to celebrate Morning Prayer on ordinary days

On weekdays Morning Prayer is celebrated as follows: Psalm 66 is said without an antiphon, drawing it out a little as is done on Sunday so that all may be present for Psalm 50, which is said with an antiphon. Afterwards, two other psalms are said according to custom, namely, on Monday Psalm 5 and Psalm 35, on Tuesday Psalm 42 and Psalm 56, on Wednesday Psalm 63 and Psalm 64, on Thursday Psalm 87 and Psalm 89, on Friday Psalm 75 and Psalm 91, and on Saturday Psalm 142 and the canticle from Deuteronomy, divided into two sections with each section followed by the *Gloria*. On other days the canticle is from the Prophets as the Roman Church sings on these days. Psalms of praise follow; then a lesson from the Apostle said by heart, the responsory, the hymn, the verse, the canticle from the Gospel, and the litany with which the office concludes.

4100

Because of possible scandals, the morning and evening offices should never conclude without the Lord's Prayer being said aloud. In this way the brothers may cleanse themselves of failings of this type, doing so by reason of the promise found in this prayer when they say: *Dimitte nobis simul et nos dimittimus.*² At other celebrations, however, only the last part of this prayer is said [aloud] so that all may answer *Sed libera nos a malo.*³

4101

xiv. How the night office is said on the feasts of the saints

On the feasts of the saints and on all solemnities, the night office is to be celebrated as we said it should be celebrated on Sunday, except that the psalms, the antiphons, and the lessons proper to the day are used. Their number is that indicated previously.

4102

xv. When the Alleluia is said

From holy Easter till Pentecost the Alleluia is always said, both in the psalms and in the responsory; from Pentecost to the beginning of Lent it is said every night at the nocturns with the six latter psalms only.

4103

Every Sunday, except during Lent, the canticles as well as Morning Prayer, Prime, Terce, Sext and None are said with the Alleluia, but at

4104

---

g. For "direct" psalmody, see R. Taft, *The Liturgy of the Hours*, 139.
2. Matt 6:12.   3. Matt 6:13.

Vespers with the antiphon. Except from Easter to Pentecost the responsories are never said with the Alleluia.

xvi. How the Work of God is prayed throughout the day

4105   As the prophet says, "Seven times a day I have praised you."[4] This sacred number of seven is thus observed by us when we perform the duties of our service at Morning Prayer, Prime, Terce, Sext, None, Vespers, and Compline because concerning these hours during the day it was said, "Seven times a day I have praised you."[5] As to the night offices the same prophet said, "At midnight I arose to praise you."[6] Therefore at these times let us praise our Creator "for the judgments of his justice,"[7] that is, at Morning Prayer, Prime, Terce, Sext, None, Vespers, Compline, and "at night let us rise to praise him."[8]

xvii. How many psalms are to be sung at these hours

4106   We have already treated the psalmody for the night and morning hours; now let us consider the following hours.

4107   At Prime three psalms are said separately, not under one *Gloria*. The hymn for this same hour is said after the verse *Deus in adjutorium*[9] before beginning the psalms. After finishing the three psalms, one lesson is said, then the verse, the *Kyrie eleison*, and the dismissal.

4108   At Terce, Sext, and None the prayers follow this order, namely, the verse, the hymn proper to the hour, three psalms at each hour, the lesson, the verse, the *Kyrie eleison*, and the dismissal. If the community is larger, the psalms are chanted with antiphons; but if it is smaller, they are sung directly.[h]

4109   For the afternoon gathering there are four psalms with antiphons. After these psalms, a lesson is recited, then the response, the hymn, the verse, the canticle from the Gospel, the litany, the Lord's Prayer, and the concluding prayer.

4110   At Compline three psalms are said, directly, without antiphons. Afterwards, there is the hymn proper to this hour, a lesson, the verse, the *Kyrie eleison*, and then the blessing with the concluding prayer.

xviii. The order in which the psalms are to be sung

4111   First, there is the verse *Deus in adiutorium meum intende, Domine ad adiuvandum me festina*[10] with the *Gloria*; then the hymn proper to each hour.

4112   At Prime on Sunday the four sections of Psalm 118 are said. At the other hours, namely, Terce, Sext, and None, three sections of the same psalm are said. Yet at Prime on Monday three psalms are said, namely, Psalm 1, Psalm 2, and Psalm 6. And so each day at Prime till Sunday three psalms are said in consecutive order up to Psalm 19, yet dividing into two Psalm

---

h. See note g above.

4. Ps 119:164.   5. Ibid.   6. Ps 119:62.   7. Ps 119:164.   8. Ps 119:62.   9. Ps 70:1.
10. Ibid.

9 and Psalm 17. In this way it will always happen that the Sunday night office always begins with Psalm 20.

At Terce, Sext, and None on Monday the remaining nine sections of Psalm 118 are said, three sections at each of these hours. Having thus completed Psalm 118 in two days, namely, Sunday and Monday, on Tuesday for Terce, Sext, and None are sung three psalms each, from Psalm 119 to Psalm 127, that is, nine psalms. These psalms are always repeated identically till Sunday at these hours, keeping on all these days a uniform arrangement for the hymns, the lessons, and the verses, so that Sunday always begins with Psalm 118.

4113

Each day at Vespers four psalms are sung. The brothers begin with Psalm 109 and go to Psalm 147; not said, however, are those psalms reserved for the other hours, namely, Psalm 117 to Psalm 127 and Psalm 133 and Psalm 142. The rest are said at Vespers. Since three psalms are lacking, the longer psalms are divided, namely, Psalm 138, Psalm 143, and Psalm 144. Psalm 116, because it is short, is joined to Psalm 115. The order of psalmody for Vespers being thus arranged, what remains is said as directed above, namely, the lessons, the responsories, the hymns, the verses, and the canticles.

4114

At Compline each day the psalms are repeated, that is, Psalm 4, Psalm 90, and Psalm 133.

4115

The arrangement of the psalms for each day being thus organized, all the other psalms will be distributed equally among the seven night offices, dividing those that are longer so that twelve occur each night.

4116

We call special attention to the fact that if this allocation of the psalms does not please, then anyone may establish another arrangement which is thought to be better, provided that all 150 psalms of the Psalter are said each week, and that this distribution always starts from the beginning at the night office on Sunday. Monks who during the course of the week fail to chant the complete Psalter with its customary canticles are lax in their devotion since we read that our holy fathers promptly did in one day what we, being lukewarm, are called to do in one week.

4117

xix. How to recite the psalms

We believe that the divine presence is everywhere and that "the eyes of the Lord look upon the good and the evil in every place."[11] However, it is especially when we assist at the Work of God that we should most strongly believe this.

4118

Furthermore, we should always remember what the prophet said: "Serve the Lord with awe."[12] Also, "Sing wisely."[13] And, "I will sing to you in the presence of the angels."[14] Consider how we should act in the presence of God and of God's angels, and, when we stand to sing the psalms, how our minds should be in tune with our voices.

4119

---

11. Prov 15:3.   12. Ps 2:11.   13. Ps 47:7.   14. Ps 138:1.

xx. Reverence when praying

4120   If when we wish to present a request to powerful individuals, we do so only with humility and reverence, then how much more are we to beseech the Lord God of the universe in all humility and with the purest devotion! Know that we are heard not by the abundance of our words but by the purity of our hearts and by the tears of our sorrow. Wherefore prayer should be brief and pure unless it is perhaps lengthened by the inspiration of divine grace. In a community, however, prayer should always be short, and when the superior gives the sign, all are to rise together.

XLI. The hours when the brothers are to take their meals

4121   From holy Easter till Pentecost the brothers will take their meals at the sixth hour and have supper in the evening.

4122   Starting from Pentecost and throughout the summer, if the monks are not required to labor in the fields and if the summer heat does not bother them, they will fast on Wednesday and Friday till the ninth hour. On other days they will dine at the sixth hour. But if they have to work in the fields or if the summer's heat is excessive, it is necessary to have dinner at this sixth hour. The abbot is to provide for this and thus arrange all things so that souls are saved and that the brothers do what they should do without having any reason to complain.

4123   From the ides of September to the beginning of Lent they will always dine at the ninth hour.

4124   During Lent, up till Easter, the meal will be in the evening. This, however, should be so arranged that the light of the lamp need not be required; everything is to be concluded while it is still daylight. At all times the hour for the meal, whether for dinner or for supper, will be sufficiently early so that all can be done while it is still daylight.

XLII. No one is to speak after Compline

4125   The monks are always to cultivate silence, especially during the night hours. Also at all times, whether it be a fast-day or a day when there is a midday meal, as soon as they have risen from the evening meal they are to sit together while someone reads to them the Conferences or the Lives of the Fathers or something else that edifies those listening; however, not the Heptateuch or the Books of Kings because it is not good for weak souls to hear this part of the Scriptures at such a time; these books can be read at other times.

4126   If it is a day of fast, then shortly after Vespers they are to gather for the reading, as we have said. Four or five pages are to be read or as much as time allows so that during the time used for this all the monks—including those engaged in some assigned task—may come together. Once all have gathered, they will celebrate Compline, and once Compline is completed no permission is granted to speak to anyone. Whoever breaks this rule of silence is to be severely punished unless he had to tend to the needs of guests or that the abbot perhaps had given him a command. But even this should be done with the greatest seriousness and moderation.

XLIII. Those arriving late for the Work of God or for meals

As soon as the signal for the Work of God is heard, the monks leave 4127 whatever they are doing and hurry with all speed, yet with decorum, so that there be no room for levity. Nothing is to be preferred to the Work of God.

Those at the night offices who arrive after the *Gloria* of Psalm 94, 4128 which for this reason is to be much drawn out and prayed slowly, are not to take their places in the choir but are to stand in the last place or in a place assigned by the abbot for such careless ones. In this way they may be seen by the abbot and by all until, the Work of God being concluded, they make satisfaction through public penance. The reason why we believe they should remain in the last place or be set apart is so that all can see them and so that they might correct themselves as a result of shame. If, however, they remained outside the oratory, it might happen that some monk would go back to sleep, or seat himself without, passing the time in gossiping and giving "chance to the devil."[15] Better that they enter so as not to lose everything and so that they might correct themselves for the future.

At the hours of the day, those who are late for the Work of God, arriving 4129 after the verse and the *Gloria* of the first psalm which is said after the verse according to the rule given above, are to stand in the last place and are not allowed to join the choir of those doing the psalmody till they have made satisfaction, unless, perhaps, the abbot has given them permission to do so, with the understanding that satisfaction be made afterwards. [. . .]

XLIV. Those who are excommunicated; how they are to make satisfaction

Whoever is excommunicated from the oratory and the table for a seri- 4130 ous sin is, after the Work of God is completed in the oratory, to lie down on his stomach before the door of the oratory and remain there saying nothing, face down, at the feet of all who are exiting from the oratory. He is to do this till the abbot has judged that satisfaction has been made. When the abbot so commands, he is to cast himself at the feet of the abbot, and next at the feet of all so that they may pray for him. And then, if the abbot orders it, he will be admitted back to the choir in the place decided by the abbot; yet he should not presume to intone a psalm or a lesson or anything else in the oratory unless the abbot again allows him to do so. And at all the hours, when the Work of God has ended, he will prostrate himself in the place where he stands and in this way make satisfaction till the abbot releases him from this penance. [. . .]

---

15. See Eph 4:27; 1 Tim 5:13.

xlv. Those who make a mistake in the oratory

4131   Anyone who makes a mistake while reciting a psalm, a response, an antiphon, or a reading, and does not humble himself before all by making satisfaction, is to undergo a more severe punishment for not having desired to correct through humility the fault he committed out of negligence. As to the children, they are to be corporally chastised [*vapulent*] for such a fault.

xlvii. Giving the signal for the time of the Work of God

4132   Announcing the hour, whether during the day or during the night, is a task entrusted to the abbot; he does this himself or entrusts this function to an attentive brother so that everything is done at its proper time.

4133   Those who have been ordered to do so are to intone the psalms or the antiphons in their turn after the abbot. No one, however, should presume to sing or to read unless he is so capable of performing such an office that those listening are edified. This is to be done with humility, gravity, and reverence, and upon the abbot's command.

xlviii. Daily work

4134   Idleness is the enemy of the soul. Therefore at certain times the brothers should occupy themselves with manual work; at other hours with the divine reading.

4135   We believe, then, that these two activities should be well distributed during the day as follows: from Easter to the calends of October the monks go out to labor as is necessary from the first till about the fourth hour. From the fourth hour till the sixth hour, when they will celebrate Sext, they devote themselves to reading. After the sixth hour, however, upon getting up from the table, they are to rest in their beds in complete silence, or if someone wishes to read for himself, he will do so in a way that disturbs no one. None will be celebrated earlier, about the middle of the eighth hour, and the monks will work at whatever is necessary till Vespers. If, however, local circumstances or poverty require that they gather the harvest themselves, they should not become downcast, for by labor they are truly monks, living by the work of their hands as did also our fathers and the apostles. Yet for the benefit of the faint-hearted all is to be done with moderation.

4136   From the calends of October till the beginning of Lent, they should devote themselves to reading till the end of the second hour. Terce is to be said at the second hour, and then, till the ninth hour, all are to carry out their assigned tasks. When, however, the first signal is given for the hour of None, they are to cease working and prepare themselves for the second signal. After the meal they devote themselves to reading or to the psalms.

4137   During Lent from morning till the end of the tenth hour, they do their appointed tasks. During these days all will receive a book from the library, and they are to read them through in sequence. These books are to be distributed at the beginning of Lent.

Above all, one or two of the senior brothers will be appointed to go 4138
about the monastery during the time when the brethren are engaged in
reading, and they shall observe whether there might be a slothful brother
engaged in idleness or useless talk rather than applying himself to the
reading. Such a brother not only harms himself but also distracts others.
If such a one is found—God forbid—he is to be reprimanded once, twice.
If he does not correct his ways, he will be subject to the correction of the
Rule so that others may fear. A brother is not to join another brother at un-
seemly times.

On Sunday, likewise, all are to devote themselves to reading, except 4139
those with appointed tasks.

If someone is negligent and lazy to the point of not wishing or not being 4140
able to meditate or read, he will be assigned some task so that he may not
remain idle. [. . .]

IL. Observing Lent

Although the life of a monk should always be an observance of Lent, 4141
yet since such virtue belongs only to a few, we advise that during these
days of Lent, the monk guard his life with all purity and at the same time
wash away all the failures of other times. This will be done if we refrain
from all vices, if we devote ourselves to tearful prayers, to reading, to
sorrow of heart, and to abstinence. And so during these days let us add
something to our ordinary service: special prayers, abstaining from food
and drink, so that each may freely and with the joy of the Holy Spirit go
beyond what is prescribed, namely, to deprive the body of some food,
drink, sleep, speech, merriment, and with the joy of spiritual desire to look
forward to holy Easter.

Each monk is to inform his abbot as to what he is offering, and it is to be 4142
done with the abbot's approval.

L. Brothers who work a long distance from the oratory or who are on a
journey

The brothers who work at too great a distance and who cannot go to 4143
the oratory at the desired hour—the abbot himself judging whether this
is true—will celebrate the Work of God where they are working, doing so
while kneeling out of fear of God.

Likewise, those sent on a journey will not omit the appointed hours but 4144
will celebrate them as best they can and will not fail to fulfill the obligation of the divine service.

LII. The oratory of the monastery

The oratory is to be what its name signifies and is not to be used for any 4145
other purpose. When the Work of God is completed, all will depart from it
in complete silence and with reverence toward God so that a brother who
desires to pray by himself is not prevented from doing so by the miscon-
duct of others. But if a monk desires to pray alone in private, he is to enter

with simplicity and pray, not loudly, but with tears and dedication of the heart. Whoever does not act in this way will not be allowed to remain in the oratory after the Work of God has ended so that, as we said, another may not be hindered from praying.

LVIII. The manner of receiving the brothers

4146   [. . .] In the presence of all and before God and his saints the person to be received is to promise, in the oratory, stability, conversion of life, and obedience so that if he should ever do otherwise, he will know that he is condemned by God, whom he mocks.[16] He is to write down his promise in the name of the saints whose relics are in the oratory and of the abbot who is present there. He is to write down this petition with his own hand. Now if he is unlettered, he can request another to write it down for him, the novice placing a mark upon the document which he personally lays on the altar. When it has been placed there, the novice begins the verse, "Uphold me, O Lord, according to your word and I shall live; and let me not be confounded in my expectations."[17] All repeat this three times, adding the *Gloria Patri*. Then the novice brother prostrates at the feet of all and asks for their prayers. From that day forward he is considered to be a member of the community. [. . .]

LX. Priests desiring to live in the monastery

4147   If a priest petitions to be admitted to the monastery, consent will not be given too hastily. But if he tenaciously persists in his request, he should know that he will have to observe the complete discipline of the Rule and that nothing will be relaxed for his benefit as is written, "Friend, why did you come?"[18] Nonetheless, he may stand next to the abbot, give the blessing, and conclude the prayers, provided the abbot allows him to do so. [. . .]

LXII. Priests of the monastery

4148   If the abbot desires to have a priest or a deacon ordained, he is to choose from among the monks someone fitting to exercise the priestly office. The ordained person is to guard against arrogance and pride; he should do only what the abbot has ordered, knowing that now he is all the more subject to the Rule. [. . .]

LXIII. Order in the community

4149   [. . .] The order of rank in the monastery will be determined according to the time when a monk entered religion or according to the merit of each monk's life, or as the abbot shall direct. [. . .] And so according to the rank the abbot has established or which the brothers themselves have, they are to receive the peace, receive Communion, intone the psalms, and stand in choir. [. . .]

---

16. See Gal 6:7.   17. Ps 119:116.   18. Matt 26:50.

LXVII. Brothers sent forth on a journey

The brothers who set forth on a journey are to commend themselves   4150
to the prayers of all the brethren and of the abbot. After the last prayer of
the Work of God, there is to be a commemoration of all who are absent.
On the day they return from a journey and once the Work of God has concluded, at each canonical hour they are to prostrate upon the floor of the
oratory and request the prayers of all because of their failings, lest seeing
evil or hearing frivolous speech should have suddenly overtook them on
the way. [. . .]

156. RULE OF PAUL AND STEPHEN[†]

The author (or authors) of this monastic rule, which appears to have been
redacted in Italy, remains anonymous.

v. Those who hold the first places in the choir begin the psalm verses.   4151
If they are impeded by sickness, the abbot appoints others to do so. Then
once they begin, all, if possible, together with one voice join in the first or
second syllable so that there be no discord among the singers, something
that ordinarily results from an inept beginning and from a conflict between voices that seem to battle one another.

vi. The younger monks, especially those who are still striving to learn   4152
the psalms, will say them carefully and according to their rank in the
choir. [. . .]

vii. If possible we are to sing the psalms in a measured fashion so that   4153
we neither excessively fall behind nor rush ahead. The pace is always to
be moderate, without either lengthening or shortening the syllables. Since
the time, the hour, and the circumstances pertain to the will and authority
of the superior, who is to examine and judge them, so he has the right to
slow down or accelerate the psalmody when, in accord with his judgment,
he gives a sign to do so. Likewise if he desires to raise or lower the pitch.
Nonetheless, the psalmody is to be rendered in unison, coming as it were
from one mouth. May no one without the superior's permission presume
either to exceed or to change the correct rendering of the psalmody, either
by singing in a very loud fashion—something that too frequently leads
thoughtless souls to a haughty and arrogant vanity—or by disordered
haste. Nor will the superior, without true necessity, presume to avail himself of his ability to regulate the psalmody, knowing that he will be held
accountable to the Lord who said, "Sing the psalms wisely."[1]

viii. With God's help we should refrain from sleep during the Work of   4154
God. We should listen to what the prophet said: "Cursed be the one who

---

[†] Translated from *Règles monastiques d'Occident: IVe–VIe siècle, d'Augustin à Ferréol*,
trans. and ed. V. Desprez, Spiritualité orientale 9 (Maine-et-Loire, France, 1980)
349ff.

1. Ps 37:8.

is negligent in doing the Lord's work,"[2] and also, "They have slept their sleep and all the rich have found nothing in their hands."[3]

4155   x. In the morning after Prime, no one is to return to bed except on Sundays and feasts. On these days, if one is more tired than usual because of observing the vigil and due to the heat of the previous day, those among us who so desire may after Prime spend a little more time in bed. This is not allowed at just any time of the year, only during the summer months. [. . .]

4156   xii. The Work of God, which the brothers will say at the appointed hours wherever they are laboring, is observed in a disciplined way, with fear, and in common. The monk does not plunge ahead as he wishes under the pretext of or for the sake of his work. Nor does a younger monk hastily presume to leap in front of an older one. As a result of such unruly self-conceit, the Work of God, which should be carried out with fear, will be sung foolishly, not wisely. Unless restrained with great effort, the spirits and voices of some of the brethren, infected by such a practice, can no longer be in unison with those in the oratory. With simple love we exhort you to rid yourselves of such evil, for God will then hear you: "He has sent his angel and has taken me from the midst of my father's sheep."[4]

4157   xiii. At the hour when we are to receive the Lord's holy Body and Blood, may we who are present—excused are those who have a reason for not being there, a reason known by the superior—hasten to cry out, "Free us from evil."[5] Care is always to be taken that we do not receive the holy Body and Blood unworthily, namely, unto judgment.[6]

4158   xiv. May no one in this community presume to sing, learn, or say the responses and antiphons, as some are wont to sing on an ornate tone, doing so as they wish, and not taking them from the canonical Scriptures. [. . .] "Only sing what you read is to be sung," as blessed Augustine has written; "do not sing what you read is not to be sung."[a] What the Lord desired to reveal to us through his prophets and apostles is not to be rendered in praise so that it differs from what he himself has prescribed. What is to be sung, let us not change into prose or into a lesson-like recitative. What is written to be a reading, let us not be so bold as to turn into a trope and ornate melody. We are to offer God the sacrifice of praise and thanksgiving according to the manner he prescribed.[7] [. . .]

157. JOHN THE DEACON

Not to be confused with the ninth-century John the Deacon who was one of the three biographers of Pope Gregory I (WEC 4:**165**), the John who wrote this Letter to Senarius was, according to some, Pope John I (523–25), a native of Tuscany.

---

a. Augustine, Rule II.4 (WEC 3:**98-V**).

2. Jer 48:10.   3. Ps 75:5, LXX.   4. Ps 151:4, LXX.   5. Matt 6:13.   6. See 1 Cor 11:29.   7. See Tob 8:19; Ps 50:14, 23.

CPL no. 950 * Altaner (1961) 554 * Altaner (1966) 464 * Steidle 237

157-A. *Letter to Senarius*[†]

This letter is addressed to a nobleman of Ravenna who had previously submitted a number of liturgical questions to Rome.

II. You wrote, "I ask why a person is made a catechumen before bap-   4159
tism. Or what is the meaning of the word 'catechumen' or 'catechesis'? Or what Old Testament rule preceded this? But if it is a new rule, then does it find its origin in the New Testament? Likewise, what is a scrutiny? Why are infants scrutinized three times before the Pasch? Why is so much attention and care given to the scrutinies?" Etc.

III. Here is my answer. I trust that you sufficiently know that at the be-   4160
ginning of the world the whole human race, so to speak, underwent death due to the collusion of the first parent. Freedom from it could only come through the grace of the Savior, who, before time begotten of the Father, did not for our sake reject being born in time as the son of his mother alone. So there is no doubt that before a person is born again in Christ, he or she is held bound by the power of the devil. Unless one is freed from the devil's bonds and renounces the devil among the first elements of the faith by a true profession, he or she cannot obtain the grace given by the saving bath. And so it is fitting to first enter the classroom of the catechumens. It is said that the word "catechesis" comes from the Greek and means "instruction." One is instructed by the Church's ministry which imposes a blessing, namely, a laying on, of the hand so that one might know who he or she is or will be: from being condemned, a person is made holy; from being unjust, one becomes just; and finally a servant becomes a son or daughter. In this way whoever was lost in the first parent is restored by the gift of a second parent and possesses the paternal inheritance. There is an exsufflation and exorcism so that the devil may be put to flight and an entrance provided for Christ our Lord. Freed from the power of darkness, one is transferred to the kingdom of the glory of the love of God.[1] Those who for a long time were vessels of Satan now become dwelling places of the Savior. An exsufflation is given because the ancient deserter merits such disgrace. There is an exorcism, namely, the devil is adjured to depart and leave and acknowledge the arrival of him who stood erect in the happiness of Paradise of him whose image the devil cast down by his evil persuasion. Catechumens receive blessed salt to signify that just as all meat is preserved by salt, so by the salt of wisdom and of preaching God's word, the mind, so drenched and weakened by the waves of the world, might, once the moisture of inner corruption has been wiped away,

---

[†] Translated from *Analecta Reginensia: extraits des manuscrits Latins de la Reine Christine conservés au Vatican*, ed. A. Wilmart, ST 59 (Vatican City, 1933) 171–78.

1. See 1 Cor 1:13.

attain stability and permanence through the pleasant working of divine salt. This is brought about by frequent impositions of the hand and, out of respect for the Trinity, by thrice invoking over a person's head the blessing of the Creator.

4161   iv. Henceforth encouraged and making progress, those who during the exsufflation renounced the snares and pomp of the devil merit to receive the words of the creed which has been handed down from the apostles, so that who was previously called a catechumen is now also called a *competens* or an *electus*. These are conceived in the womb of Mother Church and already begin to live even though they have not completed the period of holy birth. Then, according to ecclesiastical custom, follow the frequent scrutinies. We scrutinize their hearts as to what they believe, as to whether the sacred words after the renunciation of the devil are implanted in their minds; as to whether they have recognized the future grace of the Redeemer; as to whether they confess that they believe in God the almighty Father. And when their responses show that this is true, then according to what is written, "One who believes with the heart is justified; one who confesses with the mouth is saved,"[2] their ears as well as their nostrils are anointed with the oil of sanctification: the ears because through them faith enters the mind since, as the apostle says, "Faith comes through hearing, and what is heard comes through the word of God."[3] Thus, the ears, provided with a certain wall of holiness, might allow nothing harmful, nothing that might recall what is from the past.

4162   v. When their nostrils are touched, they are warned that as long as their nostrils breathe the spirit of this life, they must remain in God's service, obeying his commandments. As that holy man said, "The Lord lives, the Lord who has taken away my judgment, and the Almighty who has led my soul to bitterness; as long as breath remains in me and the spirit of God is in my nostrils, my lips will not speak iniquity nor will my tongue engage in lying."[4] The anointing of the nostrils has yet a further meaning. Because the oil is blessed in the name of the Savior, so may the nostrils be led to his spiritual aroma by internally experiencing a certain undescribable sweetness. In this way may they delight in singing, "Your name is like oil that is poured out; we will run after the aroma of your ointments."[5] Made safe by this mystery, may they admit nothing of the world's pleasures, nothing that might impair the mind.

4163   vi. The breast—this being the seat and dwelling place of the heart—is then anointed with the oil of consecration so that the catechumens might understand that they, having already rejected the devil, are to obey Christ's commandments with a firm conscience and a pure heart. They are also enjoined to come forward, completely naked, so that having put aside the deadly and carnal clothing of the world, they acknowledge that they are taking upon themselves a way of life in which nothing harsh,

---

2. Rom 10:10.   3. Rom 10:17.   4. Job 27:2–4.   5. Cant 1:3.

nothing harmful, is found. Down through the years the Church has carefully established this even though the ancient books give no evidence of such a custom. And so once the elect or the catechumens have advanced in faith by means of what might be called spiritual vehicles, it is then necessary that they be made holy by the one and only baptismal bath. In this sacrament the baptized person is made perfect by a triple immersion. And rightly so. For those who approach to receive baptism in the name of the Trinity should at least signify this Trinity by a triple immersion and acknowledge that one is in debt to him who on the third day rose from the dead.

Then, once the baptized have put on white garments, each person's   4164
head is anointed with holy chrism. In this way the baptized are able to understand that the kingdom and a priestly mystery have met in them. Priests and kings were once anointed with the oil of chrism so that, on the one hand, the priests might offer sacrifice, and on the other hand, so that the kings might govern the people. For more fully expressing the priestly image, the newly-baptized person's head is adorned with a beautiful linen cloth since priests in days past always adorned their heads with a type of mystical veil. So all who have been reborn are clothed with white garments to signify the mystery of the risen Church just as our Lord and Savior was transfigured on the mountain before some of the disciples and prophets, as is said, "His face glowed like the sun; his garments became as white as snow."[6] This prefigured the future splendor of the resurgent Church, concerning which it is written, "Who is it who rises up?"[7] Thus the newly-baptized wear white garments; although the infancy of their first birth has been darkened through the rag of the ancient error, so, wearing a wedding garment, may they hasten to the table of the heavenly bridegroom as new people.

VII. Not to overlook anything, I must clearly state that all this is also   4165
done for the young who, due to their tender age, understand nothing of what is happening. You should also know that they, whether brought by their parents or by others, and who were condemned by the sin of another, are saved by the faith of others.

You ask that I explain why the holy chrism can be consecrated only by a   4166
bishop, this not being granted to the presbyter. And rightly so. The bishop holds the rank of the high priest; the presbyter holds that of the second priest. Every bishop is a priest; not every priest can be called a bishop. In the Old Testament, not to mention elsewhere, they differed even by their clothing, priests wearing four mystical garments which were also worn by the high priest, the high priest wearing four other garments which priests were not allowed to wear. Furthermore, only the high priest was permitted—and only once each year[8]—to enter the holy of holies. And so among the New People the bishop has the power to ordain presbyters. Therefore

---

6. Matt 17:2.   7. Cant 3:6; 8:5.   8. See Heb 9:7.

the power of blessing and anointing is retained in this tradition as agreeing with the very origin of ecclesiastical orders.

4167   VIII. We must not overlook that a prayer of consecration said by a priest does not have the same words of blessing as a prayer spoken by a bishop. For if nothing special were reserved to the bishop, then his rank would appear to be unimportant. Although words may differ, the consecratory blessing is the same. It should not upset you if at times necessity requires, as is said to happen at present throughout Africa, that presbyters prepare the holy chrism; it would, however, be disturbing if this were done contrary to episcopal authority. And so it is evident that whatever is now done by bishops can be done by presbyters in cases of great necessity and when so determined by a higher order.

4168   IX. Do you also wish to know why the Catholic Church does not baptize heretics who return to it? Allow me to say that the question here concerns those who have not been baptized in the full name of the Trinity. If a person confessed only the Father and denied the Son and the Holy Spirit, or if a person confessed only the Son and denied the Father and the Holy Spirit, then he or she is certainly to be baptized. Now if the Father and the Son are confessed but the Holy Spirit is denied, then he or she is to be cleansed at the mystical font as is required by the Lord who said, "Go, baptize all nations in the name of the Father and of the Son and of the Holy Spirit."[9] If some have truly accepted the name of the Trinity and yet differentiate in regard to equality as was done at the time of Arius,[a] in no way are they to be [re-] baptized since they have followed the Lord's rule even though they appear to have erred. This is why they are to be instructed rather than baptized; after the bishop's blessing they are to be incorporated into the womb of the Church so that through the love by which God and neighbor are truly loved, they might recognize what they lacked and what was completed in them. As to the Pelagians,[b] the Eutychians[c] and the Nestorians,[d] what happens here is understood by all, this being common knowledge as you will be able to grasp more fully once you have read the *Book of Heresies*.[e]

---

a. Arius (ca. 260–336): a priest in Alexandria, noted as a preacher and for his holiness, who denied the unity and consubstantiality of the three persons of the Trinity and consequently the full divinity of Christ. This Arian doctrine was condemned by the Council of Nicaea (WEC 2:**71-C**).

b. Pelagians: members of a heretical movement promoted by Pelagius (b. ca. 354), who although British, lived in Rome, and who promoted the heresy that a person can be saved by one's personal merits alone.

c. Eutychians: another name for the Monophysites, those believing that in Christ there is only one nature, not two.

d. Nestorians: Christians believing that two separate persons exist in Christ, one human and the other divine.

e. See Augustine (WEC 3:**98-S**).

9. Matt 28:19.

x. Acolytes differ from exorcists in that the latter do not have the power   4169
to carry the sacraments and to minister these to the priests; lacking only
the imposition of the hand, they are called exorcists; they do whatever
else pertains to the rank of acolytes. Acolytes receive and then carry to the
priests the vessels containing the sacraments. An exorcist may become an
acolyte, but in no way may an acolyte be reduced to the rank of an exorcist. If an acolyte excels in carrying out his duties, he can be made a subdeacon, namely, someone who carries the sacred cup used by the bishop
when offering the mystery of the Lord's Blood. Furthermore, if a subdeacon serves in a blameless manner, he may be promoted to the most holy
dignity of the diaconate or the presbyterate. [. . .]

xii. You ask why milk and honey are placed in the most sacred cup that   4170
is offered with the sacrifice on the paschal Sabbath. The reason is found
in the Old Testament and which in figure has been promised to the New
People: "I will lead you into the land of promise, a land flowing with milk
and honey."[10] And so the land of promise is the land of the Resurrection, a
land leading to everlasting happiness; it is nothing other than the land of
our body which in the resurrection of the dead attains glorious incorruption and peace. Therefore this form of the sacrament is offered to the baptized so that they may understand that only the baptized, not others, share
in the Lord's Body and Blood, that they receive the land of promise, that
beginning this journey they, like children, are nourished with milk and
honey so that they may sing, "How sweet are your words to my face, O
Lord, sweeter than honey to my mouth."[11] The newly born, namely, those
who have put aside the bitterness of sin, those who at their first birth were
nourished with the milk of corruption and who in the beginning shed
tears, at their second birth receive within the Church the sweetness of milk
and honey so that nourished by such sacraments they may be made holy
by the mysteries of an incorruption that lasts forever.

xiii. You also asked why in the Roman church the Alleluia is sung till   4171
Pentecost. You should know that some things exist in the Catholic Church
that bind a Christian as, for example, the authority of the New and Old
Testaments. We also have what has been established by the fathers, for
example, the canons of Nicaea[f] and the like. Likewise, there are other
things that each church holds as its own, these having been given to it by
its elders, namely, things the Roman church—faith and Catholic peace
being intact—does not hold in common with other churches in the same
region. Here one fasts on all Saturdays, a practice not apparently followed
in the East. Here seven altars are arranged, something not attempted
elsewhere. In different churches things are done in various ways so that
all the churches form a garment of the queen concerning whom it is said,
"At your right hand stood a queen clothed in golden vesture."[12] Therefore

---

f. See WEC 2:**71-C**.
10. Deut 31:20.   11. Ps 119:103.   12. Ps 45:9.

do not be disturbed if you see here something done to praise God which elsewhere is legitimately done differently. Whether the Alleluia is sung till Pentecost, which among us is surely the custom, or whether as elsewhere the Alleluia is sung throughout the whole year, it is the Church singing its praise of God. Among us there is paschal restraint so that, as it were, with greater joy and renewed spirits we might joyfully return to our praise of God as expressed by our singing of the Alleluia—in Latin "Praise the Lord." Daily the voice of people using other words resounds; for example, "Praise the Lord from the heavens, praise him in the heights."[13] Or, "Praise him, all his angels."[14] Or, "Praise the Lord, all nations."[15] Therefore when God is praised in any way with a faithful heart, it is the Alleluia that is being sung.

4172   xiv. A further question remains to be answered. If someone who is baptized departs this life without the chrismal anointing and the bishop's blessing, is it or is it not held against that person? In this regard I would like to hear what the more learned have to say.[g] [. . .]

158. PSEUDO-MAXIMUS OF TURIN

A set of three homilies or treatises on baptism have come down to us under the name of Maximus of Turin. Preached (or written?) about 550, these pieces are generally considered to be the work of an unknown bishop from northern Italy who was acquainted with John the Deacon's Letter to Senarius (WEC 4:**157-A**).

CPL nos. 220ff.

B. Capelle, "Les 'Tractatus de Baptismo' attribués à s. Maxime," RB 45 (1933) 108–18.

158-A. Treatises on Baptism[†]

158-A-1. TREATISE 1

4173   Beloved, it is with the greatest concentration and attentiveness that we should listen to all that God tells us. This is especially true for what we will say to you today. The catechumens have been dismissed; only you remain as my audience.

4174   We will not speak about all that Christians have in common; no, we will specifically focus on the heavenly mysteries. One cannot be given an explanation of these mysteries till he or she has actually experienced them. With how much more reverence you should listen to what we will say since what is entrusted to the baptized and to the faithful who are

---

g. John continues on but does not really present his answer before the text, which unfortunately is incomplete, ends.

13. Ps 148:1.   14. Ps 148:2.   15. Ps 117:1.

† Translated from PL 57:771–74.

listening is much greater than what the catechumens are accustomed to hear. Beloved, be not surprised if we said nothing to you concerning these mysteries while they were being celebrated, if we did not immediately explain what we were doing. [. . .]

First, we smeared your ears with the oil of blessing; but recognize that   4175
according to church tradition this is done by all Christ's Catholic priests. The beginning of faith and of all holy instruction gains access to the soul through the ears. Understanding results from hearing. No one can understand the sacraments of faith without hearing the one who preaches, for as the apostle said, "How will they hear without the one who preaches?" Also, "Faith comes from hearing, hearing through the word of God."[1] Rightly, then, does this oil sanctify all the body's sense organs. Without it, faith cannot possess the soul. At the same time those who come to baptism are to keep themselves undefiled, avoiding very evil and foul words, not slandering their neighbor. Like the deaf, they are not to listen to those who utter obscenities or shameless things. Thus they fulfill what the Scripture says: "Fence in your ears with thorns and listen not to a wicked tongue."[2] [. . .]

Once your ears have been anointed with the blessed oil, you are placed   4176
among those who listen with wisdom so that rightly retaining God's words and carrying out what you have heard, you might on the day of judgment hear Christ saying to you, "Come, blessed of my Father, receive the kingdom prepared for you from the beginning of the world."[3] [. . .]

Your nose also did we anoint with the blessed oil. We did this to have it   4177
understood that those who come to baptism are admonished to keep integral and inviolate the sacrament of such a great mystery. They are to do so till death, for as long as they breathe the spirit of life through the nose they are not to fall away from the worship and service of Christ our Lord. [. . .]

The anointing of the nose also has a more simple explanation. The   4178
aroma of the oil, which is blessed in the name and by the power of Christ, calls you to a spiritual sense of smell, not one of the body but of the soul. By means of the senses you are able with inestimable fragrance to experience the aroma of Christ; delighted by being addressed by him and following in his footsteps, may you be worthy to imitate what the choir of believers says to God: "We will run after you, for the odor of your ointments."[4]

158-A-2. TREATISE 2[†]

[. . .] Previously we spoke to you only about what we did before you   4179
entered the holy font. [. . .]

Without reservation you renounced all the devil's works and pomp;   4180
you rejected diabolical fornication.

---

1. Rom 10:14, 17.   2. Sir 28:24.   3. Matt 25:34.   4. Cant 1:4.
† Translated from PL 57:775–76, 778.

4181   You went down into the sacred font, the font of life, the font of redemption, the font sanctified with heavenly power. Thus made holy, it sanctifies
by washing away sins. You should not judge this water with your eyes but
with your mind. For even though this water may appear to be common
water, its effect, however, proceeds from God's grace and power, God who
created the waters so that by the hidden strength of his power he might
wash away sins that are unseen. The Holy Spirit is indeed active in the
water so that those who before baptism were accused of various sins and
were to burn in hell with the devil will after baptism merit to enter the
kingdom of heaven. Thus the Lord, expressing the power of such a great
sacrament, said in the Gospel, "No one can enter the kingdom of God
without having been born of water and the Holy Spirit."[1]

4182   Before we washed your body in this font we asked, "Do you believe in
God the Father almighty?" You replied, "I believe." Again we asked, "Do
you believe in Jesus Christ his Son, who was conceived of the Holy Spirit
and born of the Virgin Mary?" Each of you replied, "I believe." Again we
asked, "Do you also believe in the Holy Spirit?" You likewise replied, "I
believe." We did all this according to the command of our Lord and Savior Jesus Christ who, before ascending to his heavenly Father, said to the
disciples, namely, his apostles, "Go, baptize all nations in the name of the
Father and of the Son and of the Holy Spirit, teaching them to do all that I
have commanded you."[2] No one upon hearing the Father, the Son, and the
Holy Spirit believes that we are acknowledging three Gods. May such a
sacrilege be far removed from our faith. As God himself attests, we know
that there is only one God, who says, "I am God and there is no other than
me."[3] Elsewhere, "Hear, O Israel, the Lord is your God; God is one."[4] Also,
"God is in heaven above, and there is no other."[5] We honor and believe in
three persons, namely, the Father, the Son, and the Holy Spirit. There is
one power, one substance, one eternity, one will, one deity, and we adore
the whole Trinity of the one God. [. . .]

4183   Rightly you were immersed three times since you were baptized in the
name of Jesus Christ who on the third day rose from the dead. This three-
fold immersion signifies a type of the Lord's burial through which we in
baptism are buried with Christ and in faith will rise with him so that, our
sins being washed away, we may live in imitation of him. [. . .]

158-A-3. TREATISE 3[†]

4184   Thus far we have spoken of the mysteries that were celebrated either
before the sacrament of baptism or during baptism itself. Now we will treat
those things that complete the holy institution for those who have been
baptized. After the bath we poured on the head chrism, namely, the oil of

---

1. John 3:5.   2. Matt 28:19.   3. Isa 45:5; see also Hos 23:4.   4. Deut 6:4.
5. Deut 4:39.
† Translated from PL 57:777–79.

sanctification, by which the Lord confers the royal and priestly dignity upon the baptized. In the Old Testament those chosen as priests and kings were anointed upon the head with holy oil; from God some received the power to rule, others that of offering sacrifice. Just as holy David and the other kings were anointed by the prophets, so by the oil of sanctification they were changed from being private citizens unto royalty. Thus we sing in the psalm, "Like oil on the head which runs down onto the beard, the beard of Aaron."[1] In the Old Testament oil conferred a temporal kingdom and a temporal priesthood. In such a case the life of service ended after a few years. But the chrism, namely, the anointing given you, has conferred the dignity of the priesthood which, once having been given, never ends. [. . .]

All the sacraments being completed, we handed down to you by word   4185
and deed the command of Christ. We washed the feet of each, summoning you to imitate our example and that of our Lord and Savior Jesus Christ so that just as we washed your feet, you also should wash the feet of your comrades and guests. We teach you to be not only hospitable but also to be humble, thus honoring those to whom you extend hospitality so that you not be ashamed to carry out the role of being their servants. [. . .]

159. VIGILIUS, POPE

In 537 Pope Silverius, accused of treason, was imprisoned. Elected to succeed him was Vigilius, a deacon and a member of a prominent Roman family.

As pope, Vigilius was involved in various religious disputes. The most famous of these concerns was the "Three Chapters," a decree issued by the emperor Justinian (527–65), who wished to extend a gesture of reconciliation toward the Monophysites. This three-part decree, seen as being anti-Nestorian, condemned (1) the writings and person of Theodore of Mopsuestia (WEC 3:**138**), (2) the writings of Theodoret of Cyr (WEC 3:**139**) against Cyril of Alexandria (WEC 3:**148**), and (3) the letter of Ibas of Edessa to Maris. The bishops of the East assented; those of the West were very unhappy with the document, seeing it as contrary to the decisions taken at the Council of Chalcedon (WEC 3:**137**). Vigilius would not approve the decree but then, summoned by the emperor to Constantinople in 548, somewhat unwillingly condemned the decree, while nonetheless upholding the decisions of Chalcedon. Vigilius then withdrew his condemnation while awaiting a discussion of the matter at the General Council of Constantinople (553). Here the decree was again condemned with Vigilius concurring. The pope died in 555 on his way back to Rome.

CPL nos. 1694ff. * Altaner (1961) 555 * Altaner (1966) 464–65 * Bardenhewer (1908) 639–40 * Bardenhewer (1910) 550 * Bardenhewer (1913) 5:281–83 * Bautz 12:1383–87

---

1. Ps 133:2.

* Steidle 228–29 * CATH 15:1118–20 * CE 15:427–28 * DCB 4:1144–51 * DPAC 2:3591 * DTC 15.2:1868–1924, 2994–3005 * EC 12:1416 * EEC 2:870 * EEChr 2:1161 * LTK 10:787–88 * NCE 14:664–67 * NCES 14:509–11 * ODCC 1697–98

B. Capelle, "'L'aqua exorcizata' dans les rites romains de la dédicace au VIe siècle," RB 50 (1938) 306–8. * A. Chavasse, "Messes du Pape Vigile (537–555) dans le sacramentaire léonien," EphL 64 (1950) 161–213; 66 (1952) 145–215. * S. Agrelo, "La simbologia de la luz en el 'Sacramentario Veronense': Estudio histórico-literario," Ant 50 (1975) 5–123. * A.A.R. Bastiaensen, "Un formulaire de messe du sacramentaire de Vérone et la fin du siège de Rome par les Goths (537–538)," RB 95 (1985) 39–43.

159-A. Letter to Profuturus[†]

There exist twenty-six letters and documents, mostly concerned with the "Three Chapters" controversy. Among these is the pope's letter to Profuturus, the metropolitan of Braga, who submitted a now lost letter to Vigilius requesting papal clarification on several matters. The pope's response formed the basis of a decretal, which entered the Spanish collection of church law.

4186   II. As to the solemn celebration of baptism, whatever apostolic authority has either ratified or observes your holiness evidently permits to those subject to you. There is, we believe, a new error occurring in this regard. Catholics everywhere when concluding the psalms say, "Glory to the Father and to the Son and to the Holy Spirit." But some, as you have indicated, remove the one syllable conjunction "and," thereby attempting to diminish the perfect word of "Trinity" as they say, "Glory to the Father and to the Son, to the Holy Spirit." Although reason may evidently teach us that removing one syllable shows in a certain way that the person of the Son and that of the Holy Spirit are one, nonetheless for demonstrating the error of those who do this, we merely need point out that the Lord Jesus designated the baptism of believers to be celebrated by invoking the Trinity, for he said, "Go, teach all nations, baptizing them in the name of the Father and of the Son and of the Holy Spirit."[1] He did not say, "In the name of the Father and of the Son, of the Holy Spirit." Rather, he commanded that with equal distinctions the Father and the Son and the Holy Spirit are to be named. It is evident that those who weaken this profession stray from the Lord's teaching. Persisting in error, they cannot be our associates.

4187   III. As to those who, having already received the saving grace of baptism, are baptized again by the Arians[a] [. . .], their reconciliation does not

---

[†] Translated from PL 69:17–18.

a. Arians: followers of Arius (ca. 260–336), a priest in Alexandria, who denied the unity and consubstantiality of the three persons of the Trinity and consequently the full divinity of Christ. This doctrine was condemned by the Council of Nicaea (WEC 2:**71-C**).

1. Matt 28:19.

take place through the imposition of the hand whereby the Holy Spirit is invoked but through that imposition whereby the fruit of penance is acquired and which is completed by restoring Holy Communion.

ɪᴠ. Concerning the construction of a church, if it has been destroyed, it is to be rebuilt. If the service of consecration is to be repeated in that place in which there were no relics of the saints, there is no reason why exorcised water cannot be sprinkled, although it is the Mass that consecrates churches. Therefore if a basilica dedicated to the saints has been restored from its foundations, surely it is fully consecrated by celebrating Mass there. If the relics of the saints have been removed, the building is sanctified by replacing them and by celebrating Mass. 4188

ᴠ. [. . .] At no time, on no feast, do we have a set of various prayers for celebrating Mass. We always consecrate the gifts offered to God according to the same text. Yet when we celebrate the paschal feast, the Lord's Ascension, Pentecost, Epiphany, and the feasts of the saints, we add formulas that are suitable for each of the days; through these we commemorate the holy solemnity and those whose birthdays are being celebrated. We then continue in the customary way. And so we direct that the text be added after that of the canonical prayer which we, through God's favor, have received from apostolic tradition. And so that your charity may know in which places we join what is fitting for the feasts, we likewise are enclosing the prayer used for the paschal feast. [. . .] 4189

ᴠɪ. If any bishop or presbyter, contrary to the Lord's command, does not baptize in the name of the Father and of the Son and of the Holy Spirit, but in the one person of the Trinity, or in two or three Fathers, or in three Sons or in three Paracletes, he is to be removed from the Church of God. 4190

160. PELAGIUS I, POPE

Son of a noble family, Pelagius was a church official under Pope Agapetus I (535–36) and then under Pope Vigilius (WEC 4:**159**). It was a time when the Roman emperor Justinian, in an attempt to placate the Monophysites, issued in 543 an edict known as the "Three Chapters," a document condemning certain theologians considered sympathetic to Nestorius and thus hated by the Monophysites. The bishops of the East assented to the decree. But Pope Vigilius, summoned to appear before the emperor as well as before his advisor Pelagius, vacillated between approving and rejecting Justinian's condemnation. Upon the death of Vigilius on June 7, 555, at Syracuse while returning to Rome, Pelagius became the emperor's choice for the Roman See. But due to hard feelings aroused by the "Three Chapters" controversy as well as rumors that Pelagius played a part in the demise of Vigilius, Pelagius was hard-pressed to find bishops willing to ordain him to the episcopate, which indeed did take place on April 16, 556.

As pope, Pelagius is especially known for his charitable deeds, for the construction of various churches and shrines, and for his attempts, generally successful, to heal a schism that developed in northern Italy as a result of the "Three Chapters" affair. He died on March 3, 561.

CPL nos. 1698ff. * Altaner (1961) 555–56 * Altaner (1966) 465–66 * Bardenhewer (1910) 550–51 * Bardenhewer (1913) 5:283 * Bautz 7:166–67 * Steidle 229 * CATH 10:1087–90 * CE 11:602–3 * DCB 4:295–98 * DPAC 2:2737 * DTC 12.1:660–69 * EC 9:1077–78 * EEC 2:666–67 * EEChr 2:890 * LTK 8:10–11 * NCE 11:55–56 * NCES 11:59–60 * TRE 26:176–85

160-A. Letters

160-A-1. LETTER TO THE BISHOPS OF TUSCANY[†]

4191   [. . .] How can you believe that you are not separated from universal communion if you fail to mention my name during the sacred mysteries? [. . .]

160-A-2. LETTER TO TULIANUS, BISHOP OF GRUMENTUM[††a]

4192   [. . .] If he [the deacon Latinus] can hasten here before the holy day [the Pasch] so that on Saturday itself after the baptisms that occur during that great night, he with God's grace can be ordained. [. . .]

160-A-3. LETTER TO LAWRENCE, BISHOP OF CIVITAVECCHIA[†††a]

4193   [. . .] And so we exhort Your Grace to watch over the [persons to be ordained] and diligently inquire whether or not they have acted according to the canons. If you find them blameless, and if you find praiseworthy witnesses who can testify as to their lives, then when *mediana septima Paschae*[b] comes, and if the Lord shall desire and if we are alive, do not delay moving them through the respective offices. Let the presbyter take care never to celebrate the sacred mysteries without mentioning my name and your name. [. . .]

161. CASSIODORUS

Cassiodorus (*Flavius Magnus Aurelius Cassiodorus Senator*) was born ca. 490. The son of a distinguished family in Calabria in southern Italy, he received a classical education and spent many years in public service. Shortly after 540 he retired to the monastery of Vivarium on the family

---

[†] Translated from PL 69:398.

[††] Translated from PL 161:472.

a. Grumentum: a town thirty-three miles south of Potenza in southern Italy.

[†††] Translated from PL 69:416.

a. Civitavecchia: a port northwest of Rome and located on the Tyrrhenian Sea.

b. *Mediana septima Paschae*: it has been suggested that this phrase refers to the week following the fourth Sunday of Lent; see G.C. Willis, *Essays in Early Roman Liturgy*, Alcuin Club Collections 46 (London, 1964) 101–4.

estate, a monastery he founded. However, it is not known whether he became a monk. It was in this monastic setting that Cassiodorus not only wrote on various religious subjects but also encouraged the monks to collect, translate, and copy the literary works of others, thus preserving these documents for posterity. He died ca. 583.

CPL nos. 896ff. * Altaner (1961) 584–86 * Altaner (1966) 486–88 * Bardenhewer (1908) 633–37 * Bardenhewer (1910) 545–48 * Bardenhewer (1913) 5:264–76 * Bardy (1930) 195–97 * Bautz 1:953–55 * Labriolle (1947) 2:786–91 * Labriolle (1968) 506–9 * Steidle 238–40 * Tixeront 359–62 * CATH 2:618–21 * CE 3:405–7 * DCB 1:416–18 * DHGE 11:1349–1408 * DictSp 2.1:276–77 * DPAC 1:617–19 * DTC 2.2:1830–34 * EC 3:1004–9 * EEC 1:149–50 * EEChr 1:219–20 * LTK 2:970–71 * NCE 3:184 * NCES 3:208–9 * ODCC 296 * PEA (1894) 3.2:1672–76 * PEA (1991) 2:1004–7 * RACh 2:915–26 * TRE 7:657–63

G. Morin, "L'ordre des heures canoniales dans les monastères de Cassiodore," RB 43 (1931) 145–52.

161-A. Commentary on the Psalms[†]

Probably composed over many years, this tract, greatly depending on Augustine's Exposition, (WEC 3:**98-O**) treats in a highly allegorical manner all 150 psalms.

Psalm 97 [a]
Conclusion of the Psalm

Why is it that we find frequent mention of musical instruments in the psalms, instruments that do not seem to charm the ears of those listening as much as to rouse the hearing of our hearts? Because this sound and rhythm of the flutes are not found in the sacred mysteries as celebrated at the present time, we should carefully inquire as to the spiritual meaning involved here. Music is a discipline that examines how sounds differ from and agree with each other. Music is correctly used to express images of spiritual things because through the power of music harmony exists within disharmony. When we sing a psalm or when we obey God's commands, we are controlled by the grace of the sweetest harmony. If you carefully consider the reasons for this, you will discover that every person living under the rule of the Creator is not exempt from this harmony. Therefore we are commanded to sing to the Lord without ceasing, to sing a psalm with harp accompaniment, to sing a psalm with the harp, to make a joyful sound with hammered flutes and horns so that there can be no doubt that these most delightful instruments show us the agreement of praiseworthy deeds.

4194

[†] Translated from CCL 98:881, 1132.
a. Enumeration of the psalms according to the LXX.

Psalm 118

4195   164. "Seven times a day I will sing your praise for the judgments of
your justice." If we desire to direct our attention to the number "seven,"
we see that this number signifies the seven times that the pious devotion
of the monks is consoled: Matins, Terce, Sext, None, Vespers, Compline,
and the Nocturns. This is attested by the hymn of Saint Ambrose that is
sung at the sixth hour.[b] Now if you are looking for a spiritual explanation of "seven," notice that this number expresses a continuous activity.
For example, "I will bless the Lord at all times; his praise will ever be on
my lips."[1] So it is that each week, which always revolves in this number,
extends for us the longest period of time since all that occurs in the dura-
tion of the world is enclosed in this number. For example, "seven" is used
as an indefinite number in the text, "A just man falls seven times and rises
again. The just man falls any number of times, but whenever he falls, he
inevitably rises again."[2] [. . .]

162. *LIBER DIURNUS*[†]

The *Liber diurnus Romanorum Pontificum* is a collection of formulas used by
the papal chancery as introductions and conclusions to letters and miscel-
laneous documents issued by the pope. Most of these formulas date from
the late sixth century to the late eighth century. It is disputed whether the
collection that has come down to us in various manuscripts is itself an
official book or, as some have argued, more a training manual for clerics
who would eventually work in the papal office.

CPL no. 1626 * Altaner (1961) 565 * Altaner (1966) 472–73 * CATH 3:901–2 * CE
9:215–16 * DACL 9.1:243–344 * DCA 1:983–84 * DDC 4:1307–14 * DPAC 2:1943–44 *
EC 7:1262–67 * EEC 1:485 * LTK 6:882 * NCE 8:694 * NCES 8:534–35

4196   VI. [. . .] In no way is the bishop to receive Africans who indiscriminately present themselves for ecclesiastical orders because some of these
are Manichaeans,[a] others are proven to have been frequently baptized.

---

b. Some see this reference as applying to the hymn *Bis ternas horas explicans*,
which can be found in A.S. Walpole, *Early Latin Hymns: With Introduction and Notes*
(London, 1922), hymn no. LXXXII, pp. 294–98. Lines 9–12 read, "*ut septies diem vere/
orantes cum psalterio/laudesque cantantes Deo/laeti solvamus debitum.*" However, there
is no universal agreement that this hymn was written by Ambrose.

1. Ps 36:2.   2. Prov 24:16.

† Translated from *Liber diurnus Romanorum Pontificum*, ed. T.E. von Sickel (Vienna, 1889) 6, 77–78.

a. Manichaeans: followers of Mani (ca. 216–76), born in Persia, who preached a
dualistic doctrine based on an ancient conflict between light and darkness, between
good and evil; his disciples—found in Egypt, Rome, and elsewhere—practiced a
severe ascetic life, e.g., always refraining from meat.

[. . .] As to what the Church receives of the offerings of the faithful, let the bishop divide these into four portions: one portion he may keep for himself; the second he is to distribute to the clergy that they be zealous in their duties; the third is to be given to the poor and members of the lower class; the fourth he will set aside for church construction. Divine judgment will be his guide in all this. The ordination of priests or deacons will be celebrated only at the fasts of the first, fourth, seventh, and tenth months and during Lent on Saturday evening of the *mediana* week.[b] The sacrament of most holy baptism will be celebrated only on the feast of the Pasch and at Pentecost, except for those in danger of death; so that they not be eternally lost, it is fitting that they be assisted with suitable remedies. [. . .]

LXXIV. [. . .] I pledge and promise that at all times and on each day I will celebrate vigils in the church, from the first cockcrow till morning, together with all orders of my clergy in such a way that on the shorter nights, namely, those between the Pasch and the equinox of 24 September, there will be three readings, three antiphons, and three responses; from this equinox to the other, namely, the vernal, equinox and till the Pasch, there will be four readings with their responses and antiphons. We promise God that on Sundays during the year we will have nine readings with antiphons and responses. I promise that the litanies will always be observed by me twice a month. [. . .]   4197

163. *LIBER PONTIFICALIS*[†]

The *Liber pontificalis* is a collection of biographical notices of the bishops of Rome. Each entry follows the same pattern: name of the pope, place of origin, name of his father, etc., and concluding with the time of vacancy before the next pope was elected. The notices for earlier popes are generally quite brief; for those of later popes the notices are, in reality, short books. The list begins with Peter and concludes with Honorius II (d. 1130).

The history of the text, written by numerous minor officials of the papal court, is complex and involves various editions and textual layers, some the work of contemporaries, others the product of pious memories or imaginations. According to Louis Duchesne, a first edition of the work, ending with Hormisdes (514–23), was redacted shortly after 530. Although the original has been lost, an attempt has been made to reconstruct it on the basis of summary versions of the primitive text.[a] A second edition was redacted during the pontificate of Vigilius (WEC 4:**159**) with further material eventually being added to this edition.

Determining the historical veracity of the liturgical information scattered throughout the work is not always possible. At times historical terms

---

b. *Mediana* week: the week following the fourth Sunday of Lent.

† Translated from *Le liber pontificalis: texte, introduction et commentaire*, vol. 1, trans. and ed. L. Duchesne (Paris, 1957) 121ff.

a. See Duchesne, *Le liber pontificalis*, 47–108.

of comparison are simply lacking. At times it is impossible to determine, and especially when duplicates are given, whether the pope's decree concerned only the papal liturgy, that of the Roman titular churches, that of churches under strong Roman influence, or that of distant churches.

CPL nos. 1568, 1682 * Altaner (1961) 564–65 * Altaner (1966) 472 * Bardenhewer (1908) 657–58 * Bardenhewer (1910) 565 * Bardenhewer (1913) 5:301–2 * Steidle 274 * Tixeront 355–56 * CATH 7:545–47 * CE 9:224–26 * DACL 9.1:354–460 * DCB 3:713–16 * DPAC 2:1947 * EC 7:1278–82 * EEC 1:486 * EEChr 2:679–80 * LTK 6:883–84 * NCE 8:695–96 * NCES 8:535 * ODCC 977 * PEA (1894) 13.1:76–81 * PEA (1991) 7:139–40

P. Lejay, "Le Liber pontificalis et la messe romaine," RHL 2 (1897) 182ff. * P. Jeffery, "The Introduction of Psalmody into the Roman Mass by Pope Celestine I (422–432): Reinterpreting a Passage in the 'Liber pontificalis,'" ALW 26 (1984) 147–65. * A. Chavasse, "Les grands cadres de la célébration à Rome 'In urbe' et 'Extra muros' jusqu'au VIIIe siècle," RB 96 (1986) 7–26.

4198   II. Linus [ca. 70], born in Italy, [. . .]. As instructed by blessed Peter, he decreed that a woman when entering a church is to have her head covered. [. . .]

4199   VI. Evaristus [ca. 100], born in Greece, [. . .] divided the *tituli*[b] in the city of Rome among the priests, and he ordained seven deacons to watch over the bishop when he recites [the eucharistic prayer] in order to determine that he is speaking correctly. [. . .]

4200   VII. Alexander [ca. 110], born in Rome, [. . .] inserted the institution narrative[c] [*passionem Domini*] into what the priest says when he celebrates Mass. [. . .] He decreed that water with salt be blessed for sprinkling the people's homes.

4201   VIII. Sixtus [ca. 117–ca. 127], born in Rome, [. . .] decreed that the sacred vessels used for ministry be touched only by the ministers. [. . .] He decreed that within the celebration [of Mass] the people sing—with the priest beginning—the "*Sanctus, sanctus, sanctus Dominus Deus Sabaoth*" etc.[d]

4202   IX. Telesphorus [ca. 127–ca. 137], born in Greece, [. . .] decreed that a fast of seven weeks should be kept before the Pasch, and that Mass be celebrated at night on the day of the Lord's birth, for no one would ever presume to celebrate Mass before the office [*cursum*] of the third hour, the hour when our Lord ascended the cross; also that the hymn of the angels, namely, the "*Gloria in excelsis Deo*," is to be sung before the sacrifice.[e] [. . .]

---

b. *Tituli*: the word *titulus* had various meanings in classical and ecclesiastical antiquity, here signifying a parish church where priests and other clergy carried out the religious ceremonies.

c. Some suggest the translation "theme of redemption."

d. The decree regarding the *Sanctus* appears only in the first edition of the *Liber pontificalis*, perhaps simply being overlooked by the redactor of the later version.

e. In the first edition the *Gloria* is restricted to the Christmas night Mass; in the second edition it is sung on all Sundays and feasts.

xi. Pius [ca. 140–ca. 154], born in Italy [. . .]. During Pius' episcopacy   4203
Hermas[f] wrote a book which contains the order the angel of the Lord imposed on Hermas when the angel came to him in shepherd's garb; he, the
angel, commanded that the Pasch be celebrated on the Lord's Day.[g] He
determined that a heretic converting from the Jewish heresy be received
and baptized. [. . .]

xiii. Soter [ca. 166–75], born in Campania, [. . .] decreed that no monk   4204
should touch the sacred pall nor burn [*ponoret*] incense in the holy church.[h]

xv. Victor [189–98], born in Africa, [. . .] decreed, like Eleutherius,[i] that   4205
the holy Pasch be celebrated on the Lord's Day. [. . .] He decreed that in
cases of necessity a person coming from paganism is to be baptized wherever that person might be, whether the baptism take place in a river, in
the sea, or in a spring, provided that the Christian confession of faith [the
creed] has been distinctly professed. [. . .] When priests questioned him
concerning the paschal cycle, he decreed that the Pasch be celebrated on
the Lord's Day;[j] having discussed this with the presbyters and bishops and
after holding a meeting to which Theophilus the bishop of Alexandria was
invited, the holy Pasch was to be observed between the fourteenth and
twenty-first days of the first lunar month. [. . .]

xvi. Zephyrinus [198–217], born in Rome, [. . .] declared that a   4206
cleric, a deacon, and a priest were to be ordained in the presence of all
the clerics and the lay faithful. He legislated concerning the church,
and that glass patens be held before the priests in the church and that
ministers should hold these patens while the bishop is celebrating
Mass with the priests standing before him;[k] Mass is to be celebrated in
this manner with the clergy remaining for all of it, although the bishop
can lawfully excuse them; and that a presbyter is to receive from what
is consecrated a consecrated crown [the eucharistic bread] to be given
to the people. [. . .]

xvii. Callistus [217–22], born in Rome, [. . .] decreed that three times   4207
each year, on Saturdays, there should be a fast from corn, wine, and oil according to the prophecy.[l] [. . .]

xxi. Fabian [236–50], born in Rome, [. . .] divided the regions among   4208
the deacons, and he made seven subdeacons who were to look out for the

---

f. Hermas: see WEC 1:**10**.

g. Confer WEC 4:4205. The Roman custom of celebrating the Lord's resurrection
on Sunday precedes Pius I; see Eusebius, *Church History* V.xxiv.14 (WEC 2:2025).

h. Confer WEC 4:4220.

i. There is nothing in the notice of Eleutherius concerning the day on which the
Pasch was to be observed.

j. Confer WEC 4:4203.

k. The text here in places is somewhat obscure.

l. In the first edition and in several manuscripts of the second edition the text
adds, "during the fourth, seventh, and tenth months."

seven notaries so that these would faithfully gather intact the acts of the martyrs. [. . .]

4209   xxiv. Stephen [254–57], born in Rome, [. . .] decreed that priests and deacons are not to wear the sacred vestments as daily garb but only when they are in church. [. . .]

4210   xxvii. Felix [269–71], born in Rome, [. . .] decreed that Mass be celebrated over the memorials of the martyrs.[m] [. . .]

4211   xxviii. Eutychianus [275–83], born in Tuscany, [. . .] decreed that the only fruits of the earth to be blessed upon the altar [during the eucharistic prayer] are to be beans and grapes. [. . .] He also decreed that whoever of the faithful buries a martyr should never do so without wearing a dalmatic[n] or *collobium*,[o] this having been brought to his attention. [. . .]

4212   xxix. Caius [283–96], born in Dalmatia, [. . .] decreed that in receiving ecclesiastical orders a person deserving to be bishop should first be a doorkeeper, a reader, an exorcist, an acolyte [*sequens*], a subdeacon, a deacon, a presbyter, and then ordained a bishop.[p] [. . .]

4213   xxxii. Eusebius [310], born in Greece, [. . .] found heretics in the city of Rome whom he reconciled by imposing hands. [. . .]

4214   xxxiii. Miltiades [310/311–14], born in Africa, [. . .] decreed that for no reason whatsoever should the faithful fast on Sunday or Thursday just because the pagans observed a holy fast on these days. And Manichaeans[q] were discovered in the city. From that day on he initiated the practice whereby consecrated offerings from what the bishop consecrated should be distributed to the churches, this being called the *fermentum*.[r] [. . .]

4215   xxxiv. Silvester [314–35], born in Rome, decreed that a presbyter not reconcile any Arian[s] who converted, but only the bishop of the designated place; and also that chrism be prepared by a bishop and, this being an episcopal privilege, that he sign a person who had been baptized at the hands of the heretics. Furthermore, he decreed that the presbyter should

---

m. The practice actually antecedes Felix; see Prudentius, *Peristephanon* xL.v.171ff.

n. *Dalmatic*: a tunic-like garment today worn by the deacon.

o. *Collobium*: a tunic without sleeves.

p. Confer WEC 4:4215. Perhaps more of an ideal than a reality.

q. Manichaeans: followers of Mani (Manes) (ca. 216–76), who was born in Persia and who preached a dualistic doctrine based on an ancient conflict between light and darkness, between good and evil; his followers, found in Egypt, Rome, and elsewhere, observed a highly ascetic life, e.g., always refraining from meat.

r. Confer WEC 4:4216. The *fermentum* was the name given to the portion of the consecrated bread at the Roman episcopal Mass sent on Sunday to the priests of the Roman churches to be placed in their chalices as a symbol of the unity of the local church.

s. Arian: a follower of Arius (ca. 260–336), a priest in Alexandria, who denied the unity and consubstantiality of the three persons of the Trinity and consequently the full divinity of Christ. This Arian doctrine was condemned by the Council of Nicaea (WEC 2:**71-C**).

anoint the baptized when taken out of the water,[t] doing so because of the risk of death. [. . .] He decreed that deacons wear dalmatics in church and that their left arms be covered with a woolen cloth.[u] [. . .] He decreed that the sacrifice of the altar is not to be celebrated on a silk or dyed cloth but only on a pure linen cloth just as the body of our Lord Jesus Christ was buried in a clean linen cloth. In this way Mass is celebrated. He decreed that any person who desires to serve or to assist the Church should be a reader for thirty years, an exorcist for thirty days, an acolyte for five years, a guardian of the martyrs for ten years, a deacon for seven years, a presbyter for three years, thus approved in every way, also by outsiders. Having only one wife, a wife blessed by a priest, he should attain the episcopal order [. . .] with the consent of all the clergy, with no cleric or member of the faithful objecting. [. . .]

XL. Siricius [384–99], born in Rome, [. . .] decreed that no presbyter should celebrate Mass every week unless he receives the *fermentum*,[v] namely, the indicated consecrated [portion] from the designated bishop of the place. He discovered Manichaeans in the city; these he sent into exile. He declared that converts from Manichaeism who return to the Church should in no way receive Communion but should be sent to a monastery and held there for life; punished by fasting and prayers, and proven by every test till the day of death; *viaticum*[w] is to be given them through the graciousness of the Church. He decreed that a heretic should, in the presence of the whole church, be reconciled by the imposition of the hands.[x] [. . .]   4216

XLI. Anastasius [399–401], born in Rome, [. . .] decreed that as often as the holy Gospels are read, priests are not to be seated but are to stand and bow. [. . .]   4217

XLII. Innocent [401–17], born in Albanum, [. . .] decreed that one born of a Christian mother is to be born again through baptism, namely, is to be baptized, something Pelagius[y] was condemning. [. . .] He decreed that Saturday be a day of fasting because our Lord was placed in the tomb on Saturday and the apostles fasted.   4218

XLIII. Zosimus [417–18], born in Greece, decreed [. . .] that deacons should cover their left arms with a linen cloth;[z] permission was granted to bless the [paschal] candle in the parishes. [. . .]   4219

---

t. The text is not very clear as to which chrismation is meant. The postbaptismal anointing? Or the anointing accompanying the consignation?

u. Confer WEC 4:4219.

v. Confer WEC 4:4214.

w. *Viaticum*: the Eucharist given to those in immediate danger of death.

x. Confer WEC 4:4213.

y. Although British by birth (ca. 354), Pelagius taught in Rome, where he promoted the heresy that a person can be saved by one's own merits alone.

z. Confer WEC 4:4215.

4220   XLIV. Boniface [418–22], born in Rome, [. . .] decreed that no woman or nun is to touch or wash the holy pall, nor to burn incense within the church, such being done only by a minister.[aa] [. . .]

4221   XLV. Celestine [422–32], born in Campania, [. . .] decreed that the 150 psalms of David be antiphonally sung before the sacrifice, something not done formerly when only the letter of blessed Paul and the Gospel were read. [. . .]

4222   XLVII. Leo [440–61], born in Tuscany [. . .] decreed that while offering the sacrifice [*intra actionem sacrificii*] there be said the *"sanctum sacrificium"* etc.[bb] He decreed that a nun not receive the blessing of the head veil till she has lived a life of virginity for sixty years. [. . .]

4223   LI. Gelasius, [492–96], born in Africa, [. . .] composed hymns in the meter used by Ambrose.[cc] [. . .] He also wrote carefully worded prefaces and prayers for the sacraments. [. . .]

4224   LIII. Symmachus [498–514], born in Sardica [. . .] decreed that on every Lord's Day or birthday of the martyrs the *Gloria in excelsis* hymn be sung.[dd] [. . .]

4225   LIV. Hormisdas [514–23], born in Campania, [. . .] taught the psalms to the clergy. [. . .]

164. SYNOD OF ROME (595)[†]

Held under the presidency of Gregory I (WEC 4:165) on July 5, 595, this synod of twenty-three bishops and numerous priests and deacons approved by acclamation six canons.

Hefele (1905) 3.1:235–36 * Hefele (1871) 4:426–27 * DCA 1:1816–17

4226   Canon 1. It has long been customary in the Roman church to ordain cantors as deacons, and, furthermore, to use them for singing rather than for preaching and caring for the poor. As a result at divine services a good voice is more appreciated than a good life. Consequently no deacon may henceforth sing in the church except for the gospel at Mass. The remaining lessons and psalms shall be sung by subdeacons or, if necessary, by those in minor orders.

4227   Canon 4. The custom has developed at the funeral of a pope to cover his body with dalmatics, which are then torn into pieces by the people and are held in great honor and preserved as relics, whereas clothes with which the apostles and martyrs were covered are less honored. This is to be corrected.

---

aa. Confer WEC 4:4204.

bb. The initial words of the addition still remain in the *Supra quae* section of the Roman Canon.

cc. See WEC 2:**53-T**.

dd. Confer WEC 4:4202.

† Translation (modified) from Hefele (1871) 4:426–27.

165. GREGORY I, POPE

Gregory ("the Great"), born ca. 540 in Rome of a patrician family, became prefect of that city in 572/573. After his father's death, he devoted himself to the monastic life and consequently established seven monasteries on family land, six in Sicily and one in Rome (Saint Andrew). In 579 Gregory was sent by Pope Pelagius II to Constantinople as a type of emissary. Returning to Rome in 585/586, he became an advisor to Pelagius, whom he reluctantly succeeded as bishop of Rome in 590.

As a pope who understood the power of diplomacy, Gregory did much not only on a religious level but also politically. He organized the possessions of the Roman Church; developed relations with the Lombards, the Franks, and the Visigoths; and sent missionaries to the Anglo Saxons in Britain. Advancing the claims of the Roman See as being the ultimate authority in the Church, he strongly objected to the patriarch of Constantinople calling himself the "Ecumenical Patriarch," and referred to himself as the *servus servorum Dei*. Gregory died in 604.

Gregory initiated certain liturgical reforms of the Roman Mass. And although some formulas in the *Gregorian Sacramentary* may reflect his literary hand, the actual redaction of this book seems to have occurred under Pope Honorius I (625–38). It has been proposed that Gregory instituted a reform of the Roman schola. However, there is no evidence that he played a role in developing the chant that traditionally has been called "Gregorian."

CPL nos. 1708ff. * Altaner (1961) 556–64 * Altaner (1966) 466–72 * Bardenhewer (1908) 650–57 * Bardenhewer (1910) 559–65 * Bardenhewer (1913) 5:284–302 * Bardy (1930) 197–201 * Bautz 2:296–304 * Hamell 160–62 * Jurgens 3:308–25 * Labriolle (1947) 2:804–15 * Steidle 229–33 * CATH 5:229–32 * CE 6:780–87 * DACL 6.2:1753–76 * DCB 2:779–91 * DHGE 21:1387–1420 * DictSp 6:872–910 * DPAC 2:1698–1707 * DTC 6.2:1776–81 * EC 6:1112–26 * EEC 1:365–68 * EEChr 1:488–91 * LTK 4:1010–13 * NCE 6:766–70 * NCES 6:478–84 * ODCC 706–7 * PEA (1894) 7.2:1868–70 * PEA (1991) 4:1216–17 * RACh 12:930–51 * TRE 14:135–45

LITURGICAL TEXTS/SACRAMENTARY

L. Beauduin, "La Pentecôte," QL 3 (1912/13) 241–53. * B. Capelle, "Les préfaces du missel romain: la préface de Noël," QLP 18 (1933) 273–83. * C. Callewaert, "Texte liturgique composé par s. Grégoire," EphL 52 (1938) 189–91. * B. Capelle, "Note sur le lectionnaire romain de la messe avant s. Grégoire," RHE 34 (1938) 556–59. * C. Callewaert, "S. Grégoire, les scrutins et quelques messes quadragési-males," EphL 53 (1939) 191–203; repr. in *Sacris erudiri* (Steenbrugge, 1940) 659–71. * F. Vandenbroucke, "La collecte pour la fête de s. Michel: son sens, son origine," QLP 25 (1940) 163–69. * C. Callewaert, "Les étapes de l'histoire du 'Kyrie': S. Gélase, s. Benoît, s. Grégoire," RHE 38 (1942) 20–45. * L. Brou, "Les oraisons du troisième dimanche de Carême," ParL 32 (1950) 111–18. * H. Ashworth, "Did St. Gregory the Great Compose a Sacramentary?" SP 2 = TU 63 (1957) 3–16. * H. Ashworth, "Did St. Augustine Bring the *Gregorianum* to England?" EphL 72 (1958)

39–43. * H. Ashworth, "The Liturgical Prayers of St. Gregory the Great," Tra 15 (1959) 107–61. * B. Fisher, "Die Lesung der römischen Ostervigil unter Gregor der Grosse," in *Colligere Fragmenta*, Texte und Arbeiten 2, Beiheft (Beuron, 1962) 144–56.

MASS

C. Lambot, "Le Pater dans la liturgie apostolique d'après s. Grégoire," RB (1930) 265–69. * T. Michels, "Woher nahm Gregor der Grosse die Kanonbitte 'diesque nostros in tua pace disponas'?" JL 13 (1933) 188–90. * C. Callewaert, "Les étapes de l'histoire du 'Kyrie': s. Gélase, s. Benoît, s. Grégoire," RHE 38 (1942) 20–45. * C. Coebergh, "La messe de s. Grégoire dans le sacramentaire d'Hadrien: essai d'explication d'une anomalie notoire, suivie de remarques sur la Mémoire des Défuncts et le développement du culte des saints confesseurs à Rome du Ve au VIIIe siècle," SE 12 (1961) 372–404. * R. Chéno, "'Ad ipsam solummodo orationem': comment comprendre la lettre de Grégoire à Jean de Syracuse," RSPT 76 (1992) 443–55. * E. Gridde, "S. Grégoire le Grand et Mgr. Duchesne à propos de la récitation du Pater à la messe," BLE 55 (1954) 164–66.

PENANCE

J. Tixeront, "La doctrine pénitentielle de s. Grégoire le Grand," BALAC 2 (1912) 241–58. * A. Lagarde, "La doctrine pénitentielle du pape Grégoire," RHL, n.s., 8 (1922) 118–26.

ORDERS

J.A. Eidenschink, "The Election of Bishops in the Letters of Gregory the Great, with an Appendix on the Pallium," diss., Catholic University of America Canon Law Studies 216 (Washington, D.C., 1945). * S.L. Greenslade, "'Sede vacante' Procedure in the Early Church," JThSt, n.s., 12 (1961) 210–26. * L.J. Patsavos, "The Image of the Priest according to the Three Hierarchs," GOTR 21 (1976) 55–70.

MUSIC: PLAINSONG

G. Morin, "Le rôle de s. Grégoire le Grand dans la formation du répertoire musical de l'Eglise latine, à propos d'un récent discours de M. Gevaert," RB 7 (1890) 62–70. * G. Morin, "En quoi consista précisément la réforme grégorienne du chant liturgique," RB 7 (1890) 193–204. * G. Morin, "Les témoins de la tradition grégorienne," RB 7 (1890) 289–323. * E. Soullier, "Causeries sur le plain-chant. II. S. Grégoire," *Etudes religieuses, philosophiques, historiques et littéraires* 50 (1890) 272–86. * P. Batiffol, "L'origine du 'Liber responsalis' de l'église romaine," RQH 55, n.s., 11 (1894) 220–28. * W. Corney, "The Gregorian Tradition," DR 23 (1904) 44–60. * G. Lefebvre, "S. Grégoire et le chant grégorien," *Bulletin paroissial liturgique* 2 (1920) 29–31. * R. van Doren, "S. Grégoire le Grand et le chant romain," QLP 12 (1927) 35–44, 264–66.

MUSIC: USE OF ALLELUIA

C. Callewaert, "L'oeuvre liturgique de s. Grégoire: la septuagésime et l'alleluia," RHE 33 (1937) 306–26. * J. Froger, "L'alleluia dans l'usage romain et la réforme de s. Grégoire," EphL 62 (1948) 6–48. * E. Wellesz, "Gregory the Great's Letter on the Alleluia," *Annales musicologiques* 2 (1954) 7ff.

MUSIC: OTHER TOPICS

S.J.P. van Dijk, "Gregory the Great, Founder of the Urban Schola Cantorum," EphL 77 (1963) 345–56.

OTHER TOPICS

G. Gassner, "Das Selbstzeugniss Gregors des Grossen über seine liturgischen Reformen," JL 6 (1926) 218–23. * L.J. Crampton, "St. Gregory's Homily XIX and the

Institution of Septuagesima Sunday," DR 86 (1968) 162–66. * J.M. McCulloh, "The Cult of Relics in the Letters and 'Dialogues' of Pope Gregory the Great: A Lexicographical Study," Tra 32 (1976) 145–84. * R.A. Markus, "The Sacred and the Secular: From Augustine to Gregory the Great," JThSt, n.s., 36 (1985) 84–96. * P. Jounel, "Le culte de s. Grégoire le Grand," EOr 2 (1985) 195–209.

165-A. Letters

Approximately 850 of Gregory's letters and official documents, many written by Gregory himself and others penned by the Roman bureaucracy, have come down to us. Most are found in the *Register of Letters* (*Registrum Epistolarum*), formed from three independent collections, which in turn were extracted from the official Roman archives. The *Register* is divided into fourteen books, one for each year of Gregory's pontificate. Abbots, monks, bishops, deacons, monarchs (male and female)—all were recipients of Gregory's advice and direction.

165-A-1. BOOK I. LETTER 41. TO LEANDER, BISHOP OF SPAIN[tab]

[. . .] As to the triple immersion at baptism, I can give no truer response   4228
than what you believe in the same faith, namely, that diverse customs do not harm the holy Church. By being immersed a third time we signify the sacrament of being buried for three days; and so when the infant leaves the water for the third time, what is expressed is the resurrection after three days. But should anyone perhaps believe that by a triple immersion we venerate the highest Trinity, there is nothing against immersing only once the person being baptized since there is only one substance in three substances, and so no one can be blamed for immersing the infant at baptism either three times or only one time since a triple immersion signifies the persons of the Trinity, one immersion signifying the singleness of God. But if till now heretics when baptizing immerse an infant three times, I believe that you should not do likewise since heretics, dividing the immersions, also divide the Divinity. And when one does what they do, they can only boast that they have changed your custom. [. . .]

165-A-2. BOOK I. LETTER 45. TO VIRGIL OF ARLES AND TO THEODORE, BISHOP OF MARSEILLES, IN GAUL[tta]

[. . .] It has been brought to our attention that a large number of the   4229
Jews living in that district have been taken to the font of baptism more

---

[†] Translated from *Registre des lettres. Grégoire le Grand*, vol. 1, ed. P. Minard, SChr 370 (Paris, 1991) 198–99.

a. Written in April 591. Leander: bishop of Seville 579–600.

b. Dates are those found in *The Letters of Gregory the Great*, 3 vols., trans. and ed. J.R.C. Martyn (Toronto, 2004).

[††] Translated from SChr 370:228–29.

a. Written in June 591.

by the use of force than by preaching. I believe that the intent of this type of action is, to be sure, praiseworthy. I also agree that it flows out of love for our Lord. Yet unless this same intention is accompanied by a suitable display of Holy Scripture, I fear (God forbid) that either no reward will be given or else losses may follow regarding some of the souls we desire to be saved. When anyone approaches the baptismal font not because of the attractiveness of the preaching but under constraint, that person returns to his or her former superstition from which he or she appeared to receive new birth, thus dying in a worse state. [. . .]

165-A-3. BOOK II. LETTER 31. TO JOHN, BISHOP OF SQUILLACE[ta]

4230   [. . .] We command you not to ordain anyone unlawfully. Do not permit a bigamist to receive holy orders. The same is true for a man whose wife was not a virgin. Do not accept an illiterate person, one infected on any part of his body, a penitent, a person bound to a court or to any form of subjection. Should you find any of these, I beg you not to ordain them. For no reason receive Africans indiscriminately or any unknown strangers who desire ecclesiastical ordination. Some Africans are Manichaeans;[b] others have been rebaptized;[c] and it has been shown that most foreigners, even when in minor orders, are only seeking more glory. [. . .]

165-A-4. BOOK II. LETTER 35. TO FELIX, BISHOP OF AGROPOLIS [. . .][tta]

4231   Since the churches of Velia, Buxentum, and Blanda, which are situated close to you, lack, as we understand it, any control by a bishop, we enjoin Your Fraternity to visit them. [. . .] As to the sacred vessels of these churches, carefully inquire as to where they are located. Finding them, hasten to inform us so that we, with God's help, might arrange them with proper knowledge.

165-A-5. BOOK II. LETTER 38. TO JOHN, BISHOP OF RAVENNA[ttta]

4232   [. . .] When you state that an ordained person should be again ordained, this is quite ridiculous and contrary to what, I believe, you really

---

[†] Translated from *Registre des lettres. Grégoire le Grand*, vol. 2, trans. and ed. P. Minard, SChr 371 (Paris, 1991) 376–79.

a. Written in July 592. Squillace: a town in southern Italy.

b. Manichaeans: followers of Mani (ca. 216–76), who preached a dualistic doctrine based on an ancient conflict between light and darkness, between good and evil.

c. Namely, the Donatists: a schismatic Christian group in Africa whose members emphasized the Church as being one holy body and who rejected sacraments celebrated by those outside Donatism.

[††] Translated from SChr 371:382–83.

a. Written in July 592. Felix: otherwise unknown. Agropolis: a town located in southern Italy on the Gulf of Taranto.

[†††] Translated from SChr 371:390–93.

a. Written in July 592.

know. [. . .] Just as someone who has already been baptized is not to be baptized again, so a person once consecrated is not to be consecrated again in the same order. Should a person come to the priesthood with a lesser fault, he should receive penance for this fault, and yet his status should be preserved. [. . .]

165-A-6. BOOK III. LETTER 7. TO JOHN, BISHOP OF LARISSA[†a]

[. . .] The second point brought against him [Stephen, a deacon at Thebes] seems to concern infants who were forbidden by his order from receiving holy baptism and who thus died in darkness, with the filth of sin not washed away. But not a single witness who testified against him claimed that he knew that anything of this kind had been brought to the attention of Bishop Hadrian. They said they learned this from the mothers of infants, mothers whose husbands had been excommunicated, as they say, because of their crimes. But they admitted that those children had not approached the time of death unbaptized, as the insidious suggestion of the accusers had implied, since it was determined that the infants had been baptized in the city of Demetrias.[b]

4233

165-A-7. BOOK IV. LETTER 9. TO JANUARIUS, BISHOP OF CARALIS[††a]

[. . .] Bishops are not to presume to seal [*signare*] children to be baptized [*baptizandos*[b]] twice on the forehead with chrism. Rather, presbyters are to anoint those to be baptized on the breast so that afterwards bishops may anoint them on the forehead. [. . .]

4234

165-A-8. BOOK IV. LETTER 18. TO MAURUS, ABBOT AT SAINT PANCRAS[†††a]

[. . .] We have learned that the Church of Saint Pancras, which was entrusted to the care of presbyters, has been frequently neglected. The people going there on Sunday to celebrate Mass [*missarum sollemnia*] return home, complaining that no priest was present there. For this reason and after much consideration we have determined to remove the presbyters and with God's grace establish for this church a monastic congregation of monks. We do this so that the abbot who is in charge may give thorough care and attention to this church. We have also deemed it fitting

4235

[†] Translated *S. Gregorii Magni Registrum Epistularum*, vol. 1, ed. D. Norberg, CCL 140 (Turnhout, 1982) 154.

a. Written in October 592. Larissa: a town in Thessaly, a region in eastern Greece.

b. Demetrias: a city in Thessaly.

[††] Translated from CCL 140:226.

a. Written in September 593. Caralis: today Cagliari in Sardinia.

b. Some manuscripts read *baptizatos*, namely, "those who have been baptized."

[†††] Translated from CCL 140:236–37.

a. Written in March 594. Church of Saint Pancras: located on the Via Aurelia in Rome.

to appoint you, Maurus, as abbot over this monastery. [. . .] You are to see to it that the work of God [*Opus Dei*] is celebrated each day over the body of Saint Pancras. [. . .]

165-A-9. BOOK IV. LETTER 26. TO JANUARIUS, BISHOP OF CAGLIARI[ta]

4236   [. . .] I have heard that some have been offended by the fact that we have forbidden presbyters to anoint with chrism those who have been baptized. We did so in accord with the ancient practice of our church. But if any are completely disturbed by this, we allow, where bishops are lacking, even presbyters to anoint with chrism the foreheads of those who have been baptized.

165-A-10. BOOK V. LETTER 5. TO VENANTIUS, BISHOP OF LUNI[tta]

4237   [. . .] It has come to our attention that, after being removed from his priestly order because of his sinful lapse in faith, he has presumed to return to practicing his priestly ministry and to offering the Body of Christ to almighty God. If you find that this is what took place, you must deprive him of the holy Body and Blood of our Lord and force him to do penance in such a way that right up to the day of his death he remains in the same state of excommunication, and receives the last rites only at the time of his death. But if you discover that he is doing such penance, he is to be pardoned so as to receive Communion with the laity before he dies. [. . .]

165-A-11. BOOK V. LETTER 57A. GREGORY'S DECREE TO THE CLERGY IN THE BASILICA OF SAINT PETER THE APOSTLE

In the perpetual reign of our Lord Jesus Christ . . .[a]

165-A-12. BOOK V. LETTER 61. TO MARINIANUS, BISHOP OF RAVENNA[ttta]

4238   [. . .] We have agreed to allow you to use the pallium.[b] [. . .] You will remember to use it in no other way except in your own church in the city, once the laity arrive, and as you go from the sacristy for the celebration of Mass. Once this is finished, you will carefully replace it in the sacristy. You are not permitted to wear it outside the church except four times a year during the litanies. [. . .]

[†] Translated from CCL 140:245–46.

a. Written in May 594. Cagliari: today the capital of Sardinia.

[††] Translated from CCL 140:270.

a. Written in September 594. Luni: a town in Etruria in northwest central Italy.

a. Some collections include this letter, which publishes the canons endorsed at the Synod of Rome in 595 (WEC 4:**164**).

[†††] Translated from CCL 140:363.

a. Written on August 15, 595.

b. Pallium: a white woolen band worn over the chasuble as a sign of episcopal authority.

165-A-13. BOOK VII. LETTER 17. TO SABINIAN, BISHOP OF ZARA[ta]

[. . .] By means of this letter we urge you not to share Communion with 4239
Maximus[b] and not to mention his name during Mass. [. . .]

165-A-14. BOOK VIII. LETTER 23. TO FANTINUS[tta]

[. . .] We have learned that many Jews, inspired by God's grace, de- 4240
sire to be converted to the Christian faith; someone must go to them at
our command. And so we enjoin you, by reason of the authority given
you and with no excuses, to hurry to them. With God's help nurture
their desire by means of your exhortations. But should the period before
the paschal solemnity be long and dreary, and if you discover that they
want to be baptized now, then speak to our brother, the bishop of that
area, so that—God forbid—a long delay may not cause them to change
their minds. Speak to him so that they, having done penance and abstained as prescribed for forty days, may be baptized by him under the
protection of the mercy of the Almighty God on the Lord's Day or on
any other feast that may occur. The times are perilous. Danger threatens.
And so may we not delay the fufillment of their desires. In addition, if
you ascertain that any of them are too poor to buy garments for themselves, we desire that you supply them with clothing for their baptism;
the expense is to be charged to your accounts. But should they choose to
wait for the holy season of the Pasch, speak again to the bishop that they
may be placed among the catechumens; may he often visit them, care for
them, and motivate them by his admonitions so that the more distant is
the anticipated feast, the more they may prepare themselves for it and
fervently desire it. [. . .]

165-A-15. BOOK VIII. LETTER 28. TO EULOGIUS, BISHOP OF ALEXANDRIA[ttta]

[. . .] Other than what Eusebius[b] has in his books pertaining to the 4241
acts of the martyrs, I am not aware that our church's archives contain any
collections. The same holds true for libraries located in the city of Rome
with the exception of a few things found in a single manuscript. We indeed know the names of almost all the martyrs, with their passions being

---

[t] Translated from CCL 140:468.

a. Written in April 597. Zara: a town in Dalmatia, a region bordering on the Adriatic Sea.

b. Namely, Maximus of Salona (today Split on the Dalmatian coast), a bishop
with whom Gregory was often in conflict.

[tt] Translated from *S. Gregorii Magni Registrum Epistularum*, vol. 2, ed. J. Norberg,
CCL 140 A (Turnhout, 1982) 543–44.

a. Written in 598. Fantinus: bishop of Catane in Sicily.

[ttt] Translated from CCL 140 A:549–50.

a. Written in July 598. Eulogius: bishop of Alexandria 580–607/608.

b. Eusebius of Caesarea (ca. 260–ca. 340): church historian (WEC 2:**81**).

gathered together in one volume and assigned to be read on particular days. On these days we commemorate them as we celebrate Mass. Yet in this volume there is nothing indicating who the martyr was, how the martyr suffered; all that we find are the martyr's name together with the place and day of his or her passion. Consequently, as I said, many countries and provinces are known to have been crowned with martyrdom on their particular days. But we believe you have these. However, we have searched for what you wanted to be sent to you. Even though we have not found it, we will continue to search and, if it can be found, we will send it to you. [. . .]

165-A-16. BOOK VIII. LETTER 37. AUGUSTINE'S QUESTIONS TO GREGORY THE GREAT AND HIS REPLIES[t][a]

First Question of Augustine

4242   My first question, most blessed father, concerns [. . .] the offerings of the faithful which are received at the altar. Into how many sections are they to be divided and how shall the bishop distribute them in the church?

Answer of Blessed Gregory, pope of the city of Rome.

[. . .] It is the Apostolic See's custom to enjoin bishops at the time of their ordination that each gift received be divided into four portions: one for the bishop and his household for purposes of hospitality and entertainment; another for the clergy; a third for the poor; and a fourth for repairing churches. [. . .]

Third Question of Augustine

4243   Since there is only one faith, why do various customs exist in the churches, for example, one way of celebrating Mass followed by the church at Rome and another by those of Gaul?

Answer of Blessed Pope Gregory

Your Fraternity is acquainted with the practice of the church at Rome, the church that gave you nourishment. I approve of your selecting carefully whatever may be found to be more agreeable to Almighty God, whether in the Roman church or that of Gaul, or in any church whatsoever, and of your introducing by a special institution whatever you have been able to gather from many churches into the church of the English, a church still new in the faith. We are not to love things for places but places for things. Accordingly, choose from each church whatever is godly, religious, and righteous. Collecting them, as it were, into a small

---

† Translated from PL 76:1183ff.

a. Presumably written soon after 600. Augustine (d. between 604 and 609), who was sent by Gregory as a missionary to the Anglo-Saxons in Britain, became the first archbishop of Canterbury. Many doubt the authenticity of this letter.

pot, put them on the table of the English so that they also may become accustomed to them.

Eighth Question of Augustine
When great distances prevent bishops from easily assembling, may a   4244
bishop be ordained without other bishops being present?
Answer of Blessed Pope Gregory
Indeed in the church of the English, where till now you are the only
bishop, it is impossible for other bishops to be present. But when bishops
come from Gaul, they will assist you as witnesses at the episcopal ordination. However, it is our desire that you ordain bishops in England so that
long distances may not separate them from one another; in this way there
will be no reason why they cannot gather when any one bishop is to be
ordained. It is very useful that other pastors be present when they can
come together without difficulty. And so when, God willing, bishops are
ordained not far from one another, no bishop is then to be ordained unless three or four bishops are present [. . .] so that they may rejoice at the
promotion of him who is ordained bishop and may together pray to the
Almighty Lord for his protection.

Tenth Question of Augustine
Is a pregnant woman to be baptized or if she has already given birth, how   4245
much time should pass before she is allowed to enter a church? Or, so that
her child may not die unexpectedly without baptism, how many days must
pass before it is baptized? [. . .] Or, if she is having her period, may she enter
a church or receive the sacrament of Holy Communion? Or may a man who
has had intercourse with his wife enter a church before being washed with
water or even approach the mystery of Holy Communion? [. . .]
Answer of Blessed Pope Gregory
[. . .] Is there any reason why a pregnant woman should not be baptized since bodily fruitfulness is not sinful in the eyes of Almighty God?
[. . .] As to the number of days that must pass before a woman after delivery may enter a church, you have learned from the Old Testament that she
should refrain for thirty-three days if the child is a male, sixty-six days if a
female.[1] [. . .] In danger of death it is permitted to baptize without delay
a woman who is giving birth, even during the birth itself. The same is true
for the child, even while it is being born. [. . .]
Do not forbid a woman who is menstruating from receiving the sacra-   4246
ment of Holy Communion. However, if out of great reverence she refrains
from doing so, she is to be praised; but should she receive, she is not to be
judged. [. . .] A man sleeping with his wife should not enter a church unless he has washed himself with water; even if he washes, he should not
enter immediately. [. . .]

---

1. See Lev 12:3–5.

165-A-17. BOOK IX. LETTER 26. TO JOHN, BISHOP OF SYRACUSE[ta]

4247   Someone coming here from Sicily told me that some of his friends—I don't know whether they were Greeks or Latins—were, as if moved by zeal for the holy Roman church, complaining about the way I arranged [the divine services]. They said, "How can he restrain the church in Constantinople when in every way he follows that church's usages?" And when I asked, "What practices of theirs do we follow?", he replied, "It is due to you that the Alleluia is sung during Masses outside the season of Pentecost. You made a decision that the subdeacons process without liturgical garb, that the *Kyrie eleison* be said, and that the Lord's Prayer be recited immediately after the canon." My answer was, "In none of these things have we followed the practice of another church."

4248   As to the Alleluia being sung here, this is said to come from the church at Jerusalem through the tradition of blessed Jerome[b] at the time of Pope Damasus[c] of blessed memory. And so in this matter we have somewhat limited a former tradition, one handed down to us from the Greeks.

4249   Furthermore, as to my being responsible for subdeacons walking in procession without wearing liturgical garb, this was the Church's ancient tradition. But one of our popes—I don't know which one—had them process while wearing linen tunics. Have your churches received their usage from the Greeks? If not, then what is the origin of the custom of having subdeacons process in linen tunics unless this practice has been received from their mother, namely, the church at Rome?

4250   Furthermore, we neither have said nor do we now say the *Kyrie eleison* as it is done by the Greeks; they say it together, but among us it is said by the clerics with the people responding. As often as the *Kyrie eleison* is said, the *Christe eleison* is also said, a practice in no way found among the Greeks.

4251   Additionally, in daily Masses we suppress some things that are usually said, and we say only *Kyrie eleison, Christe eleison* so as to devote ourselves a little more to these words of petition.

4252   The Lord's Prayer we say immediately after the [eucharistic] prayer since it was the custom of the apostles to consecrate the offering by that same prayer only. It seemed to me highly unsuitable that we should say over the offering a prayer composed by a scholastic and not say over his Body and Blood the very prayer composed by our Redeemer. Yet among the Greeks the Lord's Prayer is said by all the people; with us by the priest only.

4253   In what way, then, have we followed the practices of the Greeks since we have either restored our own ancient practices or instituted

---

† Translated from CCL 140 A:186–87.
a. Written in October 598. Syracuse: a city in southeast Sicily.
b. Jerome. See WEC 3:**145**.
c. Damasus. See WEC 2:**52**.

new and profitable ones? In these, can anyone show that we are imitating others? [. . .]

165-A-18. BOOK IX. LETTER 148. TO SECUNDINUS, AN ANCHORITE MONK[ta]

[. . .] At the end of your letter you asked what reply should be given   4254
to those who ask you about the souls of little babies who die without the
grace of baptism. Your question was, "If the body is held by original sin,
how will a soul given by God be guilty, a soul that still has not consented
to sin in its actual body?" But on this matter, your Charity, so very charm-
ing to me, should know that among the holy fathers there has been no
small inquiry over the origin of the soul, but it remains uncertain whether
it descended from Adam or is in fact given to individuals, and the fathers
have admitted that the question is insoluble in this life. [. . .] What is not
uncertain is that unless one has been reborn with the grace of baptism the
chains of original sin bind every soul. On this it is written that "He is not
clean in his sight, not even an infant of one day on earth."[1] Here David
says, "I was conceived in iniquities and my mother gave birth to me in
sin."[2] On this, truth itself says, "Unless one is born again from the water
and the Holy Spirit he or she will not enter the kingdom of God."[3] Here
the apostle Paul says, "For as in Adam all die, even so in Christ shall all
be made alive."[4] Why therefore cannot an infant who has done nothing
be pure in the sight of almighty God? Why was the psalmist, born of a
legitimate marriage, born in wickedness? Why is a man not clean unless
he has been purified by the water of baptism? Why do all die in Adam if
the chains of original sin do not hold them? But because the human race
became rotten to its very roots in its first parents, it drew aridity in its
branches, and thus everyone is born with sin since the first man was unwilling to remain without sin. [. . .]

165-A-19. BOOK IX. LETTER 209. TO SERENUS, BISHOP OF MARSEILLES[tta]

[. . .] I have learned that your Fraternity saw some people adoring   4255
images, and that you smashed these images and threw them out of the
churches. We certainly applaud you for having had the zeal not to allow
anything made by human hands to be adored, but we judge that you ought
not to have smashed such images. Pictures are provided in churches for
the reason that those who are illiterate may at least read by looking at the
walls, what they cannot read in books. Therefore your Fraternity should

---

† Translated from *S. Gregorii Magni Registrum Epistularum*, vol. 2, ed. D. Norberg,
CCL 140 A (Turnhout, 1982) 703–4.

  a. Written in May 599.

  1. See Job 14:1–5. 2. See Ps 51:5. 3. John 3:3. Gregory added the words "from
. . . the Holy Spirit." 4. 1 Cor 15:22.

  †† Translated from CCL 140 A:768.

  a. Written in July 599.

have preserved them and should have prohibited the people from adoring them, so that the illiterate might have a way of acquiring a knowledge of history and so that the people would in no way sin by adoring a picture.

165-A-20. BOOK IX. LETTER 220. TO AREGIUS, BISHOP IN GAUL[t][a]

4256   [. . .] You asked that we allow you and your archdeacon to use the dalmatic.[b] [. . .] By the tradition of our authority we grant your request and allow you and your archdeacon to wear the dalmatic; such we have sent to you, carried by our most beloved son and abbot Cyriacus. [. . .]

165-A-21. BOOK XI. LETTER 3. TO BISHOP ECCLESIUS[tt][a]

4257   [. . .] Your Fraternity must carry out the office of visitor for churches so that you can reach without too much effort those being baptized there. [. . .]

165-A-22. BOOK XI. LETTER 21. TO MARINIANUS, BISHOP OF RAVENNA[ttt][a]

4258   [. . .] Furthermore, I neither encourage nor warn you but strictly command that you do not presume to fast at all, since the doctors say that this is totally unsuitable for such an ailment unless perhaps some major religious festival demands fasting. I allow it on five occasions each year. You must also refrain from nightly vigils. Let someone else recite the prayers that are usually said over the wax-tapers in the city of Ravenna or the expositions of the Gospel that are given by priests during the solemn feast of Easter. [. . .]

165-A-23. BOOK XI. LETTER 27. TO THEOCTISTA, A PATRICIAN[tttt][a]

4259   [. . .] But if there are those who suggest that sins are removed by baptism only in a superficial manner, then what is more lacking in faith than such a claim? In this way they hasten to destroy the very sacrament of faith by which the soul is chiefly bound to the mystery of heavenly purity, so that when completely absolved from all sins, it may cling to him alone, about whom the prophet says, "But it is good for me to draw near to God."[1] For certainly the crossing of the Red Sea was a form of holy baptism, in which the enemy was dead in the rear but others were found

---

[t] Translated from CCL 140 A:792.

a. Written in July 599.

b. Dalmatic: a liturgical garment with wide sleeves and two stripes, worn on special occasions.

[tt] Translated from CCL 140 A:861.

a. Written in September 600.

[ttt] Translated from CCL 140 A:892.

a. Written in February 601.

[tttt] Translated from CCL 140 A:910–12.

a. Written in February 601.

1. Ps 73:28.

opposite them in the wilderness. Likewise, the past sins of those who are bathed in holy baptism are all remitted since these sins die behind them like the Egyptian enemy. But in the wilderness we find other enemies because while we live this life, before we reach the promised land, many temptations wear us out and hasten to obstruct our way as we travel through the land of the living. Therefore, anyone who says that sins are not completely removed by baptism should say that the Egyptians were not truly dead in the Red Sea. But if one admits that the Egyptians were truly dead, then one has to admit that sins are totally dead through baptism because in our absolution truth certainly is stronger than a shadow of truth. In the Gospel the Lord says, "He that is washed does not need to wash, but is totally clean."[2] And so if sins are not totally removed by baptism, how is one that is washed totally clean? For a person cannot be called totally clean if something remains from his or her sins. [. . .]

There are some who say that penance for a sin should be done for any   4260 three-year period, and after three years one should live a life of pleasure. These have not yet learned the message of true faith nor the precepts of Holy Scripture. [. . .] Great is the virtue of penitence against sin but only if one perseveres in that penitence. [. . .] To show true penance is to lament one's sins and to avoid those sins that have to be lamented once again. [. . .]

165-A-24. BOOK XI. LETTER 31. TO ALL THE BISHOPS IN SICILY[ta]

[. . .] We know that our enemy[b] is in a hurry to invade Sicily with every   4261 effort. But so that the multitude of our sinners may not provide them with success as they undertake this invasion, let us turn with all our hearts to the remedies of our Redeemer, and as we cannot resist our enemies with courage, let us meet them with tears. [. . .] And so, my dearest brethren, I exhort you to proclaim a litany for every week, each Wednesday and Friday, without any excuse and to beg for the help of heavenly protection against the assaults of barbaric cruelty. But to open a path for your prayers to the ears of God, you must show more vigilant concern that your voices be supported by your actions. [. . .]

165-A-25. BOOK XI. LETTER 52. TO BISHOP QUIRICUS AND THE OTHER BISHOPS OF THE CATHOLIC CHURCH IN SPAIN[tta]

[. . .] We have learned from the ancient teaching of the fathers that   4262 when heretics who were baptized in the name of the Trinity return to the

---

2. John 13:10.
[t] Translated from CCL 140 A:919–20.
a. Written in February 601.
b. Namely, the Lombards.
[tt] Translated from CCL 140 A:952–53.
a. Written on July 1, 601.

Holy Church, they are to be reconciled to the bosom of Mother Church either by anointing with chrism, by the laying-on of the hand, or simply by a profession of faith. And so the West reconciles Arians[b] to the Church through the imposition of the hand, whereas the East does so through anointing with the holy chrism. The Monophysites[c] and others are received solely through a true confession when the holy baptism they received among the heretics receives the power to cleanse them, doing so either when they accept the Holy Spirit through the imposition of the hand or when through the profession of the true faith they are united with the holy and universal Church. There are also the true heretics who were in no way baptized in the name of the Trinity, like the Bonosians[d] and the Cataphrygians,[e] the former not believing that Christ is the Lord, the latter perversely believing that an evil man named Montanus[f] was the Holy Spirit. Many others are like them. When they come to the holy Church, they are baptized because what they received when they were in error was not given in the name of the holy Trinity.

165-A-26. BOOK XI. LETTER 56. TO MELLITUS, ABBOT IN FRANCE[ta]

4263   [. . .] Tell Bishop Augustine that I have long been giving consideration to the case of the Angles, namely, that the pagan temples in that country should not be torn down even though the idols found in these temples should be destroyed. May water be blessed and sprinkled in these places. Build altars and deposit relics in them since, provided these same temples are well constructed, we must change them from being places where idols are worshiped to places where the true God is served. In this way when the people see that these temples are not being destroyed, they may remove error from their hearts and, knowing and adoring the true God, they may hasten with more familiarity to their

---

b. Arians: followers of Arius (ca. 260–336), a priest in Alexandria who denied the unity and consubstantiality of the three persons of the Trinity and consequently the full divinity of Christ; the teaching of Arius was condemned by the Council of Nicaea (WEC 2:**71**-**C**).

c. Monophysites: followers of a heresy holding that in Christ there is only one nature, not two; a heresy condemned by the Council of Chalcedon (WEC 3:**137**).

d. Bonosians: followers of Bonosus, a late fourth-century bishop of Sardica in Illyrium.

e. Cataphrygians: an alternative name given to the Montanists; it refers to the place where the movement originated, namely, Phrygia.

f. Montanus: a native of Phrygia; during the years 155–60 he founded a movement that stressed the imminence of the parousia. Fasting, almsgiving, and in general a strong ethical rigorism were practiced as a preparation for the end.

† Translated from CCL 140 A:961–62.

a. Mellitus: sent by Gregory to Britain in 601 to assist Augustine, he eventually became the third archbishop of Canterbury.

accustomed places. Since they habitually slay many oxen as a sacrifice to the demons, they should also have some solemnity of this kind, even though altered, so that on the day of dedication or on the anniversaries of the holy martyrs whose relics are placed there, they may fashion for themselves tents of the tree branches around these churches that were formerly temples. [. . .]

165-A-27. BOOK XII. LETTER 6. TO JOHN, SUBDEACON AT RAVENNA[ta]

[. . .] I have not been at all pleased about what some have told me, namely, that my most reverend brother and fellow-bishop Marinianus is having my commentary on blessed Job read in public at vigils. This treatise is not for the public, and it hinders rather than assists poorly educated listeners. Tell him that he should have a commentary on the psalms read during the vigils; this would especially teach the laity who are listening on how to live correctly. [. . .]

4264

165-A-28. BOOK XIII. LETTER 1. TO HIS BELOVED CHILDREN, THE CITIZENS OF ROME[tta]

[. . .] On the Lord's Day earthly toil should cease. All attention is to be given to prayer so that if anything is done poorly during the previous six days, by prayers expiation may be made on the day of the Lord's resurrection. [. . .]

4265

165-A-29. BOOK XIV. LETTER 2. TO VITALIS, DEFENDER OF SARDINIA[ttta]

[. . .] You wrote that our brother and fellow-bishop, Januarius, during the time when he celebrates the sacrifice of the Mass, frequently suffers such great distress that he is barely able to return to the passage in the Canon where he just left off. From this you say that many doubted as to whether they should receive Communion from what he consecrated. But they must be advised that they should in no way be afraid, but should receive with full faith and security since a person's sickness neither changes nor pollutes the blessing of the holy mystery. And yet that brother of ours should be secretly exhorted in every way not to continue whenever he feels an attack coming on so that he does not thereby make people despise him and does not tempt the weak to sin. [. . .]

4266

[†] Translated from CCL 140 A:975–76.
a. Written in January 602.
[††] Translated from CCL 140 A:992.
a. Written in September 602.
[†††] Translated from CCL 140 A:1068.
a. Written in September 603.

165-A-30. APPENDIX 4. CONCERNING THE GREATER LITANY IN THE BA-SILICA OF SAINT MARY[ta]

4267   The solemnity of the annual devotion, most beloved, advises us that we should celebrate that litany known by all as the greater one, with concerned and devoted minds, and with the Lord's help through which we may deserve to be purged to some extent of our errors as we request his pity. It is indeed right for us to consider, most beloved children, with what diverse and continuous calamities we are afflicted for our sins and offenses; also to consider how the medicine of heavenly piety comes to our rescue afterwards. Therefore, when next Friday arrives, may we depart the Church of Saint Lawrence the Martyr, called Lucina, and hurry to the Church of Saint Peter, prince of the apostles, praying to our Lord with hymns and spiritual songs, so that we may celebrate the holy mysteries there and deserve to offer him thanks, insofar as we are able, for his benefits, both past and present.

165-A-31. APPENDIX 9. DECLARATION FOR THE SEVENFOLD LITANY[tta]

4268   [. . .] Dearest brethren, tomorrow at first light let us come together with contrite hearts and emended lives as with tears we celebrate the sevenfold litany in accordance with the plan shown below. None of you must go out into the fields for work on the land; none must presume to do any business at all so that gathering at the Church of the Holy Mother of God, may we who have all sinned together now all weep together for our evil deeds. So may the strict Judge himself, as he sees that we are punishing our own faults, spare us from the sentence of condemnation pronounced against us.

4269   There follows: "Let the procession of clergy go out from the Church of Saint John the Baptist; that of the men, from the Church of the blessed martyr Marcellus; that of the monks from the Church of the Blessed Martyrs John and Paul; that of the nuns from the Church of the Blessed Martyrs Cosmas and Damian; that of the married women from the Church of the Blessed Protomartyr Stephen; that of the widows from the Church of the Blessed Martyr Vitalis; and that of the poor and infants from the Church of the Blessed Martyr Cecilia." [. . .]

165-B. Dialogues[ttt]

Gregory's *Dialogues* (*Dialogi de vita et miraculis patrum Italicorum*) were written to show that Italy was not devoid of holiness. In four books the author uses visions, miracles, and prophecies to present models of

---

[t] Translated from CCL 140 A:1096.

a. Written in September 591.

[tt] Translated from CCL 140 A:1103–4.

a. On an occasion when the Tiber overflowed.

[ttt] Translated from *Dialogues. Grégoire le Grand*, vol. 2, trans. and ed. A. de Vogüé and P. Antin, SChr 251 (Paris, 1978) 206ff.; vol. 3, SChr 265 (Paris, 1980) 188ff.

excellence in the spiritual life: Book II is devoted completely to Benedict of Nursia (WEC 4:**155**); Book IV focuses on the immortality of the soul.

II.xxiii.2–5. Not far from his [Benedict's] monastery two religious   4270
women of noble birth resided in their house. A certain godly man took
care of their daily needs. As is often true, nobility of birth too often leads
to vulgarity of soul. [. . .] Having endured their insults for quite some
time, the man went to blessed Benedict and told him how the religious
women treated him. At once the man of God warned the women to curb
their sharp tongues, adding that he would excommunicate them should
they fail to do so. In fact, he did not pass a sentence of excommunication
properly so-called on them; he was just threatening them.

But they made no change in their conduct. A few days afterwards the   4271
two nuns died and were buried in the church. When Mass [*missarum sollemnia*] was celebrated there and when the deacon pronounced the customary, "If there are any who will not receive, let them depart," the nurse,
who was accustomed to bring for them offerings to the Lord, saw them
rise from their tombs and leave the church. Having often seen them depart
when the deacon gave this invitation, she remembered what the man of
God told them while they were still alive when he said that he would refuse them Communion if they did not correct their speech and actions.

Then with great sorrow she made all this known to the servant of   4272
God, who immediately with his own hands gave an offering, saying,
"Go and have this offered to the Lord for them, and no longer shall they
remain excommunicated." When the deacon as customary cried out that
non-communicants should depart, they were no longer seen exiting the
church. Since they did not leave with those who did not receive Communion, it was certain that they had received Communion from the Lord
through the Lord's servant.

III.xxxvi.1–3. [. . .] When I was at the royal court of Constantinople as   4273
a papal envoy, Maximian and his monks, moved by friendship, came to
visit me.

When he was returning to my monastery in Rome, a violent storm arose   4274
on the Adriatic Sea. [. . .] The waves roared high in the tempest, threatening them with destruction. [. . .] The passengers were terrified. Death was
not just close; it was imminent. After exchanging the sign of peace, they
received the Redeemer's Body and Blood, and each recommended himself to God, asking that God kindly receive their souls, the God who had
handed over their bodies to such a frightening death.

IV.lvii.1–7. Can anything benefit souls after death?   4275

Although sins cannot be pardoned after one has died, the offering of the   4276
salutary victim aids many souls even after death to such an extent that at
times the very souls of the deceased are seen to require this.

Bishop Felix, of whom I spoke above, says that he learned the following   4277
from a holy priest. Till his death two years ago this priest resided in the

diocese of Centumcellae[a] where he was in charge of the Church of Saint John in Tauriana. Considering it beneficial for his health, he bathed in the hot springs of Tauriana.

4278   One day upon entering the baths he discovered a man he did not know who was most helpful by unlatching his shoes, caring for his clothing, and providing him with towels after the bath, in short, providing the utmost service. This happened frequently.

4279   One day this priest, going to the bath, said to himself, "This attendant is so devoted to me; I must repay him in some way." Accordingly, he brought with him two crown-shaped loaves of bread. When the priest arrived at the bath, the attendant served him as usual. Afterwards, once the priest was again fully dressed and about to depart, he offered the man the bread as a gift, asking that the attendant accept it as a blessing, for he offered it as an expression of his appreciation.

4280   But the man, sad and upset, answered, "Father, why are you giving me this bread? It is holy. I cannot eat it. I who stand before you was once in charge of this place. But because of my sins I was sent back here to be a servant. Now if you desire to help me, then offer this bread to almighty God and intercede on my behalf, I who have sinned." [. . .]

4281   The priest spent the whole week praying and supplicating. Daily he offered the saving victim. When he returned to the bath, he could not locate the man. This demonstrates how beneficial to souls is the offering of the sacred victim. The spirits of the dead seek this from the living and give signs indicating that pardon is obtained through it.

4282   IV.LVII.8–16. [. . .] There was a monk named Justus, skilled in medicine, who took care of me in my monastery and sat with me during my frequent illnesses. Now when Justus became gravely ill, he was cared for by his brother Copiosus, who still practices medicine here in Rome.

4283   Justus, seeing that his final hour had arrived, told his brother that he had hidden away for himself three gold pieces. This deed could not be concealed from the brothers. Carefully searching among the entire supply of drugs, they discovered the gold pieces buried among the medicines.

4284   As soon as I learned that a monk living in common with us had perpetrated such an evil deed, I could not simply overlook this misdeed since our monastic rule required the brothers to follow a strict common life. No monk was to have any personal possessions. Greatly pained, I asked myself what I might do to correct the dying man and to give an example that could guide the living.

4285   I sent for Pretiosus, the monastery's prior, and said to him: "See that no brother visits the dying man or speaks any words of consolation to him. When Justus, at the point of death, clamors for the brothers, let his natural brother Copiosus tell him that all the brothers consider him to be an abomination because of the three gold pieces he had hidden. At least at

---

a. Centumcellae: today Civitavecchia, an Italian port city on the Tyrrhenian Sea.

the time of death his soul will experience bitter compunction for his sin, and he will be cleansed from the sin he has committed. When he has died, do not bury him in the monastery's cemetery. Rather, make as you wish a trench in a manure pile and throw his body into it. Fling the gold pieces into the grave after him and have all the brothers cry out together, 'May your money perish with you.'[1] Then cover him with earth."

My goal was twofold: to benefit both the dying man as well as the brothers who were living. The bitterness of his death was to bring him forgiveness; such a condemnation of avarice was to deter others from ever surrendering to this sin.   4286

And it worked. When this brother was about to die, he anxiously at-   4287
tempted to commend himself to the brothers, but none would listen or speak to him. Copiosus explained the reason for such treatment, and so Justus began to lament abundantly for his sin. Thus it was that Justus, truly contrite, died. He was buried as I had prescribed. Terrified by such a sentence, the brothers, one by one, began to bring to the monastery's storeroom the smallest and most ordinary articles, even those allowed by the monastery's rule. They were very much afraid of keeping anything that might cause them to be reproached.

Thirty days passed after his death when I began to feel great sympathy   4288
for the deceased Justus. Deep was the sorrow I felt when considering his punishment. So I searched for a way to ease his suffering. I summoned Pretiosus, the prior of our monastery, and said to him with sadness, "Justus, your deceased brother, has now been suffering the pain of fire for a long time. We must extend our love to him. We must do all we can to gain his release. Beginning today, offer the holy sacrifice for his intention, doing so for thirty consecutive days. Not a single day is to pass without the sacrifice being offered for his pardon." Immediately the prior agreed and left.

Immersed in other affairs, we lost count of the days. One night the de-   4289
ceased Justus appeared in a dream to his brother Copiosus, who asked him, "How are you, my brother?" Justus answered, "Till now things have been very miserable, but at present I am well because today I received Communion."

Copiosus quickly hurried off to tell this to his monastic brothers who,   4290
exactly counting the days, discovered that this was the thirtieth consecu-tive day on which the sacrifice had been offered for him. Copiosus did not know that the brothers were offering the sacrifice for Justus, nor did the brothers know that Copiosus had seen Justus in a vision. And so at the very moment when all became aware of what had occurred, they under-stood that the vision and the completion of the thirty Masses occurred simultaneously. It was obvious that the deceased brother had escaped punishment because of the salutary offering.

---

1. Acts 8:20.

4291   V.LIX.6–LXI.2. [. . .] We must remember that the benefits of the holy victims are useful only for those deceased who, having led good lives, merit assistance even after death through the good deeds others perform for them.

4292   However, it is much safer to do for oneself during life the good we hope others will do for us after our death. It is better to depart the world as a free person rather than to seek liberty after being in chains. Consequently we should completely despise the present age, considering it to be already lost, and offer our sacrifice of tears to God each day as well as daily offer his sacred Body and Blood.

4293   In a unique way this sacrifice has the power to save the soul from eternal death since it mystically renews for us the death of the only-begotten Son. Although "risen from the dead and dying no more, death having no more power over him,"[2] yet in himself immortal and incorruptible, he is again offered for us in the mystery of the holy sacrifice. Where his Body is eaten, there his flesh is distributed for the salvation of the people. No longer is his blood poured into the hands of the pagans but into the mouths of his faithful followers.

4294   May we consider how the sacrifice offered for us even imitates in itself the passion of the only-begotten Son for the pardon of our sins. Can any of the faithful doubt that at the precise moment of the offering, at the voice of the priest, the heavens open and choirs of angels are present at the mystery of Jesus Christ? At the altar the lowliest is united with the highest; earth is united to heaven; the visible and the invisible become one.

165-C. Homilies on the Gospels

Divided into two books, Gregory's forty homilies on the gospel pericopes were probably written in 590–91.

165-C-1. BOOK I. HOMILY 16. ON MATTHEW 4:1–11 (1ST SUNDAY OF LENT)[†]

4295   5. [. . .] This reading is appropriate for the present days when we begin the forty days of *Quadragesima*. We have heard of our Redeemer's fast of forty days. We must first consider why this fast is observed for forty days. Moses fasted forty days to receive the law for the second time.[1] Elijah fasted forty days in the desert.[2] And the Creator of the human race, coming to us, refrained from taking any kind of food for forty days. As far as possible we also use the period of *Quadragesima* to afflict our bodies by fasting. Why do we observe the number forty when we fast except that the power of the Decalogue is completed in the four books of the Gospel? Four times ten is forty; we complete the ten commandments when we truly observe the four books of the holy Gospel.

---

2. Rom 6:9.

[†] Translated from *Homiliae in Evangelia. Gregorius Magnus*, ed. R. Etaix, CCL 141 (Turnhout, 1999) 113–14.

1. See Exod 34:28.   2. See 1 Kgs 19:8.

The number "forty" can have another interpretation. Our mortal bodies   4296
are supported by four elements. Through bodily pleasure we go against
the Lord's commandments. These are received in the Decalogue, and it is
fitting that we, who reject these commandments through bodily desires,
should afflict our bodies forty times.

There is something else that we can understand about the forty days of   4297
Quadragesima. There are six weeks—forty-two days in all—between the
present day and the joyous paschal celebration. Now if we subtract the six
Sundays from this time of fasting, there remain only thirty-six days. Since
there are 360 days in a year, when we afflict ourselves for thirty-six days,
we give, as it were, a tithe of the year to God. We, living for ourselves during the year we have received, can by fasting mortify ourselves for our
Creator during a tenth of this time. Beloved, since we are instructed to
offer him a tithe of what we own, hasten to offer him a tithe of your days
also. [. . .]

165-C-2. BOOK II. HOMILY 8. ON LUKE 2:1–14 (CHRISTMAS)[†]

1. Because, the Lord willing, we will celebrate three Masses today, we   4298
cannot speak at length on the gospel reading. Yet the birth of our Redeemer compels us to say a few words. [. . .]

165-C-3. BOOK II. HOMILY 26. ON JOHN 20:19–31 (OCTAVE OF THE PASCH)[††]

4. [. . .] And so at the very giving of the Holy Spirit it is said, "Whose   4299
sins you shall forgive, they are forgiven, and whose sins you shall retain,
they are retained."[1] It is a pleasant task to meditate on these disciples, on
such humble labors to which they were called, and on the highest glory
to which they were led. See how they are not only personally made safe
but how they receive the power of binding and of loosing others; and how
they share in the sovereignty of the heavenly tribunal so that taking the
place of God for some they retain sins and for others they remit sins. [. . .]

5. Certainly it is the bishops who hold the place [of the first disciples] in   4300
the Church today; those who have obtained the office of ruling receive authority to bind and to loose. It is a great honor, and yet its weight is heavy.
It is difficult for a person who does not know how to regulate his own life
to judge the life of another. It often happens that one may hold the rank
of a judge here below, and yet that person's life hardly agrees with such
a position. Frequently one condemns the innocent or frees others while
he himself is bound. Often in binding and loosening one's subjects, a
person follows his personal desires and not the merits of the case. Consequently, those exercising authority in accord with their own likes and not

---

[†] Translated from CCL 141:54.
[††] Translated from CCL 141:221–23, 226.
1. John 20:23.

according to the conduct of one's subjects, deprive themselves of the very power of binding and of loosening. Often a pastor will give evidence of prejudice, showing hatred toward, or bestowing favor upon, one or the other neighbor. But those who rely on their personal likes or dislikes are unable to judge their subjects in a just manner. [. . .]

4301   6. As a consequence, cases must first be carefully weighed, and only then is the power of binding and loosening to be used. First to be considered is the sin that preceded, or the nature of the penance that followed this sin so that the priest's sentence may absolve those visited by the all-powerful God through the grace of compunction. The absolution given by the presider is only valid [*vera*] when it follows the judgment of the internal judge. This is shown by the raising of the man who was dead for four days, clearly demonstrating that the Lord first calls and gives life to the dead person by saying, "Lazarus, come forth."[2] After he came forth alive, he was loosened by the disciples, as is written, "And when the one who was bound with bandages had come forth, he said to the disciples, 'Untie him and let him go.'"[3]

4302   10. [. . .] We have completed the paschal solemnities, but we are to live so that we may merit to reach the eternal feasts. Every temporal feast is transitory. Being present at these solemnities, you must take care not to be separated from the eternal solemnity. What does it profit you if you are present at human festivals and yet happen to be absent from the feasts of the angels. The present solemnity is a shadow of those to come. Each year we celebrate it so that we may be brought to the solemnity that is celebrated not yearly but continually. When celebrated at its appointed time, today's feast refreshes our memories with a desire for the feast that is yet to come. [. . .]

165-C-4. BOOK II. HOMILY 37. ON LUKE 14:25–33 (FEAST OF A MARTYR)[†]

4303   8. [. . .] It is said that not long ago a man was captured by his enemy and was then taken away to a distant location. For quite a long time he was held in chains. When he failed to return from captivity, his spouse believed that he had died. Every week she had the sacrifice offered for him as if he were deceased. As often as she did this, he was freed from his chains in captivity. Much time passed. But upon his return he related all this to his wife since he wondered why it was that his chains were removed on particular days and at particular times. His wife then realized that this took place on the days and at the times the sacrifice was offered. Beloved, consider this and realize that the holy sacrifice can free the bonds of our hearts because when one person offered it for another, it was able to loosen chains on the body.

---

2. John 11:43.   3. John 11:44.
† Translated from CCL 141:354–55.

10. Beloved, many of you know of Cassius, bishop of the city of Narni.[a]   4304
Each day he offered sacrifice to God so that scarcely a day of his life went
by without his presenting the propitiatory victim to God. His life was in
harmony with the sacrifice. Having given away all his possessions as an
alms, when it was time to sacrifice, he was overcome with tears and
offered himself with great sorrow of heart. [. . .]

GAUL

166. ORIENTAL RULE[†]

This Rule was probably redacted ca. 515 in the monastery of Condat, a
foundation established by Romanus (ca. 390–ca. 460). The text, borrowing
from the Rule of Saint Pachomius (WEC 2:**86-A**) and the Second Rule of
the Fathers, seems to have had a limited diffusion.

CPL no. 1840 * CPG no. 2403

12. No one will find a pretext to dispense himself from going to the   4305
gatherings for the office and for psalmody. Whether one is in the monastery, in the field, on a voyage, or doing whatever type of service, the time
for prayer and psalmody is not to be neglected.

167. AVITUS OF VIENNE

Avitus (*Alcimus Ecdicius Avitus*) was born ca. 450 of a noble Roman family at Vienne. Succeeding his father, Hesychius (*Isychius*), Avitus was ordained bishop of that city sometime between 490 and 494. He had good
relations with King Gundobad, whose son, Sigismund, Avitus won over to
orthodoxy from Arianism. A rigid opponent of heretical teaching, he was
no less a strong defender of the primacy of the bishop of Rome. The year
of Avitus's death is usually placed between 518 and 523.
    Avitus wrote both prose and poetry. Among the latter are his *On Virgin-
ity*, written for his sister, and a long poem entitled *De spiritualis historiae
gestis*. Most notable among his prose works are the various letters that
still prove to be a valuable source for understanding the early period of
Merovingian history.

CPL nos. 990ff. * Altaner (1961) 568–69 *Altaner (1966) 475 * Bardenhewer (1908)
609–11 * Bardenhewer (1910) 526–27 * Bardenhewer (1913) 5:337–45 * Bardy (1930)
176–77 * Bautz 1:311 * Labriolle (1947) 2:748–52 * Labriolle (1968) 487–89 * Steidle
242–43 * Tixeront 334–35 * CATH 1:1134–35 * CE 2:161 * DCB 1:233–34 * DHGE
5:1205–8 * DPAC 1:459–60 * DTC 1.2:2639–44 * EC 2:552–53 * EEC 1:105 * EEChr
1:157–58 * LTK 1:1320 * NCE 1:1138 * NCES 1:946–47 * ODCC 139

---

a. Narni: a city in Umbria south of Spoleto.
    † Translated from *Les règles des saints Pères*, vol. 2, ed. A. de Vogüé, SChr 298
(Paris, 1982) 469.

167-A. Letters

The corpus of Avitus's ninety-six letters treats a variety of political, ecclesiastical, and social topics.

167-A-1. LETTER 3. TO KING GUNDOBAD[†]

4306   [. . .] In the churches of the major cities [found in the East] supplication is customarily made during the initial rites of the Mass. With such devotion and spirit the cry of the harmonious people rises up. [. . .]

167-B. Homilies

Although a collection of Avitus's homilies once existed, it has been lost. All that survive are three complete sermons together with various extracts and fragments.

167-B-1. HOMILY ON THE ROGATIONS[††]

4307   Like a well-traveled footpath there runs, not only through Gaul but through almost the whole world, the refreshing river of the rogational observance. The earth, so infected by sin, is cleansed by a fruitful stream of yearly satisfaction.

4308   We have a special reason for joyfully keeping this observance since early on it began here as a fountain that benefits all. [. . .]

4309   I know that many of us remember why people were terrified at that time. Frequent fires, continuous earthquakes, nocturnal noises—all seemed to threaten the whole world with utter destruction. Wild animals from the forest joined domestic ones in populous areas. Only God knows whether this was an optical illusion or the persuasion of exaggeration. Whatever the case, the people considered each to be equally grotesque, whether taming the hearts of the beasts, whether the optical illusions so horribly produced for the eyes of those who were so terrified.

4310   This resulted in various feelings and opinions among the people and among those of various social classes. Some, hiding their true feelings, attributed to natural disasters what they refused to relinquish because of their sorrow. Others, in a more healthful way, interpreted the new evils as fitting signs of their own perversity. Who would not fear in the repeated fires the storm that afflicted Sodom?[1] Who would not fear in the trembling planets either the collapse of the city's roofs or the threatening destruction of the earth? Who seeing—or believing that one saw—the naturally timid deer entering the courtyard through the narrow gates would not fear the imminent judgment of being forsaken?

[†] Translated from PL 59:210–11.
[††] Translated from PL 59:289–92.
1. See Gen 19:24.

And what else? Both in public and in private people were fearfully dis- 4311
cussing all this till the night of the solemn vigil during which, as annual
custom requires, the Lord's resurrection was to be celebrated. With one
spirit all awaited the wealth of labor, the end of evil things, the safety of
those afflicted by fear. And so the venerable night arrived, one whose solemn prayer would lead to public forgiveness.

But soon a more striking noise was heard—akin to the snapping sound 4312
of a whip. Since the people had experienced almost everything possible,
they thought that complete chaos would follow. During the evening the
main public building, located on the city's summit, began to burn. The
flames were terrible. And so the joy of the feast was interrupted by news
of the approaching crisis. Terrified, the people fled the church since all
feared that the flames from the burning citadel would strike their own
property and homes.

The invincible bishop remained before the festive altars and, kindling 4313
the power of his faith, by the flood of his tears restrained the power of
the fire, now held in check. No longer in despair, the people returned to
the church where, now that the fires were extinguished, the beauty of the
tapers could be seen. Certainly there was no further delay in obtaining the
medicine of sorrow.

It was then during the night of the Pasch that the priest Mamertus,[a] my 4314
predecessor, my spiritual father by baptism—whom my father succeeded
not many years ago after the death of Mamertus—conceived the Rogations.
It was then and there that Mamertus, silently and with God, determined
what the world today loudly implores by means of psalms and prayers.

Once the paschal solemnity was over, it was in a secret meeting that 4315
Mamertus discussed not what should be done but how and when it
should be done. Some believed that the senate of Vienne, composed at
that time of numerous illustrious members, was incapable of adopting
what was new since it could hardly agree on things that were old. But
the godly and solicitous pastor, abounding with the salt of wisdom, first
prayed in order to soften the souls of his flock, souls that needed to be
tamed. He did this rather than employing speech to soothe the ear. And
so he explained the arrangement of the observance, indicating its order
and showing how fruitful it would be. For someone who by nature was
both religious and clever, it was not enough to propose this institution that
would favor the obedient, without from its very beginning giving it the
bond of custom. God inspired the hearts of the sorrowful, and so Mamertus was heard, supported, and exalted by all.

The present period of three days was selected between the feast of the 4316
Ascension and its Sunday[b] as if the solemnities on both sides formed an
appropriate border. The bishop, testing the initial fervor of the people,

---

a. Mamertus: bishop of Vienne (d. ca. 475).
b. Actually, the Sunday before the Ascension is meant.

feared that the observance would at its very beginning be held in contempt by those hesitating to observe it. He indicated that the prayer of the first procession was to occur at the basilica which at that time was closer to the city walls. [. . .]

4317   Afterwards the churches in Gaul followed this commendable example. Yet the observance is not celebrated by all on the same days when it was established among us. Nor was it of great concern as to which days were selected provided that the psalmody was performed with the annual shedding of tears. However, with growing love for the Rogations and with increasing agreement among the priests, concern for a universal observance resulted in a unified time, namely, the present days. [. . .]

168. CAESARIUS OF ARLES

Caesarius of Arles (ca. 470–542) was surely the most important bishop in southern Gaul during the early sixth century. Born in the Burgundian diocese of Chalons-sur-Sâon, he entered the island monastery of Lérins when he was twenty years old. Leaving Lérins for health reasons, he went to Arles (called the "Gallic Rome"), where, while continuing to live the spirit of the monastic life, he was ordained a priest. Before being made a bishop, he was superior of the monastery of Trinquetaille in a suburb of Arles. As archbishop Caesarius played a significant role in several local councils, e.g., that of Agde (WEC 4:**176-A**), which devoted itself to reforming church discipline, and that of Orange in 529, which condemned Semipelagianism. Caesarius was not a great theologian in the line of Augustine but a true shepherd interested in the religious welfare of his flock. The archbishop's lifestyle, we are told, was simple, and his sermons evidence a special love for the poor.

Although a somewhat substantial corpus of writings are ascribed to him, Caesarius is most noted for his numerous homilies. The famous *Statuta ecclesiae antiqua* (WEC 3:**125**) was once, and incorrectly, attributed to him.

CPL nos. 1008ff. * Altaner (1961) 569–71 * Altaner (1966) 475–77 * Bardenhewer (1908) 611–13 * Bardenhewer (1910) 527–28 * Bardenhewer (1913) 5:345–56 * Bautz 1:842–43 * Jurgens 3:282–85 * Labriolle (1947) 2:773–76 * Labriolle (1968) 497–99 * Steidle 243–44 * Tixeront 333–34 * CATH 2:841–43 * CE 3:135–37 * DCB 1:376–78 * DHGE 12:186–96 * DictSp 2.1:420–29 * DPAC 1:653–55 * DTC 2.2:2168–85 * EC 3:1353–54 * EEC 1:138–39 * EEChr 1:202–3 * LTK 2:878–79 * NCE 2:1046–48 * NCES 2:848–49 * ODCC 261–62 * PEA (1894) 3.1:1302–4 * PEA (1991) 2:926 * TRE 7:531–36

G. Morin, "Les 'Statuta ecclesiae antiqua' sont-ils de s. Césaire d'Arles?" RB 30 (1913) 334–42. * G. Morin, "Le symbole de s. Césaire d'Arles," RB 46 (1934) 178–89. * A. Chavasse, "L'onction des infirmes dans l'église latin du IIIe siècle à la réforme carolingienne: les textes," RevSR 20 (1940) 64–122, 290–364. * K. Berg, "Die Werke des hl. Caesarius von Arles als liturgiegeschichtliche Quelle," diss. (Rome, 1946). * H.G.J. Beck, *The Pastoral Care of Souls in South-East France during the Sixth Century*, Analecta Gregoriana 51 (Rome, 1950). * J. Gaudemet, "La discipline pénitentielle en Gaule du IVe au VIIe siècle," RDC 3 (1953) 233–38. * R. Metz, "La consécration des vierges en Gaule, des origines à l'apparition des livres liturgiques," RDC 6 (1956) 321–39. * C. Gindele, "Die Satisfaktionsordung von Caesarius und Benedikt bis Donatus," RB 69 (1959) 216–36. * M.C. McCarthy, *The Rule for Nuns of St. Caesarius of Arles: A Translation with a Critical Introduction*, Studies in Mediaeval History, n.s., 16 (Washington, D.C., 1960). * C. Vogel, "La paenitentia in extremis chez Césaire évêque d'Arles," SP 5, TU 80 (Berlin, 1962) 416–23. * C. Vogel, "Un problème pastoral au VIe siècle: la paenitentia in extremis au temps de Césaire, évêque d'Arles," in *Parole de Dieu et Sacerdoce* (Paris, 1962) 123–37. * A. Voog, "Le péché et la distinction des péchés dans l'oeuvre de Césaire d'Arles," NRTh 84 (1962) 1062–80. * H. Angles, "S. Césaire d'Arles et le chant des hymnes," LMD, no. 92 (1967) 73–78. * A. de Vogüé, "La règle de S. Césaire d'Arles pour les moines: un résumé de son règle pour les moniales," RAM 47 (1971) 369–406. * S. Felici, "La catechesi al popolo di s. Cesario di Arles," in *Valori attuale della catechesi patristica* (Rome, 1979) 169–86. * C. Munier, "La pastorale pénitentielle de s. Césaire d'Arles," RDC 34 (1984) 235–44. * R. Taft, *The Liturgy of the Hours in East and West: The Origins of the Divine Office and Its Meaning for Today* (Collegeville, 1986) 100–113, 150–56, 180–82. * R.M. Leikam, "'Psallentes et orantes': la doctrina espiritual sobre la oración de la igelesia en los Sermones de s. Cesáreo de Arlés," EOr 11 (1994) 153–80.

168-A. Monastic Rules

Caesarius is credited with writing two rules for religious, one for monks and another for virgins or nuns. A relationship exists between the two, although not all agree as to its exact nature. The documents depend much on the Rule of Saint Augustine (WEC 3:**98-V**), the writings of John Cassian (WEC 3:**118**), and the monastic customs at Saint Lérins. Although rather strict and pedantic, the two rules by Caesarius well reflect the monastic spirituality of the time.

168-A-1. RULE FOR MONKS[†]

This Rule is shorter than that for nuns. It appears to have been written over the course of a number of years, perhaps 534–42.

xx. During vigils,[a] from the month of October till the Pasch, there are two nocturns and three *missae*. At each a brother is to read the lessons and pray; he is to read another three and pray; he is to read three more and stand.　4318

xxi. Chant [*dicite*][b] an antiphon, a response, and another antiphon; the antiphons are to follow the order given in the Psalter. Matins is next: on a direct　4319

[†] Translated from *Oeuvres monastiques*, vol. 2, trans. and ed. A. de Vogüé and J. Courreau, SChr 398 (Paris, 1994) 218–20, 223.

a. For an explanation of the terminology (e.g., *antiphona*, vigil, *missa*, response, *directaneus*, *Duodecima*, etc.) used in this Rule as well as in that for nuns or virgins, see R. Taft, *The Liturgy of the Hours*, as noted above; also M.C. McCarthy, *The Rule for Nuns of St. Caesarius of Arles*, 70–80.

b. Here and in other instances the Latin *dicitur* or *psallitur* does not necessarily mean "said" or "recited" in our sense of the term. It can also mean "sung" or "chanted."

tone [*directaneus*] is sung "My God and my King, I will extol you."[1] Then all the morning psalms are said in order, together with their antiphons.

4320   Each Sunday there are six *missae*. During the first the account of the Resurrection is read during which no one is to be sitting. When the *missae* have been concluded, Matins is said. On a direct tone you say the psalm "My God and my King, I will extoll you."[2] Then the "Give thanks."[3] Then the "Let us sing"[4] and the "Praise the Lord, my soul."[5] Next the Canticle of Blessing,[6] the "Praise the Lord in the highest"[7] the *Te Deum laudamus*, the *Gloria in excelsis Deo*[8] and the verse. This is done each Sunday.

4321   XXII. From the holy Pasch till the month of September there is only a Wednesday and Friday fast. From the month of September to Christmas one fasts every day. Again, during the two weeks preceding Lent, one will fast each day except on Sunday when because of the Lord's resurrection, all fasting is strictly forbidden. Whoever fasts on Sunday sins. From Christmas to the second week before *Quadragesima* there is a fast on Monday, Wednesday, and Friday. From there to the Pasch one fasts on all days except on Sundays. Whoever fasts on Sunday sins. [. . .]

4322   XXV. Each Saturday, each Sunday, and all feasts have twelve psalms, three antiphons, and three lessons: one from the prophets, one from the apostle, and the third from the Gospels.

168-A-2. RULE FOR VIRGINS[†]

The final draft of this Rule, composed for the nuns of the monastery of Saint John the Baptist in Arles, dates from 534. Caesarius's sister was a member of this community.

4323   XV. During the vigils,[a] so that there be no drowsing off through inactivity, effort will be made to prevent distractions while listening to the lessons. If a sister begins to fall asleep, she will be told to stand while the others are seated; in this way she can ward off the languor of sleep so that she not be found to be either lukewarm or negligent in doing the Work of God [*Opus Dei*].

4324   XXII. When you pray to God with psalms and hymns, may the words of your voice be those of your heart. Whatever work you are undertaking, when you are not reading always reflect on a text of holy Scripture. [. . .]

4325   LXVI. With God's help "sing with wisdom."[1] Also, being principally inspired by the rule of the monastery of Lérins, we have judged it good to insert in this booklet a directive on how to chant the psalms.

---

1. Ps 145:1.   2. Ibid.   3. Ps 118:1.   4. Exod 15:1.   5. Ps 146:1.   6. See Dan 3:32–90.   7. Ps 148:1.   8. See Luke 2:14.

[†] Translated from *Oeuvres monastiques*, vol. 1, trans. and ed. A. de Vogüé and J. Courreau, SChr 345 (Paris, 1988) 190ff.

a. See note a under Caesarius's Rule for Monks.

1. Ps 47:7, LXX.

On the first day of the Pasch there are twelve psalms at Terce with their Al- 4326
leluias and their antiphons; there are three lessons, the first from the Acts of
the Apostles, the second from the Apocalypse, and the third from the Gospel;
then the hymn *Iam surgit hora tertia.* At Sext there are six psalms with an antiphon; the hymn *Iam sexta sensim volvitur*; and the lessons. Likewise at None
are said[b] six psalms with an antiphon, the hymn *Ter hora trina volvitur*, the
lesson, and the versicle. At the *lucernarium* [Vespers] there is the short psalm
which is said directly, three antiphons, and the hymn *Hic est dies verus Dei.*
This hymn is sung throughout paschal week at Matins and at Vespers.

And at the *Duodecima* the *Sol cognovit occasum suum*[2] comes first; then 4327
eighteen psalms; three antiphons; and the hymn *Christe precamur annue.*
On the next day at the *Duodecima* hour the hymn *Christe qui lux es et dies* is
said. Furthermore, these two hymns are always said in turn. As to the lessons during this paschal office at *Duodecima*, one lesson on the Resurrection is from the apostle, the other from the Gospels.

During the nocturns eighteen psalms are sung, the minor antiphons 4328
with their Alleluias; then two lessons; a hymn; and a versicle. In this way
all seven days are celebrated.

After the Pasch these same nocturns are said till the calends of October; 4329
up to the calends of August vigils take place only on Fridays and Sundays.
After the Pasch till Pentecost only one meal is taken on Friday; after the
Duodecima there are six *missae*, namely, eighteen readings are said by memory; then eighteen psalms; and then three antiphons. The nocturns are followed by three *missae* taken out of the book, this lasting till daybreak.

LXVII. Fasting. From Pentecost till the calends of September decide for 4330
yourselves the manner in which you will fast. In other words, the monastery's mother superior, who is to take into account what is feasible according
to each one's health, will endeavor to act with restraint in this matter. From
the calends of September to the calends of November a fast is observed on
Monday, Wednesday, and Friday; there is also a fast from the calends of November to the Lord's Nativity except on feasts and Saturdays. A fast of seven
days is observed before the Epiphany. From the Epiphany to the week before
Quadragesima there is a fast on Mondays, Wednesdays, and Fridays.

LXVIII. On Christmas and on the Epiphany a vigil is kept from the third 4331
hour of the night till dawn. Preceding the nocturns are six *missae* from
the prophet Isaiah; after the nocturns six *missae* from the Gospel. On the
Epiphany before the nocturns there are six *missae* from Daniel and after
the nocturns six *missae* from the Gospels.

On weekdays at Terce, Sext, and None there are six psalms with an- 4332
tiphons, hymns, lessons, and versicles. On Sunday and Saturday there
are six psalms at Terce; these are followed by three lessons, one from the
prophet, another from the apostle, and the third from the Gospels. After

---

b. See note b under Caesarius's Rule for Monks.
2. Ps 104:19.

the lessons there are six psalms, one antiphon, a hymn, and a versicle. On all feasts one adds three antiphons to the twelve psalms said at Terce; the lessons are related to the subject matter, namely, to the feast.

4333   LXIX. From the calends of October till the Pasch a second nocturn is added, namely, eighteen psalms, two lessons, and a hymn. Added at the beginning of the first nocturn is the *Miserere mei Deus secundum magnam misericordiam tuam,*[3] and at the end *Rex aeterne domine.* At the second nocturn is the *Magna et mirabilia.*[4] On the following night at the first nocturn is sung the *Media noctis tempus est;* and on the next night *Aeterne rerum conditor.* Begin the second nocturn with the *Miserere mei Deus miserere mei.*[5]

4334   After the nocturns three prayers are read; an antiphon is sung; a response; and another antiphon. Then up to dawn there are four *missae.* If possible, this number is not to be reduced. Never should the sisters be awakened earlier, never later. Then are said the canonical morning psalms, on ordinary days with antiphons, on feasts with the Alleluia.

4335   On all Sundays there are six *missae* followed by Matins. First say the small psalm in a direct fashion, the *Confitemini*[6] with an antiphon, *Cantemus domino*[7] and all the psalms of Matins with the Alleluias. On Saturdays and on all feasts a vigil is observed. On these solemnities, once Matins is finished, the hymn *Te Deum laudamus* is sung. One goes to the outer oratory and says the small psalm in a direct fashion, then the canticle *Cantemus domino,*[8] then the blessing of the three young men.[9] After the blessing there is the hymn *Gloria in excelsis.*[10] Then Prime is said with its six psalms, the hymn *Fulgentis auctor aeteris,* two readings, one from the Old Testament and the other from the New Testament, and the versicle. This is the procedure for Sundays, Saturdays, and major feasts.

4336   At Vespers the same is done: in the outer oratory a short psalm is sung in a direct fashion. This is followed by three antiphons; then the hymn—on one day the *Deus qui certis legibus,* on the following day the *Deus creator omnium.*

4337   On all Sundays the gospels are read during the vigils, but during the first *missa* the gospel of the Resurrection is always read, on the following Sunday another Resurrection text; likewise for the third and fourth Sundays. And when this first *missae* on the Resurrection is read—the first *missa* always concerns the Resurrection—no one is allowed to sit. But during the next five *missae* all sit as is customary.

4338   When the feasts of the martyrs are celebrated, the first *missa* is from the Gospel, the others from the passions of the martyrs. On ordinary days at vigils the books of the New and Old Testaments are read according to their order. In winter there are three *missae* after the *nocturns.*

4339   Above all else, the lessons during the vigils are to be regulated in such a way as to always desire more. This is why at each oration only two, three

---

3. Ps 51:1.   4. Rev 15:3–4.   5. Ps 51:1.   6. Ps 117:1.   7. Exod 15:1.
8. Ibid.   9. Dan 3:52–90.   10. See Luke 2:14.

at the most, pages are to be read aloud. Should it happen that the nuns arrive later for the vigils, only one page is read or whatever the abbess judges appropriate. She is to make the decision, and when she gives the sign, the nun who is to read immediately rises in order to complete the appointed *missae*. Curb the length of the vigil so that those in good health may not become sleepy afterwards.

At all times the sisters will read after Matins till the second hour. Then they will go about their tasks.   4340

LXX. When one among you dies, some of the sisters will keep watch over her till midnight, reading from the apostle. After midnight those who have kept vigil will go to bed where they remain till Matins; those who will keep vigil for the rest of the time will read one *missa* from the Gospels, the others from the apostle. This is the procedure for an elderly nun who has departed this light [*de hac luce*] on earth. Should the nun be a young person, the *missae* are from the apostle and last till Matins.   4341

Above all, at the death of a sister take care to inform the holy bishop of this so that he and the clerics of Saint Mary might bring her, with psalmody and holy devotion, to the basilica where she is to be interred.   4342

168-B. Sermons

Attributed to Caesarius are 238 sermons (Dom Germain Morin, OSB, spent his life preparing the definitive edition of these pieces, now available in CCL 103 and 104), some, however, of uncertain authenticity. These homilies are simple, popular in style, at times relying on the writings of others, and show that Caesarius indeed merits to be called the "greatest moral preacher since Augustine."

168-B-1. SERMON 1. THE HUMBLE ADVICE OF A SINNER[†]

xv. Perhaps it is difficult for some of my lords, the bishops, themselves to preach. If so, why should they not introduce the ancient custom of the holy ones, a custom which up to the very present is in a salutary way maintained in areas of the East, namely, to have for the salvation of souls the homilies of the ancient fathers read in the churches through the ministry of the holy priests? Should we think that some refuse to entrust this to their fellow-presbyters? May God not suffer that we suspect, much less believe, this. Rather, let us believe that all the bishops, filled with a holy zeal according to the example of blessed Moses, might say with a free conscience, "May he grant us that all the people were prophets."[1]   4343

In truth, I say that even if priests capable of doing this are lacking, it is neither inconsistent nor unfitting that a deacon be instructed to read aloud in church the homilies of the holy fathers; if it is appropriate for a deacon   4344

[†] Translated from *Sermons au peuple*, trans. and ed. M.-J. Delage, SChr 175 (Paris, 1971) 254–56.

1. Num 11:29.

to read the words of Christ, it should not be judged unfitting for a deacon
to read what Saint Hilary [WEC 2:58], Saint Ambrose [WEC 2:53], Saint
Augustine [WEC 3:98], or the other fathers preached. [. . .]

168-B-2. SERMON 6. PEOPLE SHOULD BE EAGER TO HEAR THE HOLY READINGS[†]

4345   III. Someone might say, "I am a farmer and so I am always occupied
with working the land; I can neither listen to nor read the holy text." Now
how many men and women in rural areas know by heart and sing aloud
diabolical and shameful love songs! They can remember what the devil
teaches them; they cannot remember what Christ shows them. How much
more easily and preferably and better it would be for the unlettered, both
men and women, to learn the creed, to memorize and frequently say the
Lord's Prayer, some antiphons, Psalms 51 and 91, thereby joining their
spirits to God and freeing them from the devil? In fact, just as evil songs
send one into the darkness of the devil, so holy songs show forth the
light of Christ. Let no one say, "I cannot remember what I heard read in
church." Surely if you wish to do so, you can; begin by wishing it, and you
will immediately understand. [. . .]

168-B-3. SERMON 12. AN EXPOSITION OF FAITH[††]

4346   3. [. . .] At baptism we are asked whether we renounce the devil, his
pomps, and his works; freely we answer that we do renounce them. Since
infants cannot promise this by themselves, their parents stand as guarantors for them. [. . .]

168-B-4. SERMON 13. ON THE FULL PRACTICE OF THE CHRISTIAN LIFE[†††]

4347   I. My brothers and sisters, let us now reflect more deeply on why we are
Christians and on why we bear Christ's cross on our foreheads. It is not
sufficient for us to have received the name Christian and then fail to do
the things Christians do. [. . .] If you repeat a thousand times that you are
a Christian and over and over again sign yourself with the cross of Christ
and yet do not bestow alms as you are able, [. . .] then the name Christian
will avail you nothing.

4348   II. [. . .] As I already said, give alms to the poor as you are able. Present
the offerings that are to be sanctified on the altar. A person who is well-off
should be ashamed to receive Communion from another's offering. Those
capable of doing so ought to present candles or the oil to be placed in
the lamps. Learn the creed and the Lord's Prayer and teach these to your
children. I do not understand how any can call themselves Christians by

---

[†] Translated from SChr 175:324.
[††] Translated from SChr 175:402–4.
[†††] Translated from SChr 175:416–28.

signing their foreheads and then neglecting to learn the few brief lines of
the creed or the Lord's Prayer. [. . .]

iii. Attend church every Sunday. Now if the unhappy Jews observe   4349
the Sabbath with such great devotion that they refrain from bodily work
on that day, so all the more should Christians have time for God alone
on the Lord's Day and gather at church for the salvation of their souls!
When you meet at church, pray for your sins, do not quarrel, cause neither disputes nor scandals; those who quarrel or cause disputes or scandals when they come to church harm their souls by arguing in a place
where they could have been cured through prayer. When standing in
church do not make small talk but patiently listen to the reading of the
holy texts; whoever wants to chatter in church will have to give an account for this sin in regard to themselves and others, for they, not listening to God's word, prevent others from doing so. Give the church a tenth
of your fruits. [. . .]

When some infirmity unexpectedly occurs, the sick should receive   4350
Christ's Body and Blood; may they humbly and faithfully seek the
blessed oil from the presbyters and with it anoint their sick bodies so
that what Scripture says might be fulfilled in them: "Are any of you
sick? May they have the presbyters come and pray over them, anointing
them with oil; and may the prayer of faith save the sick person and may
the Lord raise them up; and anyone who has sinned will be forgiven."[1]
My brothers and sisters, notice that those who hasten to church when
they are sick deserve to receive both bodily health and the pardon of
sins. Since we can find a twofold benefit in church, why do some miserable people try to bring numerous evils upon themselves by recourse to
charmers, springs, trees, diabolic phylacteries, magicians, diviners, or
soothsayers?

iv. [. . .] Continually admonish your neighbors and relatives always   4351
to strive to say what is good and proper lest by slandering, by speaking
evil, by leading choirs on holy feastdays, by publicly singing dissolute
and shameful songs, they appear to wound themselves by means of their
tongues with which they should be praising God.

These unfortunate and miserable people who neither are afraid nor   4352
blush to dance or do pantomime before the very churches of the saints,
even if they come to church as Christians, depart as pagans. Just notice
what kind of Christians are those who, coming to church in order to pray,
neglect prayer and are not ashamed to speak the sacrilegious words of the
pagans. Reflect, then, my brothers and sisters, on whether it is right that
the mouth of a Christian, into which the Body of Christ enters, should sing
dissolute songs, which are like the poison of the devil. [. . .]

v. Although I believe that due to divine inspiration and thanks to your   4353
admonitions, this evil custom, a vestige of the profane practice of the

---

1. Jas 5:14–15.

pagans, has disappeared from these areas, yet if you know any people who still engage in this most scandalous and shamelessness custom of disguising themselves as old women or stags, reprove them strongly so that they may repent for having committed this sacrilege. And if at the eclipse of the moon, you notice that some people, even now, are emitting loud cries, you should admonish them. Show them what a great sin they are guilty of when they by a bold sacrilege strongly believe that their cries and evil deeds can protect the moon which in fact is darkened at certain times by God's will. And if you still see people worshiping springs or trees and, as I have already said, if they are also consulting magicians, diviners, or charmers, if they wear or have their own family members wear devilish phylacteries, magic marks, herbs, or charms, severely reproach them since those who sin in this way forfeit the sacrament of baptism.

4354   We have heard that the devil has so seduced certain men and women that the men do not work on Thursday nor do the women spin wool on this day; so do we solemnly declare before God and the angels that all who willingly observe this practice, if they do not correct their ways through a long and arduous penance, will themselves be condemned to burn with the devil. These poor unfortunate ones who in honor of Jupiter refrain from working on Thursday are neither ashamed nor do they fear, as I surely believe, to do this same work on the Lord's Day. This is why you should admonish all whom you recognize as being guilty of acting in this manner. If they do not wish to repent, do not speak or eat with them. Furthermore, as to those who are subject to you, you might even whip them so that they will at least fear bodily punishment even if they do not think about the salvation of their souls. [. . .]

168-B-5. SERMON 16. THE QUALITIES OF GOOD AND BAD CHRISTIANS[†]

4355   II. [. . .] A good Christian is a person who, coming to church, presents an offering which is to be placed on the altar and gives to the poor—according to his or her means—either some money or a slice of bread. [. . .] That man is a good Christian who at the approach of each holy feast, so that he might more safely receive Communion, observes for many days chastity with his wife. In this way having a free and certain conscience, he can presume to approach the Lord's altar with a chaste body and a clean heart. Also good Christians are those who know by heart the creed and the Lord's Prayer and have taught them to their sons and daughters so that these also may faithfully retain them.

4356   III. [. . .] Indeed can those who hardly ever come to church call themselves Christians and, when they do come, do not remain standing in order to pray for their sins but make excuses for themselves or while there incite quarrels or fighting?

[†] Translated from SChr 175:454–56.

168-B-6. SERMON 19. ON THE CHRISTIAN LIFE AND SACRAMENTS[†]

III. [. . .] When the holy solemnities occur, observe chastity even with   4357
your own wives for many days beforehand so that you may approach the
Lord's altar with a safe conscience.

When you come to church do not stir up quarrels or scandals. Do not   4358
become intoxicated. Do not sing impure songs for dancing since it is not
right that your mouth, into which the Eucharist of Christ enters, should
utter diabolical words. Standing in church, faithfully make petition because of your sins. Silently and quietly listen to the divine lessons that
are read. Do not gossip in church because those who desire to engage in
harmful tales will be held guilty for their own sins and for those of others
since they are not listening to, nor do they allow others to listen to, God's
commands. Give to your church a tenth of all your fruits since it is right
that God, who has given you everything, should receive a tenth for the
poor through almsgiving, for he said, "Whatever you have done to the
least of these you have done unto me."[1]

Above all, learn by heart the creed and the Lord's Prayer and teach   4359
them to your children, for I do not believe that we should call someone
a Christian who has failed to learn by heart the few lines of the creed.
But perhaps some say that they cannot remember this. How great is the
wretchedness of the human race if we are unable to learn just a few words
whereas men and women are able to learn lewd songs and sing them
without shame.

IV. Upon coming to the church, present the offerings that will be conse-   4360
crated on the altar. If you have something and yet bring nothing, how will
you rightfully receive Communion from the offering brought by a poor person? Above all, show honor to your priest. Speak no evil regarding one another since it is written, "The detractor will be snatched from the land of the
living."[2] May no one be persuaded to worship an idol or to drink what is
offered to idols. The baptized must avoid profane things. No one is to marry
his maternal aunt, his cousin, or his wife's sister, for it is wrong that we be
lost through such vile dissipations coming from diabolical gratifications.

May no person take wicked delight in presuming to have recourse to or   4361
to pose questions to sorcerers, magicians, diviners, or enchanters regarding any kind of sickness. Whoever acts in this evil way and does not do
penance forfeits the sacrament of baptism. May no one presume to observe
Thursday in honor of Jupiter by refraining from work. My brothers and
sisters, I swear that no one, be it a man or a woman, should ever follow this
evil custom lest he or she be judged by the Lord on the day of judgment to
be among the pagans, not among Christians, for they sacrilegiously trans-
fer to the day of Jupiter what should be done on the Lord's Day.

[†] Translated from SChr 175:486–90.
1. Matt 25:40.   2. Prov 20:13, LXX.

4362   v. In addition, as often as any type of sickness befalls anyone, they should hasten to the church, receive the Body and Blood of Christ, and be anointed with the oil blessed by the presbyters. They are to request that these presbyters and the deacons pray over them in the name of Christ. If they do this, they will receive not only bodily health but also the forgiveness of sins. As the Lord graciously promised through the apostle James, "Are any of you sick? May they have the presbyters of the Church come and pray over them, anointing them with oil; and may the prayer of faith save the sick person."[3] Why should anyone kill his or her soul by having recourse to magicians, diviners, enchanters, and diabolical phylacteries when both soul and body can be cured by the prayer of the presbyter and the blessed oil? Bodily sickness is linked to the health of the soul; in this world God scourges those whom he loves.[4]

168-B-7. SERMON 33. ON TITHES[†]

4363   iv. As is also true for other feasts, it is with joy that we desire to celebrate the birth of Saint John the Baptist. Since this very illustrious solemnity is close at hand, may all of us during the several days preceding it observe perfect chastity and virtue so that all of us can celebrate this feast with joy, meriting to approach the Lord's altar with a conscience that is unencumbered and pure. I plead with you, and I adjure you by the terrible day of judgment, to warn all your neighbors, all your family members, and all who are subject to you; may you most severely reprimand them out of zeal for God. May none be so bold during the feast of Saint John as to bathe in springs or in pools or in rivers, whether at night or early in the morning since this unhappy custom still endures to the present from pagan rites. In fact, not only souls but—and this is worse—also bodies most frequently die in that sacrilegious bath so that such people, unconcerned about saving the soul, do not fear even the death of the body. Nevertheless, we trust in God's mercy that only a very few, or perhaps none at all, will dare permit this evil action in the future.

4364   My brothers and sisters, take care that your household members do not sing evil or licentious songs since it is not right that from their mouths, into which the Eucharist of Christ has entered, should come forth an impure or amorous song. [. . .]

168-B-8. SERMON 50. ON THE TASK OF DESIRING MORE ARDENTLY HEALTH OF SOUL RATHER THAN HEALTH OF BODY, AND ON AVOIDING SOOTHSAYERS[††]

4365   i. [. . .] Many grieve when their bodies begin to grow weak; yet if their souls are not merely wounded but are dead, they are not aware of this and

---

3. Jas 5:14–15.   4. See Heb 12:6.

[†] Translated from *Sermons au peuple*, vol. 2, trans. M-J. Delange, SChr 243 (Paris, 1978) 178–80.

[††] Translated from SChr 243:416–20, 422.

do not complain. And when they are sick in body, if only they would hasten to church and seek the medicine of Christ's mercy; yet some, no matter what kind of sickness it may be—and this is most deplorable—seek out soothsayers, diviners, and enchanters, and wear diabolical phylacteries and magic signs.

Often they receive these charms from clerics and religious, who in 4366 reality are not clerics or religious but helpers of the devil. My brothers and sisters, see how I beseech you not to accept these evil things even if offered by clerics because Christ's healing is not in these objects, only the devil's poison. The body is not healed by them; the unfaithful soul is destroyed by the sword of unfaithfulness. Even if you are told that the phylacteries themselves contain holy things and holy verses, may no one think, may no one expect that health will come from them because even if some are cured because of these phylacteries, this is due to the cunning of the devil. If at times the devil removes bodily infirmity, it is because he has already brought the soul to ruin.

The devil hopes to kill not so much the body as the soul; it is to test 4367 us that he is permitted to afflict our body with some infirmity so as to kill our soul when afterwards we agree to hand over our bodies to magicians and phylacteries. This is why on occasion phylacteries appear to be effective and useful since when the devil has struck a consenting soul, he no longer goes after the body. In fact, those who make phylacteries, those who request that they be made, and those who consent to them, show that they are pagans. If they fail to do an appropriate penance, they cannot escape punishment. But you, my brothers and sisters, you are to request health from Christ, who is the true light. Hurry to church, anoint yourselves with the blessed oil, receive the Eucharist of Christ. If you do this, you will receive not only health of the body but also that of the soul.

III. My brothers and sisters, [. . .] when you stand in church do not 4368 spend your time in telling useless stories. There are—and this is worse— certain men and especially women who talk in church to such a degree that they themselves do not hear God's word and do not allow others to hear it. On the day of judgment they will have to answer for this, both in regard to themselves and in regard to others. [. . .]

168-B-9. SERMON 55. A SERMON REPRIMANDING THOSE WHO ON FEASTS
SIN THROUGH DRUNKENNESS [. . .]†

1. My dear brothers and sisters, I am overjoyed and I thank God that 4369 on the holy feasts you come to church with pious devotion. Even though we, by God's grace, rejoice at your devotion, yet there are many concerning whose ruin we are sad. I have in mind those who, upon arriving in

---

† Translated from SChr 243:466–68, 470–72.

church, desire more to argue than to pray. Whereas they should be attentively listening in church to the divine lessons with the utmost of piety,
they plead their cases outside the church and attack one another with
various calumnies. At times—and this is even worse—there are those
who are inflamed with extreme anger so that they argue with the greatest intensity and most shamefully injure and accuse one another. It is not
even rare that they attack one another with their fists and feet. It would
have been better for these people not to have come to church rather than
to call down God's anger upon themselves by such evil deeds. They arrive at church with only minor sins; they leave for home with many major
sins. And so, even though my soul rejoices because of your devotion,
nonetheless, I ask you, who are upright and sober, who follow righteousness, who love chastity, and who are merciful, I ask you to pardon me and
to be patient with me, for it is necessary that I reprimand these negligent
and tepid individuals who come to the feast so that they can pass the time
with harmful gossip, not receiving there in the church the holy reading
with a faithful heart.

4370   II. There are also others who come to the feasts of the martyrs only to
become intoxicated, to dance, to sing evil songs, to lead choirs, and to
dance in a diabolical fashion; by doing so they bring ruin upon themselves
and others. Those who should be doing the work of Christ attempt to do
that of the devil. Not love of God but a love for debauchery usually brings
them to the feast. They apply themselves not to giving an example of good
works, not to the medicine of the faith, but to the poison and snares of the
devil; those who await or imitate such as these condemn their own souls
to perpetual punishment.

4371   IV. When you gather at church, do not become involved with things
that can increase your sins. Pass your time not with disputation but with
prayer, thus obtaining God's grace by supplication rather than offending
him by your quarreling. Do not drink to excess; do not erase your names
from heaven by drinking toasts. What is worse is that many not only make
themselves drunk but even encourage others to drink more than they
should. And what is still more serious, there are even some clerics who do
this. [. . .]

4372   When you come to church or gather for the feasts of the martyrs, by
almsgiving store up in heaven what you would customarily waste because of gluttony and intoxication. When present for a feast or a Mass,
listen with faith and joy to the holy readings; what you hear you should
commit to memory and with God's help strive to carry out. Do not busy
yourselves with idle gossip in church; do not chatter with one another.
This, in fact, occurs often enough, especially among women who, in
church, chatter idly to such a degree that they themselves do not hear
the holy readings and do not permit others to do so. As such, they will
have to render an unfavorable account both for themselves and for others. [. . .]

168-B-10. SERMON 64. A WARNING NOT TO BE NEGLIGENT IN HAVING RE-COURSE TO THE HEALING OF PENANCE IN THE CASE OF SERIOUS SINS[†]

II. My brothers and sisters, consider this: even if we do not allow our-selves to be snatched away by serious sins, there are the small sins to which, so much the worse, we pay no attention or which we surely count as nothing. Now if we group all these together, I know not how many good works would be required to outweigh them. May we consider what we have done since we have reached the age of reason, namely, swearing, lying, cursing, uttering calumnies, speaking evil, hatred, anger, envy, evil desires, gluttony, sleeping to excess, thinking evil things, concupiscence of the eyes, pleasure of the ears, afflicting the poor; let us remember that we have been tardy in visiting Christ in prison or have rarely done so, that we have been negligent in welcoming strangers, that we have neglected to wash the feet of our guests as we promised to do at baptism, that we have visited the sick less frequently than we should have, that we have failed to use all our resources in calling those at discord back to harmony, that we desired to eat while the Church was fasting, that while standing in church during the reading of the holy lessons we concerned ourselves with frivo-lous stories, that while chanting the psalms or while at prayer we have at times been distracted, that at banquets we have not always spoken holy words but at times have uttered indecent ones.

4373

Suppose we gather together these and similar sins, sins that can hardly be numbered, sins committed from the time we reached the age of reason, even if we exclude major sins, how many armies of good works and of what quality would redeem them if God's severity and justice were not mitigated by the divine mercy made powerful by reason of a humble and sincere penance added to the giving of alms according to our means?

4374

Since the sins I have just mentioned—sins that no one can escape—greatly oppress us, and since crimes and capital sins perhaps entangle us, I do not know how we can conscientiously assume a false security by failing through deadly negligence to seek the remedy of penance. Tossed about on the sea of this world by innumerable waves, we long delay seek-ing out the port of penance, not understanding that despair is born from a multitude of sins, a despair from which the reins of sin are shamelessly released. And so are fulfilled the words, "The evil person upon reaching the depth of sins condemns."[1]

4375

III. Someone says, "Once I reach old age or find myself seriously ill, then I will request penance." To be sure, such penance is not useless; certainly it is helpful if accompanied by generous almsgiving, by pardon-ing one's enemies, by requesting the forgiveness of all whom one has

4376

[†] Translated from *Sermons au peuple*, vol. 3, trans. M.-J. Delange, SChr 330 (Paris, 1986) 96–102.

1. Prov 18:3, LXX.

wronged. Now if such people recover, they should humbly and faithfully perform this penance for as long as they live, doing so with all their strength, with cries and groans, and by joining it to liberal almsgiving.

4377   Being wise, you should reflect in the midst of all this whether it is right that you, who were at the service of vices and sins during your whole life, should when being half-dead rise up to seek life. Would you want your servant to act in this fashion toward you, your servant who as long as he is strong and young, is at the service of your enemies, and as soon as old age approaches, then wishes to return to your service? And so it is not right that you do to your Lord what you do not wish to endure from your servant. Indeed, we know many who when in good health frequently say that they wholeheartedly desire penance but yet do not want penance immediately and so depart life lacking this remedy. Sinners are also afflicted by the punishment of being forgetful of themselves when dying since they were forgetful of God when they were in good health. In fact, it is doubtful whether those not desiring to seek the remedy of their souls when this was possible will afterwards merit to receive it, even if at that time they so desire.

4378   iv. And so, my dear brothers and sisters, may we think wisely and beneficially of the time of judgment and of the day when we must render an account; may we show sorrow for the rest of our lives, doing so with groaning and sighing because of our major crimes and sins. As to our small sins, whether those committed in the past or those we continue to commit, let us atone for them by assiduous prayer and more generous almsgiving. Just as the daily wounds of sin are not lacking, so the remedies of almsgiving and prayer are never lacking. In fact, if we punish ourselves with our own severity, we will ward off the sentence of the judge to come. Those who do not spare themselves because of their sins are immediately granted pardon by God. Those who separate themselves for a time from Communion because of their guilt will not be rejected from the heavenly altar since it is written, "Be the first to admit your iniquities so that you may be justified."[2] [. . .]

168-b-11. sermon 67. concerning those who in public request penance[†]

4379   i. Beloved, each time that we see some of the brethren make a public request to do penance, we can and should, under God's inspiration, stir up in ourselves the deep feeling of divine fear. Who, in fact, would not rejoice, would not delight, would not give thanks with all one's strength to see sinners becoming angry at their sins, proclaiming them aloud, so that what they were accustomed to defend most shamelessly, they begin to accuse themselves of for their salvation?

---

2. Prov 18:17, LXX.
† Translated from SChr 330:124–35.

They henceforth begin to associate themselves with God, and therefore   4380
they no longer want to be the defenders of their sins but to be the accusers. Since God abhors sins, as soon as people, abandoning them, begin to
hate them and separate themselves from sin, they are joined to God. Those
who receive penance in public could have done so in private. Yet in light
of the vast number of their sins, they lack sufficient strength to cope with
them by themselves. For this reason they desire to seek the assistance of
all the people. [. . .]

Beloved, notice that it is no little matter that the person who receives   4381
penance is clothed with a hairshirt, which is made from the hair of goats.
Because goats resemble sinners, those who receive penance in public declare that they are not lambs but goats, saying and affirming this by what
they are wearing. They say: "Look at me, all of you, and pour forth all
your dutiful tears for me, a miserable sinner; what I am outwardly, that
I am inwardly; henceforth I no longer desire to appear externally as if I
were a righteous person and to hide iniquities and plundering within.
Henceforth, like the bent-over publican, I do not dare look upward toward
heaven but humbly offer the wounds and deformities of my sins to the
heavenly doctor so that he might heal them. This is why I ask that all of
you request his mercy on my behalf so that he might completely cure the
decay of my sins and call me back to true health."

"I fear, in fact, that what the Lord said of the hypocrites may also be   4382
said of me, 'They come to you dressed like sheep but inwardly there are
ravenous wolves.'[1] This is why, as I already said, what I am within, so I
show myself without. Till now I adorned myself outwardly with precious
clothing; yet internally my soul was covered with the leprosy of sins. Consequently, clothed with a hairshirt and requesting penance with my whole
being, I ask that through your prayers I might merit to be freed from the
paralysis of my sins. Again and again I implore you—since under God's
inspiration you know how to weep with those who weep—that your piety
be moved to cry and to lament for the remission of my sins. I believe that
with this infinitely merciful judge your holy prayers will be able to obtain
for me the pardon of sins."

II. [. . .] My brothers and sisters, notice that when people request pen-   4383
ance, they ask to be excommunicated. When they are received into penance, each is covered with a hairshirt and is then placed outside. They
request excommunication because they deem themselves unworthy to
receive the Lord's Eucharist. Additionally, they desire to be excluded from
that altar for a period of time so that they might merit to reach the heavenly altar with a clear conscience. Furthermore, they want to be separated
from Christ's Body and Blood so that they, now guilty and ungodly, may
by their humility deserve to receive Communion at the holy altar.

---

1. Matt 7:15.

4384   III. Beloved, even those who so faithfully request penance with a contrite and sorrowful heart should place their trust in the intercession of all the people; and yet, with God's assistance, they themselves should not fail to be totally concerned with their own salvation. They are not to say in their hearts, "Look at all the people who have prayed for my iniquities. Already I can and should feel safe." May no one who does penance think, much less express, this. But with God's help may penitents, insofar as they are able, trust in the prayers of others as they strive to devote themselves to fasting, almsgiving, prayer, humility and love, holy works; may they visit the sick, bring together those who are in conflict with one another, welcome strangers, humbly wash the feet of venerable travellers, refrain from calumny and slander. Unless allowed by sickness, they are not to drink wine. But if due to old age or an ailment of the stomach, this is not possible, may they listen to the apostle who says, "Use a little wine for the sake of your stomach."[2]

4385   Some penitents, so that they can eat meat, wish to be reconciled immediately. To be sure, those who desire or presume to eat meat without being compelled by sickness certainly do not receive penance with true sorrow. And so penitents, even after being reconciled, are not to eat meat at any time, whether when eating alone or with others. Let them find potherbs or beans or fish. They are not to partake of other foods. I mention this because, and what is worse, some penitents are eager to eat meat and to drink wine, perhaps at times even to excess. [. . .]

168-B-12. SERMON 72. EPHREM'S ADMONITION ON PRAYER AND HARMFUL SPEECH[†]

4386   I. [. . .] My dear brothers and sisters, with joy I thank God that you faithfully hasten to church in order to hear the holy readings. Yet if you want to fully complete your progress and our joy, arrive there earlier. When the nights are so long, those who are not restrained by sickness harm their souls by coming late to church. Beloved, if merchants, goldsmiths, blacksmiths, and other artisans awake early to provide for material necessities, should we not arise early before daybreak to hurry to church in order to merit the forgiveness of our sins.

4387   If people in business are accustomed to rise early for monetary gain, why don't we do likewise out of love for eternal life? There are those who at times expose themselves to winds and storms, who suffer numerous dangers, who on occasion endure severe hunger and thirst. If they patiently bear all this because of what is perishable, then why does it bother us to keep watch for the sake of eternal life?

4388   So this is why I ask you to arrive earlier, and once there, to occupy yourselves with praying and chanting the psalms rather than with idle or

---

2. 1 Tim 5:23.

† Translated from SChr 330:178–82.

harmful gossip. As to those who come to church for the purpose of useless conversation, it would have been better for them not to have come at
all. Those busy with gossiping do not themselves chant the psalms, do not
permit others to do so, nor do they listen to the holy readings. Because of
this those who come to church with small sins return home with greater
ones; by idle talk they harm themselves in the very place where through
prayer and psalmody they should have been able to provide remedies for
themselves and others.

11. Above all, my dear brothers and sisters, when we devote ourselves   4389
to prayer, we should supplicate silently and quietly; those desiring to pray
aloud seem to forcefully remove the fruit of prayer from all those standing
nearby. Only sobs, sighs, and groans should be heard. [. . .]

168-B-13. SERMON 73. AN ADMONITION IN WHICH ALL THE PEOPLE ARE
URGED TO FAITHFULLY REMAIN IN CHURCH TILL THE DIVINE MYSTERIES
HAVE BEEN CELEBRATED[†]

1. My dear brothers and sisters, with paternal kindness I ask and remind   4390
you that no one, whenever there is a Mass on Sunday or on another major
feast, is to leave the church before the divine mysteries have ended. Even
if there are many whose faith and devotion cause us to rejoice, nonetheless, more numerous are those who, less concerned about their soul's
salvation, depart the church immediately after the holy readings; there
are others who during these readings are so concerned with harmful and
worldly stories that they themselves do not hear the readings and do not
allow others to do so. We would blame these less if they had not come to
church, for they are convicted of offending God in the place where they
should have merited the pardon of their sins.

11. So I ask you, my beloved, to receive our humble suggestion not only   4391
patiently but also willingly. If you notice closely, you will understand that
the Mass does not take place when the holy lessons are read in church but
when the gifts are offered and when the Lord's Body and Blood are consecrated. You can hear the prophets, the apostles, and the gospels read at
home, either by yourselves or by others. Therefore it is only in the house
of God that you can see and hear the consecration of Christ's Body and
Blood. This is why those desiring to participate in the whole Mass for a
spiritual gain should remain in church with a humble attitude and a contrite heart till the Lord's Prayer has been said and the people have been
blessed.

When, in fact, most people or, worse yet, almost all of them leave the   4392
church after the readings, to whom will the priest say, "Lift up your
hearts"? Or how will these people reply that they have lifted them up on
high when they go out into the streets in both body and heart? Or how
will they exclaim with both joy and fear, "Holy, holy, holy, blessed is he

---

[†] Translated from SChr 330:190–98.

who comes in the name of the Lord"? Or when the Lord's Prayer is said, who will humbly yet truthfully cry out, "Forgive us our sins as we forgive those who sin against us"?[1] Surely even those who remain in church, if they do not forgive those who sin against them, say aloud the Lord's Prayer more unto judgment than for a remedy since they do not put this prayer into practice and since it is useless for them to say, "Deliver us from evil," considering that they themselves do not cease doing evil. Now if those within the church are in danger when they are unwilling to carry out what they promise, what about those whom either insatiable desire or love for this world keep so entangled that they cannot spend a single hour in church?

4393   It is not enough that throughout the whole week they concern themselves with the necessities of life or perhaps, and more likely, with what they simply desire: furthermore, after an hour or two during which they seem to be present in the church more in body than in soul, and turning their backs to the sacrifices and priests of God, they immediately return to embrace the pleasures of this world without knowing what awaits them or what they have left behind. They follow the darkness and desert the light; they embrace the shadows and despise the truth; they reject the sweetness of Christ and seek the bitterness of the world, loving vanity and pursuing falsehood.[2] In truth, those who are in a hurry to leave the church are ignorant of the good that is found in the celebration of the Mass.

4394   III. Now if a king or some other powerful person should invite these to a meal, I would like to know whether they would dare depart before the meal has ended. Even if no person restrains them, their gluttony does. Why do we not leave a banquet given by a human person before it is completely finished if it is not because we wish to fill up our stomachs, perhaps more than is fitting, and also because we fear giving offense? Now why do we so quickly depart the spiritual and divine banquet? I fear saying this lest some become angry, but I will do so anyway because of the danger to myself and to you: we act in this way because we do not care about feeding the soul, because we neither fear God nor respect others.

4395   Certainly, by God's mercy, all are not guilty. On the contrary, there are many who with great devotion do not leave church till the people have been blessed and who do not fail to pray humbly, not only for themselves but for others as well. God rewards those to whom he has granted such great devotion that they remain in church. But his just judgment condemns those who are negligent. This is why, my brothers and sisters, you are to admonish those who do not wish to say the Lord's Prayer and to receive the blessing; do not cease to reprimand them by telling them and most assuredly threatening them that it profits them nothing to hear the holy readings if they depart before the end of the divine mysteries. Yet we cannot nor should we blame those who must attend to public necessities

---

1. Matt 6:12.   2. See Ps 4:2.

or are unable to stay because of some illness. However, these should look to their own consciences as to whether they leave because of necessity or simply because they want to depart.

iv. Again and again I ask and beseech you: may no one on Sunday and   4396
especially on major feasts depart the church till the divine mysteries have been completed except perhaps those mentioned above whom serious sickness or public duty hinder from staying longer.

My brothers and sisters, truly do I say that it is very harmful and al-   4397
most totally ungodly for Christians to lack respect for the Lord's Day, a respect with which we see the Jews observing the Sabbath. In fact, if these unfortunate ones so observe the Sabbath that on this day they dare do no earthly work, so much the more should those who have been redeemed "not with gold or silver but with the precious blood of Christ"[3] pay atten- tion to their price, dedicate to God the day of the Resurrection, and most attentively care for the salvation of their souls. Finally, if on Sunday we ne- glect to engage in reading and prayer to God, we do not sin lightly against him; the evil is greater if for a space of one or two hours during the cele- bration of the divine mysteries we lack the patience to remain standing in church. But what is worse is that the love of this world so intoxicates us that its changing shadows and the delights of worldly desires constantly drag us to those vain and false joys which give rise to true grief.

v. And so I again ask that none of you leave church before the divine   4398
mysteries have been completely celebrated; so act in church that none of you pass the time by engaging in idle words or gossip. [. . .]

168-B-14. SERMON 74. AN ADMONITION THAT THE PEOPLE REMAIN FOR THE WHOLE MASS[†]

i. My dear brothers and sisters, if you wish to discover and diligently   4399
see how much sorrow and how much bitterness afflict me when I see that you do not desire to remain at Mass till its end, you might take pity both on yourselves and on me. Those who understand what happens in church during the celebration of the divine mysteries recognize the great amount of evil done by those who without any great necessity leave church be- fore the Mass is finished. This is why, if you wish to free me from sorrow of the spirit and if you wish to deliver yourselves from sin, you should not disregard my plea; you should fear what the Lord said to his priests, "Whoever hears you hears me, and whoever despises you despises me."[1] Those who neither fear nor are ashamed to hasten out of church before the end of Mass surely sin twice: by not assisting at the divine mysteries, and by distressing and expressing disdain for the priest who is concerned about them.

---

3. 1 Pet 1:18–19.
† Translated from SChr 330:200–206.
1. Luke 10:16.

4400   If we would humbly ask you to perform some worldly and difficult task, we believe that you would lovingly obey. Yet when we call you not to earthly activities but to those of heaven, not to temporal things but to those that eternally profit the soul, we are not seeking any transitory gain but are calling you to the treasures of heaven. Reflect, then, on the danger in which remain those who fail to heed us. My dear brothers and sisters, what causes me so much distress is that when you leave church, it is not that you are causing me bodily harm but, desiring that you be perfect, I know that you have seriously sinned against God.

4401   II. And so again and again I ask—even though I am completely unworthy to extend the Lord's invitation—that when you come to church, you remember that you come not to an earthly banquet in which is served food destined for human consumption, but you come to a heavenly and spiritual banquet in which the bread of angels is served. Do not reject or despise the Lord's banquet so that he not despise you in the joy of his kingdom. You should, in fact, fear the words of the Gospel in which he himself has declared unworthy of his banquet those who refused the invitation to come to the wedding feast, and so he commanded that others be invited.[2] It should not be considered as something indifferent but as something to be feared that those who refused to come because of the impediments of the world were judged unworthy of it by the Lord's own mouth. This is why, so that the same not also be said of us, we, as I have already asked, are to be patient for one or two hours till the food of souls is placed on this spiritual table, till the sacramental and spiritual gifts be consecrated.

4402   When the Lord's Prayer has ended, you are not blessed by a man. Yet it is through a man that you receive with a thankful and godly spirit, with a humble body and a contrite heart, the dew of the divine blessing so that according to the Lord's promise "the fountain of water flowing unto life eternal"[3] exists in you.

4403   III. Diverse and varied occupations do not allow all to remain in church; bodily infirmity afflicts some; for others public necessity calls; as to others, their own desires bind and hold them like prisoners. Right now how many are out in the streets or in the courtyards of the churches where they are engaged in legal disputes or business dealings! How many at church entrances or in sacristies are engaged in calumnies or hateful speech. Among them we usually find a good number of clerics. What benefit can these people obtain from the Holy Scriptures when they do not even allow the sound of the Scriptures to reach their ears? Yet what Scripture says is fulfilled in them, for "like deaf asps they close their ears so that they do not hear the voice of the charmers."[4]

4404   This is why you—having received God's fear and love and coming to church with great devotion—should most frequently admonish those who

---

2. See Matt 22:1–10.   3. John 4:14.   4. Ps 58:4–5.

have not desired to do so or were unable to do so. Warning them, you should advise them to fear what has been written, "The burdens of the world have made them unhappy."ᵃ We do not say that they should not be concerned about what to eat or what to wear. What we ask is that for one or two hours, during which the lessons are being read and the divine mysteries are being celebrated, they do not leave the church. May they labor as much for their souls as they do for their bodies. May they provide for the soul's needs more than for those of the body since what has been created in God's image is better than what has been formed from the mud of the earth. [. . .]

ɪᴠ. Therefore, my dearest brothers and sisters, I ask that you carefully   4405
carry everything you have heard, everything you have freely received under the Lord's inspiration from my preaching, that you carry it to wherever you go, to your neighbors and friends who cannot come to church with you or, even worse, perhaps do not even wish to; bring it to those who accompany you only to leave immediately. Just as I would be guilty if I neglected to tell you this, so you also, if you do not remember what you have heard in order to teach others, should fear that you will have to give an account for them. [. . .]

168-ʙ-15. sᴇʀᴍᴏɴ 75. ᴘʀᴀɪsᴇ ᴏғ ᴘsᴀʟᴍᴏᴅʏ ᴀɴᴅ ᴀɴ ɪɴᴠɪᴛᴀᴛɪᴏɴ ᴛᴏ ᴘᴇʀsᴇᴠᴇʀᴀɴᴄᴇ†

ɪ. Words fail me when I try to express the joy the Lord has given me be-   4406
cause of your holy and faithful devotion. For a number of years I desired and wholeheartedly longed for the good Lord to inspire you with this custom of chanting the psalms. And so I praise my God and, as best I can, I continue to thank the God who graciously granted my desire. In fact, when I desired that you chant the psalms as was done in other nearby towns, God so prepared your spirit that you with the Lord's help did so even better.

What should we now do in the midst of our joy if not to petition the   4407
Lord with all our strength to graciously allow us to complete what he graciously allowed us to begin? May he deign to grant a happy perseverance to those whom he has given such a holy devotion to psalmody. Because it is not the person who begins but "whoever perseveres to the end that will be saved,"¹ you also, insofar as you are able, should by the sorrow of your heart light the flame of love, which began to burn faithfully within you so that it may not cool through any negligence.

ɪɪ. Above all, apply yourselves not only through prayer but also   4408
through holy meditation to make your own the words of the psalms you sing and to allow the Holy Spirit, who speaks to you through your lips, to

---

a. *Visio Pauli* 10 and 40, James, *Apocrypha Anecdota*, p. 14, line 25; p. 33, line 15.
† Translated from SChr 330:210–14.
1. Matt 10:22.

dwell in your hearts. Truly it pleases and is greatly agreeable to God when the mouth faithfully chants the psalms. If one's life agrees with one's lips, then the psalmody is truly good. May what we say agree with what we do. In this way our words will not bear testimony against bad conduct, and what we say will not contradict us. If what we say differs from what we do, then our evil conduct immediately destroys what the mouth is seen to build up.

4409   May you, my brothers and sisters, be occupied not only with the sweetness of the chant but also by the meaning of the words so that, just as the melody of the chant may charm the ears, so may the words be sweet to the heart, for as Scripture says, "How sweet are your words to my mouth, O Lord."[2] Also, "The words of the Lord are more to be desired than gold or any precious stone, and sweeter than honey or the honeycomb."[3] As to those who when chanting the psalms pay attention only to the beauty of the chant and the harmony of its sound and are not as attentive as they should be to the meaning contained therein, their ears receive transitory food; God's word does not reach their souls. Doing this is like chewing on the wax and not at all tasting the sweetness of the honey.

4410   III. But you, my brothers and sisters, as I suggested above, are to pay special attention to the power found within the psalms. When you chant a psalm verse that reads "May the proud be put to shame because they have unjustly done evil against me,"[4] you should try to flee pride so as to escape eternal confusion. And when we chant "You put an end to those who are disloyal to you,"[5] we should attempt to flee from all evil desires. When we sing "Blessed are those who day and night meditate on the law of the Lord,"[6] may we reject as if they were the devil's poison useless undertakings and biting jests, hateful and even wanton conversations; may we frequently read again the holy lessons or, if we cannot read, may we eagerly and often listen to those who do read them. [. . .]

168-B-16. SERMON 76. AN ADMONITION TO KNEEL FOR PRAYER AND TO BOW AT THE BLESSING[†]

4411   I. Beloved, I petition and with paternal affection exhort you that at the beginning of each prayer you should immediately bend down or bow the head, except those whom infirmity perhaps restrains from kneeling. What is to be gained by faithfully chanting the psalms when, once the psalmody has ended, you do not wish to supplicate God? May each of us, then, when the psalmody has been completed, most humbly petition the Lord so that with God's assistance we might merit to put into practice the words we have uttered. Beloved, chanting the psalms is like sowing a field; saying a prayer is to labor once again by burying and then covering over the seed. In fact, if someone sows in a field yet fails to entirely cover

---

2. Ps 119:103, LXX.   3. Ps 19:10.   4. Ps 119:78.   5. Ps 73:27.   6. Ps 1:2.
[†] Translated from SChr 330:218–22.

up the seed, then the birds will come—that is, the fleeting, vain, and useless thoughts of this world—to seize what was sown in the heart. No one
should cease praying as soon as the chanting of the psalms has ended, not
if one wishes that the harvest of divine mercy be of profit in the field of
that person's heart.

II. My brothers and sisters, I ask that as often as you pray at the altar   4412
you bow your heads. Doing so, you will avoid what was written about the
Pharisee[1] who, standing erect, praised his own merits. Take care, dearly
beloved, that while some are at prayer, others are not occupied with useless tales so that the latter not wound themselves with what should have
been remedies and not perish in the place where they should have been
saved. Those acting in this way will have to give an unfavorable account
on the day of judgment, both in regard to themselves and in regard to
those whom they impeded. This also, my brothers and sisters, I both exhort and request: each time you are told to bow down for the blessing, you
should not find it difficult to incline your heads, for you are not bowing to
another human being but to God.

III. Surely, dearly beloved, I rejoice at your fervent devotion; and yet   4413
there are some, indeed quite a few, who arrive late for the vigils, and as
soon as God's word is read they immediately leave. I ask that you exhort
them, and by your holy and salutary counsel to rouse them to imitate
you as they should. For how long, my brothers and sisters, do we seem to
keep them occupied? You yourselves see that it is hardly for half an hour.
We do not want the poor and all the workers to be late for work. So each
time there is a sermon, Psalm 50 is to be said more quickly. In this way the
people will not depart the church later than usual; they will always leave
at the accustomed time. [. . .]

168-B-17. SERMON 78. AN ADMONITION TO OBSERVE SILENCE IN CHURCH[†]

I. A few days ago and motivated by paternal affection I suggested   4414
something regarding those with sore feet or those suffering from sickness
of any kind. I requested that when the long passions [of the martyrs] are
read or at least when there are some particularly long readings, those unable to stand should humbly and silently sit in order to listen attentively
to the reading. But at present some of our daughters—all or at least most
of them being in good health—believe that they should frequently act likewise. In fact, when someone begins to read aloud the word of God, they
want to stretch out as they would in bed. If only they would be content
to lie down and with thirsting hearts silently receive the word of God.
May they not be so occupied with gossiping that they fail to hear what is
being preached and do not allow others to hear it. This is why, my dear
daughters, I ask and exhort you by paternal affection that when either the

---

1. See Luke 18:10–14.
† Translated from SChr 330:238–40.

lessons are read or God's word is being preached no one is to lie down unless perhaps constrained to do by a very serious sickness; in such a case do not lie down but rather sit and, listening attentively to what is being preached, receive it with an eager heart.

4415   II. My brothers and sisters, tell me, I ask you, what do you believe has more value, the word of God or the Body of Christ? If you wish to respond truthfully, you should indeed answer that the word of God is not worth less than the Body of Christ. We take such great care when Christ's Body is given to us so that nothing of it might fall from our hands onto the ground. We are to be just as careful that God's word, which is given us, not perish from our hearts while we are thinking or speaking about something else. Those who hear the word of God with negligence will be no less guilty than those who through negligence allow Christ's Body to fall to the ground.

168-B-18. SERMON 80. AN EXHORTATION TO THE PEOPLE THAT EACH ONE IS TO STRIVE HARDER TO PRAY IN CHURCH[†]

4416   I. My dear brothers and sisters, whenever you gather in church, refrain from silly speech and worldly stories; with an eager and thirsting heart listen to the holy readings. Whoever comes to church and neglects to pray or chant the psalms would have done better by not coming at all. Whoever behaves improperly in church seems to be bodily present, and yet the heart is far distant. And what is worse, a person does not sin alone or in only one thing by not listening to the holy readings and by not allowing others to hear them; surely one must be punished for all those to whom an occasion of sin was given.

4417   And this, my beloved, I say to both men and women, to religious and to the laity, to those who are placed among the faithful as well as to those at the altar. Should someone want to converse with a friend, there is sufficient time to do this after departing from the church. Do not pass your time with useless stories; do not seek death in the house of life. Do not inflict wounds on yourself in the very place where you should receive remedies; rather, faithfully prepare the holy receptacles of your heart for the streams of living water, that is, faithfully prepare for the Lord's lessons so that his words may be fulfilled in you: "Whoever believes in me, living waters will flow from within him."[1]

4418   II. My dear brothers and sisters, may we now cry out in the church so that afterwards we will not have to cry out in vain in Gehenna. Let us listen to what the prophet says, "Sing, sing psalms to our God."[2] May those who are able to sing psalms do so; those unable to do so are to praise God within themselves, doing so in their hearts and rejoicing with those who are chanting the psalms. Furthermore, may they keep silent so that their talking not

---

[†] Translated from SChr 330:254–58.

1. John 7:38.   2. Ps 47:6.

impede those who are chanting the psalms. "Cry out," says the prophet, "cease not. Lift up your voice like a trumpet."[3] We also should cry out so that our psalmody and our prayer in church drive off our adversary the devil, who is troubled by our holy cry. The devil customarily inserts himself, if not in the behavior at least in the thoughts and words of those who are silent or who converse about frivolous and meaningless things. Those whom the devil sees chanting the psalms and praying, those who engage the heart as well as the voice in praising God, these he cannot surprise by any cunning.

And so, my dear brothers and sisters, when we enter the church we 4419
should fight for Christ rather than for the adversary; we should serve God rather than the world. In fact, whoever faithfully prays and sings psalms in church is proven to offer God an odor of sweetness from the holy thurible of the heart. [. . .]

168-B-19. SERMON 86. ON THE MATERNITY OF HOLY REBECCA[†]

5. [. . .] My brothers and sisters, I especially ask and invite you to try 4420
to rise earlier for the vigils; faithfully come to Terce, Sext, and None. Especially throughout Lent and up to the end of the Pasch[a] observe chastity even with your wives. Distribute to the poor what you would have eaten at noon. Be at peace with one another and reconcile those whom you know to be at discord. Welcome strangers. Be not ashamed to wash their feet. May a Christian not blush to do what Christ deigned to do. Freely give alms to the poor as you are able, "for the Lord loves a joyful giver."[1]

As to the impediments of the world, if you cannot completely remove 4421
them, at least somewhat diminish them so that you can devote yourselves to the readings and to prayer, thereby abundantly filling the holy receptacle of your heart with spiritual wine, namely, with the word of God. Once all your crimes and sins have been repudiated, it is with a free and sincere conscience that you can serve God. And when the paschal feast arrives, having faithfully and joyfully extended charity not only toward those who are good but also toward those who are bad, may you with a pure heart and chaste body approach the table of the Lord in joy and exultation. May each of you merit to receive the Lord's Body and Blood not unto judgment but for healing the soul. [. . .]

168-B-20. SERMON 130. ON ELISEUS AND THE AXE[††]

v. The time is approaching when we will hand over the creed to the 4422
catechumens. Receiving them as sons or daughters in baptism, you know

---

3. Isa 58:1.

[†] Translated from *Sermons sur l'Ecriture*, trans. J. Courreau, SChr 447 (Paris, 2000) 164–66.

a. To the end of Easter week or the end of the Easter season.

1. 2 Cor 9:7.

[††] Translated from *Sermons*, vol. 1, ed. G. Morin, SChr 103 (Paris, 1953) 537–38.

that we will be responsible for them before God. Therefore instruct them to prepare the creed so that those who are older may recite it back by themselves; as to the little children who will receive the creed, it may be given back either by you or by others. [. . .] Above all, have not only your children but also your whole household memorize the creed; those failing to do so show that they are tepid and negligent Christians. Let no one give excuses, saying that they cannot memorize, for there are many, men and women, who have learned indecent songs by heart for their own destruction and that of others. Can any dare say that they cannot retain the few lines of the creed? [. . .]

168-B-21. SERMON 136. ON WHAT IS WRITTEN: THE SUN KNOWS THE HOUR OF ITS SETTING[†]

4423   I. Dearly beloved, this psalm [Psalm 104], which is said throughout the whole world in churches and monasteries at the twelfth hour, is so well-known that almost all people are acquainted with it, the vast majority of them knowing it by heart.

168-B-22. SERMON 147. AN EXPLANATION OF THE LORD'S PRAYER[††]

4424   VI. The prayer continues, "Give us this day our daily bread."[1] Whether we petition the Father for what is necessary to sustain the body—bread signifying all that is necessary for us—or whether we understand this to be the daily bread you will receive from the altar, we rightly ask that God give it to us. What is it that we ask for unless it is that we do no evil that can separate us from this bread? The word of God, preached daily, is bread; and since it is not bread for the stomach, it is, therefore, bread for the soul. Once life has ended, we will not seek the bread sought by those who are hungry, nor will we have to receive the sacrament of the altar because we will be there with the Christ whose Body we receive; nor will the words we address to you have to be said; nor will the Scriptures have to be read as we will see him since he himself is the Word of God. [. . .]

4425   VII. In this life we petition for what follows, namely, "Forgive us our sins as we forgive those who sin against us."[2] In baptism all our debts, namely, all sins, are forgiven us. But no one can live on earth without sin, even though one may live without having committed serious faults that separate us from the [eucharistic] bread. Since no one can live on this earth without sins and since we can be baptized not twice but only once, in this prayer we have the daily washing by which our sins are forgiven each day, yet only if we do what follows, namely, "As we forgive those who sin against us."[3]

[†] Translated from CCL 103:560.

[††] Translated from *Sermons*, vol. 2, ed. G. Morin, CCL 104:603–4. Much of this sermon is not by Caesarius.

1. Matt 6:11.   2. Matt 6:12.   3. Ibid.

168-B-23. SERMON 156. ON THE TEN VIRGINS[†]

IV. [. . .] Virgins should [. . .] occupy themselves with reading and   4426
keeping vigil. Unless sickness prevents, they should arise as quickly as
possible in order to keep vigil.

Whether in church or at table or in any place whatever, they should take   4427
pains to demonstrate what pertains to obedience and humility. If they see
someone who is sad, they should offer consolation; if they see disobedience, they should not cease to rebuke.

168-B-24. SERMON 170. ON THE SAMARITAN WOMAN AND ON NOT DELAYING BAPTISM[††]

4. [. . .] Not all know God's gift because not all desire the living water.   4428
Those desiring this water would never delay the sacrament of baptism.
Consequently, those who postpone baptism so that they can commit many
crimes and sins judge themselves and give testimony concerning their
lives. My people, do not delay the remedy of your salvation because you
do not know when you will be asked for your soul. [. . .]

168-B-25. SERMON 179. AN ADMONITION ON THE GOSPEL TEXT "WHOSE WORK ABIDES WILL BE REWARDED [. . .]."[†††]

II. Even though the apostle has mentioned numerous capital sins,   4429
we—so that we not appear to despair—will briefly list what they are:
sacrilege, murder, adultery, false witness, theft, robbery, pride, envy, avarice, and—if it persists—anger, drunkenness, as well as slander. Those
who know that they are guilty of these sins and do not rightly perform a
long penance, provided time for this is permitted them, and who are not
generous in almsgiving, and who do not refrain from these sins, cannot
be cleansed in that transitory fire spoken of by the apostle but will be tor-
tured without relief by eternal flames.

III. All of us, however, know what the lesser sins are. Since there is not   4430
enough time to list all of them, we mention only some. Those eating or
drinking more than necessary know that this is a less serious sin; those
who say more than is fitting or remain silent for longer than they should;
those who are rude to a poor beggar; those in good health who desire to
eat while others are fasting; those who oversleep and thus arise late for
church; a man who has relations with his wife and yet does not desire
to have children—surely such are sins. [. . .] There can be no doubt that
these and similar acts are lesser sins. As I already said, sins like these are

---

[†] Translated from CCL 104:638.

[††] Translated from CCL 104:698. Not all sections of this sermon appear to be the
work of Caesarius.

[†††] Translated from CCL 104:724–26.

without number, afflicting not only the whole Christian people but even all the saints. [. . .]

4431   IV. [. . .] If we, being sorrowful, do not thank God, if we fail to redeem our sins by our good works, then we will remain in that purifying fire [*in igne purgatorio*] till these lesser sins are consumed like wood or straw or hay. [. . .]

168-B-26. SERMON 187. A HOMILY TO BE GIVEN ON THE TENTH OR FIFTEENTH DAY BEFORE THE LORD'S NATIVITY[†]

4432   I. Dearly beloved, close is the day on which we joyfully celebrate the birth of the Lord our Savior. Consequently I ask and admonish that insofar as possible we, with God's assistance, work so that with a pure and sincere conscience and with a pure heart and a chaste body we may approach the altar of the Lord and merit to receive his Body and Blood, not unto judgment but as spiritual remedy. [. . .]

4433   IV. Therefore, just as you should always abstain from adultery and from most pitiable concubines, so you should abstain from your wives for a number of days in order to prepare yourselves to celebrate the Lord's birth and the other feasts. [. . .]

168-B-27. SERMON 188. A HOMILY TO BE GIVEN BEFORE THE NATIVITY OF THE LORD[††]

4434   III. As I have often advised, when the Lord's nativity or any other feast is celebrated, you are not only to avoid consorting with concubines but are also, for a number of days beforehand, to abstain from your wives. Put aside all anger. Past sins are forgiven through almsgiving and penance. Feel hatred toward none. [. . .]

4435   IV. Although it is always proper to give alms, it is especially on the holy solemnities that we should do so more generously. More frequently summon the poor to the banquet, for it is not right that on a holy solemnity some of the Christian people—all of whom belong to the same Lord—should have much to eat while others suffer from the danger of hunger. We and all the Christian people are servants of the one Lord. One price has been paid for all of us. We have all entered the world in the same condition. We will all exit the world in the same way. If we all act well, we will all arrive at the same happiness. Why should not the poor person, who will join you in attaining the state of immortality, not receive your old tunic? Why should the poor person, who with you merited to receive the sacrament of baptism, be unworthy to receive your bread? Why should the person who comes with you to the banquet of the angels be unworthy to receive your leftover food? [. . .]

[†] Translated from CCL 104:763–65.
[††] Translated from CCL 104:768–69.

168-B-28. SERMON 192. ON THE CALENDS OF JANUARY†

I. My dear brothers and sisters, the day of calends, called the calends of   4436
January, receives its name from a certain wretched and irreligious man by
the name of Janus, once the leader and chief of the pagans. The ignorant and
unlearned, fearing him as if he were a king, began to worship him like a god.
They gave him unlawful honor while dreading his royal power. Surely the
foolish and the ignorant at that time believed that the more exalted human
beings ranked among the gods; and so the worship of the one true God was
transferred to the many names of the gods or rather to those of the demons.
And so, as I already said, they named the day of today's calends from the
name of Janus, desiring to confer divine honor on this man. They assigned
him the end of one year and the beginning of the next. And because for them
the calends of one year was said to complete one year and begin the next,
they placed this Janus, as it were, at the year's beginning and ending, so
that one would believe that he ended one year and initiated the next. This is
why the ancient worshipers of idols gave him a form having two faces, one
looking straight ahead, the other looking directly behind. The former was
understood as to be facing the past year, the latter facing the approaching
year. And so these foolish people by assigning him two faces, while desiring
to make him a god, turned him into a monster; for what is monstrous in animals they wished to be a prominent feature of their god. [. . .]

II. This is why the pagans, having perverted the order of things, pres-   4437
ently cover themselves with obscene disfiguring; in this way those who
worship turn themselves into what is being worshipped. Throughout
these days miserable people and, even worse, some of the faithful assume
corrupt forms and terrible appearances; I don't know whether I should
laugh or cry on their account. Can any wise person believe that those willing to turn themselves into small stags or wild beasts are of sound mind?
Some clothe themselves with animal skins; others put on the heads of wild
animals, making merry and delighting in the fact that they look so much
like animals that they do not appear to be human. [. . .]

IV. Our venerable forebears saw that most members of the human race   4438
were slaves to gluttony and dissipation during these days, raging as they
were with drunkenness and evil dancing. Consequently our ancestors
decreed for the whole world that a public fast be declared throughout all
the churches. They did this so that these poor individuals might realize
that the evil they had committed was so great that all the churches had to
observe a fast because of their sins. [. . .]

168-B-29. SERMON 196. ON THE BEGINNING OF LENT††

I. My dear brothers and sisters, the season of Lent draws near through   4439
God's mercy. And so I ask you, beloved, that with God's help we may

---

† Translated from CCL 104:779–81.
†† Translated from CCL 104:792–93.

celebrate these days, which are healthful for the body and medicinal for the soul, in such a holy and spiritual way that our observance of this holy Lent may bring us not to judgment but to perfection. If we act negligently, if we become involved in too many activities, if we do not wish to be chaste, if we do not participate in fasting, vigils, and prayer, if we do not read or listen to others reading the holy Scriptures, then what should have been our medicine is turned into our wounds; what should have been our remedy becomes our judgment.

4440   II. And so I ask you, my brothers and sisters, to rise up at an early hour for the vigils; gather especially for Terce, Sext, and None. May none remove themselves from this holy work unless sickness, public need, or what is clearly a great necessity occupy them. Nor is it enough that you hear the holy readings only in church; read them at home or have them read by others and gladly listen to them. Recall, my brothers and sisters, what our Lord said, "What will it profit them if they gain the whole world but give up their life?"[1] Especially remember and constantly fear what is written: "The world's burdens have made them miserable."[a] And so when at home act in such a way that you do not neglect your soul. Should you be incapable of more, at least try to labor as much for your soul as you do for your body.

4441   IV. Therefore, my dear brothers and sisters, it is by fasting, reading, and prayer that we during these days of Lent should store up food for our souls as if for the whole year. For although you frequently and faithfully hear with God's help the holy lessons throughout the whole year, during these days we should rest from the waters and waves of this world and have recourse to the port of Lent. Silently and quietly we should receive the holy readings into the receptacle of our hearts. [. . .]

168-B-30. SERMON 197. A HOMILY OF SAINT FAUSTUS ON THE FAST OF LENT[†]

4442   III. Therefore, my brothers and sisters, during these few days may the "burdens of the world" disappear, burdens which according to the Scriptures make many negligent persons miserable; may bodily joys vanish; may the many poisonous allurements of this world cease. May joys of the body diminish so that spiritual gains may be prepared for the soul since Scripture says, "Woe to you who are laughing now, for you will be hungry."[1] Also, "Blessed are those who mourn, for they will be consoled."[2] May holy reading replace the time you squandered by your mad addiction to table games. May discourses on Holy Scripture replace harmful stories, biting jokes, and poisonous slander. During the time when we once used

---

a. *Visio Pauli* 10 and 40, James, *Apocrypha Anecdota*, p. 14, line 25; p. 33, line 15.
1. Matt 16:26.
† Translated from CCL 104:800–801.
1. Luke 6:25.   2. Matt 5:4.

to hunt—and this to the loss of our souls—may we visit the sick, inquire about those in prison, welcome travellers, and call to harmony those at odds with one another. Beloved, if we do this, we can then provide medicines from what we utilized to inflict wounds upon ourselves.

iv. Especially on fast days may we expend on the poor what we were accustomed to eat at noon; in this way may no one prepare extravagant meals or delicious banquets and seem to have changed rather than to have removed from the body an abundance of food. Nothing is gained if the fast is prolonged throughout the day, and then afterwards the soul is destroyed by food that is sweet and abundant. A mind that has been filled immediately becomes sluggish, and the drenched earth of our body spouts forth thorns of unlawful pleasure. Therefore may food be moderate, and may the stomach never be overly satisfied. May we always think more of food for the soul than of food for the body. [. . .] 4443

v. As is customary, willingly listen to the holy readings in church and do so again at home. If some are so busy as to be unable to attend to the Holy Scriptures before eating at noon, they should not hesitate to read again something of them when they take a bit of food by themselves in order that just as the body is nourished with food, so the soul is refreshed with the word of God. [. . .] 4444

168-B-31. SERMON 199. ON THE DISCOURSE IN WHICH IT IS SAID, "SHARE YOUR BREAD WITH THE HUNGRY"[†]

i. My dear brothers and sisters, I ask that during this proper and most holy time of Lent no one presume to take food except on Sundays. To fast at other times is either a remedy or a reward; not to fast during Lent is a sin. May forgiveness be granted to those who fast at other times. May those who are able to fast during this season but who fail to do so be punished. [. . .] 4445

ii. Fasting, my dear brethren, is good; almsgiving is better. For those who can do both, both are good. Yet if one cannot fast, it is better to give alms. If fasting is impossible, almsgiving without fasting suffices. Fasting without almsgiving in no way suffices. Therefore if someone cannot fast, almsgiving without fasting is good; if a person can fast, then fasting with almsgiving is a double good. Fasting without almsgiving is not good unless perhaps it is done by a poor person who has nothing to give. If one has nothing from which to give, then good will suffices. [. . .] 4446

vi. As we suggested above, my dear brothers and sisters, the abundance of our almsgiving is like a lamp lacking oil. For just as a lamp that is lighted without oil can emit smoke but cannot give light, so fasting without almsgiving certainly punishes the body but does not illuminate the soul with the light of charity. Meanwhile, as to what we should now do, my brothers and sisters, may our fast be such that we use for the poor the 4447

[†] Translated from CCL 104:803–4, 806–7.

food that we would have eaten at noon. Doing this, we do not store up in our purses what we could have eaten but rather store up in the stomachs of the poor. The treasury of Christ is the hand of the poor. [. . .]

4448   VII. [. . .] I believe that through God's inspiration you always observe chastity with your wives several days before the approaching feasts. [. . .] If with God's help you do this all through Lent till the end of the Pasch, then, clothed with the light of charity on that most holy solemnity of the Pasch, purified by almsgiving, adorned with prayer and vigils and fasts as if with heavenly and spiritual pearls, being at peace not only with your friends but also with your enemies, approaching the Lord's altar with a free and sincere conscience, you will be able to receive his Body and Blood not unto judgment but as a remedy.

168-B-32. SERMON 207. ON THE LITANIES[†a]

4449   I. My dear brothers and sisters, approaching are the holy and spiritual days which are medicine for our souls. Those desiring to heal the wounds of their sins should not despise this salutary medicine. [. . .] So that we may be able to conquer God's enemy, we should provide ourselves with the arms of fasting, vigils, and prayers.

4450   II. Although we always have need of fasting, vigils, and prayers, especially during these three days which the Church regularly celebrates throughout the whole world, none are to absent themselves from the holy assembly; may no one, occupied with worldly affairs, leave the church, which is the school of heavenly medicine; may none desert the spiritual camp. As you know, those who fight on behalf of a worldly king and, on the eve of battle, desert the army because of fear, not only fail to receive glory and the prize but also fail to evade the danger of the present life. Those who do not frequent the church during these three days will be considered like deserters from the royal army. Except for those who are sick or who must do a necessary task, all who desert God's people on these days should know that they will receive from the heavenly king not a reward but a reproach, not glory but shame. To be sure, those who desert and flee the heavenly camp will receive eternal confusion. [. . .]

4451   III. Throughout the whole year the wounds of sin destroy us. For this reason we should faithfully hurry to church on these three days so that with a contrite heart and a bowed body we may seek God's mercy, so that on these three days we may recall the wounds of our sins—the medicine of sorrow being received as a spiritual antidote for restoring original health. Not only during these days but at all times flee as if they were a

---

† Translated from CCL 104:828–31.

a. Sermons 207, 208, and 209 were given on or shortly before what are called Rogation Days, celebrated on the three days before the Ascension. Called "minor litanies," these observances of prayer and fasting were established in 470 by Mamertus, the bishop of Vienne (see WEC 4:4314–16).

school of sin, table games, which are contrary to the health of the soul. May no one intentionally be preoccupied with other things. May none busy themselves with hateful tales so as not to turn what could have been medicine into wounds. During these three days may no one either take blood or accept a potion unless a very serious illness requires this. Except for the sick, for whom a chicken is always permitted, may our meals be akin to those taken during Lent; and by reading, psalmody, and prayer may we seek spiritual food for the soul rather than delights of the body. In this way may we, completely free for God and requesting divine mercy, merit to be cured of all infirmities, to be saved from sins, and to be freed from frequent floods of water through God's mercy. [. . .]

iv. Again and again I ask that those who hurry to the beehive of the   4452
church, as if to the most sweet honeycomb of Christ, be like most prudent bees and prepare within themselves cells from the various readings of the Holy Scriptures where they receive the holy and heavenly honey. As to those who come late and leave early, neither are they content to wait till the divine mysteries are finished nor are they reputed to be among the swarm of bees belonging to Christ. They do not make spiritual honey from good works, but through pride and contempt they impede it for themselves, and by the example of evil conduct they cause others to fall. Those who truly love God, those who hurry to church and leave late persevere in good works. Rejecting hateful and worldly fables like a deadly poison, they sing psalms and pray. Contemptuous of the bitterness of the world, they need to be in the church where they receive the sweetness of Christ. Neglectful are those who not only come late to church but also leave before the divine mysteries are completed and while there, engaging in worldly and poisonous fables, they do not pray, neither chanting the psalms nor allowing others to do so. May these amend their ways so that they do not prepare for themselves death where they could have found life. [. . .]

168-B-33. SERMON 208. ON THE LITANIES[†]

i. We should know and understand that these days are to be days of   4453
compunction and penance. Consequently it is not fitting for us to indulge in merriment or in any reckless and inappropriate guffawing, fearing what the Lord says in the Gospel, "Woe to you who laugh, for you will cry and mourn."[1] Also, "The end of joy may be sorrow."[2] It should not seem harsh that we urge you on to sorrow and mourning rather than to happiness and joy. [. . .]

iii. May none seek any occupation for themselves that causes them to   4454
be absent from the assembly in the church. Surely the wounds of sin are loved by those who during these three days fail to gain spiritual medicine

---

[†] Translated from CCL 104:832–33.
1. Luke 6:25.   2. Prov 14:13.

for themselves by means of fasting, prayer, and psalmody. Abundant are
the sins we have accumulated during the space of one year. Therefore
during these three days may we strive to do what pertains to the purga-
tion and brilliance of the soul. Do not absent yourselves from gathering
in church; the time we spend there is not so long that we cannot endure
it. Just as those who do not withdraw themselves from the Church's assembly during these six hours are known to provide a greater remedy
for the soul, so those who for purposes of greed or for doing what is less
necessary do not wish to be present, inflict wounds upon themselves out
of what could have been salutary medicine; they burden themselves with
what could have lifted them up. [. . .]

168-B-34. SERMON 209. ON THE LITANIES[†]

4455   IV. Approaching are days that are medicinal for the soul, namely, the litanies. During these days the wounds of sin, wounds human frailty is wont to
incur throughout the rest of the year, are with God's help completely cured
by means of prayer, vigils, fasting, and almsgiving. My brothers and sisters,
I ask you, I warn you, and I call upon you to witness that during these three
days, from Wednesday to Friday, none should absent themselves from gathering in church unless prevented by sickness. It is enough that during the
year we concern ourselves with what is necessary and useful for the body;
but during these days may we more attentively reflect on our soul's salvation. All are to eat as we customarily do during Lent. These fasts are beneficial to the soul since what is saved through fasting is given to the poor and to
travellers. Those who willingly hear me and desire to carry out what I humbly suggest will quickly rejoice over the condition of their wounded souls.
Those who do otherwise will be doubly guilty: they despise a father who
humbly admonishes, and they do not seek the remedy for their souls. [. . .]

168-B-35. SERMON 229. ON THE FEAST OF A CHURCH[††]

4456   VI. No one, my brothers and sisters, is to be refused the sacrament of
baptism, especially if such a person seems to be close to death due to
bodily sickness. However, it is good and permitted that those in good
health be allowed to postpone baptism till Easter; yet according to the
Church's rule they are to fast and keep vigil during the days of Lent and
are to come forward for the anointing and the imposition of the hand.
Those who desire that their children be baptized on another feast should
come to the church seven days beforehand and there fast and keep vigil;
as I said above, they should have their children come for the anointing
and the imposition of the hand, and in this way baptism is received in its
rightful order. Those who do this not only obtain baptism for their children but also gain for themselves the forgiveness of sins through fasting

---

[†] Translated from CCL 104:836–37.
[††] Translated from CCL 104:910.

and keeping vigil. As I said, those not wishing to do this and who bring the children to be baptized immediately before the baptism itself should know that they have committed no small sin because they have failed to bring the children for the anointing and the imposition of the hand. Dearly beloved, know that before God you are the guarantors of the children you have brought to be baptized. May you, therefore, always strive to counsel and admonish them so that they may live chastely, justly, and soberly. Above all, teach them the creed and the Lord's Prayer, by word and example encouraging them to do good works. [. . .]

169. THIRD RULE OF THE FATHERS[†]

This Rule, written shortly after 533 and borrowing from the legislation of Caesarius of Arles (WEC 4:**168**) and various local councils, e.g., Agde (WEC 4:**176-A**), Orleans I (WEC 4:**176-B**), and Orleans II (WEC 4:**176-G**), comes from southern Gaul.

CPL 1859b * CPG 2403

vi. At the time for prayer and once the signal has been given, whoever does not immediately lay aside whatever he is doing—for nothing is to be preferred to the Work of God [*Opus Dei*]—will be reprimanded by the abbot or the dean, and if he does not prostrate himself to request pardon, he will be excommunicated. 4457

170. CYPRIAN OF TOULON

A native of Marseilles, a close friend and a disciple of Caesarius of Arles (WEC 4:**168**), Cyprian was ordained bishop by Caesarius. He was present at the Council of Orange (529) and other Merovingian councils, where he was a strong opponent of Semipelagianism. Cyprian's death occurred before 549.

CPL nos. 1020ff. * Altaner (1961) 569 * Altaner (1966) 476 * Bardenhewer (1913) 5:356 * Tixeront 338 * CATH 3:402–3 * CE 4:582–83 * DCB 1:756 * DHGE 13:1161 * DPAC 1:683 * EC 3:1692 * EEC 1:212 * LTK 2:1366–67 * NCE 4:566 * NCES 4:460 * ODCC 442 * PEA (1894) 4.2:1942

170-A. Life of Caesarius of Arles[††]

At the request of Caesaria, the sister of Caesarius, several disciples of the bishop of Arles collaborated in writing this biography, Cyprian alone probably being responsible for all or most of Book I.

[†] Translated from *Les règles des saints Pères*, vol. 2, trans. and ed. A. de Vogüé, SChr 298 (Paris, 1982) 537.
[††] Translated from PL 67:1016–17, 1022.

4458   I.iv.31. From there [Rome] he returned to Arles where psalm-singing
accompanied his entrance into the city. [. . .] On this day he went to the
church where he was to bestow the blessing at Vespers. All of a sudden
one of the women—she was trembling, wailing, foaming at the mouth—
rushed forward into the church where she terrified all. Apprehended by
members of the crowd, the unfortunate woman was taken to the holy man
before the altar. The people implored that her affliction be taken away
and that she be restored to good health. Then, as customary, he prostrated
while praying for her. Placing his hand on her head, he anointed her face
and all her senses with the holy oil. This being done, the affliction was expelled in the name of Christ, never again to return.

4459   I.iv.45. As customary, the holy man was engaged in prayer, reading, and
almsgiving. On Sundays and feasts he constantly preached. Frequently he
gave homilies at Matins and Vespers for the benefit of those coming from
the outside so that no one could plead ignorance. [. . .] He also decreed
that those who have just married are not—out of reverence for the blessing given in the basilica—to consummate their marriage till after three
days.[1] [. . .]

170-B. Letter to Maximus, Bishop of Geneva[†][a]

4460   [. . .] But in the hymn[b] which the whole Church throughout the world
has received and sings, daily do we profess, "You are Christ, the King of
glory; you are the eternal son of the Father." [. . .]

171. AURELIAN OF ARLES

Ordained bishop of Arles in 546, Aurelian established in his diocese a
monastery for men and a convent for women. Influenced by the directives of Caesarius of Arles (WEC 4:**168**), he wrote rules for each congregation. A great lover of the martyrs and confessors, Aurelian enriched
the oratories of these foundations with many relics, including, we are
told, a relic of the True Cross. Referring to himself as "Aurelian the Sinner," he assisted at the Council of Orleans in 549. Aurelian died in Lyons
ca. 550.

CPL nos. 1844ff. * Bardenhewer (1913) 5:356 * Tixeront 337 * CATH 1:1070 * DHGE
5:741 * DPAC 1:446 * EC 2:407–8 * EEC 1:102 * LTK 1:1253 * NCE 1:1079 * NCES
1:895

R. Taft, *The Liturgy of the Hours in East and West: The Origins of the Divine Office and
Its Meaning for Today* (Collegeville, 1986) 100–113.

---

    1. See Tob 6:18.
    † Translated from *Epistolae Merowingici et Karolini Aevi*, vol. 3 (Berlin, 1892) 436.
    a. Written between 524 and 533.
    b. Namely, the *Te Deum.*

171-A. Rule for Monks[†]

Aurelius wrote this Rule for the Monastery of the Holy Apostles and Martyrs, a foundation he established in 547.

xx. No one will become the godfather of an infant. 4461

xxii. In every service, whether it be singing[a] the psalms or reading or 4462
working, the brothers will take turns, except for the holy abbot, the elderly,
and small children. Also the sick who are absolutely incapable of getting up
from bed; they will not be forced to do what they lack the strength to do.

xxviii. No one will be allowed to return to bed after Matins; but once 4463
Matins is completed, Prime is said immediately; then all engage in reading
till the third hour.

xxix. At vigils during which there is a reading, work with your hands 4464
[by weaving] bulrushes, hemp, or anything similar, in order to avoid
sleeping. But if it is a Sunday or a feast, whoever is overcome by sleep will
be told to stand, the others remaining seated, so that he might chase away
the torpor of sleep and not show that he is tepid or negligent during the
Work of God.[1]

xxx. When the signal is given, all put aside their work and hasten like 4465
very shrewd bees flying to the beehive. Whoever arrives late will be subject to correction.

xxxi. During the psalmody may your holy souls be careful not to 4466
be distracted in spirit; furthermore, may they not allow themselves to
speak or work but to sing with wisdom,[2] for as the prophet says, "I will
sing and understand."[3] Also, "I will sing with the spirit but also with
understanding."[4] Fearing this evil, "Cursed be the one who undertakes
God's work with negligence."[5]

lvi. We have judged it fitting to insert in this booklet the following ordi- 4467
nance according to which you should sing the psalms.

On the first day of Easter, at Terce, the *Kyrie eleison* is said three times, 4468
and there are twelve psalms: namely, four brothers take turns each saying two psalms plus a third Alleluia psalm. After the psalms there is the
Kyrie eleison followed by six antiphonal psalms;[b] then three readings, the
first taken from the Acts of the Apostles, the second from the Apocalypse,
and the third from the Gospel; then the hymn *Iam surgit hora tertia* and the
capitulum; then the *Kyrie eleison*. Likewise, at every divine office the *Kyrie*

[†] Translated from *Règles monastiques d'Occident: IVe–VIe siècles, d'Augustin à
Ferréol*, trans. and ed. V. Desprez, Vie monastique 9, Collection spiritualité orientale
et vie monastique (Bégrolles-en-Mauges, 1980) 234ff.

a. Here and in other instances the Latin *dicitur* or *psallitur* does not necessarily mean
"said" or "recited" in our sense of the term. It can also mean "sung" or "chanted."

b. For an explanation of the terminology (e.g., *antiphona*, vigil, *missa*, response,
directaneus, *Duodecima*, etc.) used in this Rule, see R. Taft, *The Liturgy of the Hours*.

1. See Jer 48:10. 2. See Ps 47:8. 3. Ps 101:2. 4. 1 Cor 14:15. 5. Jer 48:10.

eleison is said three times: before the office begins, after the psalms, and after the *capitulum*.

4469   Sext has the same number of psalms; the hymn [the invitatory] *Iam sexta sensim volvitur*, the reading from the Gospel; and the *capitulum*. The same pattern is followed at None where the hymn is the *Ter hora trina volvitur*. At the *lucernarium* [Vespers] a small section of the psalm is sung *indirectum*, namely, *Regna terrae, cantate Deo, psallite Domino*,[6] and on the following day: *Laudate, pueri, Dominum*;[7] three antiphonal psalms; the hymn *Hic est dies verus Dei*; and the *capitulum*. This hymn is sung throughout Easter week at Matins and at the *lucernarium*.

4470   At the *Duodecima* a small section of the psalm is sung *indirectum: Sol cognovit occasum suum*.[8] Then six brothers will take turns reciting two psalms with their Alleluia psalms; three antiphonal psalms; two readings, one from the Apostle, the other from the Gospel. At the nocturns of paschal week all the elements of the office follow the number that we indicated for the *Duodecima*.

4471   At Matins, first of all, in the direct mode: *Exaltabo, Deus meus et Rex meus*.[9] Next the *Iudica me, Deus*[10] and the *Deus, Deus meus, ad te de luce vigilo*[11] with the Alleluia. Then the *Cantemus Domino*[12] with the Alleluia followed by the *Cantemus Domino*[13] in the same manner. Then: *Lauda, anima mea, Dominum. Laudate Dominum quoniam bonus est psalmus. Lauda, Jerusalem, Dominum*:[14] all three with the Alleluia. Then the Blessing [of the Three Infants][15] is said. After the Blessing: *Laudate Dominum de coelis; Cantate Domino canticum novum. Laudate Dominum in sanctis ejus*,[16] with the Alleluia. *Magnificat anima mea Dominum*[17] with antiphons or with the Alleluia; the hymn *Gloria in excelsis Deo* and the *capitulum*. Throughout all Easter week Matins is concluded in this manner; likewise on Sundays and on all the principal feasts when there is no work.

4472   On ordinary days at the nocturns there is first said the *Miserere mei, Deus, secundum magnam misericordiam tuam*[18] in the direct mode; then eighteen psalms; three small antiphonal psalms; two readings, from the Apostle or from the Prophets; and the *capitulum*.

4473   Once the nocturns have been completed, Matins is said. In summer, namely, after Easter and up to the calends of October, the same pattern is followed. On Saturday after the nocturns two *missae* are said during the summer, three in winter. For on Sunday in every season, summer as in winter, the nocturns are followed by six *missae*. Should any rise late for the vigils, only what the abbot has decided will be read. Once the abbot gives the signal, the reader will immediately stand so that the canonical number of *missae* can be assured.

---

6. Ps 68.   7. Ps 113:1.   8. Ps 104.   9. Ps 145.   10. Ps 43.   11. Ps 62.   12. Ps 118. 13. Exod 15:2–18.   14. Pss 145–47.   15. Dan 3:57–88.   16. Pss 148–50.   17. Luke 1:46–55.   18. Ps 51.

Beginning with the calends of October, other nocturns will be added. 4474
At the first nocturn the *Miserere mei, Deus, secundam magnam misericordiam
tuam;*[19] at the second the *Miserere mei, Deus, miserere mei*[20] is sung directly;
then Psalm 19, two readings from the Prophets or Solomon. The hymn
for the first nocturn is *Rex aeternae Domine;* for the second nocturn *Magna
et mirabilia.* After the nocturns and as the night becomes longer, each day
is to have four *missae* taken from the book. A brother will read three or
four pages, according to the size of the book. If the writing is fine or the
size of the book is large, three pages are read; if small, four pages; then
one prayer. He will again read so much, and then all stand and say an antiphonal psalm taken in sequence from the Psalter; then a response; then
an antiphonal psalm. Another brother will take his turn doing the reading;
and once the three *missae* have been completed, the canonical psalms of
Matins follow, namely, first the canticle sung antiphonally; then in a direct
manner the *Judica me Deus,*[21] the *Deus, Deus meus ad te de luce vigilo,*[22] the
Laudate Dominum, quoniam bonus es,[23] and the *Lauda Jerusalem, Dominum.*[24]
Then antiphonally the *Laudate Dominum de coelis,* the *Cantate Domine canticum novum,*[25] and the *Laudate Dominum in sanctis ejus.*[26] Then the hymn
Splendor paternae gloriae which is replaced on the following day by the
Lucis conditor; then the *capitulum* and the *Kyrie eleison* twice. This is how
the office concludes on all ordinary days.

After Matins two psalms are said at Prime; then the hymn *Fulgentis* 4475
auctor aetheris; two readings, one from the Old Testament, the other from
the New Testament; and the *capitulum.* After this all read till the third
hour; the rest of the day they will do their work according to what the
Lord says, "My Father works till now, and I also am working."[27] Also the
Apostle: "I work with my own hands."[28] Also, "Whoever does not work
is not to eat."[29] For it is written, "The way of the lazy is overgrown with
thorns."[30] Also, "Throw the useless servant into the darkness without."[31]

At Terce on ordinary days twelve psalms are sung; one antiphonal 4476
psalm; the hymn *Iam surgit hora tertia;* the reading; and the *capitulum Fiat,
Domine.*[32]

Sext has the same number of psalms with an antiphonal psalm; the 4477
hymn *Surgit hora tertia;* the reading; and the *capitulum.*

The same pattern is followed at None but with the hymn *Tera hora trina* 4478
volvitur.

At the *lucernarium,* in every season, on feasts, and on ordinary days, 4479
first the psalm is sung directly; then two antiphonal psalms; the third is
always said with the Alleluia. On one day the hymn will be the *Deus qui
certis legibus;* the next day it will be the *Deus creator omnium;* the *capitulum*
follows.

---

19. Ibid.   20. Ps 57.   21. Ps 43.   22. Ps 63.   23. Ps 147:1–11.   24. Ps 147:12–20.
25. Pss 148–49.   26. Ps 150.   27. John 5:17.   28. 1 Cor 4:12.   29. 2 Thess 3:10.
30. Prov 15:19.   31. Matt 25:30.   32. Ps 33:22.

4480   At the *Duodecima* there are eighteen psalms; one antiphonal psalm; the hymn; the reading; and the *capitulum.*

4481   When you go to bed, you will say Compline in the place where you are. First Psalm 91 is said in the direct way; then the usual *capitulla.*

4482   LVII. At Christmas and on the Epiphany all rise at the third hour of the night and recite a nocturn and [at Christmas] do six *missae* from Isaiah the prophet; there is also a second nocturn, and there may be six other *missae* from the Gospel. Likewise at the Epiphany: first a nocturn; and then six *missae* from Daniel the prophet; and the nocturns; and likewise six *missae* taken from the Gospel. Matins follows the pattern we have described for Easter and Sundays. On the feasts of the martyrs there are three or four *missae.* The first *missa* is from the Gospel; the others are passions of the martyrs. Each Saturday, after the *Duodecima* there are six *missae* from the book and three *missae* after the nocturns. Each Saturday at Matins there is the *Sing to the Lord*[33] and the *Te Deum laudamus.* At Terce there are three readings, one from the Prophets, one from the Apostle, and the third from the Gospels. Each Sunday after the nocturns during the reading of the first series of readings, namely, the narrative of the Resurrection, no one is allowed to sit but all remain standing. On the following Sunday another narrative of the Resurrection is read; thus Sunday after Sunday all four narratives of the Resurrection are read. After Terce the Our Father is said, and all receive Communion while singing the psalms. Act in like manner on feasts. As to what pertains to the Mass, it will take place when the holy abbot judges it to be opportune.

4483   LVIII. When a brother dies, several brothers will keep vigil in the oratory up to midnight, and there will be a number of *missae* from the Apostle. After midnight, those keeping vigil will take their rest, and others will keep vigil in turn. Inform the holy bishop of this death so that he might give the order to transport the body to the place of burial. Should the bishop decline to do so, ask the clerics from any church to lead the procession and give them the *eulogia.*

171-B. Rule for Virgins[†]

Aurelius wrote this Rule for the nuns of Saint Mary Monastery.

4484   XVI. No one will become [. . .].[a]

4485   XVIII. In every service [. . .].[b]

4486   XXIII. At vigils no one is to sleep, but if it is Sunday or a feast, she who is overcome with sleep will stand, the others remaining seated so as to be

---

33. Exod 15.

[†] Translated from Desprez, *Règles monastiques,* 253ff.

a. This paragraph is the same as no. XX in Aurelian's *Rule for Monks* (WEC 4:4461).

b. This paragraph is the same as no. XXII in Aurelian's *Rule for Monks* (WEC 4:4462).

able to chase away the numbness of sleep and show that she is not tepid or negligent during the Work of God.

xxiv. When the signal is given [. . .].^c   4487

xxv. During the psalmody [. . .].^d   4488

xxxviii. The community will recite the day and the night cursus of the   4489
office, namely, Matins, the vigils, the nocturns, Vespers, and the office of
Duodecima, in the basilica of Saint Mary. If the winter is harsh, in the basilica say only Matins, Vespers, and the office of the twelfth hour; but the
second hour, Terce, Sext, and None are in the interior oratory because of
those who desire to engage in prayer or wish to meet the abbess or visit
with their parents.

xli–xlii. We have judged it [. . .]^e   4490

172. GREGORY OF TOURS

Son of a distinguished family which produced several bishops, Gregory
was born on November 30, 538, in Clermont (today Clermont-Ferrand).
He was ordained bishop of Tours in 573. At that time Tours was the religious center of Gaul. Living conditions, however, were unsettling, for the
town saw a succession of political masters; the times were often lawless
with bands of Teutonic tribes roaming the countryside; social structures
were disintegrating.

Nevertheless, Gregory received a good religious education. However,
the study of rhetoric and profane literature was not stressed, this unfortunately being reflected in his writings. As a historian, albeit one who preferred to relate what he saw and heard rather than explore the why and
the wherefore, he has left us an excellent picture of religious and civic life
in Merovingian Gaul.

CPL nos. 1023ff. * Altaner (1961) 571–72 * Altaner (1966) 477–78 * Bardenhewer
(1908) 643–47 * Bardenhewer (1910) 553–57 * Bardenhewer (1913) 5:357–66 * Bardy
(1930) 205–8 * Bautz 2:339–40 * Jurgens 3:305–6 * Labriolle (1947) 2:791–98 * Labriolle
(1968) 509–15 * Steidle 244–45 * Tixeront 338–41 * CATH 5:262–65 * CE 7:18–21 *
DACL 6.2:1711–53 * DCB 2:771–76 * DHGE 22:47–48 * DictSp 6:1020–25 * DPAC
2:1721–22 * EC 6:1158–59 * EEC 1:365 * EEChr 1:498–99 * LTK 4:1026–27 * NCE
6:798–99 * NCES 6:522–23 * ODCC 714 * PEA (1894) 7.2:1867–68 * PEA (1991) 4:1217
* RACh 12:895–930 * TRE 14:184–88

P. de Puniet, "La liturgie baptismale en Gaule avant Charlemagne," RQH 72, n.s.,
28 (1902) 382–423. * J. des Graviers, "La date du commencement de l'année chez

---

c. This paragraph is the same as no. xxx in Aurelian's *Rule for Monks* (WEC 4:4465).

d. This paragraph is the same as no. xxxi in Aurelian's *Rule for Monks* (WEC 4:4466).

e. The order of the office is, at least for the most part, the same as that for monks, nos. lvi–lvii (WEC 4:4467–68), the only difference being that the nuns say six psalms rather than twelve at Prime, Terce, Sext, and None.

Grégoire de Tours," REF 32 (1946) 103–6. * "Les rites de la dédicace en Gaule ('Miraculorum libri III' 1, 46; 'Miraculorum libri VIII' 8, 20)," LMD, no. 70 (1962) 146–48. * D. Aupest, "L'observation du repos dominical d'après Grégoire de Tours," Imp, n.s., 4 (1967) 19–33.

172-A. History of the Franks[†]

This history, in ten books, begins with the creation of the world and ends with the death of King Guntram in 591.

4491   II.vii. [. . .] One night a poor man, intoxicated with wine, was asleep in a quiet corner of the basilica of Saint Peter the Apostle. When, as customary, the doors were closed, he was not observed by the watchman. Rising during the night, the poor man, terrified by lights shining brightly throughout the whole building, searched for a means of escape to the outside. He pulled the bars of one door, then another, but soon came to realize that everything was locked. So he laid down on the floor and fearfully waited for a time to escape when the people would gather for the morning hymns. [. . .]

4492   II.xxii. Holy Sidonius[a] was so gifted in speech that he often improvised. One day it happened that he went to the church of the monastery we mentioned previously [Saint-Cyr in Clermont], being invited there for a feast. Someone maliciously had removed the book customarily used for the holy rites. Sidonius was so prepared that he correctly carried out the whole ritual of the feast. All were amazed and those present believed this feat was carried out by an angel, not by a man. I described all this in greater detail in the preface of the book I wrote concerning the Masses composed by him.[b]

4493   II.xxiii. When Sidonius was devoting himself to the things of the Lord and was leading a holy life in the world, two presbyters rose up against him and took away from him all power regarding church property, thus reducing him to a very impoverished way of life and submitting him to the greatest insult. The merciful God did not long allow him to endure such unpunished injustice. On the previous night one of these two most evil men—a man who was unworthy to be called a priest—threatened to remove Sidonius from his own church. Rising from sleep the next morning, this man heard the bell that called to Matins. [. . .]

4494   II.xxxi. [. . .] Remigius[c] commanded that the baptismal pool be prepared. The streets were adorned with colored banners; the churches were

---

[†] Translated from *Gregorii Episcopi Turonensis Libri Historiarum X.*, ed. B. Krusch and W. Levison, Scriptores Rerum Merovingiarum, vol. 1, part 1, 2nd ed. (Hanover, 1951) 49ff.

a. Sidonius: namely, Sidonius Apollinaris (WEC 3:**122**).

b. This is now lost.

c. Remigius: bishop of Rheims in northeastern France; little is known of his life.

decorated with white cloths; the baptistery was prepared; the aroma of balsam spread everywhere; aromatic candles burned brightly; and the whole temple of baptism was filled with a divine aroma. God filled those who were present with such grace that they thought they were favored with the scent of paradise. The king, Clovis,[d] asked that the bishop baptize him first. Like some new Constantine, Clovis proceeded to the pool in order to wash away the sore of his old leprosy and by flowing water to be purified from the filthy stain he bore for so long. [. . .] Clovis, confessing that he believed in the all-powerful triune God, was baptized in the name of the Father and of the Son and of the Holy Spirit and marked with holy chrism in the sign of Christ's cross. At the same time more than three-thousand of his soldiers were baptized. Also his sister, Albofled. Shortly thereafter she died and went to the Lord. [. . .] Another sister, Lanthechild, converted from the Arian heresy[e] and, having confessed that the Son was equal to the Father and the Holy Spirit, received the chrism.

II.xxxiv. [. . .] In his holy homily written on the Rogations that are cele-   4495
brated before the Lord's triumphant ascension, Avitus[f] says that these were established by Mamertus,[g] the bishop of Vienne. When he wrote this homily, Avitus was bishop of the same town. At the time of Mamertus the people were frightened by numerous unnatural events. There were frequent earthquakes; savage packs of stags and wolves entered through the city gates; and, according to what he wrote, these animals, fearing nothing, took over the whole city. Such events lasted the whole year. When the days of the paschal solemnity arrived, all the people looked forward to God's mercy. Their hope was that the days of the great solemnity would bring an end to the terror. But on the very vigil of the holy night when holy Mass was being celebrated, the royal palace, situated within the city, was burning with divine fire. People were terrified. They exited the church, believing that the whole town would be incinerated or that the earth would open up, thus devouring them. The holy bishop lay prostrate before the altar, with tears and pleas imploring God's mercy. What else is there to say? The prayer of this renowned bishop ascended to heaven on high, and his tears extinguished the fire burning in the palace. Meanwhile the feast of the Ascension was approaching, as I already said. Mamertus instructed the people to fast; he established a manner for praying, a period of time for making requests and for giving alms to the poor. Thereupon the terrors came to an end. Notice of what happened spread throughout

---

d. Clovis: Frankish king 481–511 of the Merovingian dynasty.

e. Arianism: a doctrine propagated by Arius (ca. 260–336), a priest in Alexandria, who denied the unity and consubstantiality of the three persons of the Trinity and consequently the full divinity of Christ. Arianism was condemned by the Council of Nicaea (WEC 2:71-C).

f. Avitus of Vienne (WEC 4:167).

g. Mamertus: fifth-century bishop of Vienne in Narbonne.

all the provinces with bishops everywhere imitating what this bishop did out of faith. Up to the present time and in the name of God this is celebrated in all the churches with compunction of heart and spiritual sorrow.

4496   III.xxxi. Audofleda and Amalasuntha[h] were both members of the Arian sect. As was customary among the Arians, royalty when approaching the altar received from one cup, with ordinary people receiving from another cup. [. . .]

4497   IV.xvi. [. . .] Saint Tetricus[i] was at that time the bishop of Langres. [. . .] His priests placed three books upon the altar, namely, the Prophets, the Apostles, and the Gospel. [. . .] They agreed that at Mass each would read whatever was found where the book was opened. [. . .]

4498   VI.xl. [. . .] The Spanish envoy arrived in Tours for the holy Pasch. I inquired whether he was of our religion. He answered that he believed what Catholics believe. Then, going with us to the church, he was present at Mass but neither exchanged the peace with us nor received Communion from the sacred sacrifice. [. . .]

4499   VIII.iii. [. . .] Once the meal was half-over, the king ordered my deacon, who chanted the responsorial psalm at Mass on the previous day, to sing. [. . .]

4500   VIII.iv. [. . .] On the holy day of the Pasch, when my brother Sigibert was standing in the church, the deacon came forth with the holy book of the gospels. A messenger from the king arrived. The messenger and the deacon who was reading the gospel said the same thing, "A son is born to you." The people responded to both when they replied, "Glory to God almighty." The child was baptized on the holy day of Pentecost and at Christmas was made king. [. . .]

4501   X.i. [. . .] While preparations were being made for his blessing, a plague devastated the people, causing Gregory[j] to exhort the people to do penance in the following words.

The Oration of Pope Gregory to the People

4502   "[. . .] Beloved, with contrite hearts and with amended lives may we gather at dawn on Wednesday to observe the sevenfold litanies. [. . .] Let the clergy with the presbyters of the sixth region go from the Church of the Holy Martyrs Cosmas and Damian. Let all the abbots with their monks proceed from the Church of the Holy Martyrs Protase and Gervase with the presbyters of the fourth region. May all the abbesses with their nuns depart from the Church of the Holy Martyrs Marcellinus and Peter with the presbyters of the first region. All the children should proceed from

---

h. Audofleda and Amalasuntha: Audofleda (d. 526) was the sister of Clovis and the wife of Theodoric, King of Italy; Amalasuntha was the daughter of Audofleda and Clovis.

i. Tetricus: bishop of Langres in eastern France (d. 572/573).

j. Gregory: bishop of Rome (WEC 4:**165-A-31**).

the Church of the Holy Martyrs John and Paul with the presbyters of the second region; all the laity from the Church of the Protomartyr Stephen with the presbyters of the seventh region; all the married women from the Church of the Holy Martyr Clement with the presbyters of the third region so that going forth from the individual churches with prayers and tears they might gather at the Basilica of Blessed Mary Ever Virgin, the Mother of our Lord Jesus Christ, and there with many tears and lamentations may they supplicate the Lord, requesting that our sins be pardoned."

Having said this, Gregory gathered together various groups of priests 4503 and enjoined them to sing psalms and seek the Lord's mercy for three days. At the third hour all the choirs of the psalm-singers came to the church, singing the *Kyrie eleison*, which they had sung throughout all the streets of the city. My deacon, who was present for this, relates that while the people were uttering supplications to the Lord, eighty of them fell down and expired. But Gregory continued to preach to the people who did not cease praying.

X.xxx. [. . .] In the town of Limoges[k] many people were destroyed by 4504 the divine fire because they did harm to the Lord's Day by carrying out public business on that day. Sunday is a holy day because in the beginning it was the first day to see light created, and it shined forth as a witness of the Lord's resurrection. For this reason Sunday should be most faithfully observed by Christians with no public business being done on it. [. . .]

X.xxxi.1. At times Gatianus,[l] the first bishop [of Tours] [. . .] secretly 4505 celebrated the solemn mysteries with just a few Christians, concealing himself in various hiding places. [. . .]

X.xxxi.5. Perpetuus[m] instituted fasts and vigils to be observed through- 4506 out the year and which are still observed by us today. Their order is as follows:

Fasts
After Pentecost, Wednesday, and Friday till the Nativity of Saint John;[n] 4507
From 1 September to 1 October, two fasts each week;
From 1 October to the burial of Saint Martin,[o] two fasts each week;
From the burial of Saint Martin till the Lord's Nativity on earth, three fasts each week;
From the birth of Saint Hilary[p] till the middle of February, two fasts each week.

---

k. Limoges: city in southwestern France.

l. Gatianus: most historians consider Litorius (337/338–70) as the first bishop of Tours.

m. Perpetuus: bishop of Tours 458/459–488/489.

n. Nativity of Saint John: June 14.

o. Burial of Saint Martin: November 11.

p. Birth of Saint Hilary: January 13.

4508   Vigils
At Christmas, in the cathedral;
At Epiphany, in the cathedral;
On the Nativity of Saint John, in the Basilica of Saint Martin;
On the anniversary day of the episcopate of Saint Peter,^q in his basilica;
On 27 March, the resurrection of Jesus Christ, in the Basilica of Saint
Martin;
On the Pasch, in the cathedral;
On Ascension, in the Basilica of Saint Martin;
On Pentecost, in the cathedral;
On the Passion of Saint John,^r in the baptistery of the basilica;
On the feast of the holy apostles Peter and Paul,^s in their basilica;
On the feast of Saint Martin,^t in his basilica;
On the feast of Saint Simphorian,^u in the Basilica of Saint Martin;
On the feast of Saint Litorius,^v in his basilica;
Likewise on the feast of Saint Martin,^w in his basilica;
On the feast of Saint Bricius,^x in the Basilica of Saint Martin;
On the feast of Saint Hilary,^y in the Basilica of Saint Martin. [. . .]

172-B. Eight Books of Miracles (Octo Miraculorum Libri)

This is the title given to a collection, compiled by Gregory himself, of eight
previous works.

172-B-1. *GLORY OF THE MARTYRS (IN GLORIAM MARTYRUM)*[†]

Written ca. 590, this work relates the miracles of the Lord, of the apostles,
and of various Gallican martyrs.

4509   xxiv. On the plain of Osset[a] is located a very ancient pool, sculpted
from various types of marble and built in the form of a cross. Over this
pool Christians constructed a tall and gleaming building. When the holy
day after the circle of the year was approaching—the day on which the
Lord, having dismayed the one who would hand him over, and the day
on which he gave his disciples the mystical supper—the people and

---

q. Episcopate of Saint Peter: February 22.
r. Passion of Saint John: August 29.
s. Feast of Peter and Paul: June 29.
t. Feast of Saint Martin: July 4.
u. Feast of Saint Simphorian: August 22.
v. Feast of Saint Litorius: September 13.
w. Feast of Saint Martin: November 11, second feast of this saint.
x. Feast of Saint Bricius: November 3.
y. Feast of Saint Hilary: January 13.
[†] Translated from PL 71:725–26, 781–82.
a. Osset: located near Seville in Spain.

the bishop gathered there; they had already detected the scent of a holy aroma. After a prayer by the bishop there was a command that the temple's doors be immediately sealed. On the third day, namely, on [Easter] Saturday, the people gathered for baptism. Coming with his citizens, the bishop inspected the seals and opened the doors. Behold! The pool which was empty when they left, was found to be full. [. . .] Once the water had been sanctified by means of an exorcism and sprinkled with chrism, the people drank from it to manifest their devotion. Then for the sake of its salvation each family took home a vessel full of this water in order to protect its fields and vineyards by sprinkling them. No matter how many jars were filled, the amount of water never decreased. As soon as the first child was immersed, the amount of water began to decrease. And once all had been baptized, the water receded. Just as the water flowed from an unknown source, so it disappeared in a way unknown to me.

LXXXVI. We weep and mourn for our sins since we do not know whether   4510
we are indeed sinless when we approach the altar of the Lord. [. . .] I recall what happened when I was a young man. It was the day when we were recalling the suffering of Polycarp,[b] the great martyr, and Mass was being celebrated in Rion, a village near the city of Clermont. His passion together with the other readings contained in the priestly canons were read. The time for offering the sacrifice arrived, and the deacon, taking the tower in which the [soon to be] mystery of the Lord's Body is contained, began to carry it toward the door. He entered the temple in order to place the tower on the altar. But the vessel, escaping from his hands, flew into the air. As he advanced toward the altar, the deacon could not grab hold of the vessel. The reason why this happened is, I believe, that his conscience was stained. Some say that the deacon was guilty of adultery. This event was observed by one priest and three women, one of whom was my mother. I confess I was present at the time of this feast but I did not merit to see what happened.

LXXXVII. The priest Epachius,[c] rashly presuming to do what he was un-   4511
worthy of doing, was struck by God's judgment and fell down. He went to the church in order to celebrate the vigils of the Lord's birth. At each of these hours he left God's temple and returned home where he wantonly drank from intoxicating vessels; many stated that he was drinking on that night after cockcrow. But since he was of senatorial origin and since no one in that town of Riom was of more noble rank according to worldly standards, it fell upon him to celebrate Mass. This poor man, already inebriated with wine, did not hesitate to do what a person could not do without fear, without a frightened conscience. Indeed, having pronounced the sacred words, having broken the sacrament of the Lord's Body, he took

---

b. Polycarp of Smyrna (WEC 1:**13**).

c. Epachius: probably a priest who lived at Clermont toward the end of the fifth century.

and distributed it to others so that they might eat it. Soon, neighing like a horse, he fell down, his mouth foaming and spitting out the portion of the sacred mystery that he could not break apart. He was carried from the church by his servants.

172-B-2. *MIRACLES OF SAINT JULIAN (DE VIRTUTIBUS S. JULIANI)*†

Written between 581 and 587, this piece is, as it were, a catalog of some fifty miracles attributed to Saint Julian, who was martyred in 304 and buried at Brioude, some forty miles south of Clermont. The basilica containing his relics was a popular pilgrimage destination.

4512   xx. The feast of Saint Julian had arrived, and a certain man who was present noticed that the holy basilica was aglow with numerous decorations. Evil in mind, he desired what, once obtained, he could not conceal. Therefore as the people were departing the church after Vespers [*post gratiam vespertinam*], he, lingering in a corner of the basilica, hid himself. [. . .]

4513   xxiv. Much later it was the feast of Saint Julian, and my father together with his whole family was hastening to this joyful solemnity. During the journey Peter, my older brother, was afflicted with a burning fever, so much so that he was unable to eat or to do anything else. He suffered throughout the whole trip. No one knew whether he would recover or expire. We arrived at the place and upon entering the basilica we venerated the tomb of the holy martyr. My sick brother knelt on the pavement and requested a cure from the glorious martyr. Completing his prayer, he returned to the place where we were staying. Once there the fever somewhat lessened. When night came, we hurried to the vigils. Peter requested that he also be brought there. He laid down before the tomb and spent the whole night praying to the martyr. When these night vigils came to an end, he requested that the dust surrounding the tomb be collected and be given to him in a drink or be suspended from his neck. Once this was done, his burning fever disappeared. [. . .]

172-B-3. *MIRACLES OF SAINT MARTIN (DE VIRTUTIBUS S. MARTINI)*††

Martin, born ca. 315/336, was elected bishop of Tours ca. 371. He died in 397. This listing of miracles attributed to him contains four books (the last never having been completed).

4514   II.xiv. [. . .] Palatina, a young girl, was stricken with paralysis, thus being unable to walk. [. . .] Her father brought her to Tours where he placed her at the feet of blessed Martin. Lying there three months, she sought alms from those passing by. On the feast of this illustrious saint and while I was saying Mass, she was faithfully praying in the location I mentioned above. While I was engaged in carrying out the holy

---

† Translated from PL 71:813, 815–16.
†† Translated from PL 71:946ff.

ceremonies—I was saying the preface [*contestationem*] concerning the wonders of our holy Lord—she suddenly began to cry aloud and weep, indicating that she was in pain. But when the preface was completed and all the people were proclaiming the *Sanctus* in praise of the Lord, the nerves that were bound were loosened; she stood up and thus, before all the people and with the Lord's help, she on her own power approached the holy altar to receive Communion. She remains in good health up to the present day.

II.xxix. Two blind men arrived from Bourges. Their eyelids were closed, joined together by a liquid. They fell down, praying at the feet of the holy lord Martin. This occurred on his feast when all the people were present and while the stories of miracles were being read from his *Life*. [. . .] 4515

II.xxx. [. . .] On Sunday during the celebration of Mass this [mute] woman was standing in the church with the rest of the people. While the Lord's Prayer was being said, her mouth was opened and she began to sing this holy prayer with the others. [. . .] 4516

II.xlvii. [. . .] A cripple came to Tours shortly before the feast of the bishop [4 July]. Praying, he was kneeling before the tomb. Toward the end of Mass[a] [*expletis missis*] the people began to receive the most holy Body of the Redeemer. Suddenly his knees were set free, and he stood up. With all looking on, he gave thanks and on his own walked to the holy altar. [. . .] 4517

II.xlix. It was the feast of Saint Martin, a day when all the people had gathered. Among them was a man with a crippled arm. He kissed the holy tomb with his lips, moistened it with his tears, and with his voice requested the help of the blessed confessor; his faith remained strong as he awaited the customary assistance. Then the priests arrived to carry out the solemn rites of the Mass; there was a reader whose task it was to read, and who took the book and began reading the life of the holy confessor. Immediately the man's arm was healed. [. . .] 4518

172-B-4. LIVES OF THE FATHERS (LIBER VITAE PATRUM)[†]

This, the most well-known of Gregory's hagiographical works, was written soon after 593. The book treats twenty-three notables of Gaul, some being Gregory's own relatives.

vi.7. Let us come to the time when the Lord commanded that Gallus[a] be taken from this world. Ill health had confined Gallus to bed where an internal fever consumed all his members; as a result he had lost both his hair and his beard. The Lord revealed to him that he would expire after three days. So Gallus gathered his people, broke the [eucharistic] bread for all, and in a holy and pious manner distributed Communion. The third day 4519

a. Some would translate *expletis missis* as "At the end of the consecratory prayer."
† Translated from PL 71:1034ff.
a. Gallus: Gregory's uncle and a bishop of Tours (d. 554).

arrived, this being the Lord's Day, and the people of Auvergne began to mourn deeply. As day dawned Gallus asked what was being sung in the church. He was told that they were singing the blessing [the *Benedicite*]. When Psalm 50[b] and the Blessing had been sung, and when the Alleluia with the *capitulum* were finished, he completed all of Matins. When the office was finished, he said, "Farewell, my beloved!" He then extended his arms and sent to the Lord his spirit, which was intent upon reaching heaven. [. . .]

4520   VIII.4. One morning Saint Nicetius[c] rose early for Matins. He waited for the two antiphons and then entered the church where, after he sat down, the deacon began to sing the response. But Nicetius, being disturbed, said, "Be silent! Be silent! O friend of injustice, do not presume to sing." No sooner had he said this than the deacon's mouth closed and he was silent. And the holy man, having ordered that the deacon come before him, said, "Did I not forbid you to enter God's church? Why have you heedlessly presumed to do so? Why did you sing the Lord's songs?" All present were astounded, for they knew nothing of the deacon's evil. However, the demon in the deacon cried out, saying that the holy man was greatly tormenting him. He had indeed presumed to sing in church. Although not recognized by the people, his voice was recognized by the holy one whose harsh words condemned the demon, not the deacon. The holy man, imposing hands, chased out the demon and restored the deacon to his senses.

4521   XIII.3. [. . .] After Lupicinus[d] died, a certain lady took his body, washed it, and clothed it with fitting garb. She wanted to take it to the town of Trézelle.[e] The people of Lipidiacum,[f] however, were opposed to this, saying, "Our soil nourished him; so his body should belong to us." [. . .] The woman took away the holy body of Lupicinus by force and began to carry it on a bier to Trézelle. She placed crowds of psalm-singers with crosses, candles, and sweet-smelling incense along the route. Seeing this, the people, moved with penance, told the woman, "We have sinned by opposing you, for we truly know that this is God's will; we request that we not be excluded from the burial service but be allowed to participate in it." The woman permitted them to follow; both groups of people came together and went to Trézelle where Mass was celebrated. It was there that they buried the body with the greatest honor and joy. [. . .]

4522   XVI.2. One Sunday when Saint Venantius[g] was invited to celebrate Mass, he said to his brothers, "My eyes, being very weak, I am unable to see the

---

b. Psalm 50, LXX.

c. Nicetius: bishop of Tours 525/526–ca. 569.

d. Lupicinus: bishop of Lyons in the late fifth century.

e. Trézelle: located in the province of Auvergne.

f. Lipidiacum: located in the region of Aquitaine in southwest Gaul.

g. Venantius: namely, Venantius Fortunatus (WEC 4:**173**).

book. For this reason have another presbyter do all this." The presbyter did so, with the holy man standing close beside him. The moment arrived when the holy offering was, following Catholic custom, to be blessed by the sign of the cross. Venantius saw that a ladder was, as it were, placed at one window of the apse, and upon it was an elderly man descending, a man venerable with the honor of a cleric. With his right hand he blessed the sacrifice offered on the altar. This occurred in the basilica of Saint Martin and was observed only by Venantius. [. . .]

One Sunday the same Venantius, having completed his prayers and supported by a little staff, was returning from the basilica of the saints. In the middle of the courtyard of the blessed confessor he stopped to listen, eyes wide open and ears intent upon heaven. Then, moving forward, he began to groan and sigh. Questioned by his companions as to what was wrong or whether he had seen something divine, he said, "Woe to us who are unskillful and lazy. Behold! In heaven the Mass is well in progress, and we, slothful as we are, have not begun [to celebrate] the sacrament of this mystery. Truly I have heard the voices of the angels in heaven proclaiming the *Sanctus, Sanctus* in praise of the Lord." And Venantius ordered that Mass be immediately celebrated in the monastery. [. . .]

4523

172-B-5. *GLORY OF THE CONFESSORS (DE GLORIA CONFESSORUM)*[†]

This is the counterpart to Gregory's *In Gloria Martyrum*. The work, treating saints who were not martyrs, dates from 587.

xx. [. . .] Under God's inspiration I decided to faithfully dedicate a very elegant room, one used by Saint Eufronius[a] as a storeroom. The chamber was to be used for prayer. It was beautifully decorated with an altar located in the customary place. One night I observed a vigil in the holy basilica, and early in the morning I went to the little room so that I might bless the altar I had set up. Returning to the basilica, I moved Martin's holy relics together with those of the martyrs Saturninus[b] and Julian[c] and those of blessed Illidius,[d] doing so with brightly shining candles and crosses. Present were many presbyters, deacons in white vestments, a large number of distinguished citizens, together with people of lesser rank. [. . .]

4524

xxii. [. . .] Maximus[e] desired to cross the Saône, but his boat was swamped and it sank. This priest was in the water. He had around his

4525

[†] Translated from PL 71:812ff.

a. Eufronius: bishop of Tours 556–73.

b. Saturinus: an early martyr at Toulouse.

c. Julian: martyred in 304 and buried at Brioude, some forty miles south of Clermont.

d. Illidius: late fourth-century bishop of Clermont.

e. Maximus: abbot of a monastery in Lyons.

neck the book of the gospels used for the weekly liturgy as well as the dish and the cup. But the divine goodness did not permit God's own to perish. At God's command Maximus was rescued from this peril. [. . .]

4526   xlvii. Two presbyters were buried in one and the same basilica but on opposite walls: the tomb of one was on the south, that of the other on the north. The clerics began to sing psalms as they celebrated the office. Doing so, they formed two choirs, each choir singing psalms to the Lord; each presbyter's voice joined the communal singing of the psalms. Thus one choir was enlarged by the assistance of one presbyter's voice, the other choir strengthened by the voice of the other presbyter. So great was the sweetness of this harmony that it delighted those listening. [. . .]

4527   xlviii. [. . .] Not far from here is the village of Rion in which there was a Catholic church. When the Goths came, they took possession of this church. Next door to the church was a large house. When the Paschal Vigil arrived, the heretical priests baptized the infants in our church so that the people might more easily be associated with this sect, the [Catholic] priest not being allowed to enter this building. This priest, however, came up with a clever idea. While the heretics were baptizing in our church, he, ready to serve, began to baptize in their house. God's punishment followed. The infants whom the heretics baptized—twenty infants in all—all died by the end of the Pasch. Seeing this, the heretics, fearing that their house was becoming a church, returned the church to the presbyter. Those whom the presbyter baptized did not die with the exception of one infant who was called by the Lord after having attained a proper age.

4528   lxv. In Lyons there once lived two people, a man and his wife, members of an influential senatorial family. Being childless, they named the church as their heir. The husband, being the first to die, was buried in the Basilica of Saint Mary. The woman visited the church for a whole year where she diligently prayed, every day being present for Mass. Making offerings in memory of her husband, she was confident that through the Lord's mercy her deceased husband would enjoy rest on each day she made an offering for his soul. For this reason she always presented some wine from Gaza[f] to be used for the sacrifice in the holy basilica. The subdeacon was a worthless fellow, reserving the wine from Gaza for himself. In the cup he presented [what seemed to be] most bitter vinegar. The woman, however, did not always come forward to receive the gift of Communion. And so it pleased God to reveal this deception. The husband appeared to his wife [in a dream] and said, "Alas, alas, my dearest wife, why has my labor in this world so come to naught that now at the offering I taste vinegar?" She replied, "I have not forgotten your love. I have always obtained the most exceptional Gaza wine to be offered in God's sanctuary for your repose." She then awoke, marveled at what she had seen, and did not forget it. As

---

f. Gaza wine: a wine produced in Gaza (Palestine) and highly esteemed by the Gauls.

was customary, she rose for Matins. When this was completed and when Mass had been celebrated, she approached the saving cup. Tasting the vinegar contained in it, she thought her teeth would have fallen out had she not so quickly swallowed the liquid. She then reproached the subdeacon. What had been done sinfully and deceitfully was corrected. [. . .]

173. VENANTIUS FORTUNATUS

Born ca. 530 at Trevisio near Venice, Venantius was educated at Ravenna, where he was well instructed in the classical authors as well as in the Scriptures. After frequent travels (e.g., a pilgrimage to the tomb of Saint Martin of Tours), he eventually was ordained, becoming chaplain of a community of nuns. In 596 he was elected bishop of Poitiers, dying there shortly after the turn of the century.

A prolific writer, Venantius has left us numerous prose and poetic compositions. But he is especially known for his poetry, being called the "first of the medieval poets."

CPL nos. 1033ff. * Altaner (1961) 601–3 * Altaner (1966) 499–501 * Bardenhewer (1908) 647–50 * Bardenhewer (1910) 557–59 * Bardenhewer (1913) 5:367–77 * Bardy (1930) 178–81 * Labriolle (1947) 2:756–61 * Labriolle (1968) 491–94 * Steidle 204–5 * Tixeront 344–45 * CATH 4:1458–60 * CE 6:149 * DACL 5.2:1892–97 * DCB 2:552–53 * DPAC 2:3556–58 * DTC 6.1:611–14 * EC 12:1177 * EEC 2:862–63 * EEChr 2:1158 * LTK 10:582–83 * NCE 5:1034–35 * NCES 5:823 * ODCC 1685

B. Capelle, "'Regnavit a ligno,'" QLP 7 (1922) 92–95. * J. Szövérffy, "'Crux fidelis . . .': Prolegomena to a History of the Holy Cross Hymns," Tra 22 (1966) 1–41. * B.K. Braswell, "Kleine textkritische Bemerkungen zu frühchristlichen Hymnen," VC 29 (1975) 222–26. * D. Norberg, "Le 'Pange Lingua' de Fortunat pour la croix," LMD, no. 173 (1988) 71–79.

173-A. Life of Queen Radegunde[†]

Radegunde (d. 587), of royal birth and the wife of King Lothar I (a man of a decidedly unsavory character), eventually fled the court, became a nun, and established a monastery for female religious outside Poitier. Here she lived a life of good works and became a friend of Venantius, who, more interested in edification than in factual accuracy, wrote her biography.

16. [. . .] Making the offerings with her own hands, she never failed to distribute these in the holy places. [. . .]   4529

174. COLUMBANUS

Columbanus (Columban), born ca. 543, was a monk of the monastery of Bangor, located in County Down in northeastern Ireland. Saint Comgall

---

[†] Translated from PL 88:370.

was abbot of this community. With twelve companions and with the abbot's permission, Columbanus departed Ireland for Gaul ca. 585/590, where he established several monastic foundations, first at Annegray, then at Luxeuil and Fontaines. Well received by the king, Guntram, this missionary monk had less than cordial relations with the local clergy, especially since he adhered to various Irish religious customs, for example, observing the Celtic date of Easter. Imprisoned and then banished in 610 for condemning the immoral activity of the king, Thierry II, Columbanus went to Switzerland, then to Milan, and finally to Bobbio in northern Italy, where he founded a monastery in 614, only to die a year later in 615.

CPL nos. 1107ff., 1117ff. * Bautz 1:1104–5 * CATH 2:1317–21 * CE 4:137–40 * DCB 1:605–7 * DDC 3:1005–24 * DHGE 13:313–20 * DictSp 2:1:1131–33 * DPAC 1:736–37 * DTC 3.1:370–76 * EC 3:1996–98 * EEC 1:186–87 * EEChr 1:270–71 * LTK 2:1268 * NCE 3:1036–37 * NCES 3:863–64 * ODCC 379–80 * TRE 8:159–62

C. Gindele, "Die Satisfaktionsordung von Caesarius und Benedikt bis Donatus," RB 69 (1959) 216–36. * A. Verheul, "La prière monastique chorale avant Benoît: son influence sur le culte en occident: la prière des heures avant la Règle et dans la Règle de s. Benoît," QL 62 (1981) 227–42. * A. Verheul, "Les psaumes dans la prière des heures: hier et aujourd'hui," QL 71 (1990) 261–95.

174-A. Rules

Two monastic rules are attributed to Columbanus. The first, the *Regula Monachorum*, probably redacted in Ireland and then in Gaul, is more concerned with the internal aspects of monastic life, although attention is paid to the prayer life of the monks. Corporal punishment is often called for, even in cases of minor fractions of the monastic way of life.

The second rule, the *Regula Coenobialis*—Columbanus seems to be responsible for only its first nine chapters—complements the general principles given in the *Regula Monachorum*.

It has been suggested that primitively these two rules formed but one document.

174-A-1. REGULA MONACHORUM[†]

4530   VII. As to the synaxis, namely, the canonical order of the psalms and prayers, a number of distinctions are to be made since what is done has been handed down to us from various sources. Therefore according to the nature of a person's life and the rotation of the seasons, the same will be reflected in my writing. Given the changing of the seasons, there will not be any uniformity. The office should be longer for long nights, shorter

---

[†] Translated from *Sancta Colombian Opera*, ed. G.S.M. Walker, Scriptores Latini Hiberniae, no. 2 (Dublin, 1957) 128, 130, 132.

for short nights. And so—and here we concur with our elders—from 24 June on and as the night grows longer, the office begins to increase from twelve *chora*,[a] the shortest number of psalms being on Saturday and Sunday up to the beginning of winter, namely, 1 November. On such days twenty-five antiphonal psalms are sung. [. . .] These always follow third after the non-antiphonal psalms so that in this way the whole psalter is sung within the course of these two nights. The remaining nights during the winter are less burdensome, with only twelve *chora*. At the conclusion of winter and gradually during each week of spring the number of psalms is reduced by three so that there are only twelve antiphonal psalms on the holy nights, namely, the daily winter curses of thirty-six psalms, with twenty-four during spring and summer, this extending to the autumn equinox, namely, 24 September. Then the synaxis is like that of the spring equinox, 25 March, when with its alternating changes it slowly increases and decreases. It is in this way that we keep vigil according to our abilities, especially since the Author of our salvation commands that we watch and "pray always."[1] And Paul commands that we "pray without ceasing."[2] But since the manner of canonical prayer is to be known by all who assemble at the appointed hours for common prayer—the monk praying in his own cell afterwards[3]—our elders determined that there be three psalms at each of the day's hours, work being interrupted for this. Versicles are to be added, the first being for our own sins, then for the whole Christian people, then for the priests and others of the holy people who are consecrated to God, then for those who give alms, then for peace among kings, and finally for our enemies so that God not count it as a sin that they persecute and disparage us because "they know not what they do."[4] At night's beginning there are twelve psalms; likewise twelve are sung at midnight; toward morning there are twenty-four psalms, as we have said, during the time when the night is short; more, as already indicated, during the night of the Lord's Day and on the Sabbath vigil—on these occasions seventy-five psalms are individually sung during a single office.

There are certain Catholics for whom the canonical number of psalms   4531
is twelve, whether it be during long nights or short nights. They observe this rule four times during the night: at night's beginning, at midnight, at cockcrow, and at morning. During the winter a curse like this seems small to some; during summer it is found to be rather burdensome and oppressive since with its frequent rising and retiring it results not so much in exhaustion as it does in weariness. During the most holy nights, those of the Lord's Day and of the Sabbath, three times this number of psalms is prayed in the morning, namely, thirty-six psalms. [. . .]

---

a. *Chora*: as explained by Columbanus, a unit of three psalms, the first two being without antiphons, the third being antiphonal.
1. Luke 21:36.   2. 1 Thess 5:17.   3. See Matt 6:6.   4. Luke 23:34.

174-A-2. *REGULA COENOBIALIS*[†]

4532   IX. [. . .] All, once they have heard the sound that begins each day's assemblies, are to wash before entering the oratory unless they have done so previously. To be appointed is a cantor who leads the psalmody; also a subcantor. The monks do not kneel but only bow. Those having seniority are in the middle of the oratory, with the others standing on the right and the left except the presider and his assistant. At each Sunday's solemnity as well as on the day that begins the Easter season a hymn to the Lord may be sung. When a monk approaches the altar to receive the Eucharist, he is to prostrate himself three times. Novices, not having been instructed, as well as all others who lack instruction, are not to approach to receive from the cup. And when the offering takes place, no one, other than when necessary, is to be forced to receive the Eucharist. On every Lord's Day and solemnity those who for some necessity have not prayed to the Lord are to pray individually. During the offering all movement is to be kept to a minimum. [. . .]

4533   All the brethren when they pray during the day and night should kneel for prayer at the conclusion of each psalm provided bodily infirmity does not hinder them from doing so. In silence they are to say, "O God, deliver me. O Lord, come to my assistance."[1] Once they have silently prayed this verse three times, they are to stand. However, during the psalmody on the Lord's Day and on the first day of the Easter season and up to the fiftieth day, although they bow slightly, they are to diligently pray to the Lord without bending their knees.

4534   XV.[a] If someone has misplaced the Eucharist and does not know where it is, there is to be a year's penance. If someone has in such a way neglected the Eucharist that it has dried out and is consumed by worms, becoming, as it were, nothing, a half year's penance is to be performed. If someone has so neglected the Eucharist that a worm is found within it and yet it remains entire, the worm is to be burned by fire and its ashes placed next to the altar; for this there is to be a penance of forty days. [. . .]

174-B. Penitential[††]

This penitential, namely, a book for confessors that lists various types of sins and their respective penalties, is modeled upon a text by the monk Finnian (WEC 4:**181-A**). Here three classes of people are considered: 2–13, the monks; 15–26, the clergy; 27–44, the laity.

[†] Translated from *Sancta Colombian Opera*, 155ff.

a. Chapters X and following appear to be later additions to the text.

1. Ps 70:2.

[††] Translated from *Le Pénitentiel de Saint Columban*, trans. and ed. J. Laport, Monumenta Christiana Selecta, no. 4 (Tournai, 1958) 91ff.

1. True penance consists in no longer committing those actions calling   4535
for penance as well as regretting sins already committed. But many—I do
not say all—because of human weakness act contrary to this rule. For this
reason it is necessary to know the system of penance. The general prin-
ciple, stated by our holy elders, is to determine the length of the fast according to the gravity of the sin.

2. If a monk sins by thought, namely, has desired to kill, fornicate, steal,   4536
eat in secret, become intoxicated, strike another, deceive, or commit whatever action of this kind or was disposed to commit such an action, he will
fast on bread and water for six months or forty days according to the gravity of the action he intended to commit.

3. If anyone has allowed himself to be carried away to actually commit   4537
actions such as homicide or sodomy, there is to be ten years of fasting. If
he fornicates only once, three years of penance. If he does so more often,
seven years of penance. If a monk abandons the monastic state and breaks
his vows but quickly returns, he will fast for three Lents. If he returns only
after many years, he will do penance for three years.

7. Anyone who is so intoxicated that he vomits or, being fully satiated,   4538
vomits the Eucharist, forty days of fast. If he does this due to sickness,
seven days of fast. If the Eucharist is allowed to fall or is lost on a voyage,
one year of fasting.

14.[+] Different sins require different penances. Doctors of the body also   4539
adapt their medicines to various types of illnesses. Differently do they
cure wounds, diseases, tumors, bruises, gangrene, blindness, fractures,
burns. In like manner the doctor of the soul should cure, by remedies appropriate to the wounds of the soul, its maladies, its sins, its sorrows, its
weariness, its infirmities. Since there are but few doctors who are perfectly
conversant as far as healing and restoring the health of the soul, we here
propose several counsels, partly according to the traditions of the elders,
partly according to our own judgment, "for imperfect is our prophecy, imperfect also is our science."[1]

15. [. . .] A cleric who commits murder and kills another will be exiled   4540
for ten years. He will then be allowed to re-enter his country on condition
that he has regularly fasted on bread and water, as attested by the bishop
or the priest who has supervised his penance and to whom he has con-
fided. [. . .]

29. A laic who has committed sodomy, namely, uniting with a man as   4541
one would with a woman, will fast seven years, the first three being on
bread and water, with salt and dry vegetables only. The other four years
he will abstain from wine and meat. In this way his sin will be pardoned,
and the confessor will pray for him and will readmit him to Communion.

[+] = later additions to the primitive text.

1. 1 Cor 13:9.

4542   33. A laic who is a thief, namely, someone who steals an ox, a horse, a sheep, or a domestic animal, will first of all return the stolen goods to its owner and, if it is his first or second such offense, will fast for three Lents on bread and water. But if the theft is habitual and if the sinner cannot return what was stolen, then there will be a fast of one year plus three Lents together with a promise not to steal again. This person will be able to receive Communion at Easter of the following year, namely, after two years, alms taken from one's labor being given to the poor and a meal being provided for the confessor. In this way the sin contracted by one's evil habit will be forgiven.

4543   39.[+] If through ignorance a laic has entered into communion with the Bonosians[a] or with other heretics, he or she will be placed among the catechumens, namely, will be separated from other Christians, and this for forty days. For two other Lents such will expiate the crime of having been in communion with the followers of an absurd heresy by placing himself or herself in the lowest rank of the faithful, namely, among the public penitents. If the guilty one has acted out of contempt, namely, after having been warned by a priest and after having received the prohibition not to soil oneself by such communion with the outcast, there will be a fast for one year and three Lents; for two years the person will abstain from wine and meat. Only after the imposition of hands by a Catholic bishop will he or she be again allowed to approach the altar.

4544   44.[+] We enjoin that all confess promptly, especially acknowledging the disturbances brought about by the passions. They are to do so before going to Mass so that no one unworthily approaches the altar, that is, not having "a clean heart."[2] It is better to delay Communion so that the heart be clean, free from self-conceit and haste, rather than to rashly approach the tribunal. Christ's altar is, in fact, a tribunal, and his Body and Blood judge those who approach unworthily. It is necessary to guard against grave and carnal sins before receiving Communion. We must also avoid internal sins and spiritual apathy before participating in the peace and in eternal salvation.

175. FERREOLUS OF UZÈS

A native of Narbonne and first mentioned by Caesarius of Arles (WEC 4:**168**) in his *History of the Franks* (6:7), Ferreolus was bishop of Uzès, where he established a monastery, in southern France. Little is known of his life. He died in 581.

CPL 1849 * CATH 4:1199–1200 * DHGE 16:1242–43 * EEC 322 * LTK 3:1244

G. Holzherr, *Regula Ferrioli* (Einsiedeln, 1961).

---

a. Bonosians: a heretical group denying, among other things, the divinity of Christ.

2. Ps 51:10.

175-A. Rule of Ferreolus[†]

XII. The psalms are always sung in sequence up to the end of the Psalter. 　4545
However, in secret and in view of one's own personal profit, each may
offer each day praise apart from the psalms that are recited in public to
the Lord. This is done in private, for one's own personal profit. God alone
is aware of this silent pondering. Also at night it is fitting to keep vigil by
reciting numerous psalms followed by prayers. In this way one fulfills the
words of the Lord, "Day and night I cry out before you."[1] Also, "Day and
night I will meditate on your law."[2]

XIII. No monk who is present [in the monastery] is to absent himself from 　4546
the night vigils during which prayer to God is sought out of devotion or is
fitting due to a feast, the only exception being sickness or necessity. [. . .] We
remind you, if it is not superfluous to do so, that all are to rise each day for
Matins; on all days may all quickly and together rise for the nocturns so that,
having assembled together, no one be found to have come late. But indeed
whoever is observed acting contrary to this directive, he alone is to fast for as
many days as the number of hours he did not keep watch with his brothers.

XV. We have judged that what is done in other monasteries be followed, 　4547
namely, that children are not to be baptized in the monastery. Nor is a
monk in any place to receive anyone's children from the holy bath: so that
he not gradually be joined to the child's parents, as often happens, in illicit
or gradually wicked familiarity. Whoever presumes to do this will be corrected as transgressing the rule.

XVIII. We strongly enjoin that the Acts of the Martyrs, namely, the pas- 　4548
sions of the holy ones, which have been carefully received and written
down, be read in the oratory in the presence of the whole community. And
so each day is not to pass unnoticed; it is to be a special day. Just as what
was formerly illustrated by the constancy of those who were martyred, so
the memory of their passion will now indicate.

176. SYNODS

176-A. Synod of Agde (506)[††]

Presided over by Caesarius of Arles (WEC 4:**168**), this meeting of thirty-
five bishops in Agde (southern France on the Mediterranean) issued forty-
seven canons.

[†] Translated from *Règles monastique d'Occident: IVe–VIe siècle, d'Augustin à Ferréol*,
trans. and ed. V. Desprez, Vie monastique 9, Collection spiritualité orientale et vie
monastique (Bégrolles-en-Mauges, 1980) 305–8, 310.

1. Ps 88:1.　2. Ps 1:2.

[††] Canons translated from *Concilia Galliae de 314 à 506*, ed. C. Munier, CCL 148
(Turnhout, 1963) 200–212.

CPL no. 1784 * Hefele (1905) 2.2:973–1002 * Hefele (1871) 4:76–86 * CATH 1:198 * CE 1:206 * DACL 1.1:871–77 * DCA 1:42 * DDCon 1:7–8 * DTC 1.1:563 * EEC 1:17 * ODCC 28

J. Deligny, "La bénédiction de la fin de la messe," RevAug 12 (1908) 316–21.

4549　Canon 12. All children of the Church must fast each day during Lent, even on Saturdays,[a] Sundays alone being the exception.[b] [. . .]

4550　Canon 13. In all churches the priest is to publicly hand over the creed[c] to the *competentes* on the same day, namely, eight days before the day of the Lord's resurrection.[d]

4551　Canon 14. Altars are not only to be anointed with chrism[e] but are also to be blessed by the priest.

4552　Canon 15. When sinners seek penance, they shall receive from the priest[f] the imposition of hands and a haircloth upon the head. However, if they do not cut off their hair[g] and change their clothes, they are to be rejected, and they are not to be accepted unless they have in truth done penance. Because of the frailty of their age young people must not lightly be admitted to penance.[h] Viaticum, however, is not to be refused to anyone who is in danger of death.[i]

---

a. See Elvira (ca. 300) can. 26 (WEC 2:1276); Dvin (527) can. 38 (WEC 4:4853); Orleans IV (541) can. 2 (WEC 4:4616).

b. See Saragossa (ca. 380) can. 2 (WEC 2:1295); Gangra (ca. 345) can. 18 (WEC 2:1955); *Statuta* (5th c.) can. 77 (WEC 3:3102); Orleans IV (541) can. 2 (WEC 4:4616); Braga I (561) ser. 1 can. 4 (WEC 4:4737); *Capitula Martini* (after 561) can. 57 (WEC 4:4692).

c. See Laodicea (between 343 and 381) can. 46 (WEC 2:1992); Braga II (572) ser. 1 can. 1 (WEC 4:4755); *Capitula Martini* (after 561) can. 49 (WEC 4:4684).

d. See Laodicea (between 343 and 381) can. 45 (WEC 2:1991); Irish Synod II (after 456) can. 19 (WEC 3:3180); Auxerre (late 6th or early 7th c.) can. 18 (WEC 4:4641); Gerunda (517) can. 4 (WEC 4:4720); Mâcon II (585) can. 3 (WEC 4:4653); *Capitula Martini* (after 561) can. 49 (WEC 4:4684).

e. See Irish Synod I (between 450 and 456) can. 23 (WEC 3:3178); Epaon (517) can. 26 (WEC 4:4581); Orleans III (538) can. 16 (WEC 4:4607); Braga I (561) ser. 2 can. 19 (WEC 4:4752); Braga II (572) cans. 5–6 (WEC 4:4758–59).

f. See Elvira (ca. 300) can. 32 (WEC 2:1279); Carthage II (390) cans. 3–4 (WEC 2:876–77); Hippo (393) *Brev. Hipp.* ser. 2 can. 30-b (WEC 2:888); *Statuta* (5th c.) can. 20 (WEC 3:3077); Toledo III (589) ser. 2 cap. 11 (WEC 4:4766).

g. See Barcelona I (ca. 540) can. 6 (WEC 4:4729); Toledo III (589) ser. 2 cap. 12 (WEC 4:4767).

h. See Orleans III (538) can. 27 (WEC 4:4608).

i. See Elvira (ca. 300) cans. 1, 6, 7, 37, 47 (WEC 2:1270–72, 1284, 1290); Ancyra (314) cans. 16, 22 (WEC 2:1432, 1435); Nicaea I (325) can. 13 (WEC 2:1453); Rome (488) Letter 7, can. 3 (WEC 3:2959); *Statuta* (5th c.) cans. 20–21 (WEC 3:3077–78); Orange I (441) can. 3 (WEC 3:3125); Vaison (442) can. 2 (WEC 3:3137); Arles II (between 442 and 506) can. 28 (WEC 3:3149); Epaon (517) can. 36 (WEC 4:4587); Orleans III (538) cans. 6, 28 (WEC 4:4605, 4609); *Capitula Martini* (after 561) can. 82 (WEC 4:4699); Gerunda (517) can. 9 (WEC 4:4722); Barcelona I (ca. 540) can. 9 (WEC 4:4732).

Canon 17. No metropolitan is to ordain a presbyter or a bishop who is not yet thirty years old, that is, before maturity is reached.[j] No blame is to be imputed if, as has happened several times, an error has been made regarding age. 4553

Canon 18. The laity who do not receive Communion at Christmas, Easter, and Pentecost are not to be considered Catholics,[k] nor are they to take their place among Catholics. 4554

Canon 19. Virgins, however much their lives and morals may be approved, are not to receive the veil before they are forty years old.[l] 4555

Canon 21. We grant permission to anyone who, outside parishes in which the rightful and ordinary gathering takes place, wishes to have an oratory in the country so that Mass is celebrated there on other feasts because of the fatigue of the household. On Easter, Christmas, Epiphany, the Ascension of Christ, Pentecost, the Nativity of Saint John the Baptist, or on other great feasts Mass is to be held only in the cities and parishes.[m] Clerics who on these feasts and without the bishop's command or permission hold Mass or wish to continue doing so are excommunicated. 4556

Canon 30. Because it is fitting that the arrangement of the Church's prayer be followed by all equally,[n] we should strive that after the antiphons, as is done everywhere, the collects are said in order by the bishop or presbyters each day; that the morning and evening hymns be sung on all days, that at the close of Matins and Vespers, after the hymns, verses [*capitella*] from the [Book of] Psalms are to be said, and that the people after evening prayer be dismissed by the bishop with a blessing. 4557

Canon 34. If Jews wish to become Catholics—their faithlessness frequently having them return to their vomit—for eight months they are to enter the church among the catechumens. When they are recognized as coming with pure faith, then at last they merit to receive the grace of baptism. But if for some reason they should within the appointed period of time become seriously and hopelessly ill, then they may be baptized. 4558

Canon 39. Priests, deacons, subdeacons, and all who are themselves forbidden to marry are not to attend the marriages of others nor frequent 4559

---

j. See Neo-Caesarea (ca. 320) can. 11 (WEC 2:1443); Hippo (393) *Brev. Hipp.* ser. 2 can. 1-b (WEC 2:881); Arles IV (524) can. 1 (WEC 4:4589); Orleans III (538) can. 6 (WEC 4:4605).

k. See Irish Synod II (after 456) can. 22 (WEC 3:3181).

l. See Carthage II (390) can. 3 (WEC 2:876); Hippo (393) *Brev. Hipp.* ser. 2 can. 1-b (WEC 2:881); Hippo (393) *Brev. Hipp.* ser. 2 can. 34 (WEC 2:891); Saragossa (ca. 380) can. 8 (WEC 2:1298); Riez (439) can. 4 (WEC 3:3122).

m. See Orleans I (511) can. 25 (WED 4:4570); Epaon (517) can. 35 (WEC 4:4586); Clermont (535) can. 15 (WEC 4:4604); Orleans IV (541) can. 3 (WEC 4:4617); Lyons IV (583) can. 5 (WEC 4:4650).

n. See Vannes (between 461 and 491) can. 15 (WEC 3:3164); Braga I (561) ser. 2 can. 1 (WEC 4:4739).

gatherings where love songs are sung and where wicked and indecent gestures are used at dances.[o] In this way those who are appointed for the holy mysteries may not be polluted by the infection of what they see and hear.

4560 Canon 43. According to the synodal decrees of our holy fathers no one is to be ordained a cleric from among the penitents;[p] and if one has already been ordained through ignorance, he will be considered like those who have married twice or have married widows. If he is a deacon, he is not to serve. If he is a presbyter, he is not to consecrate at the altar.

4561 Canon 44. The presbyter must not bless the people or the penitents in the church.

4562 Canon 47. On Sundays the laity must be present at the whole Mass so that they do not depart before the priest's blessing.[q] Should they do so, they shall be publicly rebuked by the bishop.

176-B. Synod of Orleans I (511)[†]

This meeting, summoned by Clovis, king of the Franks, brought together thirty-two bishops on July 10, 511. They issued thirty-one canons.

Hefele (1905) 2.2:1005–15 * Hefele (1871) 4:87–92 * CE 11:318 * DDCon 3:245–47 * EEC 1:555

4563 Canon 10. The following is to be observed regarding heretical clerics who conscientiously and voluntarily come to the Catholic faith and regarding churches that the perverse Goths owned till the present. If clerics are converted and integrally confess the whole Catholic faith and if they live an upright life in regard to what they do and how they act, they may, by being blessed with the imposition of the hand, receive the office for which the bishop deems them worthy. Their churches may be consecrated in the same way that our churches are customarily consecrated.[a]

4564 Canon 11. Penitents who forget the obligations of their state and return to the secular life[b] are to be excluded from Communion and from all dealings

o. See Neo-Caesarea (ca. 320) can. 7 (WEC 2:1439); Laodicea (between 343 and 381) can. 53 (WEC 2:1999); Vannes (between 461 and 491) can. 11 (WEC 3:3162).

p. See Toledo I (400?) can. 2 (WEC 3:3168); *Statuta* (5th c.) can. 84 (WEC 3:3106); Epaon (517) can. 3 (WEC 4:4575); Arles IV (524) can. 3 (WEC 4:4591); Orleans III (538) can. 6 (WEC 4:4605); *Capitula Martini* (after 561) can. 23 (WEC 4:4679).

q. See Antioch (341) can. 2 (WEC 2:1948); Orleans I (511) can. 26 (WEC 4:4571); Orleans III (538) can. 32 (WEC 4:4612); Narbonne (589) can. 12 (WEC 4:4659).

[†] Canons translated from *Concilia Galliae de 511 à 695*, ed. C. de Clercq, CCL 148 A (Turnhout, 1963) 7–12.

a. See Epaon (517) can. 33 (WEC 4:4585); Saragossa II (592) can. 3 (WEC 4:4771).

b. See Angers (453) can. 5 (WEC 3:3153); Tours I (461) can. 8 (WEC 3:3159); Vannes (between 461 and 491) can. 3 (WEC 3:3160); Epaon (517) can. 23 (WEC 4:4579); Orleans III (538) can. 28 (WEC 4:4609); Toledo III (589) ser. 2 cap. 11 (WEC 4:4766).

with Catholics. Whoever after this prohibition eats with them is deprived of Communion.

Canon 12. A deacon or a presbyter who has sinned and is removed from Communion at the altar in order to do penance may, nevertheless, baptize anyone requesting baptism[c] provided no other ministers are present or if there is a case of true necessity.   4565

Canon 14. Renewed are the ancient canons whereby the bishop appropriates for himself half of the offerings placed on the altar [in the cathedral]; half is to be distributed to the various ranks of clerics.[d] [. . .]   4566

Canon 15. The decrees of the ancient canons are to be observed concerning what is given to the parishes from the fields, vineyards, private property, and possessions [outside the episcopal city]. These fall under the authority of the bishop. As to what is placed upon the altar [in the parish], a third is always given to the bishop.[e]   4567

Canon 16. To the extent that he is able, the bishop shall present food and clothing to the poor and to the sick who because of weakness can no longer do manual labor.   4568

Canon 24. Before Easter a *Quadragesima*[f] and not a *Quinquagesima* is to be observed.   4569

Canon 25. No one is to observe Easter, Christmas, or Pentecost on one's own estate [*villa*] unless forced by illness.[g]   4570

Canon 26. When they gather in the name of God to celebrate Mass, the people must not leave the church before the end of Mass[h] and, when a bishop is present, till they have received his blessing.   4571

Canon 27. All churches will celebrate the Rogations, namely, the litanies, before the Lord's Ascension so that the three-day fast concludes at the feast of the Ascension.[i] During these three days all male and female servants will be excused from labor so that all the people may easily assemble [for liturgical prayer]. Furthermore, on these three days all abstain and eat as they do during Lent.

---

c. See Elvira (ca. 300) can. 77 (WEC 2:1294); Dvin (527) can. 18 (WEC 4:4845).

d. See Orleans I (511) can. 15 (WEC 4:4567); Braga I (561) ser. 2 can. 21 (WEC 4:4754); Braga II (572) can. 6 (WEC 4:4759); Mâcon II (585) can. 4 (WEC 4:4654).

e. See Orleans I (511) can. 14 (WEC 4:4566); Braga I (561) ser. 2 can. 21 (WEC 4:4754); Braga II (572) can. 6 (WEC 4:4759); Mâcon II (585) can. 4 (WEC 4:4654).

f. See Saragossa (ca. 380) can. 2 (WEC 2:1295); Dvin (527) can. 29 (WEC 4:4851); Orleans IV (541) can. 2 (WEC 4:4616).

g. See Agde (506) can. 21 (WEC 4:4556); Epaon (517) can. 35 (WEC 4:4586); Clermont (535) can. 15 (WEC 4:4604); Orleans IV (541) can. 3 (WEC 4:4617); Lyons IV (583) can. 5 (WEC 4:4650).

h. See Antioch (341) can. 2 (WEC 2:1948); Agde (506) can. 47 (WEC 4:4562); Orleans III (538) can. 32 (WEC 4:4612); Narbonne (589) can. 12 (WEC 4:4659).

i. These three days are called the "minor litanies," an observance of fasting and prayer established by Mamertus, bishop of Vienne, in 470; see WEC 4:4314.

4573   Canon 28. Clerics who fail to be present for this holy work [the Rogations] will be punished according to the judgment of the bishop.

4574   Canon 31. Unless he is ill, the bishop must be present [for worship] in the church that is nearest him.

176-C. Synod of Epaon (517)[†]

Thirty-four bishops, including Avitus of Vienne (WEC 4:**167**), were present for this meeting, which probably began on September 6, 517, and lasted till September 15 of the same year. Forty canons were enacted at this gathering, which many consider as the most important French synod of the century. The precise location of Epaon, apparently somewhere in the Rhone Valley, cannot be determined.

CPL no. 1068 * Hefele (1905) 2.2:1031–42 * Hefele (1871) 4:107–14 * CATH 4:281–82 * DCA 1:614 * DDCon 2:45–46 * DHGE 15:524–45 * EEC 1:555

4575   Canon 3. A person who has done penance cannot become a cleric.[a]

4576   Canon 16. Due to the salvation of souls, a salvation we desire for all, we permit presbyters to aid with the chrismation[b] those hopeless and fallen heretics who seek immediate conversion. But if they are in good health, they should obtain this from the bishop.

4577   Canon 21. Widows are not to receive the consecration given to those who are called deaconesses since this consecration is henceforth abolished throughout our region.[c] They can receive the blessing given to penitents if they become such.

4578   Canon 22. If a presbyter or a deacon commits a mortal sin, he is to be deposed from his office, confined to a monastery where, for as long as he lives, he will receive Communion [as a lay person].

4579   Canon 23. Should a sinner have been admitted to the order of penitents and, forgetful of the good that has been received, return to worldly affairs, this person is not to be admitted to Communion unless he or she returns to the penance that was wrongfully interrupted.[d]

[†] Canons translated from CCL 148 A:25–34.

a. See Toledo I (400?) can. 2 (WEC 3:3168); *Statuta* (5th c.) can. 84 (WEC 3:3106); Agde (506) can. 43 (WEC 4:4560); Arles IV (524) can. 3 (WEC 4:4591); Orleans III (538) can. 6 (WEC 4:4605); *Capitula Martini* (after 561) can. 23 (WEC 4:4679).

b. See Laodicea (between 343 and 381) can. 7 (WEC 2:1960); Orange I (441) can. 1 (WEC 3:3123); Arles II (between 442 and 506) cans. 17, 26 (WEC 3:3145, 3148).

c. See Nicaea I (325) can. 19 (WEC 2:1456); Laodicea (between 343 and 381) can. 11 (WEC 2:1964); Nîmes (394) can. 2 (WEC 2:1226); *Statuta* (5th c.) can. 100 (WEC 3:3119); Orange I (441) can. 25 (WEC 3:3136); Chalcedon (451) can. 15 (WEC 3:3379); Dvin (527) can. 17 (WEC 4:4844); Orleans II (533) can. 18 (WEC 4:4600).

d. See Angers (453) can. 5 (WEC 3:3153); Tours I (461) can. 8 (WEC 3:3159); Vannes (between 461 and 491) can. 3 (WEC 3:3160); Orleans I (511) can. 11 (WEC 4:4564); Orleans III (538) can. 28 (WEC 4:4609); Toledo III (589) ser. 2 cap. 11 (WEC 4:4766).

Canon 25. The relics of the saints are not to be placed in private chapels 4580
unless there are clerics from a neighboring parish who can frequently
sing psalms over the holy remains. If such are lacking, none are to be appointed for this task till provision has been made for their adequate food
and clothing.

Canon 26. Only altars constructed of stone are to be dedicated, and this by 4581
anointing them with chrism.[e]

Canon 27. The bishops of the province are to follow the metropolitans in 4582
the arrangement of the divine offices.[f]

Canon 28. If a bishop dies before he has absolved those whom he has ex- 4583
communicated, his successor can do so provided such persons are amend-
ing their ways or are doing penance.[g]

Canon 29. As to the lapsed, that is, those who were baptized in the 4584
Catholic Church and who through detestable deceit have become heretics,
antiquity has deemed that it is only with great difficulty that they return.
We, however, shorten the number of years and impose a penance of two
years providing they observe the following: for two years they are to observe a strict fast on Tuesdays; they are to eagerly gather in church; they
are to practice humility by standing among and praying with the penitents; they are to leave the church when the catechumens are bidden to do
so. If they wish to do this, the appointed time before being admitted to the
altar will then be relaxed. But if they believe that this is too arduous and
difficult, then they should observe the precepts of the former canons.[h]

Canon 33. So greatly do we detest the churches of the heretics that we 4585
consider them incapable of being purified; they must never again be used
for sacred purposes. We can, however, reconcile churches that have been
taken from us by violence.[i]

Canon 35. Well-to-do citizens, no matter in which city they find them- 4586
selves, are to obtain the bishop's blessing at the Easter Vigil and at the
feast of the Lord's birth.[j]

---

e. See Irish Synod I (between 450 and 456) can. 23 (WEC 3:3178); Agde (506) can.
14 (WEC 4:4551); Orleans III (538) can. 16 (WEC 4:4607); Braga I (561) ser. 2 can. 19
(WEC 4:4752); Braga II (572) cans. 5– 6 (WEC 4:4758–59).

f. See Vannes (between 461 and 491) can. 15 (WEC 3:3164); Gerunda (517) can. 1
(WEC 4:4717); Braga I (561) ser. 2 can. 4 (WEC 4:4742).

g. See Elvira (ca. 300) can. 53 (WEC 2:1293).

h. See Elvira (ca. 300) can. 1 (WEC 2:1270); Ancyra (314) cans. 1–12 (WEC
2:1422–30); Nicaea I (325) cans. 8, 11, 14 (WEC 2:1449, 1451, 1454); Valence (374)
can. 3 (WEC 2:1225); Arles II (between 442 and 506) cans. 10–11 (WEC 3:3141–42).

i. See Orleans I (511) can. 10 (WEC 4:4563); Saragossa II (592) can. 3 (WEC
4:4771).

j. See Agde (506) can. 21 (WEC 4:4556); Orleans I (511) can. 25 (WEC 4:4570);
Clermont (535) can. 15 (WEC 4:4604); Orleans IV (541) can. 3 (WEC 4:4617); Lyons
IV (583) can. 5 (WEC 4:4650).

4587   Canon 36. No one is to be excluded from the Church without a remedy or a hope of forgiveness. No one who has done penance or has undergone conversion is to be denied access to the grace of returning. But if perhaps the danger of death is imminent, the appointed time of penance is to be shortened. If the sick person, having received Viaticum,[k] should recover, it is appropriate that the appointed time [for doing penance] be observed.

176-D. Synod of Lyons II (between 518 and 523)[†]

Under Archbishop Viventiolus eleven bishops gathered at Lyons sometime between 518 and 523. They issued six canons.

CPL no. 997° * Hefele (1905) 2.2:1042–46 * Hefele (1871) 4:114–16 * DDCon 2:283–84

4588   Canon 6. Following the view of the most glorious king, we have authorized this lenient modification, namely, that Stephen together with Palladia[a] may remain praying in church up to the prayer over the people, which is said after the gospel.

176-E. Synod of Arles IV (524)[††]

Held on June 6, 524, this synod was attended by thirteen bishops. Only four canons were enacted.

Hefele (1905) 2.2:1060–62 * Hefele (1871) 4:131–32 * CATH 1:838 * CE 1:727 * DCA 1:142 * DDCon 1:36 * EC 1:1950 * EEC 1:555

4589   Canon 1. [. . .] No bishop is to ordain a deacon before the latter is twenty-five. No layman is to be ordained a bishop or a presbyter unless his conversion[a] has preceded or he is thirty years old.[b]

---

k. See Elvira (ca. 300) cans. 1, 6, 7, 37, 47 (WEC 2:1270–72, 1284, 1290); Ancyra (314) cans. 16, 22 (WEC 2:1432, 1435); Nicaea I (325) can. 13 (WEC 2:1453); Rome (488) Letter 7, can. 3 (WEC 3:2959); *Statuta* (5th c.) cans. 20–21 (WEC 3:3077–78); Orange I (441) can. 3 (WEC 3:3125); Vaison (442) can. 2 (WEC 3:3137); Arles II (between 442 and 506) can. 28 (WEC 3:3149); Agde (506) can. 15 (WEC 4:4552); Orleans III (538) cans. 6, 28 (WEC 4:4605, 4609); *Capitula Martini* (after 561) can. 82 (WEC 4:4699); Gerunda (517) can. 9 (WEC 4:4722); Barcelona I (ca. 540) can. 9 (WEC 4:4732).

†Canon translated from CCL 148 A:40.

a. After the death of his wife, Stephen, an official in Burgundy, married his wife's sister Palladia. For this Stephen was excommunicated.

†† Canons translated from CCL 148 A:43–44.

a. Conversion: undertaking a life of asceticism or celibacy?

b. See Neo-Caesarea (ca. 320) can. 11 (WEC 2:1443); Hippo (393) *Brev. Hipp.* ser. 2 can. 1-b (WEC 2:881); Agde (506) can. 17 (WEC 4:4553); Orleans III (538) can. 6 (WEC 4:4605).

Canon 2. [. . .] No metropolitan is to confer the dignity of the episcopacy   4590
upon a layman; other bishops are not to confer the honor of the presbyterate or the diaconate upon anyone who has not undergone conversion for
at least a whole year.

Canon 3. No one should dare ordain to the above honors any person who   4591
has done penance,[c] anyone who has married twice, or any man who has
married a widow.[d] [. . .]

176-F. Synod of Vaison II (529)[†]

The eleven or twelve bishops who attended this meeting on November 5,
529, reviewed previous canons and issued five new ones.

Hefele (1905) 2.2:1110–15 * Hefele (1871) 4:169–70 * DCA 2:2010 * EEC 1:555 *
ODCC 1674

E. Bishop, "'Kyrie eleison': A Liturgical Consultation I," DR 18 (1899) 294–302. *
L. Beauduin, "Le concile de Vaison (529)," QLP 6 (1924) 177–85. * E. Griffe, "Trois
textes importants pour l'histoire du canon de la messe," BLE 6 ser. 59 (1958) 65–72.

Canon 1. According to a very worthwhile custom which we know is fol-   4592
lowed throughout Italy, the presbyters appointed to rural parishes receive
young readers who are unmarried. There they reside. The presbyters, spiritually nourishing them like good spiritual fathers, teach them the psalms,
have them meditate on the holy readings, and instruct them in the law of
the Lord so that they, the presbyters, might provide for themselves worthy
successors and from the Lord receive eternal rewards. Upon reaching maturity, those readers who due to weakness of the flesh desire to marry may
do so.

Canon 2. For the building up of all the churches and for the advantage   4593
of all the people, not only in the cities but in rural areas, presbyters have
the power to preach [God's] word. If due to sickness a presbyter cannot
preach, deacons can read aloud homilies written by the holy fathers; for if
deacons are worthy to read what Christ spoke in the Gospel, why should
they be considered unworthy to read in public the writings of the holy
fathers?

Canon 3. Both in the Apostolic See [Rome] as well as throughout the prov-   4594
inces of the whole East and of Italy the pleasing and very salutary custom
has been introduced that the *Kyrie eleison* is often said with great devotion
and feeling. It pleases us that in all our churches such a holy custom be
introduced at Matins, at Mass, and at Vespers. At all Masses, whether in

---

c. See Toledo I (400?) can. 2 (WEC 3:3168); *Statuta* (5th c.) can. 84 (WEC 3:3106);
Agde (506) can. 43 (WEC 4:4560); Epaon (517) can. 3 (WEC 4:4575); Orleans III (538)
can. 6 (WEC 4:4605).

d. See Angers (453) can. 11 (WEC 3:3156).

† Canons translated from CCL 148 A:78–80.

the morning or during Lent or at those commemorating the deceased, the "Holy, holy, holy" is to be said in the same arrangement as found in public Masses because such a holy, pleasing, and desirable utterance, even if it could be said day and night, is not able to cause disdain.

4595   Canon 4. The name of the pope—that is, whoever holds the apostolic chair—is to be read aloud in our churches.

4596   Canon 5. Because of the cunning of the heretics who deny that God's Son was not always with the Father but blasphemously hold that the Son had a temporal beginning, the *Sicut erat in principio* is said in all conclusions after the *Gloria* not only in Rome but also throughout the whole East and throughout Africa and Italy.[a] And so we desire that this be done in all our churches.

176-G. Synod of Orleans II (533)[†]

The twenty-one bishops and five metropolitans who gathered on June 23, 533, in Orleans enacted twenty-one canons.

Hefele (1905) 2.2:1130–35 * Hefele (1871) 4:185–88 * CE 11:318 * DDCon 3:247–48 * EEC 1:555

4597   Canon 3. No bishop is allowed to receive anything, under no pretext whatsoever, for ordaining bishops and other clerics.[a] [. . .]

4598   Canon 14. Clerics who neglect to carry out their office or who refuse to come to church when it is their turn[b] will be deposed of their dignity.

4599   Canon 16. No one is to be ordained as a priest or as a deacon who is illiterate or who does not know how to baptize.[c]

4600   Canon 18. Henceforth the diaconal blessing will not be conferred upon women because of the weakness of their condition.[d]

---

a. See Narbonne (589) can. 2 (WEC 4:4656); Toledo III (589) ser. 1 can. 14 (WEC 4:4763).

[†] Canons translated from CCL 148 A:99–101.

a. See *Chalcedon* (451) can. 2 (WEC 3:3378); Braga II (572) can. 3 (WEC 4:4756); Barcelona II (599) can. 1 (WEC 4:4772).

b. See *Statuta* (5th c.) can. 35 (WEC 3:3083); Toledo I (400?) can. 5 (WEC 3:3169); Irish Synod I (between 450 and 456) can. 7 (WEC 3:3173); Vannes (between 461 and 491) can. 14 (WEC 3:3163); Tarragona (516) can. 7 (WEC 4:4714); Orleans III (538) can. 15 (WEC 4:4606).

c. See Hippo (393) *Brev. Hipp.* ser. 2 can. 1-c (WEC 2:881); Narbonne (589) can. 11 (WEC 4:4658).

d. See Nicaea I (325) can. 19 (WEC 2:1456); Laodicea (between 343 and 381) can. 11 (WEC 2:1964); Nîmes (394) can. 2 (WEC 2:1226); *Statuta* (5th c.) can. 100 (WEC 3:3119); Orange I (441) can. 25 (WEC 3:3136); Chalcedon (451) can. 15 (WEC 3:3379); Epaon (517) can. 21 (WEC 4:4577); Dvin (527) can. 17 (WEC 4:4844).

176-H. Synod of Clermont (535)[†]

Held on November 8, 535, in Clermont-Ferrand under the presidency of Honoratus, the archbishop of Bourges, this synod was attended by fifteen bishops and issued sixteen canons.

Hefele (1905) 2:1139–42 * Hefele (1871) 4:190–92 * DDCon 1:292–93 * EEC 1:555

Canon 3. The bodies of the deceased are not to be wrapped in linen or in other sacred cloths.

4601

Canon 7. The body of a bishop when being taken for burial is not to be covered with the cloth that is used for the Body of the Lord; a holy veil used for this purpose, although honoring the body, soils the altar.

4602

Canon 8. Objects used for divine worship are not to be handed over for use at weddings; being soiled by contact with corrupt people and by the display of worldly dissipation, they appear unworthy of use during the holy mysteries.

4603

Canon 15. If a presbyter or a deacon has no canonical position, whether in the [episcopal] city or in a [rural] parish but resides on an estate, and if he leaves the oratory where he celebrates the holy mysteries, he is not to celebrate the principal feasts—Christmas, Easter, Pentecost, and the other major feasts—other than with his bishop in the city. Furthermore, all the more well-to-do citizens are to come into town to join the bishop on these feasts.[a] [. . .]

4604

176-I. Synod of Orleans III (538)[††]

The nineteen bishops present at this meeting in 538, probably on May 7, renewed former legislation and issued thirty-three new canons.

Hefele (1905) 2.2:1155–62 * Hefele (1871) 4:185–88 * CE 11:318 * DCA 2:1527 * DDCon 3:249–51 * EEC 1:555

Canon 6. A layman must not be ordained until a year after his conversion[a] nor until he has attained the legitimate age, twenty-five years for a deacon, and thirty years for a presbyter.[b] Constant care is to be taken regarding those to be ordained clerics. Not to be promoted to the orders listed

4605

[†] Canons translated from *Les canons des conciles mérovingiens*, vol. 1, trans. and ed. J. Gaudemet, SChr 353 (Paris, 1989) 212–19.

a. See Agde (506) can. 21 (WEC 4:4556); Orleans I (511) can. 25 (WEC 4:4570); Epaon (517) can. 35 (WEC 4:4586); Orleans IV (541) can. 3 (WEC 4:4617); Lyons IV (583) can. 5 (WEC 4:4650).

[††] Canons translated from CCL 148 A:116–26.

a. Conversion: undertaking a life of asceticism or celibacy?

b. See Neo-Caesarea (ca. 320) can. 11 (WEC 2:1443); Hippo (393) *Brev. Hipp.* ser. 2 can. 1-b (WEC 2:881); Agde (506) can. 17 (WEC 4:4553); Arles IV (524) can. 1 (WEC 4:4589).

above is a man who has married twice, or has married a widow,[c] or has done penance,[d] or whose body is deformed, or who at one time or another has been tormented [by the demons] in public. But if a bishop has acted contrary to these canons, the person who was ordained will be deprived of his office. And the bishop, because of his recklessness in ordaining, will not be allowed to celebrate the [holy] office for six months. Yet if the bishop dares to ordain within this period of time, he will be excluded from the love of all the brethren for a whole year. If a cleric or lay person has given false testimony concerning promotion to orders, and if due to the bishop's ignorance an illicit ordination was celebrated, that cleric or lay person is to be denied Communion for a year. However, Viaticum is not to be denied in the case of very serious sickness.[e]

4606 Canon 15 (14). Concerning the celebration of [the pontifical] Mass, at least on major feasts it is to begin at the third hour [9:00 A.M.] so that the priests, once Mass has concluded, might more easily gather at a suitable hour for Vespers, that is, during the evening since it is neither fitting nor proper that on such feasts priests be absent from the church during the evening offices.[f]

4607 Canon 16 (15). A bishop is not to rush into a diocese of another bishop to ordain clerics that are not his own[g] or to consecrate altars.[h] Should he do this, the person he has ordained is to be deposed; altars, however, remain as they are. Whoever transgresses this canon will not celebrate Mass for a year.

4608 Canon 27 (24). The blessing of penance is not to be granted to those who are young[i] nor to those who are married without the consent of the spouse[j] and only to those advanced in years.

---

c. See Angers (453) can. 11 (WEC 3:3156); Arles IV (524) can. 3 (WEC 4:4591).

d. See Toledo I (400?) can. 2 (WEC 3:3168); *Statuta* (5th c.) can. 84 (WEC 3:3106); Agde (506) can. 43 (WEC 4:4560); Epaon (517) can. 3 (WEC 4:4575); Arles IV (524) can. 3 (WEC 4:4591).

e. See Elvira (ca. 300) cans. 1, 6, 7, 37, 47 (WEC 2:1270–72, 1284, 1290); Ancyra (314) cans. 16, 22 (WEC 2:1432, 1435); Nicaea I (325) can. 13 (WEC 2:1453); Rome (488) Letter 7, can. 3 (WEC 3:2959); *Statuta* (5th c.) cans. 20–21 (WEC 3:3077–78); Orange I (441) can. 3 (WEC 3:3125); Vaison (442) can. 2 (WEC 3:3137); Arles II (between 442 and 506) can. 28 (WEC 3:3149); Agde (506) can. 15 (WEC 4:4552); Epaon (517) can. 36 (WEC 4:4587); *Capitula Martini* (after 561) can. 82 (WEC 4:4699); Gerunda (517) can. 9 (WEC 4:4722); Barcelona I (ca. 540) can. 9 (WEC 4:4732).

f. See *Statuta* (5th c.) can. 35 (WEC 3:3083); Toledo I (400?) can. 5 (WEC 3:3169); Irish Synod I (between 450 and 456) can. 7 (WEC 3:3173); Vannes (between 461 and 491) can. 14 (WEC 3:3163); Tarragona (516) can. 7 (WEC 4:4714); Orleans II (533) can. 14 (WEC 4:4598).

g. See Angers (453) can. 9 (WEC 3:3154).

h. See Irish Synod I (between 450 and 456) can. 23 (WEC 3:3178); Agde (506) can. 14 (WEC 4:4551); Epaon (517) can. 26 (WEC 4:4581); Braga I (561) ser. 2 can. 19 (WEC 4:4752); Braga II (572) cans. 5–6 (WEC 4:4758–59).

i. See Agde (506) can. 15 (WEC 4:4552).

j. See Arles II (between 442 and 506) can. 22 (WEC 3:3147).

Canon 28 (25). A person who after receiving the blessing of penance pre-   4609
sumes to return to a worldly life[k] or to military service is to be punished
by excommunication till the time of death when Viaticum is granted.

Canon 29 (26). According to the statutes of the Apostolic See no slave or   4610
farmer is to be admitted to ecclesiastical honors unless it is first evident
by testimony or writing that he has obtained his freedom. A bishop who
knows the condition of the one ordained and still proceeds with the ordination is not to celebrate Mass for a whole year.

Canon 31 (28). The people have been told that on the Lord's Day no trip   4611
is to be taken by means of horses or oxen or vehicles, that they are not to
prepare food, that they cannot do anything related to the cleanliness of the
person's house. Surely this pertains more to Judaism than to Christianity.
We decree that on the Lord's Day it is allowed to do what was formerly
permitted. As to work in the country, that is, ploughing, caring for the
vineyards [. . .], this is not to be done[l] so that people may more easily
come to church for the grace of prayer. Those engaging in such forbidden
works are to be punished not by lay authority but by the bishop.

Canon 32 (29). No member of the laity is to leave Mass before the Lord's   4612
Prayer has been said.[m] If a bishop is present, his blessing is to be awaited.
No one bearing weapons for war is to attend the morning or evening sacrifice of the Mass. Whoever dares to do so is to be subject to the power of
the bishop as to the manner of punishment.

Canon 33 (30). Because, God willing, we come under the power of   4613
Catholic kings, from Holy Thursday up to Easter Monday, that is, for four
days, Jews shall not dare to show themselves among Christians nor for
any reason associate with Catholics.[n]

Canon 34 (31). Subject to a year's excommunication is the judge of a city   4614
or place who knows that a heretic or a follower of Bonosius[o] or a priest
from any other heresy has rebaptized a person who is Catholic,[p] and who
does not immediately restrict the rebaptizer and—seeing that we have
Catholic kings—bring this person to the king where justice will thereupon
be administered, namely, a year's excommunication.

---

k. See Angers (453) can. 5 (WEC 3:3153); Tours I (461) can. 8 (WEC 3:3159); Vannes
(between 461 and 491) can. 3 (WEC 3:3160); Orleans I (511) can. 11 (WEC 4:4564);
Epaon (517) can. 23 (WEC 4:4579); Toledo III (589) ser. 2 cap. 11 (WEC 4:4766).

l. See Laodicea (between 343 and 381) can. 29 (WEC 2:1980); Auxerre (late 6th or
early 7th c.) can. 16 (WEC 4:4640); Mâcon II (585) can. 1 (WEC 4:4651); Narbonne
(589) can. 4 (WEC 4:4657).

m. See Antioch (341) can. 2 (WEC 2:1948); Agde (506) can. 47 (WEC 4:4562); Orleans I (511) can. 26 (WEC 4:4571); Narbonne (589) can. 12 (WEC 4:4659).

n. See Mâcon I (581/583) can. 14 (WEC 4:4649).

o. Bonosius: a fourth-century bishop of Sardica whose followers were accused of
various trinitarian and christological errors.

p. See Carthage (345–48) can. 1 (WEC 2:874–75); Toledo III (589) ser. 1 can. 15
(WEC 4:4764).

176-J. Synod of Orleans IV (541)[†]

A wide representation of Gallican bishops was present for this meeting, which occurred on May 14, 541. Thirty-eight canons, several recalling past legislation, were enacted.

Hefele (1905) 2.2:1164–74 * Hefele (1871) 4.2:210–15 * CE 11:318 * DCA 2:2527 * DDC 3:251–53 * EEC 1:556

4615   Canon 1. Easter is to be celebrated by all bishops at the same time[a] and according to the table of Victorius.[b] Each year on Epiphany the date of Easter is to be announced to the people in church.[c] As often as there is any doubt regarding the feast, the metropolitan shall consult with the Apostolic See as to a decision.

4616   Canon 2. In all churches Lent is to be observed in the same manner;[d] no bishop is to allow a *Quinquagesima* or a *Sexagesima* before Easter. On Saturday all who are not sick are to observe the Lenten fast;[e] only on Sunday may one eat.[f] The statutes of the fathers have especially decreed this. Those breaking this rule will be rebuked by the bishop as transgressors of discipline.

4617   Canon 3. Should any of the more well-to-do members of the laity desire to observe Easter outside the [bishop's] city, they should know that the synod forbids this.[g] They are to observe the principal feasts in the presence of the bishop where there is a [cathedral] church. However, if necessity does not allow this, they can request leave from the bishop [to be absent]. [. . .]

[†] Canons translated from CCL 148 A:132–34.

a. See Nicaea I (325) (WEC 2:1459); Antioch (341) can. 1 (WEC 2:1947); Hippo (393) *Brev. Hipp.* ser. 1 can. 1 (WEC 2:880); Carthage V (401) can. 73 (WEC 3:2747); *Statuta* (5th c.) can. 78 (WEC 3:3103).

b. Victorius of Aquitaine in 457 composed a table for determining the date of Easter. It is found in *Monumenta Germaniae Historica, Auctores Antiquissimi*, 9, 1, 677–735.

c. See Auxerre (late 6th or early 7th c.) can. 2 (WEC 4:4630); Braga II (572) can. 9 (WEC 4:4761).

d. See Saragossa (ca. 380) can. 2 (WEC 2:1295); Orleans I (511) can. 24 (WEC 4:4569); Dvin (527) can. 29 (WEC 4:4851).

e. See Elvira (ca. 300) can. 26 (WEC 2:1276); Agde (506) can. 12 (WEC 4:4549); Dvin (527) can. 38 (WEC 4:4853).

f. See Saragossa (ca. 380) can. 2 (WEC 2:1295); Gangra (ca. 345) can. 18 (WEC 2:1955); *Statuta* (5th c.) can. 77 (WEC 3:3102); Agde (506) can. 12 (WEC 4:4549); Braga I (561) ser. 1 can. 4 (WEC 4:4737); *Capitula Martini* (after 561) can. 57 (WEC 4:4692).

g. See Agde (506) can. 21 (WEC 4:4556); Orleans I (511) can. 25 (WEC 4:4570); Epaon (517) can. 35 (WEC 4:4586); Clermont (535) can. 15 (WEC 4:4604); Lyons IV (583) can. 5 (WEC 4:4650).

Canon 4. In the offering of the holy chalice only wine mixed with water   4618
will be offered because it is judged sacrilegious to offer anything other
than what the Lord established by his most holy commands.[h]

Canon 5. A bishop is to be consecrated in the city in which his election to   4619
ordination took place and in the church over which he is to be in charge.
Clearly if the necessity of time does not allow this, although it is better
for him to be ordained in his own church, yet either in the presence of the
metropolitan or certainly with his authority, he is at least to be ordained
within his own province and by his fellow bishops.

Canon 8. As to those who, after receiving the sacrament of baptism, yield   4620
to bodily desires, fall into heresy, and, recognizing their guilt, wish to return to the unity of the Catholic faith, it is within the power of the bishop,
once he sees that they have done a fitting penance, to determine when and
how they are to be restored to their former communion.

176-K. Synod of Lyons III (between 567 and 570)[†]

This meeting, attended by two metropolitans and six bishops, produced
six canons.

Hefele (1905) 3.1:182–84 * Hefele (1871) 4:387–88 * DDCon 2:284–85

Canon 6. During the first week of the ninth month [November], before   4621
its first Sunday, all churches and parishes shall henceforth observe the
litanies[a] just as, according to the decree of the fathers, they are observed
before the feast of the Ascension.[b]

176-L. Synod of Tours II (567)[††]

Nine bishops, meeting on November 17, 567, in the Basilica of Saint Martin in Tours, issued twenty-seven canons.

Hefele (1905) 3.1:184–93 * Hefele (1871) 4:388–94 * DCA 2:1990 * EEC 1:556

Canon 3. The Lord's Body[a] shall be placed on the altar not in a figurative   4622
fashion but in the form of a cross.

Canon 4. Whether during vigils or during Mass the laity should not pre-   4623
sume to stand among the clergy next to the altar where the holy mysteries

---

h. See Hippo (393) *Brev. Hipp.* ser. 2 can. 23-a (WEC 2:886); Auxerre (late 6th or
early 7th c.) can. 8 (WEC 4:4633).

† Canon translated from CCL 148 A:202.

a. See Gerunda (517) can. 3 (WEC 4:4719).

b. See Orleans I (511) can. 27 (WEC 4:4572).

†† Canons translated from CCL 148 A:178–92.

a. Namely, the various parts of the consecrated bread that has been broken.

are being celebrated.[b] The space between the railings [*cancellis*] is for the choir of clerics who chant the psalms. As is customary, for prayer and for [receiving] Communion the sanctuary [*sancta sanctorum*] is open to men and to women.

4624   Canon 18 (17). As to the fasts observed by the monks, the old regulations shall continue. From Easter to Pentecost, with the exception of the Rogations, a prandium[c] shall be prepared daily for them. After Pentecost they will fast completely for one whole week, and then till 1 August they will fast three times a week, on Monday, Wednesday, and Friday, except for the sick. In August there shall be a prandium daily because each day there are Masses of the saints. Throughout September, October, and November, they will fast three times a week as was said before, but in December there is to be a daily fast till Christmas.[d] From Christmas to Epiphany there shall be daily prandium because every day is a feast except during the three days at the beginning of January, during which our fathers, to oppose heathen customs, ordered special litanies so that psalms are sung in church, and at the eighth hour on the calends the Mass of the circumcision, God willing, is celebrated. From Epiphany to Lent they are to fast three times a week.

4625   Canon 19 (18). Out of honor and reverence to Saint Martin in this holy basilica as well as in all our churches, the following pattern for singing the psalms will be followed: during summer there will be six antiphons with two psalms each; during August there will be *manicationes* [quicker formulas?] since there are feasts and Masses; in September there are seven antiphons with two psalms each; in October eight antiphons with three psalms each; in November nine antiphons with three psalms each; in December ten antiphons with three psalms each; the same number in January and February till Easter; but according to individual abilities, there may be more or less. Furthermore, at least twelve psalms are appointed for Matins as prescribed by the fathers. At the sixth hour there are six psalms with Alleluias, and at the twelfth hour [*Duodecima*] there are twelve psalms also with Alleluias, which was known to the fathers through the revelation of an angel. If there are twelve psalms at the twelfth hour, why not at least twelve at Matins? Whoever says less than twelve psalms at Matins should fast till evening; he is to remain on bread and water; no other food may be taken. Whoever fails to do this is to fast for one week, every day till evening when bread and water may be taken.

4626   Canon 20 (19). [. . .] A priest who has intercourse with his wife, or a deacon with his wife, or a subdeacon with his wife, is excommunicated for a year, deposed from his clerical office, and placed among the laity.

---

b. See Laodicea (between 343 and 381) can. 44 (WEC 2:1990); Braga I (561) ser. 2 can. 13 (WEC 4:4748); *Capitula Martini* (after 561) can. 42 (WEC 4:4681).

c. Namely, a meal taken at midday.

d. See Mâcon I (581/583) can. 9 (WEC 4:4647).

With permission he may take a place among the readers in the choir of singers. [. . .]

Canon 23 (22). [. . .] There are those who on the feast of the chair of Saint Peter offer food to the dead and, returning home after Mass, revert to the errors of the heathens;[e] after having received the Lord's Body they receive the devil's consecrated food. [. . .] **4627**

Canon 24 (23). Although we have ambrosian works [hymns] in our canon, there are, however, others which in form are worthy to be sung; we wish to freely receive them, the names of their authors having been written down with their titles. Style is not to exclude what comes from faith.[f] **4628**

176-M. Synod of Auxerre (late 6th or early 7th century)[†]

This diocesan synod, presided over by Bishop Aunacarius and occurring sometime between 561 and 605, issued forty-five canons.

Hefele (1905) 3.1:214–21 * Hefele (1871) 4:409–14 * CE 2:145 * DCA 1:154 * DHGE 5:958 * DTC 1.2:2622 * EC 2:504 * EEC 1:556

Canon 1. On the calends of January [1 January] no one is to dress like a cow or a stag, nor is anyone to engage in diabolical practices;[a] on this day one may give only what is given on other days. **4629**

Canon 2. Before Epiphany all presbyters are to send their messengers [to the bishop]; they will inform the presbyters as to when Lent will begin; on Epiphany this will be indicated to the people.[b] **4630**

Canon 3. It is not permitted to sacrifice in private homes[c] or to hold vigils [in church] on feasts of the saints. [. . .] **4631**

Canon 6. About the middle of Lent presbyters are to ask for the chrism[d] and, if illness prevents one from doing this, the task is entrusted to the archdeacon or to the archsubdeacon. The chrism is carried in a *chrismarium* with a linen cloth just as one carries the remains of the saints. **4632**

---

e. See Laodicea (between 343 and 381) can. 39 (WEC 2:1988); Auxerre (late 6th or early 7th c.) can. 1 (WEC 4:4629).

f. See Laodicea (between 343 and 381) can. 59 (WEC 2:2002); Braga I (561) ser. 2 can. 12 (WEC 4:4747); *Capitula Martini* (after 561) can. 67 (WEC 4:4696).

† Canons translated from CCL 148 A:265–69.

a. See Laodicea (between 343 and 381) can. 39 (WEC 2:1988); Tours II (567) can. 23 (WEC 4:4627).

b. See Carthage V (401) can. 73 (WEC 3:2747); Orleans IV (541) can. 1 (WEC 4:4615); Braga II (572) can. 9 (WEC 4:4761).

c. See Laodicea (between 343 and 381) can. 58 (WEC 2:2001); Dvin (527) can. 16 (WEC 4:4843).

d. See *Statuta* (5th c.) can. 87 (WEC 3:3108); Toledo I (400?) can. 20 (WEC 3:3172); Vaison (442) can. 3 (WEC 3:3138); *Capitula Martini* (after 561) can. 51 (WEC 4:4686); Braga II (572) can. 4 (WEC 4:4757); Barcelona II (599) can. 2 (WEC 4:4773).

4633   Canon 8. At the divine sacrifice on the altar it is not permitted to offer
wine mixed with honey, which is called *mulsa*, or any liquid other than
wine mixed with water because it is a great sin for a presbyter to offer
anything other than wine consecrating Christ's Blood.[e]

4634   Canon 9. It is not permitted for choirs of the laity or of young girls to sing
in church; nor are banquets to be prepared in church, for "My house will
be called a house of prayer."[1]

4635   Canon 10. It is not permitted to celebrate two Masses on the same day at
the same altar. Nor is a presbyter, once a bishop has celebrated, allowed to
celebrate Mass on the same day and at the same altar.

4636   Canon 11. On the vigil of Easter it is not permitted to complete the vigil
before the second hour of the night [7:00 P.M.] because on that night it is
not permitted to drink [till] after midnight; the same is true for the Lord's
Nativity and other feasts.[f]

4637   Canon 12. Neither the Eucharist[g] nor the kiss may be given to the deceased; nor are their bodies to be covered with a veil or a cloth [*pallas*].

4638   Canon 13. The deacon is not to cover his shoulders with a veil or a cloth
[*pallas*].

4639   Canon 14. No dead body may be buried in the baptistery.[h]

4640   Canon 16. On Sunday it is forbidden to harness oxen and do other such
labor.[i]

4641   Canon 18. It is not permitted to baptize at any time other than on the feast
of Easter;[j] the only exception would be those who are seriously ill or in
danger of death, those called *grabatorii*. But if some carry their infants into
another district to have them baptized there, they [parents and children]
are not to be received in our churches; any presbyter who receives them
without our permission will be separated from communion with the
Church for three months.

4642   Canon 19. A presbyter, deacon, or subdeacon who has taken food or drink[k]
is not to serve at Mass or to be in the church during Mass.

---

e. See Hippo (393) *Brev. Hipp.* ser. 2 can. 23-a (WEC 2:886); Orleans IV (541) can. 4
(WEC 4:4618).

f. The meaning of this canon is not clear; see Hefele (1871) 2:411–13.

g. See Hippo (393) *Brev. Hipp.* ser. 2 can. 4 (WEC 2:883).

h. See Dvin (527) can. 21 (WEC 4:4848); Braga I (561) can. 18 (WEC 4:4751).

i. See Laodicea (between 343 and 381) can. 29 (WEC 2:1980); Orleans III (538) can.
31 (WEC 4:4611); Mâcon II (585) can. 1 (WEC 4:4651); Narbonne (589) can. 4 (WEC
4:4657).

j. See Laodicea (between 343 and 381) can. 45 (WEC 2:1991); Irish Synod II (after
456) can. 19 (WEC 3:3180); Agde (506) can. 13 (WEC 4:4550); Gerunda (517) can. 4
(WEC 4:4720); Mâcon II (585) can. 3 (WEC 4:4653); *Capitula Martini* (after 561) can.
49 (WEC 4:4684).

k. See Hippo (393) *Brev. Hipp.* ser. 2 can. 28 (WEC 2:887); Dvin (527) can. 24 (WEC
4:4850); Braga II (572) can. 10 (WEC 4:4762); Mâcon II (585) can. 6 (WEC 4:4655).

1. Isa 56:7; Matt 21:13.

Canon 25. No abbot or monk is to be a godfather at baptism.　4643

Canon 36. Women are not to receive the Eucharist with an uncovered hand.　4644

Canon 37. Women are not to touch the Lord's pall.[1]　4645

176-N. Synod of Mâcon I (581/583)[†]

The twenty-one bishops attending this meeting on November 1 in either 581 or 583 enacted nineteen canons.

Hefele (1905) 3.1:202–5 * Hefele (1871) 4:403–5 * CE 9:507 * DACL 10.1:751 * DCA 2:1070 * DDCon 3:2

Canon 6. An archbishop may not celebrate Mass without the *pallium*.[a]　4646

Canon 9. From the feast of Saint Martin till the Nativity of the Lord a fast　4647
is to be observed on Monday, Wednesday, and Friday.[b] Mass is to be celebrated as during Lent. [. . .]

Canon 10. Presbyters, deacons, and all other clerics are to be devotedly　4648
subject to the bishop and are not to hold or celebrate feasts other than in the service of the bishop. [. . .]

Canon 14. According to a decree of the fondly remembered King Childe-　4649
bert, from Holy Thursday till Easter permission is denied the Jews to walk on the streets or in the squares[c] as if to insult us Christians. [. . .]

176-O. Synod of Lyons IV (583)[††]

Under the presidency of Priscus, the archbishop of Lyons, seven bishops gathered on May 22, 583, and issued six canons.

Hefele (1905) 3.1:206–7 * Hefele (1871) 4:406 * DDCon 2:285–86

Canon 5. Unless afflicted with illness or having been ordered otherwise　4650
by the king, the bishop will always celebrate the Nativity of the Lord and Easter in his own church.[a]

176-P. Synod of Mâcon II (585)[†††]

Forty-three bishops gathered in Mâcon on October 23, 585, in a type of French national council and issued twenty canons.

---

1. Pall: a cloth placed on the altar and used to cover the bread and cup.

[†] Canons translated from CCL 148 A:224–26.

a. *Pallium*: a woolen band worn over the shoulder; see DACL 13:1 (1937) 935–36.

b. See Tours II (567) can. 18 (WEC 4:4624).

c. See Orleans III (538) can. 33 (WEC 4:4613).

[††] Canon translated from CCL 148 A:232.

a. See Agde (506) can. 21 (WEC 4:4556); Orleans I (511) can. 25 (WEC 4:4570); Epaon (517) can. 35 (WEC 4:4586); Clermont (535) can. 15 (WEC 4:4604); Orleans IV (541) can. 3 (WEC 4:4617).

[†††] Translated from CCL 148 A:239–42.

Hefele (1905) 3.1:208–14 * Hefele (1871) 4:406–9 * CATH 8:123 * CE 9:507 * DACL 10.1:751–52 * DDCon 3:2–6 * EEC 1:556

L. Beauduin, "La liturgie pascale," QLP 2 (1911–12) 293–304.

4651 Canon 1. We see the Christian people rashly treating with contempt the Lord's Day; they do what they are accustomed to do on other days. Therefore by means of this synodal letter we have decided that each one of us should, in our holy churches, warn those who are subject to us. Those who heed our warning will profit; but if they do not listen, they will be subject to the penalties defined by us under divine inspiration. Therefore all of you, being Christians who do not bear this name in vain, listen to our warning, knowing that it is our responsibility to watch out for your welfare and to keep you from doing what is evil. Observe the Lord's Day, a day that has given us rebirth and has freed us from our sins. May no one of you stir up disputes; may no one of you bring anyone to court; may no one imagine a necessity that requires you to put a yoke on the necks of oxen.[a] Pay attention in soul and in body to God's hymns and praises. If you find yourself close to a church, hurry there, and on the Lord's Day devote yourself to prayer and tears. On that day may your eyes and hands be lifted up toward God. The Lord's Day is the perpetual day of rest that was signified by the Law and the prophets under the figure of the seventh day. And so it is right that we celebrate this day together, a day through which we have become what we were not. Once we were slaves of sin; thanks to this day we have become children of justice. May we show our free servitude to the Lord by whose mercy we know we were saved from the prison of error, not that our Lord requires us to celebrate Sunday with bodily abstinence; he seeks obedience through which, our earthly actions crushed underfoot, he mercifully leads us to heaven. If any of you think little of this exhortation or hold it in disdain, then, as you know, you will first be punished by God as you merit, and then, implacably, you will be subject to the wrath of the bishop. If such a person is a lawyer, may he forever lose his argument. If he is a country person or a slave, he will be whipped severely. If he is a cleric or a monk, for six months he will not associate with his brothers. All these, on the one hand, render God's spirit favorable toward us and, on the other hand, remove and repel the blows of sickness and sterility. Even the night which leads us to the inaccessible light inspired from above, we use for spiritual vigils, and at that time we do not sleep as do those who are Christians in name only, but we pray and watch in holy doings that we be found worthy to inherit the kingdom of the Savior.

4652 Canon 2. Therefore our Pasch, on which our sinless high priest and pontiff was sacrificed for our sins, we are all to celebrate as a great feast. We are to

---

a. See Laodicea (between 343 and 381) can. 29 (WEC 2:1980); Orleans III (538) can. 31 (WEC 4:4611); Auxerre (late 6th or early 7th c.) can. 16 (WEC 4:4640); Narbonne (589) can. 4 (WEC 4:4657).

venerate it most zealously in every way so that during these six most holy days no one dares to do any work, but, gathered as one and intent upon singing the paschal hymns, we will assiduously be present at the daily sacrifice, praising our Creator who gave us rebirth, giving praise in the evening, in the morning, and at midday.

Canon 3. We learn from our brethren that some Christian people, not ob-   4653
serving the appointed day for baptism,[b] baptize their children on other days and on the feasts of martyrs so that on the holy day of Easter there are only two or three who will be regenerated by water and the Holy Spirit. Consequently we have decided that no one shall henceforth be permitted to commit such an abuse. Exceptions are parents desiring to have their children baptized because of a child's serious illness or approaching death. For this reason we require that all parents, now urged to leave behind their errors and ignorance, are to be present in church on the first Sunday of Lent with their children; having received the imposition of the hand on appointed days and having been anointed with holy oil,[c] may these children rejoice in the festivities of the appointed day and be regenerated by holy baptism which, if their lives be good, allows them to do priestly things and participate at each solemn celebration.

Canon 4. Participating in this holy council, we have learned from the report   4654
of our brothers that in some places certain Christians are so removed from God's law that none of them wish to carry out the legitimate obligation of obeying God in that they bring no offering to the holy altar. For this reason we decree that on all Sundays the offering upon the altar be presented by all, men and women, both the bread and the wine, so that by these sacrifices they may be freed from the burden of their sins and merit to be associated with Abel and with others who rightly present an offering. [. . .]

Canon 6. We likewise decree that no priest gorged with food or drunk   4655
with wine be allowed to touch the consecrated species [sacrificia] or celebrate Mass on ordinary days or on feasts; it is not right that bodily food be preferred to spiritual good. Whoever attempts to violate this rule will lose his dignity and rank. In fact the councils of Africa have already made a decision in similar matter, and we have judged it appropriate to join their decision to our own: "Except on Holy Thursday the sacraments are only celebrated by those who are fasting."[d] As to the remains of the consecrated species that remain in the sacristy once Mass has been completed, on

---

b. See Laodicea (between 343 and 381) can. 45 (WEC 2:1991); Irish Synod II (after 456) can. 19 (WEC 3:3180); Agde (506) can. 13 (WEC 4:4550); Gerunda (517) can. 4 (WEC 4:4720); Auxerre (late 6th or early 7th c.) can. 18 (WEC 4:4641); *Capitula Martini* (after 561) can. 49 (WEC 4:4684).

c. See Rome (ca. 400?) can. 11 (WEC 3:2958).

d. Hippo (393) *Brev. Hipp.* ser. 2 can. 28 (WEC 2:887). See also Dvin (527) can. 24 (WEC 4:4850); Auxerre (late 6th or early 7th c.) can. 19 (WEC 4:4642); Braga II (572) can. 10 (WEC 4:4762).

Wednesday and Friday some young boys [*innocentes*] are led to the church by the person in charge, and having observed the fast, they receive what remains, this being moistened with wine.

176-Q. Synod of Narbonne (589)⁺

Held on November 1, 589, at Narbonne in southern France, this Visigothic synod issued fifteen canons.

Hefele (1905) 3.1:228–30 * Hefele (1871) 4:422–23 * DACL 12.1:830–31 * DCA 2:1377–78 * DDCon 3:153 * EEC 1:556

4656   Canon 2. It is decreed that in singing the psalms the *Gloria Patri* is to be said after each psalm; longer psalms are to be divided, and the *Gloria Patri* is to be sung after each section.ᵃ

4657   Canon 4. No one, whether a slave or free, [. . .] will do any work on the Lord's Day or will yoke oxen other than in cases of necessity.ᵇ Whoever presumes to do so will, if a free person, pay the city judge six gold pieces; if the culprit is a serf, a hundred lashes will be administered.

4658   Canon 11. The bishop is not to ordain any illiterate person to the diaconate or the presbyterate, but if such a person was ordained, he is to be forced to learn.ᶜ [. . .]

4659   Canon 12. [. . .] When Mass is being celebrated, no presbyter or deacon, except in cases of illness, is to leave the altar till Mass is completed.ᵈ Neither a deacon nor a subdeacon nor a reader is to remove the alb before the end of Mass. [. . .]

4660   Canon 13. According to the canons, subdeacons, doorkeepers [*ostiarii*] and other ministers are to carry out their ecclesial duties with zeal. They are to raise the curtains at the door for their superiors. [. . .]

177. INSCRIPTION. MAINZ BAPTISTERY⁺⁺

This inscription, found among the works of Venantius Fortunatus (WEC 4:**173**), decorated a baptistery in Mainz.

⁺ Canons translated from CCL 148 A:254–56.

a. See Vaison II (529) can. 5 (WEC 4:4596); Toledo III (589) ser. 1 can. 14 (WEC 4:4763).

b. See Laodicea (between 343 and 381) can. 29 (WEC 2:1980); Orleans III (538) can. 31 (WEC 4:4611); Auxerre (late 6th or early 7th c.) can. 16 (WEC 4:4640); Mâcon II (585) can. 1 (WEC 4:4651).

c. See Hippo (393) *Brev. Hipp.* ser. 2 can. 1-c (WEC 2:881).

d. See Antioch (341) can. 2 (WEC 2:1948); Agde (506) can. 47 (WEC 4:4562); Orleans I (511) can. 26 (WEC 4:4571); Orleans III (538) can. 32 (WEC 4:4612).

⁺⁺ Translation from J. Daniélou, *The Bible and the Liturgy* (London, 1960) 36. The original citation is found in L. de Bruyne, "La décoration des baptistières paléochrétiens," in *Miscellanea Liturgica in Honorem L.C. Mohlberg*, vol. 1 (Rome, 1948) 198ff.

The hall of holy baptism, so difficult to enter, now is shining. Here it is   4661
that Christ washes away in the river the sin of Adam.

IBERIA

178. BRAULIO OF SARAGOSSA

Braulio, a student, friend, and correspondent of Isidore of Seville (ca. 560–636), was bishop of Saragossa 631–51.

Among his forty-four letters is one that concerns the liturgy of Christian initiation. It is a response to a letter written to Braulio by Eugene, once Braulio's archdeacon, who became bishop of Toledo 646–57.

CPL nos. 1230ff. * Altaner (1966) 497 * CATH 2:234–36 * CE 2:744–45 * DCB 1:333 * DHGE 10:441–53 * DictSp 1:1925–26 * DPAC 1:557 * DTC 2.1:1123–24 * EC 3:47 * EEC 1:127 * LTK 2:658–59 * NCE 2:760 * NCES 2:585–86

C. Lynch, *Saint Braulio, Bishop of Saragossa (631–651): His Life and Writings* (Washington, D.C., 1938). * T.C. Akeley, *Christian Initiation in Spain c. 300–1100* (London, 1967) 75–76.

178-A. Letters

178-A-1. LETTER FROM EUGENE TO BRAULIO[†]

I. Two things have occurred in my church that greatly distress me, and   4662
all I can do is seek your counsel. We have learned that there is a man who
acts as if he were a priest even though he has not received this office. To
apprise you of the particulars, I now present the details.

This man was most troublesome to my lord Eugene.[a] The king asked   4663
Eugene to ordain this man a presbyter. Since the bishop could not refuse
the monarch's request, he came up with a deception. Eugene led the man
to the altar but did not impose his hand. While the clerics were vigorously
singing, he pronounced a malediction rather than a blessing. This the
bishop later acknowledged to some of his dear and trusted friends, entreating them to remain silent about this during his lifetime.

Now I ask that you immediately tell me what I should do. Is he to be   4664
considered a priest? Are those whom he has baptized and anointed with
chrism[b] rightly called Christians?

II. [. . .] I have learned that in some places deacons anoint with the   4665
chrism. I am at a loss as to what we should do regarding those who have
been anointed by such deacons. Is the anointing with the holy chrism to

---

[†] Translated from PL 87:403.

a. Eugene: namely, Eugene I, bishop of Toledo 636–46.

b. The precise nature of this postbaptismal rite is debated. See C. Lynch, *Saint Braulio*, 89–94.

be repeated? If not repeated, is the oil to be considered as chrism, something perhaps done under pressure or out of ignorance. I request that your
piety inform me as to what action I should take here.

4666   III. Furthermore, some presbyters, contrary to the law and the ancient
canons, presume to sign the baptized with the chrism—if it can be called
"chrism"—that they themselves have prepared. To be sure, I do not know
what remedy to apply or how to correct the situation in regard to those
who have been so signed. Consequently I ask you to enlighten me in this
matter. [. . .]

178-A-2. LETTER OF BRAULIO TO EUGENE†

4667   II. [. . .] In your letter you wrote that in your church there are two
situations that disturb you and concerning which you don't know what to
do.

4668   You wrote about a certain man who, not having received the presbyteral rank, nonetheless functions as a presbyter. Explaining this, you say
that he was troublesome to your predecessor who, asked by the king to
ordain him a presbyter, did so because he did not wish to refuse this royal
request. And so, to use your words, he devised this deception. Leading
the man to the altar, your predecessor did not impose the hand upon him.
During the loud singing by the clerics the bishop said a malediction, not
a blessing. Your predecessor later acknowledged this to some of his dear
and trusted friends, entreating them to remain silent about this.

4669   And so you requested that I consider what you should do in these
circumstances since you do not know whether he should be considered
a presbyter and whether those whom he anointed with chrism should
rightly be called Christians.

4670   III. You requested that I, despite my ignorance in practical matters,
might solve the question. [. . .] Inquire of the man over whom the malediction was spoken whether he ever carried out the presbyteral office in
the presence of the bishop. Or was he prohibited from doing so by the
bishop? Ask whether he baptized, anointed with chrism, offered the sacrifice—being allowed to do so by the bishop who gave the malediction.

4671   In my opinion the person to be blamed is not the presbyter but the
bishop who engaged in deceit by acting fraudulently. And so it seems to
me that whoever acts badly "will bear the burden." Your holiness will
be exempt from this sin because you allow all to remain in the calling in
which you found them.[1] Why should he not be considered a presbyter
if he who did not want him to be a priest recognized him as a priest? Or
why should those whom he anointed with chrism not be called Christians
because even if the one who gives the anointing is unworthy, nonetheless,
they have still been anointed with true chrism?

---

† Translated from PL 87:407–10.

1. See 1 Cor 7:20.

Your prudence is aware that according to the ancient canons a presby- 4672
ter was not allowed to anoint with chrism. This, as we know, has been
observed in the East and throughout Italy. Later on, however, presbyters
were permitted to anoint with chrism but only with chrism blessed by
the bishop. The reason here is that the presbyters not appear to have as
their own the privilege of consecrating God's people. They do so with the
blessing and permission of the bishop acting, as it were, by the hand of the
bishop. Since this is so, is there any reason why those anointed by such a
priest, although unworthy, not be considered Catholics, being anointed
as if by the hand of the bishop since, as I said, they were anointed by the
holy and true chrism made holy by the bishop? Obviously baptism given
in the name of the Trinity is not to be repeated. Yet we are not prohibited
from using chrism to anoint heretics whom we learn did not receive a true
chrismal anointing. As I said, this priest anointed them with real chrism. I
do not believe that what he did is useless.

iv. Even more, the bishop who allowed him to function never spoke out 4673
against him. The bishop did not hesitate to hand over to him the chrism
that he himself sanctified. And thus the bishop himself did what was done
by the other. What difference does it make whether something is done
as circumstances permit or as truth requires? Because the anointing was
given in the Catholic Church, it is not to be repeated.

vii. [. . .] There is also the matter of certain priests who prepare the 4674
chrism—if it can be called "chrism"—and presume to sign the baptized
with it. I indeed confess that what, contrary to law and the ancient canons,
seems to have been consecrated by presumptuous presbyters and not by
any bishop is doubtfully consecrated. For if the heavenly Teacher and Lord
gave us bishops as his substitutes, then what they established is established
by the spirit of Christ, as the apostle says.[2] If any reject their precepts, they
reject Christ's precepts. And so it seems to me that those who have fraudulently been anointed should again be signed with the holy and true chrism.
The punishment of the guilty is left to your discretion; it is one thing to correct those who err, another to condemn those who are guilty. [. . .]

179. MARTIN OF BRAGA

Born in 515 in the Roman province of Pannonia, Martin spent his early
years as a monk in Palestine. Ordained a presbyter ca. 550, he went to Gallaecia (today in northwest Spain), where he established a monastery at
Dumio, becoming its first abbot and eventually bishop of the place. Before
572 he was made bishop of Braga (Bracara) in northern Portugal, where he
undertook to convert the Suevians from Arianism to orthodoxy.

Well educated in the writings of the Church Fathers and an admirer
of the Roman philosopher Seneca (ca. 4 B.C.–65 A.D.), Martin, who

---

2. See Acts 20:28.

presided at the Council of Braga (WEC 4:**180-G**), has left us only a rela-tively small number of literary and pastoral works, including some catechetical tracts, various moral and spiritual treatises together with two poems.

CPL nos. 1079ff. * Altaner (1961) 592–93 * Altaner (1966) 492–93 * Bardenhewer (1908) 658–60 * Bardenhewer (1910) 566–67 * Bardenhewer (1913) 5:379–88 * Bardy (1930) 209–10 * Bautz 5:915–19 * CATH 8:741–42 * Labriolle (1947) 2:816–17 * Steidle 245–46 * Tixeront 368 * CE 9:731–32 * DCB 3:845–48 * DDC 6:835–36 * DictSp 10:678–80 * DPAC 2:2129–30 * DTC 10.1:203–7 * EC 8:220–21 * EEC 1:530–31 * EEChr 2:723 * LTK 6:1423 * NCE 9:303 * NCES 9:219 * ODCC 1044 * PEA (1991) 7:965 * TRE 22:191–94

179-A. Capitula Martini[†]

Written after 561, the *Capitula Martini*—also known as the *Collectio Orientalium Canonum*—is a collection of eighty-four canons selected from both Eastern (Greek) and Western sources. The canons, at times rewritten, treat the ordination and functions of clerics (sixty-eight canons) and then focus on the laity (sixteen canons).

4675   Canon 1. The selection of those appointed to the priesthood shall not rest with the people.[a] This judgment belongs to the bishops who test the candidates to see whether they have been instructed in word, in faith, and in the spiritual life.

4676   Canon 2. It is especially fitting that the bishop be appointed by the whole council; but if this should be difficult due to a long distance to be traveled, then three of the bishops gather. With those who are present together with the absent, all giving their endorsement, the ordination then takes place. In every province it is the metropolitan bishop who is in charge of this.

4677   Canon 3. No bishop is to be ordained without the consent and presence of the metropolitan bishop. It is fitting that all the priests in the province be present. These the bishop should call together by letter. If all can gather, so much the better. But should this prove difficult, then as many as possible are to meet. Whoever cannot come should be present by means of a letter. In this way consent is given to the episcopal ordination.

4678   Canon 22. Those of an appropriate age and who were recently baptized should not be immediately promoted to an ecclesiastical order because it is fitting that they first be taught what they can learn. Such a person is to

---

[†] Translated from *Opera Omnia*, ed. C.W. Barlow, Papers and Monographs of the American Academy in Rome, vol. 12 (New Haven, 1950) 124ff.

a. See Laodicea (between 343 and 381) can. 13 (WEC 2:1965); Hippo (393) *Brev. Hipp.* ser. 2 can. 20 (WEC 2:884); *Statuta* (5th c.) can. 10 (WEC 3:3072).

spend much time after baptism being tested so that, well examined, he may be made a cleric according to the precept of the Apostle, who says, "Not a neophyte, lest being puffed up with pride, one fall into the judgment of the devil."[b1] If afterwards he should be overcome by serious sin two or three times, he is to be deposed from his rank and cease being a cleric. [. . .]

Canon 23. If necessity or need requires that a penitent be first counted among the doorkeepers or readers, he is not to read the gospel or the epistle. If, however, he has been ordained, then he is to be placed among the subdeacons so that there be no imposition of the hand, nor is he to touch holy things.[c] [. . .]   4679

Canon 41. No one is allowed to touch the Lord's sacred vessels other than the subdeacon or the acolyte; these may do so in the *secretarium*.[d]   4680

Canon 42. Women are not permitted to enter the sanctuary.[e]   4681

Canon 45. No one is allowed to read or sing the psalms from the pulpit unless ordained as a reader by the bishop.[f]   4682

Canon 48. During Lent no anniversaries of the martyrs are to be celebrated; only on Saturday and Sunday are offerings presented that commemorate these martyrs. Neither a birthday nor a wedding is permitted to be celebrated during Lent.[g]   4683

Canon 49. It is not permitted to receive anyone for baptism later than the third week before Easter.[h] On these days it is fitting that those to be baptized learn the creed and on Thursday of the last week recite it to the bishop or priest.[i]   4684

Canon 50. The fast is not to be relaxed on Thursday of the last week of Lent. Doing so dishonors the whole season. With sincerity we are to fast during the whole period of Lent, eating in a frugal manner.[j]   4685

---

b. See Nicaea I (325) can. 2 (WEC 2:1448); Arles II (between 442 and 506) can. 1 (WEC 3:3139).

c. See Toledo I (400?) can. 2 (WEC 3:3168); *Statuta* (5th c.) can. 84 (WEC 3:3106); Agde (506) can. 43 (WEC 4:4560); Epaon (517) can. 3 (WEC 4:4575); Arles IV (524) can. 3 (WEC 4:4591); Orleans III (538) can. 6 (WEC 4:4605).

d. See Laodicea (between 343 and 381) can. 21 (WEC 2:1973).

e. See Laodicea (between 343 and 381) can. 44 (WEC 2:1990); Braga I (561) ser. 2 can. 13 (WEC 4:4748); Tours II (567) can. 4 (WEC 4:4623).

f. See Laodicea (between 343 and 381) can. 15 (WEC 2:1967).

g. See Laodicea (between 343 and 381) cans. 51–52 (WEC 2:1997–98).

h. See Laodicea (between 343 and 381) can. 45 (WEC 2:1991); Auxerre (late 6th or early 7th c.) can. 18 (WEC 4:4641); Irish Synod II (after 456) can. 19 (WEC 3:3180); Gerunda (517) can. 4 (WEC 4:4720); Mâcon II (585) can. 3 (WEC 4:4653).

i. See Laodicea (between 343 and 381) can. 46 (WEC 2:1992); Agde (506) can. 13 (WEC 4:4550); Braga II (572) can. 1 (WEC 4:4755).

j. See Laodicea (between 343 and 381) can. 50 (WEC 2:1996).

1. 1 Tim 3:6.

4686   Canon 51. The bishop is always allowed to confect the chrism that is designated for his diocese.[k] Before Easter a deacon or a subdeacon is sent from the individual churches to the bishop in order to obtain the chrism.[l]

4687   Canon 52. When the bishop is present, the presbyter may not sign infants unless the bishop has directed him to do so.[m]

4688   Canon 53. A priest is not to enter the baptistery before the bishop; he always enters with the bishop unless the latter is absent or sick.[n]

4689   Canon 54. A pregnant woman desiring the grace of baptism may be baptized whenever she so desires. The mother of an infant who is born in no way shares in the child's baptism since each person must express his or her own will by a confession [of faith].[o]

4690   Canon 55. It is not permitted to offer in the sanctuary anything other than the bread, wine, and water,[p] which are blessed as a type of Christ; while he hung upon the cross blood and water flowed from his body. In Christ Jesus these three are one, this victim and offering to God unto a sweet odor.

4691   Canon 56. When the bishop or the presbyter of the town is present, priests from the countryside are not allowed to minister to the people except when the former are absent.[q]

4692   Canon 57. If a presbyter because of public penance received from a priest or because of another necessity fasts on Sunday as do the Manichaeans,[r] let him be anathema.[s] Likewise, the ancient canon handed down from the apostles holds this: on all Sundays and from Easter to Pentecost we are not to kneel or bow low; rather, we are to stand erect, looking at the Lord, for on this day we celebrate the joy of the Lord's resurrection.[t]

4693   Canon 63. Should any presbyter, deacon, or any cleric attached to a church, if he is within the city or place where the church is located, not

---

k. See Toledo I (400?) can. 20 (WEC 3:3172); Carthage II (390) can. 3 (WEC 2:876); Hippo (393) *Brev. Hipp.* ser. 2 can. 34 (WEC 2:891); Braga I (561) ser. 2 can. 19 (WEC 4:4752).

l. See Toledo I (400?) can. 20 (WEC 3:3172); Elvira (ca. 300) can. 77 (WEC 2:1294); *Statuta* (5th c.) can. 87 (WEC 3:3108); Vaison (442) can. 3 (WEC 3:3138); Auxerre (late 6th or early 7th c.) can. 6 (WEC 4:4632); Braga II (572) can. 4 (WEC 4:4757); Barcelona II (599) can. 2 (WEC 4:4773).

m. See Toledo I (400?) can. 20 (WEC 3:3172).

n. See Laodicea (between 343 and 381) can. 56 (WEC 2:2000).

o. See Neo-Caesarea (ca. 320) can. 6 (WEC 2:1438).

p. See Hippo (393) *Brev. Hipp.* ser. 2 can. 23-a (WEC 2:886).

q. See Neo-Caesarea (ca. 320) can. 13 (WEC 2:1445).

r. Manichaeans: followers of Mani (ca. 216–76), who preached a dualistic doctrine based on an ancient conflict between light and darkness, between good and evil.

s. See Gangra (ca. 345) can. 18 (WEC 2:1955); Saragossa (ca. 380) can. 2 (WEC 2:1295); *Statuta* (5th c.) can. 77 (WEC 3:3102); Agde (506) can. 12 (WEC 4:4549); Orleans IV (541) can. 2 (WEC 4:4616); Braga I (561) ser. 1 can. 4 (WEC 4:4737).

t. See Nicaea I (325) can. 20 (WEC 2:1457); *Statuta* (5th c.) can. 67 (WEC 3:3099).

meet for the daily sacrifice of psalmody at the morning and evening hours, he is to be deposed from the clerical state unless, making amends, he shows that he has merited to be pardoned by the bishop.[u]

Canon 64. No cleric, no matter who he is, is to absent himself from church on Sunday but is to be present at Mass and observe the [pre-Communion?] fast.[v]   4694

Canon 65. Neither clerics nor religious are to begin eating before the third hour of the day, nor are clerics at any time to eat bread without having sung a hymn and, after eating, without giving thanks to God the author [of all things].   4695

Canon 67. Not to be said in church are [privately] composed or common psalms.[w] Nor are the noncanonical works to be read; only the canonical books of the Old and New Testaments.[x]   4696

Canon 69. Christians are not to carry food to the tombs of the deceased and to offer it on their behalf.   4697

Canon 70. Clerics and the Catholic laity are not to receive *eulogiae*[y] from heretics because the *eulogiae* are evils rather than blessings. Nor are they to pray with heretics or schismatics.[z]   4698

Canon 82. Not to be refused are those departing the body who desire the final and necessary Communion, namely, Viaticum.[aa] But if they, having regained health and having received Communion, are again placed in a grave state of health, they are to be prayed over since they are not to receive the Sacrament till they have carried out the appointed time of penance.   4699

Canon 83. As to those who enter the church of God and due to talking do not hear the sacred Scriptures or due to dissipation fail to receive sacramental Communion, or do not follow the disciplinary rule regarding the mysteries, we decree that they are to be ejected from the Catholic Church   4700

---

u. See Toledo I (400?) can. 5 (WEC 3:3169).

v. See Hippo (393) *Brev. Hipp.* ser. 2 can. 28 (WEC 2:887).

w. See Laodicea (between 343 and 381) can. 59 (WEC 2:2002); Braga I (561) ser. 2 can. 12 (WEC 4:4747); *Capitula Martini* (after 561) can. 67 (WEC 4:4696); Tours II (567) can. 24 (WEC 4:4628).

x. See Laodicea (between 343 and 381) can. 59 (WEC 2:2002); Hippo (393) *Cod. Ver.* can. 5, *Brev. Hipp.* can. 36-a (WEC 2:879, 892).

y. For a listing of the meaning of *eulogiae* (literally, "to speak well" or "to bless"), see EEC 1:297.

z. See Laodicea (between 343 and 381) cans. 32–33 (WEC 2:1982–83); *Statuta* (5th c.) can. 82 (WEC 3:3105).

aa. See Elvira (ca. 300) cans. 1, 6, 7, 37, 47 (WEC 2:1270–72, 1284, 1290); Ancyra (314) cans. 16, 22 (WEC 2:1432, 1435); Nicaea I (325) can. 13 (WEC 2:1453); Rome (488) Letter 7, can. 3 (WEC 3:2959); *Statuta* (5th c.) cans. 20–21 (WEC 3:3077–78); Orange I (441) can. 3 (WEC 3:3125); Vaison (442) can. 2 (WEC 3:3137); Arles II (between 442 and 506) can. 28 (WEC 3:3149); Agde (506) can. 15 (WEC 4:4552); Epaon (517) can. 36 (WEC 4:4587); Orleans III (538) cans. 6, 28 (WEC 4:4605, 4609); Gerunda (517) can. 9 (WEC 4:4722); Barcelona I (ca. 540) can. 9 (WEC 4:4732).

till they do penance and show the fruit of penance, asking that, Communion having been received, forgiveness might be merited.[bb][cc]

179-B. On Triple Immersion[†]

Here Martin responds to Boniface, a Spanish bishop, who believes that the triple baptismal immersion is a response to the Arian heresy.

From Bishop Martin to Bishop Boniface. [. . .]

4701   II. According to what you have written, some of our people traveling in your lands have told you that the priests of this province confer baptism not in the one name of the Trinity but in the names of the Trinity. This, as you must know, is completely false. For in my mind whoever wanted you to believe this has either not seen bishops baptizing or certainly wanted to recall what was formerly the practice here. But I have most certainly learned that some years ago the metropolitan of this province requested from the See of blessed Peter the formula having the utmost authority.[a] Upon most carefully reading a copy [of the reply], I found it written that the person being baptized is to be dipped or immersed three times.

4702   III. You say, "Invoking the name three times and immersing three times is most certainly a practice of the Arians."[b] I reply that to be immersed three times in the one name of the Father and of the Son and of the Holy Spirit is the ancient and apostolic tradition, a tradition the priests of this province have from the authority of the bishop of Rome in written form. The bishop of Constantinople observed this practice on the very feast of Easter and in the presence of this court's delegates who were sent to the imperial court. There is also the letter from Paul the blessed Apostle which says, "There is one God, one faith, one baptism."[1] There is also Saint Jerome's treatise in which he confirms that the baptized are immersed three times with the one name being invoked only once.[c] Should you so desire, you can find this most ancient papyrus in the possession of our venerable and holy brother the priest Ausentius. Furthermore, in the *Acts of Saint Sylvester* Constantine, in a vision, was ordered to be immersed three times.[d] Many, upon hearing the Apostle say "one baptism," wish to

---

bb. See Antioch (341) can. 2 (WEC 2:1948).

cc. Some suggest that the text "deprecans ut possit communione percepta indulgentiam promereri" may be, at best, just unclear.

[†] Translated from *Opera Omnia*, ed. C.W. Barlow, 256–58.

a. See WEC 4:4190.

b. Arians: followers of Arius (ca. 260–336), a priest in Alexandria who denied the unity and consubstantiality of the three persons of the Trinity and consequently the full divinity of Christ, a doctrine condemned by the Council of Nicaea in 325.

c. Jerome, *Dialogue between a Luciferian and an Orthodox Christian* (WEC 3:3929).

d. See *Edictum Constantini Magni* (PL 8:572).

1. Eph 4:5.

understand this as pertaining to the one immersion rather than to the one Catholic faith with baptism being everywhere celebrated in one way. And then, attempting to distance themselves from the practice of the Arians, who practice triple immersion but use a single name—as is our custom— they altered the formula found in ancient tradition so that there would be only one immersion given under one name. They did not understand that a single name shows the unity of substance and that the triple immersion shows the distinction of the three persons. For if under one name there would be only a single immersion, then only the divine unity in the Father and the Son and the Holy Spirit would be shown, not the difference in persons.

iv. Now when they distance themselves from the Arians, they fail to realize that they come close to the Sabellians[e] who under one name have only a single immersion, who say that the Father is identical to the Son and the Holy Spirit, and hold that the Holy Spirit is identical to the Father. Although it does not demonstrate a distinction of the three persons in the sacrament of baptism, the impious use of three words deceitfully implies one person. As a result some of the Spaniards, "not knowing," as is written, "what they say nor concerning what they assert,"[2] and attempting to flee the Arians, unknowingly fall into another error. The Arians practice psalmody, read the letters of the apostles and the Gospels, and do many other things that Catholics do. But does this mean that we, for our part, are to reject all these things out of a desire to flee their error? Far from it! They have departed from us, as it is written, but they retain all we observe except that they diminish the divinity of God's Son and the Holy Spirit.

4703

v. Yet as we said, there are some who do not follow this reasoning and desire that there be only a single immersion. To somewhat bolster their presumptuous thinking, they claim that several councils established this practice in order to avoid any similarity with the Arians, something that is patently false. For no council, whether general or local, ever legislated as to one immersion. Now, if any claim that the contrary is true, let them produce the writing showing where, by whom, and by how many of our elders this was done. If they are unable to demonstrate this, let them confidently join us in regard to what has been handed down by the authority of the Roman See, in regard to what the ancient institution of the eastern provinces demonstrates, and what is written in the treatises of the ancient fathers and in the writings that give instruction for celebrating the sacraments, so that just as in the one name of the Father and of the Son and of the Holy Spirit, which names one God, just as we declare that the three are of one substance, so we show the distinctions between the three persons when we three times immerse believers. [. . .]

4704

---

e. Sabellians: followers of Sabellius, an early third-century Roman theologian who held that in the Divinity there is a succession of modes or operations.

2. 1 Tim 1:7.

179-C. On the Pasch[†]

This treatise—not all agree that Martin is its author—explains why the Pasch is celebrated at variable periods between the xi Calends of April (March 22) and the xi Calends of May (April 21).

4705   i. Many have attempted to explain the mystery of the Pasch. They likewise desire to make it intelligible by calculating the month, the moon, and the day, but they have left the matter somewhat obscure, either because of the impossibility of knowing or because of the impossibility of speaking; it is as if they had said nothing. I know that many are accustomed to seek more detail as to why we celebrate the Pasch on different days by following Jewish custom according to a computation of the moon. They say that it would seem better if the commemoration of the Lord's passion were celebrated in the same manner as we observe one anniversary day of our birth—a custom followed by the Gallican bishops not all that long ago—and so we should always celebrate the Pasch on the viii Calends of April [March 25], the day on which Christ's resurrection is said to have occurred. For this reason I have decided to thoroughly investigate and clearly explain the practice of our ancestors.

4706   ii. The passion of Christ redeems the creature. Concerning this the apostle said, "It was made subject to slavery not willingly but because of him who made it subject, in hope. Because it also shall be delivered from the slavery of corruption unto the freedom of the glory of God's children."[1] This creature is the spirit of life which brought all earthly and corporeal things into being. This creature is subject to the hope that it might be freed from the corruptibility of the tomb and given the freedom of the children of glory; it was made subject to slavery on the day of the world's creation, the world Christ came to save through his passion. This he did so that at that time it would be revealed that the day on which the creature had been made subject to slavery would become a day of joy. Because the sacrament of this lamb was so great that even the shadow of truth would profit for salvation by freeing the Jews from slavery under the Pharaoh—as if already prefigured was the liberation of the creature from the slavery of corruption—so the image of Christ's future passion was involved in the coming of salvation. Thus God said that during the first month of the fourteenth day of the moon the year-old spotless lamb was to be sacrificed, its blood being sprinkled on the doorsteps[2] so that the people might fear the angel of death. And during the night when the lamb was being eaten in their homes, namely, at the celebration of the Passover, they might accept freedom through the figure of slavery. That Christ was

---

   [†] Translated from *Opera Omnia*, ed. C.W. Barlow, 270–75, with assistance from *Iberian Fathers*, vol. 1, trans. and ed. C.W. Barlow, Fathers of the Church 62 (Washington, D.C., 1969) 103–9.
   1. Rom 8:20–21.   2. See Exod 12:3–11.

prefigured by the spotless lamb is easy to understand; no less obvious is that his sacrifice was intended to free us from the slavery of death. We are marked by the sign of his cross as well as by the sprinkling of his blood. For this reason at the end of the world we will be saved from the angels of death. [. . .]

III. This is what our ancestors asked: "According to what has been writ-   4707
ten, what is the first month, what is the first day, and on what day does the fourteenth day of the moon occur, the day on which the Passover meal was to be eaten?" When the Jews began this tradition, the meaning of the names of the month had not yet been determined by the movement of the moon. But once our elders had determined the time and the day of the Lord's passion and resurrection, they were able to know when the first month of the year would occur, what the first day of the month would be, when the fourteenth day of the moon would occur, and why they ought to observe the mystery of the Pasch according to the moon and the day. This was judged to be of primary importance, namely, as the years progressed, the time of the Pasch no longer coincided with the moon and the day. So it was judged better to extend the time rather than not observe the moon and the day: first, because two things would be more rightly retained; also because both of these appeared to be more preferable in their observance. Let us now show how each was determined.

IV. Let us first explain what we mean by the first month of the year; then   4708
what we mean by its first day. We say that our ancestors took their reasoning from the time of the Lord's passion and resurrection. It is handed down that the Lord rose on Sunday, the VIII Calends of April [March 25], and that he ate with his disciples on the preceding Thursday, namely, on the XI Calends of April [March 22]. The reason for this, as our elders believed, was that the creature, whom the Lord was freeing by his blood, was at the same time subjected to slavery. Consequently, we must show that the world began at this time.

V. Genesis teaches that the world began during the spring. When the   4709
dry land—called the "earth" by God—appeared, he said, "Let the earth produce every kind of vegetation: seed-bearing plants and every kind of fruit-bearing trees that bear fruit from their seeds."[3] It is during the spring that we see all things germinate, and thus the world certainly began during this season. Since spring has three months, the world's beginning is found within the middle month. Not only during the middle month but also during the middle days of this month. From the v Ides of February [February 9, the beginning of spring] there is one month till the Ides of March [March 11]. However, there are fifteen days from the v Ides of March [March 11], till the VIII Calends [March 25], namely, half a month. Thus a month and a half precede this day; a month and a half follow. As we read in Genesis, night and day were equal since "God divided the

---

3. Gen 1:11.

light from the darkness, calling the light 'day' and the darkness 'night.'"[4] The two are equally divided. And so where we find day and night being equally divided, there we find the beginning of the world. Yet there was a reason why our ancestors subtracted three days from the VIII Calends of April [March 25] in order to discover the first day of the world. According to our ancestors the XI Calends of April [March 22] was the first month and the first day of the world because three days had passed before the sun was established to govern the world. Genesis tells us that the sun and the moon were created on the fourth day.[5] And so we find that Christ rose on the VIII Calends of April [March 25] and had begun the Passover with his disciples on the XI Calends of April [March 22], the day when the creature was subjected to slavery, a slavery Christ had come to abolish by means of his passion.

4710   VI. There can be no doubt that Sunday was the first day of the world because Scripture says, "The world was made in six days and God rested on the seventh."[6] The seventh day God called the Sabbath. Consequently it is evident that Sunday was the first day of the world. We know that the moon was made full because it was created at the beginning of the night and its rule. But this, as the computation shows, cannot be repeated each year in order that, for example, the XI Calends of April [March 22] and the twenty-fourth day of the moon always fall on a Sunday. During subsequent years, however, the XI Calends of April [March 22] is the twenty-fifth day of the moon, a Monday. And so when both the moon and the day are found to be changed, it seemed correct to observe the XI Calends of April [March 22] as the world's birthday.

4711   VII. This is why our ancestors decided that a full month should be observed for celebrating the world's birthday and that the Pasch should be celebrated in whatever part of the month the day and the moon coincided. Nor did this lack scriptural authority. Moses said, "This month shall stand at the beginning of your calendar, and you shall count it as the first month of the year."[7] Saying this, he consecrated a whole month as the day of the world's birth. And so our ancestors, who established the XI Calends of April [March 22] as the birth of the world, defined the XI Calends of May [April 21] as the limit of the first month. Thus the Pasch may not be celebrated before the XI Calends of April [March 22] nor after the XI Calends of May [April 21]. But when in this month both the moon and the day coincide, namely, the fourteenth day of the moon and Sunday, then the Pasch is to be celebrated at this time. But since it often happens that the fourteenth day of the moon does not coincide with Sunday, they chose to have the moon lengthened by seven days provided that Sunday be observed with the joy of the Resurrection. So when the day occurs in this manner, we always defer the Pasch up to the twenty-first day of the moon for the sake of Sunday so that we celebrate the Pasch neither before the XI

---

4. Gen 1:4–5.   5. See Gen 1:16, 19.   6. Gen 2:2–3.   7. Exod 12:2.

Calends of April [March 22] nor after the xi Calends of May [April 21]. In this way the month and the day and the moon are maintained when celebrating the Pasch.

viii. When considering the world's birthday it is prudent that we direct   4712
our attention to the moon and the day rather than to the xi Calends of April [March 22] since a full moon sheds its light upon all night's darkness and since Sunday is the resurrection of the days of the week, returning as it does to the beginning of these days and refreshing their end. It is better that these days should be observed for the happiness of the birthday and of the liberation of the creature, especially since they are kept within the confines of the first month. Furthermore, our ancestors considered the day to have more religious importance than the moon since we pass beyond the fourteenth day of the moon but not the day of the week, our whole salvation being in the resurrection of the day. Sunday is both the beginning of days and the day of the Resurrection since it was on this day that the Lord rose. The moon, however, even though it does not fill up the whole night till the twenty-first day, still sheds its light on most of the night, leaving the darkness behind and conquering the darkness that lies ahead. For this reason our elders desired to have it extended till the twenty-first day rather than to have the Pasch celebrated before the fourteenth day since it is preferable to leave the darkness behind one's back rather than being unable to overcome the darkness that is ahead.

ix. Our elders concluded that the Pasch should be celebrated neither   4713
before the xi Calends of April [March 22] nor after the xi Calends of May [April 21]. [. . .]

180. SYNODS

180-A. Synod of Tarragona (516)†

On November 6, 516, ten bishops gathered at the port city of Tarragona, where they issued thirteen canons.

Hefele (1905) 2.2:1026–29 * Hefele (1871) 4:102–4 * DCA 2:1949 * EEC 2:814

Canon 7. If a priest and a deacon are appointed to a rural parish [*ecclesia*   4714
diocesana] together with other clerics, these two shall alternate weeks. During one week the priest, during the other the deacon, shall provide for divine service, which must consist daily of Matins and Vespers. However, on Saturday all the clerics must appear at Vespers.[a] This makes it easier for all to be present at the Sunday solemnity. On all days Vespers and Matins

---

† Canons translated from CV:36–37.

a. Irish Synod I (between 450 and 456) can. 7 (WEC 3:3173); Vannes (between 461 and 491) can. 14 (WEC 3:3163); Orleans II (533) can. 14 (WEC 4:4598); Orleans III (538) can. 15 (WEC 4:4606).

are to be celebrated because if a cleric is not present—and this is even worse—there is no one to light the lamp in the church. [. . .]

4715   Canon 8. Since it is known that many rural churches are in a bad condition, the bishop in accordance with ancient practice should visit these churches every year. If they are in disrepair, they should be repaired since, in accord with ancient custom, the bishop receives the third part [of all the offerings] from rural churches.[b]

4716   Canon 9. Should a reader marry an adulteress or continue in marriage with her, he must be excluded from the clergy unless he leaves the adulteress woman. The same is true for an *ostiarius*.

180-B. Synod of Gerunda (517)[†]

On June 8, 517, seven bishops gathered at Gerunda in northeastern Spain and there enacted ten canons.

Hefele (1905) 2.2:1029–30 * Hefele (1871) 4:105–6 * DCA 1:726–27 * DDCon 2:115–16

4717   Canon 1. The order of Mass as well as the manner of church song and of ministry at the altar shall in the whole province of Tarragona be the same as in the metropolitan church.[a]

4718   Canon 2. During the week after Pentecost, on the three days from Thursday to Saturday, the litanies are to be celebrated with fasting.

4719   Canon 3. The second litanies will begin on 1 November. If, however, one of these three days is a Sunday, then the litanies are transferred to another week.[b] They begin on Thursday and end on Saturday evening after Mass. On these days all refrain from meat and wine.

4720   Canon 4. [. . .] Catechumens are to be baptized only at Easter[c] and Pentecost.[d] The sick, however, may be baptized at any time.

4721   Canon 5. When newborn children are sick, as they often are, and do not seek their mother's milk, they should be immediately baptized on the same day they are born.[e]

---

b. See Orleans I (511) cans. 14–15 (WEC 4:4566–67); Braga I (561) ser. 2 can. 21 (WEC 4:4754); Braga II (572) can. 6 (WEC 4:4759); Mâcon II (585) can. 4 (WEC 4:4654).

† Canons translated from CV:39–41.

a. See Vannes (between 461 and 491) can. 15 (WEC 3:3164); Epaon (517) can. 27 (WEC 4:4582); Braga I (561) ser. 2 can. 4 (WEC 4:4742).

b. See Lyons III (between 567 and 570) can. 6 (WEC 4:4621).

c. See Laodicea (between 343 and 381) can. 45 (WEC 2:1991); Irish Synod II (after 456) can. 19 (WEC 3:3180); Agde (506) can. 13 (WEC 4:4550); Auxerre (late 6th or early 7th c.) can. 18 (WEC 4:4641); Mâcon II (585) can. 3 (WEC 4:4653); *Capitula Martini* (after 561) can. 49 (WEC 4:4684).

d. Some manuscripts read "the Nativity of the Lord" for "Pentecost."

e. See Carthage V (401) can. 72 (WEC 3:2746); Milevis (416) can. 2 (WEC 3:2749).

Canon 9. If any sick person has received the *benedictio poenitentiae,*[f] called
Viaticum,[g] by receiving Communion and if, after recovery, has not been
required to do public penance in the church, he may be received into the
clergy if he has otherwise had no irregularity.

Canon 10. Each day after Matins and Vespers the Lord's Prayer is to be
said by the priest.

4722

4723

180-C. *Synod of Valence (524)*[†]

Six bishops, gathering on December 4, 524 (there are those who place the
meeting in 549), in Valence on the Mediterranean, issued six canons in addition to renewing previous ones.

Hefele (1905) 2.2:1067–68 * Hefele (1871) 4:137–38 * NCE 14:515

Canon 1. [. . .] The holy gospel is to be read before the gifts are presented
or before the catechumens are dismissed[a] or after the epistle so that not
only the faithful but also the catechumens, the penitents, and all others
may hear the word of God and the preaching of the bishop. As everyone
knows, many have been drawn to the faith by hearing what the bishop
preaches.

4724

180-D. *Synod of Barcelona I (ca. 540)*[††]

Six bishops gathered ca. 540 in Barcelona, where they enacted ten brief
canons whose meanings are not always clear.

Hefele (1905) 2.2:1163–64 * Hefele (1871) 4:209–10 * DCA 1:178 * DDCon 1:139 *
DHGE 6:715 * EC 2:835–36 * EEC 1:110

Canon 1. Psalm L [the *Miserere*] is to be said before the canticle.

Canon 2. The faithful are to be blessed at Matins as well as at Vespers.

Canon 4. A deacon is not to sit when presbyters are present.[a]

Canon 5. In the presence of the bishop priests are to connect the prayers in
proper order.

4725

4726

4727

4728

---

f. See Barcelona II (599) can. 4 (WEC 4:4775).

g. See Ancyra (314) can. 22 (WEC 2:1435); Nicaea I (325) can. 13 (WEC 2:1453);
Statuta (5th c.) cans. 20–21 (WEC 3:3077–78); Arles II (between 442 and 506) can. 28
(WEC 3:3149); Orange I (441) can. 3 (WEC 3:3125); Rome (488) Letter 7, can. 3 (WEC
3:2959); Agde (506) can. 15 (WEC 4:4552); Epaon (517) can. 36 (WEC 4:4587); Orleans
III (538) can. 6 (WEC 4:4605); *Capitula Martini* (after 561) can. 82 (WEC 4:4699).

† Canon translated from CV:61.

a. See Orange I (441) can. 17 (WEC 3:3133).

†† Canons translated from CV:53.

a. See Nicaea I (325) can. 18 (WEC 2:1455); Laodicea (between 343 and 381) can.
20 (WEC 2:1972); Arles II (between 442 and 506) can. 15 (WEC 3:3144).

4729   Canon 6. Penitents are to shave their heads,[b] wear monk's clothing, and dedicate their lives to prayer and fasting.

4730   Canon 7. Penitents are not to attend banquets nor engage in business affairs; they are to lead a simple life in their homes.

4731   Canon 8. If the sick request and receive penance from the bishop, they must upon recovering live on as penitents. Hands, however, are not to be laid upon them. They are not to receive Communion till the bishop has found their life confirmed.

4732   Canon 9. The sick will receive the *benedictio viatica.*[c]

180-E. Synod of Lerida (546)[†]

In 546 (not 524 as is sometimes stated) seven bishops gathered for a provincial meeting in Lerida (Ilerda) in northeast Spain, where they passed sixteen canons.

Hefele (1905) 2.2:1063–66 * Hefele (1871) 4:132–37 * CE 9:188 * DCA 1:979 * DDCon 2:251–52 * EEC 1:483 * NCE 8:673

4733   Canon 4. Concerning those who pollute themselves through incest: as long as they persist in that detestable and illicit intimacy, they will be allowed to remain in church only till the dismissal of the catechumens. [. . .]

4734   Canon 9. Concerning those who have received sinful baptism without being forced to do so by compulsion or fear of martyrdom, the decrees of the Synod of Nicaea on sinners shall apply, namely, they must pray for seven years among the catechumens and two years among the faithful and then, through the moderating kindness of the bishop, may assist at the offering and the Eucharist.[a]

4735   Canon 13. The offerings of Catholics who allow their children to be baptized by heretics will not be received in the church.[b]

4736   Canon 14. The faithful must not eat with the rebaptized.

---

b. See Agde (506) can. 15 (WEC 4:4552); Toledo III (589) ser. 2 cap. 12 (WEC 4:4767).

c. See Elvira (ca. 300) cans. 1, 6, 7, 37, 47 (WEC 2:1270–72, 1284, 1290); Ancyra (314) cans. 16, 22 (WEC 2:1432, 1435); Nicaea I (325) can. 13 (WEC 2:1453); Rome (488) Letter 7, can. 3 (WEC 3:2959); *Statuta* (5th c.) cans. 20–21 (WEC 3:3077–78); Orange I (441) can. 3 (WEC 3:3125); Vaison (442) can. 2 (WEC 3:3137); Arles II (between 442 and 506) can. 28 (WEC 3:3149); Agde (506) can. 15 (WEC 4:4552); Epaon (517) can. 36 (WEC 4:4587); Orleans III (538) cans. 6, 28 (WEC 4:4605, 4609); *Capitula Martini* (after 561) can. 82 (WEC 4:4699); Gerunda (517) can. 9 (WEC 4:4722).

† Canons translated from CV:56–59.

a. See Nicaea I (325) cans. 8–12 (WEC 2:1449–52).

b. See Elvira (ca. 300) can. 28 (WEC 2:1277); *Statuta* (5th c.) cans. 49, 69 (WEC 3:3087, 3100).

180-F. Synod of Braga I (561)†

Meeting on May 1, 561 (the date is sometimes given as 563), in Braga, a city in northwest Portugal, the eight bishops at this provincial gathering issued two sets of canons.

CPL no. 1790 * Hefele (1905) 3.1:176–93 * Hefele (1871) 4:381–86 * CE 2:729 * DCA 1:246 * DDCon 1:207–8 * EEC 1:127 * LTK 2:625–26

Series 1

The first series of twenty-two canons condemned several aspects of the doctrine of Priscillianism, a spiritual renewal movement apparently containing various trinitarian, christological, and other errors.

Canon 4. If any do not honor Christ's birthday but fast on this day and on Sunday[a] because they do not believe that Christ was born in true human nature [. . .] let them be anathema. 4737

Canon 16. Anathema are those who on the Thursday before Easter—the day called the *Coena Domini*—do not while fasting celebrate Mass at a proper hour after None but, like the Priscillianists break the fast and celebrate the day from the third hour with Masses for the dead. 4738

Series 2

The Braga synod also issued a series of twenty-two disciplinary rules, most pertaining to liturgical celebration.

Canon 1. One and the same type of psalmody is to be used in the morning and evening offices everywhere; neither monastic custom nor private usage is to be intermingled with ecclesiastical norms.[b] 4739

Canon 2. At the vigils and Masses of festal days the same and not different lessons are to be read everywhere in church. 4740

Canon 3. Bishops are to greet the people in the same manner as do the priests, with *Dominus vobiscum* as is read in the Book of Ruth so that the people respond *Et cum spiritu tuo*. This has been the practice in all the East since the time of the apostles. The change introduced by the perverse Priscillianists is not to be adopted. 4741

Canon 4. The same order of Mass must be celebrated by all in accordance with the formulary sent in writing from Rome and received by Profuturus, formerly the metropolitan of Braga.[c] 4742

---

† Canons translated from CV:67–76.

a. See Saragossa (ca. 380) can. 2 (WEC 2:1295); Gangra (ca. 345) can. 18 (WEC 2:1955); *Statuta* (5th c.) can. 77 (WEC 3:3102); Agde (506) can. 12 (WEC 4:4549); Orleans IV (541) can. 2 (WEC 4:4616); *Capitula Martini* (after 561) can. 57 (WEC 4:4692).

b. See Vannes (between 461 and 491) can. 15 (WEC 3:3164); Agde (506) can. 30 (WEC 4:4557).

c. See Vannes (between 461 and 491) can. 15 (WEC 3:3164); Agde (506) can. 30 (WEC 4:4557); Epaon (517) can. 27 (WEC 4:4582); Gerunda (517) can. 1 (WEC 4:4717).

4743   Canon 5. None are to disregard the order of baptism as was formerly observed by the metropolitan church of Braga and which, to remove all doubt, was received by Profuturus in writing from the see of the most holy apostle Peter.

4744   Canon 9. Deacons are not to wear the *orarion*[d] under the tunic but over the shoulder so that they can be distinguished from the subdeacons.

4745   Canon 10. Not the reader but only the subdeacons ordained by the bishop are allowed to carry the holy vessels used at the altar.

4746   Canon 11. Readers are not allowed to sing psalms in church in secular garb nor are they allowed to have long hair.

4747   Canon 12. As the holy canons prescribe, no poetical compositions are to be sung in church other than the psalms of the Bible's Old and New Testaments.[e]

4748   Canon 13. No lay person, whether male or female, may enter the church's sanctuary to receive Communion; only clerics may do so.[f]

4749   Canon 16. The names of those who committed suicide by means of the sword or poison, by jumping from a high cliff or by hanging themselves, are not to be commemorated in the sacrifice, nor is the singing of the psalms to take place while their bodies are brought for burial, as many through ignorance have done. The same is true for those punished [by execution] for their crimes.

4750   Canon 17. The names of the catechumens who died before baptism are not to be mentioned during the offering, nor is the singing of the psalms to take place, as is done through ignorance.

4751   Canon 18. In no way are corpses to be interred within the churches of the holy ones.[g] If necessary, it is not unfitting to do so outside and around the walls of the church. For if cities till now have strongly forbidden that corpses be buried within them, how much more should reverence for the venerable martyrs require this?

4752   Canon 19. A priest who, after being forbidden to do so, dares to bless the chrism[h] or who consecrates churches or altars[i] shall be deposed from his office since the ancient canons forbid this.

---

d. See Laodicea (between 343 and 381) cans. 22–23 (WEC 2:1974–75).

e. See Laodicea (between 343 and 381) can. 59 (WEC 2:2002); Tours II (567) can. 24 (WEC 4:4628); *Capitula Martini* (after 561) can. 67 (WEC 4:4696).

f. See Laodicea (between 343 and 381) cans. 19, 44 (WEC 2:1971, 1990); Tours II (567) can. 4 (WEC 4:4623).

g. See Auxerre (late 6th or early 7th c.) can. 14 (WEC 4:4639); Dvin (527) can. 21 (WEC 4:4848).

h. Carthage II (390) can. 3 (WEC 2:876); Hippo (393) *Brev. Hipp.* ser. 2 can. 34 (WEC 2:891); Toledo I (400?) can. 20 (WEC 3:3172).

i. See Irish Synod I (between 450 and 456) can. 23 (WEC 3:3178); Agde (506) can. 14 (WEC 4:4551); Epaon (517) can. 26 (WEC 4:4581); Orleans III (538) can. 16 (WEC 4:4607); Braga II (572) cans. 5–6 (WEC 4:4758–59).

Canon 20. No lay person is to be made a priest until he has learned the 4753
ecclesiastical discipline for a whole year as a reader or a subdeacon and
has risen through all the grades up to the priesthood.[j]

Canon 21. What is presented by the faithful either on the feasts of the 4754
martyrs or at commemorations of the deceased is to be faithfully gathered
by a cleric.[k] At a determined time, either once or twice a year, this is to be
divided among all the clergy. If each cleric is allowed to retain for himself
what has been presented during the week, then there exists no little in-
equality from which discord arises.

180-G. Synod of Braga II (572)[†]

This meeting, attended by the bishops of three ecclesiastical provinces and
presided over by Martin of Braga (WEC 4:**179**), issued ten canons.

Hefele (1905) 3.1:194–95 * Hefele (1871) 4:395–97 * CATH 2:230 * CE 2:729 * DCA
1:246 * DDCon 1:208 * EEC 1:127 * LTK 2:625–26

Canon 1. The bishops are to visit the individual churches of their diocese 4755
and examine how the clergy celebrate the order of baptism, of Mass, and
whatever services they have in their church; if the bishop finds that the
clergy do everything correctly, then give thanks to God; if they do not, the
bishop is to instruct the ignorant; he is to command, as the ancient canons
so order, that the catechumens come twenty days before baptism for the
purifying exorcism;[a] during these twenty days the catechumens are to
receive special instruction on the creed, which is the "I believe in God the
Father almighty."[b] After the bishop has examined or instructed the clergy,
then on another day, having called together the people of the church, he
should instruct them to flee the errors of idols and various sins. [. . .]

Canon 3. As to clerical ordinations, the bishop is to accept no gift for it is 4756
written that what is freely accepted is to be freely given.[1] The imposition
of the hands is not to be sold, no matter what the price.[c] [. . .]

---

j. See Barcelona II (599) can. 3 (WEC 4:4774).

k. See Orleans I (511) cans. 14–15 (WEC 4:4566–67); Tarragona (516) can. 8
(WEC 4:4715); Braga II (572) can. 6 (WEC 4:4759); Mâcon II (585) can. 4 (WEC
4:4654).

† Canons translated from CV:81–85.

a. See Laodicea (between 343 and 381) can. 26 (WEC 2:1978); Constantinople I
(381) can. 7 (WEC 2:1460); Rome (ca. 400?) can. 11 (WEC 3:2958); *Statuta* (5th c.)
cans. 64, 95 (WEC 3:3096, 3114).

b. See Laodicea (between 343 and 381) can. 46 (WEC 2:1992); Agde (506) can. 13
(WEC 4:4550); *Capitula Martini* (after 561) can. 49 (WEC 4:4684).

c. See Chalcedon (451) can. 2 (WEC 3:3378); Orleans II (533) can. 3 (WEC 4:4597);
Barcelona II (599) can. 1 (WEC 4:4772).

1. See Matt 10:8.

4757   Canon 4. Nothing is to be requested for the small portion of balsam blessed and sent throughout the churches[d] for use during the sacrament of baptism.[e] [. . .]

4758   Canon 5. When a bishop is invited by one of the faithful to consecrate a church,[f] he is not to require that the person inviting him give any kind of gift. But if something is voluntarily offered, it will not be rejected. [. . .]

4759   Canon 6. In some places, so it is said, there are those who for reasons of personal gain and not for purposes of devotion have churches built where [only] half the gifts collected from the people are given to the clergy.[g] Thus no bishop is to dare consecrate a church[h] that has been established not to obtain the protection of the saints but for the purpose of obtaining personal wealth.

4760   Canon 7. Each bishop is to enjoin that those bringing children to be baptized and who voluntarily give an offering be received by the church. If poverty does not allow this offering to be made, no such gift will be demanded by the clergy[i] since many poor people, in view of this, do not bring their children for baptism. [. . .]

4761   Canon 9. The date of the next Pasch will be announced so that the other bishops and the rest of the clergy might each in his own church make this known by a short announcement after the gospel.[j] In this way no one can be ignorant of the beginning of Lent. At its beginning all gather in the neighborhood church and for three days process through the churches of the saints while singing the psalms and celebrating the litanies. On the third day, Mass being celebrated at the ninth or tenth hour, the people are dismissed. They are enjoined to observe the forty day fast and on the twentieth day to present the infants[k] to be cleansed by the exorcism.

---

d. See *Statuta* (5th c.) can. 87 (WEC 3:3108); Vaison (442) can. 3 (WEC 3:3138); Toledo I (400?) can. 20 (WEC 3:3172); Auxerre (late 6th or early 7th c.) can. 6 (WEC 4:4632); *Capitula Martini* (after 561) can. 51 (WEC 4:4686); Barcelona II (599) can. 2 (WEC 4:4773).

e. See Elvira (ca. 300) can. 77 (WEC 2:1294); Laodicea (between 343 and 381) can. 48 (WEC 2:1994); Toledo I (400?) can. 20 (WEC 3:3172); Rome (ca. 400?) can. 11 (WEC 3:2958); Riez (439) can. 3 (WEC 3:3121); Orange I (441) can. 2 (WEC 3:3124).

f. See Irish Synod I (between 450 and 456) can. 23 (WEC 3:3178); Agde (506) can. 14 (WEC 4:4551); Epaon (517) can. 26 (WEC 4:4581); Orleans III (538) can. 16 (WEC 4:4607); Braga I (561) ser. 2 can. 19 (WEC 4:4752).

g. See Orleans I (511) cans. 14–15 (WEC 4:4566–67); Tarragona (516) can. 8 (WEC 4:4715); Braga I (561) ser. 2 can. 21 (WEC 4:4754); Mâcon II (585) can. 4 (WEC 4:4654).

h. See note f above.

i. See Elvira (ca. 300) can. 48 (WEC 2:1291).

j. See Carthage V (401) can. 73 (WEC 3:2747); Orleans IV (541) can. 1 (WEC 4:4615); Auxerre (late 6th or early 7th c.) can. 2 (WEC 4:4630).

k. See Carthage V (401) can. 72 (WEC 3:2746); Milevis (416) can. 2 (WEC 3:2749); Gerunda (517) can. 5 (WEC 4:4721).

Canon 10. [. . .] We know that some priests, corrupted by the stench of 4762
the Priscillianist heresy, are so audacious as to consecrate the offering in
Masses for the dead after having taken some wine. Therefore, to be deposed from his office by the bishop is any presbyter who after this decree
is caught in this madness—that is, who is not fasting[l] and has taken some
food—and who has consecrated the offering on the altar.

180-H. Synod of Toledo III (589)[†]

Summoned by King Reccared to commemorate the conversion of the
Visigoths from Arianism to orthodoxy, sixty-two bishops (some of whom
were themselves Arians) gathered in Toledo and began their deliberations
on May 8, 589.

Hefele (1905) 3.1:222–28 * Hefele (1871) 4:416–22 * DCA 2:1968 * DTC 15.1:1177–78 *
EEC 2:844 * NCE 14:190 * NCES 14:100

Series 1

The bishops first issued twenty-three anathemas against Arianism and
those rejecting the teachings of the councils of Nicaea (WEC **2:71-C**), Constantinople (WEC **2:71-D**), Ephesus, and Chalcedon (WEC 3:**137**).

Canon 14. Those who do not say *"Gloria et honor Patri et Filio et Spiritui* 4763
Sancto"[a] are to be anathema.
Canon 15. Those who believe or have believed that the sacrilege of rebap- 4764
tism is something good or who practice or who have practiced it[b] are to be
anathema.

Series 2

In a further series the bishops issued twenty-three decrees [*capitula*] on
various disciplinary matters.

Capitulum 2. Out of respect for the holy faith and to strengthen the weak 4765
understanding of the faithful, at the decision of Recared the most holy and
glorious lord and king, this holy synod has determined that throughout
the churches of Spain, Gaul, and Gallaecia, the creed of the Council of
Constantinople is—according to the formula of the Eastern Churches, that
is, of the 150 bishops—to be recited so that before the Lord's Prayer it is

---

l. See Hippo (393) *Brev. Hipp.* ser. 2 can. 28 (WEC 2:887); Dvin (527) can. 24 (WEC
4:4850); Auxerre (late 6th or early 7th c.) can. 19 (WEC 4:4642); Mâcon II (585) can. 6
(WEC 4:4655).
   † Canons and *capitula* translated from CV:119–33.
   a. See Vaison II (529) can. 5 (WEC 4:4596); Narbonne (589) can. 2 (WEC 4:4656).
   b. See Carthage (between 345 and 348) can. 1 (WEC 2:874–75); Orleans III (538)
can. 34 (WEC 4:4614).

said aloud by the people so that purified by the witness of faith the hearts of the people might approach to receive the Body and Blood of Christ.

4766   Capitulum 11. We have discovered that in certain churches of Spain the canons are not followed; people do penance for their sins so that as often as they desire to sin, so often do they request the presbyter to reconcile them.[c] Therefore, in order to restrain such a cursed presumption, this holy council has ordered that penance be given according to the ancient canonical form, namely, that first the penitent is excluded from communion and is placed among the other penitents in order to return often for the imposition of the hand. When the time of expiation has ended, the bishop as it seems good may restore the person to communion. Those who return to their previous sins either during the time of penance or after their reconciliation will be punished according to the severity of the early canons.[d]

4767   Capitulum 12. Whenever someone, whether sick or in good health, requests penance from the bishop or a presbyter, the bishop or presbyter first sees to it that, if the person is a man, he first cuts his hair[e] and then is admitted to penance. If the person is a woman, she will not begin penance till she has changed her clothing, for it can often happen that after performing an easy penance, the laity again return to their sins, the very sins they were lamenting after being admitted to penance.

4768   Capitulum 22. The bodies of all the religious who have been called by God from this life are to be carried to burial only with voices singing the psalms. We totally forbid the funeral songs that are ordinarily sung to the deceased and which friends and servants accompany with a striking of their breasts. Christians, with their hope of rising, are to honor the remains by means of the divine canticles since the apostle forbids us to mourn the deceased when he says, "I do not want you to grieve over those who have fallen asleep as do the others who lack hope."[1] The Lord did not cry over the dead Lazarus but requested that he be raised up from the hardships of the present life. The bishop, if he can do so, is to prohibit all Christians from doing this, and religious should not, we believe, act any differently; it is fitting that throughout the world the bodies of the deceased Christians be buried in this manner.

4769   Capitulum 23. To be completely eliminated is the irreligious custom whereby the people on the feasts of the saints—the people who should be present at the divine services—occupy themselves with dancing and

---

c. See Carthage II (390) cans. 3–4 (WEC 2:876–77); Hippo (393) *Brev. Hipp.* ser. 2 can. 30-b (WEC 2:888); Elvira (ca. 300) can. 32 (WEC 2:1279); *Statuta* (5th c.) can. 20 (WEC 3:3077); Agde (506) can. 15 (WEC 4:4552).

d. See Angers (453) can. 5 (WEC 3:3153); Tours I (461) can. 8 (WEC 3:3159); Vannes (between 461 and 491) can. 3 (WEC 3:3160); Orleans I (511) can. 11 (WEC 4:4564); Epaon (517) can. 23 (WEC 4:4579); Orleans III (538) can. 28 (WEC 4:4609).

e. See Agde (506) can. 15 (WEC 4:4552); Barcelona I (ca. 540) can. 6 (WEC 4:4729).

1. 1 Thess 4:13.

singing lewd songs. So doing, they not only harm themselves but also intrude upon the offices of the religious. [. . .]

180-I. *Synod of Saragossa II (592)*[†]

On November 1, 592, eleven bishops met for a provincial synod at Saragossa in northeast Spain to solve several problems resulting from the conversion of the Visigoths to Catholicism.

Hefele (1905) 3.1:234–35 * Hefele (1871) 4:426–27 * CE 13:469 * DCA 2:1842 * EEC 2:755

Canon 1. A presbyter who comes to the holy Catholic Church from Arianism, whose faith is holy and strong, and who has led a chaste life, may, having been ordained as a presbyter, continue in this office, doing so in a pure and holy manner. Those who do not desire to live such a life will be deposed from the clerical office. This applies to both presbyters and deacons.   4770

Canon 3. To be consecrated anew are those churches consecrated by bishops converting from Arianism to the Catholic faith and who performed these consecrations before they themselves were ordained as Catholic bishops.[a]   4771

180-J. *Synod of Barcelona II (599)*[††]

The bishops who met for this provincial synod in Barcelona on November 1, 599, enacted four canons.

Hefele (1905) 3.1:237 * Hefele (1871) 4:428–29 * DCA 1:178 * DDCon 1:140 * DHGE 6:715–16 * EC 2:836 * EEC 1:110

Canon 1. When clerics are promoted to an ecclesiastical office, namely, when subdeacons or deacons or presbyters are blessed, neither the bishop nor any of his clerics may ask for anything. They are to remember what the Lord Jesus said: "Freely give what you have freely received."[a1]   4772

Canon 2. Likewise, when the chrism is given to the diocesan presbyters for confirming the neophytes,[b] nothing is to be accepted as payment for   4773

[†] Canons translated from CV:154.

  a. See Orleans I (511) can. 10 (WEC 4:4563); Epaon (517) can. 33 (WEC 4:4585).

[††] Canons translated from CV:159–60.

  a. See Chalcedon (451) can. 2 (WEC 3:3378); Orleans II (533) can. 3 (WEC 4:4597); Braga II (572) can. 3 (WEC 4:4756).

  b. *Statuta* (5th c.) can. 87 (WEC 3:3108); Vaison (442) can. 3 (WEC 3:3138); Toledo I (400?) can. 20 (WEC 3:3172); Auxerre (late 6th or early 7th c.) can. 6 (WEC 4:4632); *Capitula Martini* (after 561) can. 51 (WEC 4:4686); Braga II (572) can. 4 (WEC 4:4757).

  1. Matt 10:8.

this; otherwise God's grace, spoiled by paying for the blessing, will bring destruction to those who appear to be associated with Simon Magus in buying and selling.[c]

4774   Canon 3. As determined by the early canons and the prescriptions of the episcopal synodal letters, no layman is to aspire to or is to be promoted to ecclesiastical orders unless the times prescribed by the canons are followed.[d] [. . .] Now if two or three, agreed upon by clergy and people, are presented for judgment to the metropolitan and his co-bishops, the one on whom the lot falls after a preceding fast by the bishops will, Christ designating, be consecrated. Yet if any, God forbid, act differently, both those ordaining and those ordained will be deposed.

4775   Canon 4. If a virgin has freely laid aside her lay clothing, has put on the garments of a religious, and has promised to observe chastity, or if any-one of either sex upon asking receives from the bishop the blessing of penance,[e] then, if that person voluntarily marries, he or she, expelled from the church, will be separated from communion with all Catholics and even deprived of the pleasure of speaking with them.

BRITISH ISLES

181. FINNIAN

Sixth-century Ireland appears to have known two Finnians. One, and perhaps the most famous, is Finnian of Clonard (d. 549), the founder of a monastery in Leinster in eastern Ireland. The other is Finnian, bishop of Moville (d. 579). Some ascribe to the former the *Penitential of Finnian*, whereas others ascribe the work to the latter. It has even been suggested that the two Finnians are one and the same person.

CATH 4:1313–14 * CE 6:77 * DCB 2:518–19 * EEChr 1:430 * LTK 3:1294–95 * NCE 5:929 * NCES 5:735–36 * ODCC 612–13

L. Fleuriot, "Le 'saint' breton *Winniau* et le pénitentiel dit 'de Finnian,'" *Etudes celtiques* 15 (1976–78) 607–14.

181-A. Penitential[†]

This, the oldest of such books to be used by confessors, was composed toward the middle or in the latter half of the sixth century.

4776   In the name of the Father, and of the Son, and of the Holy Spirit.

---

c. See Braga II (572) can. 4 (WEC 4:4757).

d. See Braga I (561) ser. 2 can. 20 (WEC 4:4753).

e. See Gerunda (517) can. 9 (WEC 4:4722).

† Translated from C. Vogel, *Le pécheur et la pénitence au Moyen Age* (Paris, 1969) 52–62.

1. Those who sin in thought and immediately repent are to strike the breast, request God's pardon, and perform any appropriate penance in order to be cured.

2. Those who often sin in thought but hesitate to carry out their thoughts or do not know whether consent was given to such evil thoughts will request God's pardon by means of prayer and fasting, doing so day and night till their evil thoughts subside. Then they will be cured.

3. As to those who have thought about or have desired to engage in evil but lacked any possibility of doing so, the sin is the same [as if the deed were actually committed], but the penance will be different. Thus those who desired to commit an act of impurity or homicide but did not carry out this desire have already sinned within. Provided penance is done immediately, there can be a cure. The penance will consist of six months of fasting, and for one year there will be abstaining from meat and wine.

4. Those who sin through harmful words and then immediately repent—should there be no premeditation—must submit to penance. There will be a prolonged fast [i.e., of two days], and care will be taken not to sin in the future.

5. Those who argue with a cleric or with a minister of God will fast for a week on bread and water. They will humbly and sincerely seek God's pardon and that of their neighbors, and thus they will be reconciled with God and with others.

6. Should a cleric have had the scandalous intention of striking or killing his neighbor, he will fast for six months on bread and water and abstain from wine and meat. In this way he will be permitted to return to the altar [in order to offer and receive Communion].

7. If a laic should do this, he or she is to fast for seven days because the guilt of a person of this world is less serious in this world, and so one's reward will be less in the world to come.

8. If a cleric has struck a brother or a neighbor and has thereby shed blood, the sin is the same as if he had committed murder. The penance, however, is different. He will fast for one year on bread and water and will not exercise his ministry; he will pray with tears and lamentation so as to obtain God's pardon, for Scripture says, "Whoever hates his brother is a murderer,"[1] so how much more guilty is he who strikes his brother.

9. A lay person who strikes his or her brother [or sister] will do penance for forty days and give a fine as determined by a priest or a monk. Clerics, however, neither give nor receive money [in regard to penance].

10. A cleric who falls into the sin of impurity and forfeits his innocence one time only and without the people being aware of this—but not without God knowing—will fast for a year on bread and water; for two years he will abstain from wine and meat and will not exercise any ecclesiastical

4777

4778

4779

4780

4781

4782

4783

4784

4785

4786

---

1. 1 John 3:15.

function. We declare that his sins can be absolved, in secret, by penance and by a serious effort.

4787   11. A cleric who habitually sins by impurity—without the people being aware of this—will do penance for three years on bread and water and will forfeit his office; for an additional three years he will abstain from wine and meat.

4788   12. A cleric who falls so low as to kill his own child is guilty of both the sin of fornication and the sin of murder. These sins, however, can be atoned for by means of penance and good works. The guilty will do three years of penance on bread and water. In tears, lamentations, and prayers, both day and night, the cleric will request God's pardon in order to obtain the forgiveness of his sins. For three years he will abstain from wine and meat. He will forfeit his clerical office, and for the last three Lents he will fast on bread and water. Being an outcast in his own country for seven years, he will then be restored to his duties according to the judgment of the bishop or priest.

4789   13. If the cleric has not killed his child, the sin is less grave. The penance, however, is the same.

4790   14. If a cleric is friendly with a woman but has done nothing sinful, neither remaining with her nor immodestly embracing her, his penance will be as follows: for as long as he has an affection for the woman in question, he will refrain from Communion; he will do penance for forty days and forty nights till he has removed from his heart the love he has for the woman. He will then be readmitted to the altar.

4791   15. But if a cleric is friendly with many women, taking pleasure in their company, indulging in their endearments, but avoids—as he says—definite dishonor, he will do six months of penance on bread and water and will refrain from wine and meat. He will not lose his clerical office, and after a year of fasting he will be readmitted to the altar.

4792   16. The cleric who only once carnally desires a virgin or any other woman, without acting upon this, will fast for seven days on bread and water.

4793   17. The cleric who for a long time harbors evil desires but does not act upon them, either because the woman spurns him or because he is ashamed to make such advances, has already committed adultery in his heart. The sin remains in his heart, but the penance is not the same [as if he would have acted upon his desires]. The guilty cleric will fast forty days on bread and water.

4794   18. If a cleric or a woman who engages in sorcery misleads anyone by this sorcery, he or she commits a very serious sin. However, they can be saved through penance: six years of fasting, the first three on bread and water, the other three without wine or meat.

4795   19. If the sorcerer or sorceress in question has not used sorcery to end someone's life but only to arouse carnal desire, there is one year of fasting on bread and water.

20. A woman who kills another woman's infant by means of evil spells is to fast for six months on bread and water, go two years without wine and meat, and endure six Lents on bread and water. 4796

21. If a female religious gives birth to a child and her sin is known by all, she will fast on bread and water for six years, as was said for a cleric; the seventh year she will be reconciled and will then be allowed to renew her religious profession, to be garbed with white garments, and once again she can be called a "virgin." 4797

The cleric who falls in the same way may regain his office after a fast of seven years since Scripture says, "The just fall seven times and again arise,"[2] namely, after seven years of penance the fallen monk can again be called a "religious." He will henceforth take care not to lapse again since Solomon says, "The dog that returns to its own vomit is odious."[3] The same is true for a cleric who through weakness returns to his sins. 4798

22. A false oath is a sin that can be atoned for only with great difficulty. And yet it is better to do penance than to despair since God's mercy is great. The penance for this is as follows: never again to swear falsely during one's life since those doing so will not be justified, with evil descending upon them. A spiritual remedy promptly administered will ward off future punishment: seven years of penance and doing good the rest of one's life, giving freedom to a male or female serf, or distributing to the poor what has been received as a legal compensation. 4799

23. A cleric guilty of murder will undergo ten years of exile and will do seven years of penance, three years on bread and water, and will observe a more severe fast for three periods of forty days; he will abstain from wine and meat for another four years. After ten years, provided the cleric has lived a good life according to the testimony of an abbot or a priest to whom the sinner has been entrusted [in order to fulfill the penance], he can return to his native land. He will give the victim's parents compensation, placing himself in the service of the victim's mother and father and saying to them, "I will take the place of your son in whatever you order me to do." If the guilty cleric fails to make sufficient amends, he will never be received into eternity. 4800

24. But if a cleric has committed murder without premeditation, without hatred, and if he was a friend of the victim, and then giving way to the devil and the devil's instigation, has murdered, he will fast for three years on bread and water and will abstain from wine and meat for three years. His penance will be done far from his native country. 4801

25. If a cleric has once or twice committed theft, e.g., by stealing a sheep, a pig, or another animal, he will fast for a year on bread and water and return fourfold what he has taken. 4802

26. If a cleric habitually steals, he will do penance for three years. 4803

27. If a deacon or a cleric in orders lives with his sons, with his daughters, and with the woman he married before entering into orders and, as 4804

---

2. Prov 24:16.   3. Prov 26:11.

a result of carnal desire conjugally cohabits with his wife and produces a child, he is to understand that he has sinned greatly. His sin is no less than if—being a cleric from youth [and not married]—he had sinned with the woman. Consecrated to God, they have sinned after their promise of continence and have violated their vows: the cleric and his wife will fast for three years on bread and water. During three other years they will refrain from wine and meat, but each will do penance in his or her own way. After seven years they will be reunited, and the cleric will be restored to his office.

4805   28. The avaricious cleric sins greatly since avarice is a type of idolatry. It can be corrected by charity and almsgiving. Penance consists in removing this sin by practicing its opposite virtue.

4806   29. Anger, spite, calumny, unkindness, and envy, especially for a cleric, are capital sins, vices that kill the soul and plunge it into the abyss below. Penance is carried out as follows: till these vices are pulled up and removed from the human heart with the Lord's help and with our perseverance, we will request that the Lord be merciful and grant us victory over our sins. We will continue to do penance, day and night, in tears and lamentation for as long as these sins remain within us. To cure the sickness we will use remedies that are the opposite. We will cure our vices by the opposite virtues: anger by being kind and by loving God and neighbor; calumny by self-control in the way we think and act; discouragement by spiritual joy; avarice by generosity. The Scriptures say that whoever utters calumny against one's neighbors "will be uprooted from the land of the living."[4] Sorrow destroys and consumes the soul. "Avarice is the root of all evil," says the Apostle.[5]

4807   30. If a cleric is convicted of stealing from a monastery or a church, doing so under the false pretext of ransoming captives, and if he reforms, he will fast for one year on bread and water; his ill-gotten goods will be distributed and, as it were, lent to the poor.

4808   31. We order that such goods be used to ransom captives and, following the teaching of the Church, be placed at the disposition of the poor and destitute.

4809   32. If a guilty cleric does not make amends, he will be excommunicated and banished from living among Christians. He will be exiled from his own country. He will be beat unmercifully till he sincerely and definitively repents.

4810   33. As to our own goods, we should use them to assist the churches dedicated to the saints and to help all who are in need. We should receive pilgrims into our homes, for it is written that "we are to visit the sick and aid prisoners."[6] We must obey God's commandments in their least detail.

4811   34. When a sinner—it matters not whether it be a man or a woman—requests Communion at the end of life, the Body of Christ [*nomen Christi*]

---

4. Ps 52:5.   5. 1 Tim 6:10.   6. See Matt 25:44.

is not to be refused if the person promises to make amends and if he or she is doing good and meeting one's obligations. If such fail to carry out their promises [i.e., to amend], punishment will again fall upon them. As to ourselves, we will not refuse to give what we ought to give. We should never cease to snatch the prey from the mouth of the lion or dragon, namely, from the clutches of the devil, who himself never ceases to snatch away our souls. We are to assist those who are at the point of death.

35. When a layman turns back to the Lord after having sinned— whether it be impurity or murder—he will do three years of penance and will no longer bear arms except for a rod. He will leave his spouse during the first year of fasting on bread and water. After these three years he will give the priest a sum of money in order to redeem his soul, and he will provide the monks with a meal. During this meal he will be reconciled and received into communion. He can then return to his wife and be admitted to Communion. 4812

36. A layman who has had carnal relations with another man's wife or with a [consecrated?] virgin will do penance for one year on bread and water and will cease having relations with his own wife. After a year he will receive Communion. He will pay a fine for the redemption of his soul and will not fornicate in the future. 4813

37. The layman who violates a female religious, namely, deflowers her and makes her pregnant, will fast for three years, the first year doing so on bread and water. He will refrain from bearing arms and having relations with his wife. During the following two years he will abstain from wine and meat and will in no way approach his spouse. 4814

38. If the layman in question has not impregnated a virgin but only deflowered her, he will fast for one year on bread and water; for six months he will abstain from wine and meat and will refrain from having sexual relations with his spouse prior to the conclusion of his time of penance. 4815

39. A married layman who has relations with his female slave will sell her and for a year will refrain from relations with his wife. 4816

40. If a married layman makes pregnant a slave and one or more children are born, the slave is to be given her freedom, the master not being allowed to sell her. The two partners [in sin] will be separated, and the guilty man will fast one year on bread and water. As to the future, he will forsake his concubine slave and be content with his wife. 4817

41. A married man will not dismiss his wife because she is barren. They should remain together in continence, and they will be happy if they stay this way till God pronounces a just judgment upon them. If they remain like Abraham and Sarah, Isaac and Rebecca, like Anna the mother of Samuel, or like Elizabeth the mother of John, they will be happy till the last day. The apostle says, "May those who have spouses live as if they had none, for what is visible in this world will pass away."[7] 4818

---

7. 1 Cor 7:29, 31.

4819   42. A wife should not leave her husband; should she do so, she is to remain single [without remarrying] or be reconciled with her spouse.

4820   43. If a wife has committed adultery and lives with a man to whom she is not married, her husband does not have the right to marry another woman while his adulteress wife is still alive.

4821   44. If an adulterous wife does penance, her husband is bound to take her back provided she freely and clearly requests that he do so. The husband will not give her a dowry, and she will serve him as long as she lives like a slave, completely submissive and with full devotion.

4822   45. A wife dismissed by her husband will not marry another while her husband is still alive. She will wait alone, with patience and in continence, till God calms the heart of her husband. The penance for an adulterous husband or wife is one year on bread and water. The spouses will carry out their penance separately and not share the same bed.

4823   46. We prescribe continence in marriage since a marriage without continence is not a true marriage but a sin. Marriage is not given by God for the purpose of pleasure but for that of procreation. It is indeed written, "They will be two in one flesh,"[8] namely, in bodily unity for the purpose of begetting children and not for that of bodily pleasure.

4824   Each year the spouses will observe continence three times, doing so with mutual consent for a period of forty days so that they might be able to pray for the salvation of their souls. They will likewise abstain from relations from Saturday night till Sunday. Also, a man will not approach his wife if she is pregnant. But after she gives birth, they can again unite as the Apostle says.[9]

4825   47. If through negligence on the part of the parents an infant dies without baptism, this is a great sin since a soul is lost. This sin can be atoned for by penance: one year of fasting on bread and water for the parents; during this time they are not to share the same bed.

4826   48. A cleric attached to a parish who refuses to baptize a small child will fast for a year [if through his own fault the child dies without baptism].

4827   49. Whoever is incapable of baptizing is not to be called a cleric or a deacon, nor is he to receive the clerical dignity or be ordained.

4828   50. Monks are neither to baptize nor receive the offerings [for the Eucharist]. If they would be allowed to receive such gifts, then why can they not baptize?

4829   51. The man whose wife is an adulteress will not have relations with her till she has done penance, as previously stated, namely, for the period of a whole year. Likewise, a wife will not have relations with her adulterous husband till he has performed the same penance.

4830   52. Whoever loses something blessed by God will do seven days of penance.

4831   53. It is forbidden to receive Communion before the time of penance has concluded. The end. Thanks be to God!

---

8. Gen 2:24.   9. See 1 Cor 7:5.

And so, my dear brothers, these are several points relative to the remedies of penance. They agree with the teaching of the Scriptures and with the opinions of learned individuals. Inspired by my love for you, I have attempted to put these in writing, although doing so exceeded my ability. There are other teachings on these remedies and on the diversity of sins to be healed which we cannot list here due to lack of space and also due to my shortcomings. If anyone having a greater knowledge of the Scriptures should find more, we will agree to follow him.   4832

End of the book compiled by Finnian for his children so that sins might disappear from among those on earth.   4833

Chapter XII

Sixth Century. East

ARMENIA

182. SYNOD OF DVIN (527)[†]

Dvin (or Dovin), the capital of Armenia, was the site of several synods during the sixth century. Thirty-eight canons were passed at a meeting that took place in 527 (date disputed).

Hefele (1905) 2.2:1077–80 * Hefele (1871) 4:145–48

Canon 1. Gifts for priests must be brought into the church and not into the house of any priest.[a]   4834

Canon 2. Priests must receive these gifts and presents without selfishness at the sacrifice of the Mass.[b]   4835

Canon 6. Priests who do not officiate on festivals are to be deprived of their income for that day.   4836

Canon 7. Priests must not lessen the Communion chalice because of the poverty of their church.   4837

Canon 8. Nor are they to use new wine at Communion.   4838

Canon 9. The tabernacle curtain must not be brought to the house of a bride or bridegroom.   4839

Canon 10. Priests must not give baptismal water to other people, especially not to women,[c] for the baptism of their children.   4840

Canon 12. Lacking a priest, the other servants of the Church must not officiate at divine services.   4841

Canon 15. The furniture of the church shall be preserved by the archpriest, who is to live in the church.   4842

Canon 16. Baptism is to be celebrated in the church and only when necessary in a private home.[d]   4843

[†] Translation based on a summary of these canons in Hefele (1871) 4:146–48.

a. See Mâcon II (585) can. 4 (WEC 4:4654).

b. Ibid.

c. See Elvira (ca. 300) can. 38 (WEC 2:1285); *Statuta* (5th c.) can. 41 (WEC 3:3086).

d. See Laodicea (between 343 and 381) can. 58 (WEC 2:2001); Auxerre (late 6th or early 7th c.) can. 3 (WEC 4:4631).

4844   Canon 17. Married women are not to assist as deaconesses[e] at baptism.

4845   Canon 18. No deacon may baptize[f] except in cases of necessity.

4846   Canon 19. No priest must receive money for the sacrament of penance.

4847   Canon 20. A priest who violates the secrecy of confession must be anathema.

4848   Canon 21. There must be no common place of burial in the church.[g]

4849   Canon 23. The *agape* destined for the poor may not be given away by the priests at their pleasure, but must be divided immediately among the poor in the presence of the givers.

4850   Canon 24. No one must partake of anything before Communion;[h] and if the clergy know that anyone has already done so, he must not give that person Communion.

4851   Canon 29. All are required to observe the Lenten[i] and other fasts.

4852   Canon 30. On the great Sabbath of the kindling of lights[j] no one must communicate before the sacrifice of the Mass.

4853   Canon 38. Every month there shall be a day of fast on a Saturday.[k]

ASIA MINOR

183. THEODORE LECTOR

Living in the early sixth century, Theodore ministered as a reader in the Church of Sancta Sophia in Constantinople. He has left us two works: the *Tripartite History*, based on the histories of Socrates (WEC 3:**133**), Sozomen (WEC 3:**144**), and Theodoret of Cyr (WEC 3:**139**); and his *Church History*.

CPG 3: nos. 7502ff. * Altaner (1961) 276 * Altaner (1966) 228–29 * Bardenhewer (1908) 552–53 * Bardenhewer (1910) 477–78 * Bardenhewer (1913) 5:117–18 * Bautz 11:867–69 * Steidle 256 * Tixeront 302 * CATH 14:988 * DCB 4:954 * DPAC 2:3381 * DTC 15.1:232–33 * EC 11:1934 * EEC 2:827 * LTK 9:1413 * NCE 14:17–18 * NCES 13:873–74 * ODCC 1598 * PEA (1894) 5.2 (n.s.) 1869–81

---

e. See Nicaea I (325) can. 19 (WEC 2:1456); *Statuta* (5th c.) can. 100 (WEC 3:3119).

f. See Elvira (ca. 300) can. 77 (WEC 2:1294); Orleans I (511) can. 12 (WEC 4:4565).

g. See Braga I (561) can. 18 (WEC 4:4751); Auxerre (late 6th or early 7th c.) can. 14 (WEC 4:4639).

h. See Hippo (393) *Brev. Hipp.* ser. 2 can. 28 (WEC 2:887); Auxerre (late 6th or early 7th c.) can. 19 (WEC 4:4642); Braga II (572) can. 10 (WEC 4:4762); Mâcon II (585) can. 6 (WEC 4:4655).

i. See Orleans I (511) can. 24 (WEC 4:4569); Orleans IV (541) can. 2 (WEC 4:4616).

j. Namely, Holy Saturday.

k. See Elvira (ca. 300) can. 26 (WEC 2:1276); Agde (506) can. 12 (WEC 4:4549); Orleans IV (541) can. 2 (WEC 4:4616).

183-A. Church History[†]

The *Church History*, in four books of which only fragments remain, extends from the last days of Theodosius the Younger (450) to the reign of Julius I (d. 518).

32. Timothius[a] ordered that the Creed of the 318 Fathers[b] was to be recited at each [liturgical] gathering, certainly out of the disdain for Macedonius,[c] who did not, as it were, accept this creed. It was formerly recited only once each year, namely, on Good Friday, the day of the Lord's suffering, when the bishop instructs those to be baptized.

4854

184. EUTICHIUS OF CONSTANTINOPLE

Eutichius, born in Phrygia ca. 512, was patriarch of Constantinople, where he presided at the Second Council of Constantinople in 553. Deposed by the emperor in 565, he was restored to the patriarchal office twelve years later, dying shortly thereafter.

CPG 1:6937–40 * CE 5:639 * DHGE 16:94–95 * EEC 1:305 * NCE 5:643 * Tixeront 301

184-A. Sermon. On the Pasch and on the Eucharist[††]

3. [. . .] The fullness of the divinity of God's Word substantially dwells in the Lord's Body. To be sure, the breaking of the bread to be venerated stands for death. This is why the Pasch was called desirable, providing us, as it were, with salvation, immortality, and a perfect knowledge of God. [. . .]

4855

8. They act foolishly who, when the bread to be offered and the recently mixed cup are ceremonially brought forward in procession to the holy altar, say that they carry the King of Glory, even employing these words to name what they bear. Yet the bread and the cup, lacking consecration through the bishop's invocation, have not been wonderfully sanctified. Perhaps the hymns of those who do this have a meaning that is unknown to me. The great Athanasius in his sermon to the newly baptized said, "You will see the levites . . ."[a]

4856

SYRIA

185. DIONYSIUS THE PSEUDO-AREOPAGITE

It is in the sixth century that mention is first made of a corpus of writings ascribed by the collection's redactor to Dionysius the Areopagite, the convert of Saint Paul and who appears in Acts 17:34.

[†] Translated from PG 86:201–2.

a. Timothius: bishop of Constantinople 511–17.

b. Creed of the 318 Fathers: namely, the Nicene Creed.

c. Macedonius: Timothius's predecessor as patriarch of Constantinople.

[††] Translated from PG 86:2394–95, 2399–2401.

a. See WEC 2:2424.

Following the sequence of the manuscript tradition, the collection includes: (1) *The Celestial Hierarchy*, (2) *The Ecclesiastical Hierarchy*, (3) *The Divine Names*, (4) *Mystical Theology*. There are also ten letters as well as several works mentioned by the author, but they are now lost.

As early as the sixth century the authorship of these pieces was disputed. But within relatively recent years scholars generally agree that the collection does not date from apostolic times. Rather, the author uses a literary device to show that his instruction has its roots in the history and tradition of the Church. Today most believe that the author, a Syrian and perhaps a monk, had close ties with the Church at Athens.

Pseudo-Dionysius, whose language, while poetic, is at times simply obscure, endeavored to give a Christian perspective to the pagan Neoplatonism of his day. Doing so, he greatly influenced Christian reflection during the Middle Ages. As to philosophy, his influence is seen, for example, in Alcuin (730–806), Thomas Aquinas (1125–74), and Bonaventure (1221–74). His mystical thought is reflected, for example, in Bernard of Clairvaux (1091–1153), Catherine of Sienna (1347–80), and John of the Cross (1515–82).

CPG 3: nos. 6600ff. * Altaner (1961) 604–9 * Altaner (1966) 501–5 * Bardenhewer (1913) 4:282–99 * Bardenhewer (1910) 462–67 * Bardenhewer (1908) 535–41 * Bardy (1929) 183–85 * Bautz 1:1320–22 * Campbell 75–82 * Jurgens 3:300–302 * Steidle 207–8 * Tixeront 287–90 * CATH 3:620–27 * CE 5:13–18 * DCB 1:841–48 * DHGE 14:265–310 * DictSp 3:244–429 * DPAC 1:971–80 * DTC 4.1:429–36 * EC 4:1662–68 * EEC 1:238–40 * EEChr 1:335–36 * LTK 3:242–43 * NCE 11:943–44 * NCES 11:800–802 * ODCC 485 * PEA (1894) 5.1:996–98 * PEA (1991) 3:647–48 * RACh 3:1075–1121 * TRE 8:772–80

C. Pera, "'Eucharistia Fidelium,'" Sal 3 (1941) 81–117. * A. Grabar, "Le témoignage d'un hymne syriaque sur l'architecture de la cathédrale d'Edesse au VIe siècle et sur le symbolique de l'édifice chrétien," CA 2 (1947) 41–67. * P. Schepens, "La liturgie de Denys le Pseudo-Aréopagite," EphL 63:4 (1949) 357–75. * O. Rousseau, "Le sens du culte et son unité dans l'église d'orient," Ire 23 (1950) 37–51. * E. Boularand, "L'eucharistie d'après le pseudo-Denys l'Aréopagite," BLE 6 ser. 58 (1957) 193–217. * E. Boularand, "L'eucharistie d'après le pseudo-Denys l'Aréopagite," BLE 6 ser. 59 (1958) 129–69. * R. Roques, "Le sens du baptême selon le Pseudo-Denys," Ire 31 (1958) 427–49. * I.P. Sheldon-Williams, "The Ecclesiastical Hierarchy of Pseudo-Dionysius," DR 82 (1964) 293–302; 83 (1965) 20–31. * J. Moing, "Caractère et ministère sacerdotal," RSR 56 (1968) 563–89. * G. S. Bebis, "'The Ecclesiastical Hierarchy' of Dionysius the Areopagite: A Liturgical Interpretation," GOTR 19 (1974) 159–75. * W. Strothmann, *Die Sakrament der Myron-Weihe in der Schrift De Ecclesiastica Hierarchia des Pseudo-Dionysius Areopagita*, Götting Orientforschungen, 1st ser., 15 (Wiesbaden, 1977–78). * A. Schmemann, "Symbols and Symbolism in the Orthodox Liturgy," in *Theology and Diakonia: Trends and Prospects in Honor of His Eminence Iakovos on the Occasion of His Seventieth Birthday*, ed. D.J. Constantelos (Brookline, MA, 1981). * J. Thekeparampil, "Weihrauchsymbolik in den syrischen Orientforschungen," in *Typus, Symbol, Allegorie bei den östlichen Vätern und ihren Parallelen in Mittelalter*, ed. M. Schmidt, Eichstätten Beiträge 4 (Regensburg, 1981) 131–45. * P.

Rorem, *Biblical and Liturgical Symbols within the Pseudo-Dionysian Synthesis*, Texts and Studies 71 (Toronto, 1984). * S.P. Brock, "An Early Syriac Commentary on the Liturgy," JThSt, n.s., 37 (1986) 387–403. * A. Louth, "Pagan Theurgy and Christian Sacramentalism in Denys the Areopagite," JThSt, n.s., 37 (1986) 432–38. * P. Wesche, "Christological Doctrine and Liturgical Interpretation in Pseudo-Dionysius," *St. Vladimir's Theological Quarterly* 33 (1989) 53–73. * E.J.D. Perl, "Symbol, Sacrament, and Hierarchy in St. Dionysius the Areopagite," GOTR 39 (1994) 311–56. * L.M. Harrington, *Sacred Place in Early Medieval Neoplatonism* (New York, 2004).

185-A. The Ecclesiastical Hierarchy[†]

The Ecclesiastical Hierarchy examines the various orders and liturgical celebrations that lead to God. It is through the hierarch, namely, through the bishop who is the symbol of Jesus Christ, that we come to possess divine life. The work begins by introducing the origins of the ecclesiastical hierarchy (Chapter I). It then treats: the rite of illumination or baptism (Chapter II); the synaxis or the Eucharist (Chapter III); the rite of the anointing (Chapter IV); the three clerical orders—hierarch or bishop (taking the place of Jesus), presbyter, and deacon (Chapter V); those approaching to be initiated as well as the order of monks (Chapter VI); and rites for the deceased and the initiation of children (Chapter VII).

Chapter II

2. The mystery of illumination

II.2.2. When someone is inflamed by the love of things that are beyond the present world and strongly desires to share in them, he or she first approaches a person who is already baptized, requesting to be led to the hierarch [the bishop] and promising to obey all that the hierarch requires. The hierarch requests the person who has already been baptized to take charge of the candidate's formation and of all that pertains to his or her future life. [. . .]   4857

II.2.3. The hierarch, joyfully receiving these two as if carrying sheep on his shoulders,[1] first expresses his gratitude. With a grateful heart and by means of bodily prostrations he sings the praises of the one and only Source by which those who are invited are called,[2] by which those who are being saved are saved.   4858

II. 2.4. Gathering together in the holy place, all the members of the assembly are enjoined to cooperate in saving this person, in celebrating together this individual's salvation, and in giving thanks to the Divine Forgiveness. With all the clergy he reverently sings a hymn taken from the Scriptures. Then, kissing the holy table, the hierarch approaches those who are standing before him and asks why each has come.   4859

[†] Translated from *Oeuvres complètes du Pseudo-Denys l'Aréopagite*, ed. M. de Gandillac (Paris, 1942) 253ff.

1. See Luke 15:5.   2. See Matt 22:3.

4860　II.2.5. The candidates, full of love for God and following the instruction of the sponsors, repudiate their own ungodliness, their ignorance of what is truly beautiful, and their complete lack of all divine life. They ask the hierarch to pray that they might participate in God and in the divine mysteries. Then the hierarch says that the candidates are to give the total gift of themselves and are to approach God in a most perfect manner, one that is beyond reproach. Having taught the candidates the rules of living a life in God and having asked them whether they have decided to live according to these rules, the hierarch places his hands upon each candidate, thus marking him or her with the holy sign. He then tells the priests to enroll each candidate's name as well as that of each sponsor.

4861　II.2.6. Once this enrollment has been completed, the hierarch says a prayer. All the clergy recite it with him. Then the hierarch enjoins the deacons to untie each candidate's belt and remove all clothing. Next, he has the candidates face the west with hands extended in this same direction as a gesture of abjuration. He orders the candidates to breathe upon Satan and to consent to the abjuration. Three times the hierarch pronounces the formula, the aspirants repeating it each time. He has them turn toward the east, eyes upraised and hands extended upwards, ordering them to submit to Christ as well as to all God's teachings.

4862　II.2.7. After this ceremony the hierarch calls for the novices to make a triple profession of faith. When the candidates have finished this triple profession, the hierarch prays, blesses the candidates, and again imposes hands. Then the deacons completely disrobe the candidates, and the priests bring in the holy oil to be used for the anointing. The hierarch begins the anointing with three holy signings, leaving it to the priests to complete the anointing of each person's body while he himself goes to the womb of all adoption [the baptistery]. The hierarch sanctifies the water with holy prayers and consecrates it by pouring the holy oil into it three times, all being done in the form of the sign of the cross. Each time he pours the holy oil, he chants the sacred canticle inspired by God's Spirit in the prophets.[a] He then has the novices led back to him. One of the priests says aloud each candidate's name together with that of each sponsor as found written in the register. Then the candidates are led by the priests to the water and handed over to the hierarch, who is standing in a higher place. At each immersion the priests repeat the name of each candidate, whom the hierarch plunges into the water while invoking the three Divine Persons each time the candidate goes into and emerges from the water. The priests then take charge [of the newly baptized] and lead them, each to his or her sponsor, namely, to the promoter of the initiation. Together with the sponsors the priests robe the newly-baptized and lead them to the hierarch. With the sacramental oil he signs each and proclaims that each is worthy to share in the sanctifying act of giving thanks.

———————————

a. Namely, the "Alleluia."

3. Contemplation

II.3.7. Notice with me and carefully observe how appropriate are the symbols that express the holy mysteries. For us death is not—as others imagine it to be—a total dissolution of being. Rather, it is the separation of two united parts, a separation that leads the soul into what for us is an invisible world. It is here that the soul is, as it were, forever deprived of the body. The body, so to speak, is hidden under the earth where it undergoes another change, one that modifies its bodily form. And so all human form is dissolved. Thus it is right that those seeking initiation be completely immersed into the water. This signifies the death and burial whereby all form is lost. By this symbolic lesson whoever is baptized and is thrice plunged into the water learns by way of mystery to imitate this divine death, which was the burial of Jesus, the source of life, a burial lasting three days and three nights.[3] We imitate God insofar as possible when according to a deep and secret tradition of Scripture the prince of this world found nothing.[4] 4863

II.3.8. White clothing is then placed on the newly-baptized. Their courage and divinization have made them impervious to all that belongs to the realm of opposites. This is due to their vigorous thrust toward the One God. Order now replaces disorder, form replaces formlessness, and their lives now shine with the fullest of light. The consecration with the oil perfumes the initiates with a sweet odor, for the holy perfection of God's birth within them joins them to God's Spirit. But this outpouring remains inexpressible, for its work of perfuming and perfecting remains in the domain of the mind. How to intelligently understand this I entrust to those who have merited to enter into communion, on the level of the mind and in a holy and divine way, with the Spirit of God. 4864

Once these rites are completed, the bishop invites those initiated to a very holy act of thanksgiving [the Eucharist] and allows them to share in the mysteries that will make them perfect. 4865

Chapter III

1. What occurs during the synaxis

III.1. Let us continue. Since we have alluded to the synaxis,[b] it would be completely wrong to pass over this and begin by praising any other activity of the hierarchy. The synaxis, in fact, is according to our illustrious teacher the sacrament of sacraments. After having presented—thanks to the divine wisdom given us by the Scriptures and the hierarchy—the holy description of it, we, guided by inspiration and the Holy Spirit, must uplift ourselves to contemplate what truly is. 4866

Let us begin in a godly fashion by considering what is especially characteristic about this sacrament and yet is no less proper to all the other 4867

---

b. Namely, the liturgical gathering.
3. See Matt 12:40.   4. See John 12:31; 14:30; 16:11.

hierarchic sacraments. It is quite simply called "communion" since every sacramental action indeed consists in bringing together our separate lives into a life that is divine, in gathering together in divine conformity all that divides us, thus having us enter into communion and union with the One God. Yet we hold that participation in the other symbols of the hierarchy is only completed by the divine and perfecting gift of communion. It is nearly impossible that any hierarchic sacrament be celebrated without the divine thanksgiving as the major element of each particular rite; by its divine action it brings about the spiritual unification of those who receive the sacrament, without which God's mystical perfecting powers are not given, without which we cannot attain divine communion. Each of the hierarchic sacraments is imperfect in that it does not complete our communion with the One God; in itself each is imperfect since it cannot make us totally perfect. Nonetheless, the purpose of all the sacraments as well as their major element always consist in having those receiving them participate in the divine mysteries. Also, priestly learning has seen to it that the word "communion" truly signifies the very essence of what is happening.

4868   The same is no less true for the holy sacrament that produces God's birth within us since God is the Creator of light and the basis of all divine illumination, and so it is correct for us to praise this sacrament according to its proper functioning under the name of illumination. Although all hierarchic actions transmit light to the faithful, it is indeed this sacrament which first opens our eyes, its original light allowing us to view the light diffused by the other sacraments. [. . .]

2. The synaxis mystery

4869   III.2. The hierarch, once he has finished praying at the foot of the altar, begins by incensing the altar. He then walks around the holy place where the assembly gathers. Returning to the altar, he intones the singing of the psalms, and the whole assembly with its ordered ranks unites as its members join him in the psalmody. Immediately afterwards the deacon reads from the holy Scriptures. This is when the catechumens depart from the holy place, the possessed and the penitents doing likewise. Remaining are only those who are worthy of initiation into and sharing in the divine mysteries. Some of the deacons go to the doors of the church to make sure they are closed. Others carry out the various functions proper to them. Those higher in dignity together with the priests place the holy bread and the cup of blessing on the altar. This is done after the whole assembly has sung a hymn of the Catholic faith.[c]

4870   At this time the hierarch says a prayer and extends the peace to all. Those assisting exchange the ritual kiss. Then there is a reading from the holy tablet. Once the hierarch and the priests have purified their hands with water, the hierarch takes his place at the middle of the altar.

---

c. Opinions differ as to the nature of this hymn, with some suggesting the creed.

Surrounding him are those deacons who are greater in rank, these being joined by the priests. The hierarch praises the works of God and then reverently carries out the most holy mysteries. It is in this way that he publicly expresses, under the veil of sacred symbols, the divine work he came to perform. Having thus shown the gracious works of God, he prepares to receive Communion in a reverent fashion, exhorting others to imitate him. After receiving and distributing Communion, he concludes the ceremony with a prayer of thanksgiving. Although the people attend to the divine symbols alone, he, on the other hand, inspired by God's Spirit, does not cease to uplift his soul toward the holy Source of the sacramental rite, doing so in blessed and intelligible contemplation, conforming to the laws of the hierarchy and in the customary purity that should characterize his whole life in God.

3. Contemplation

III.3.1. [. . .] The chanting from the Scriptures and the readings [taken   4871 from the tablets] teach the precepts of a virtuous life and especially the necessity of completely purifying oneself of all destructive evils. The distribution, shared and done peacefully, of the same bread and of the same wine requires that the people, nourished with the same food, become one by living completely in God. It also calls to mind the memory of the Last Supper, which is the primitive symbol of every sacrament and from which the very Creator of these symbols has rightly excluded those who present themselves at the holy banquet unworthily and without having been reconciled to him. And so in a very holy and godly manner it teaches that by truly developing the custom of approaching the divine mysteries one deserves to be assimilated to them, to enter into communion with them.

III.3.4. The psalmody that accompanies almost all the hierarchic myster-   4872 ies is not to be absent in the most hierarchic mystery of them all. What the holy scriptural tablets teach to those who are capable of being divinized, what the Scriptures implant in them by the holy sacramental mysteries and by the spiritual exhortations that lead them to follow a godly life—it is these whereby God himself grants substance and order[d] to all that exists, including the hierarchy and public order as prescribed by the Law.[e] These tell of the divisions by lot, the distribution and sharing that concern God's people.[f] They impart knowledge of the holy judges,[g] of the wise kings,[h] of the priests who live according to God. They relate the powerful and resolute philosophy that enabled our ancestors to endure various and

---

d. Genesis.
e. Leviticus and Deuteronomy.
f. Numbers.
g. Judges.
h. Kings and Chronicles.

numerous misfortunes.[i] There are the wise precepts for living,[j] the song that divinely depicts God's love,[k] prophecies regarding the future,[l] the divine works of Jesus who was made man,[m] the activities and teachings of his disciples in regard to both profane and sacred things, with God inspiring them to imitate him.[n] There is also the secret and mystical vision of the inspired one who was the most beloved among the apostles.[o] Finally there is the theological explanation of the mysteries concerning Jesus, mysteries that transcend this world,[p] an explanation designed for those who are fitting for divinization and are strengthened by the holy sacraments they have received and who live in conformity to God. Then there are the divine chants whose purpose is to praise God's revelation and activity and to retell all that has been said of God and all that the people of God have done with divine help; they constitute the complete historical poem of all the divine mysteries and confer upon all who reverently hear them the lasting power of receiving and distributing all the sacraments of the hierarchy.

4873   III.3.5. Thus when the chants, which sum up the most holy truths, have harmoniously prepared our souls for the mysteries that we will soon praise, when they have brought us to unity not only with the divine realities but also with ourselves and among ourselves so that we form a single and homogenous choir of holy people, then what the psalmody first abbreviated or rather outlined is enlarged by the more numerous and clearer images and explanations found through the reading of the scriptural texts. In reflecting upon these sacred writings with a holy eye, we will see there the unity and uniqueness of an accord whose very foundation is the unity of the divine Spirit. So it is that the custom of proclaiming the New Testament after the Old Testament is justified. In fact, it seems to me that this sequence, coming as it does from God and prescribed by the hierarchy, indicates how the works of Jesus were foretold by one Testament and how the other Testament presents their realization; how one Testament has depicted the truth by means of images and how the other shows the present reality; for what is announced by one Testament is declared authentic by the events related by the other. The works of God are the culmination and completion of the words of God.

4874   III.3.6. There are those who are completely deaf to the teaching of the holy sacraments. Such do not understand images, for they have foolishly

---

i. Job.
j. The Wisdom Books.
k. The Canticle of Canticles.
l. The Prophetic Books.
m. The Synoptic Gospels.
n. The Epistles and the Acts of the Apostles.
o. The Book of Revelation.
p. The Fourth Gospel.

refused saving initiation and the birth of God in their souls. They have rejected Scripture by the deadly words, "I do not desire to know your ways."[5] But the catechumens and the possessed as well as the penitents should, according to the regulations of the holy hierarchy, listen to the psalmody and the reading of the holy Scriptures. However, they are not to be admitted to the celebration of the mysteries that follow nor to the contemplation that is reserved to the perfect eyes of those who are perfect. The hierarchy, conforming as it does to God, is full of holy righteousness. According to the merits of each person and in view of each person's salvation, it distributes a share of the mysteries that is proper and fitting for each, measuring out and proportioning gifts according to particular circumstances. The catechumens, however, have obtained only the lowest rank; not having been initiated, they do not share in the hierarchic sacrament. [. . .]

III.3.7. The crowd of the possessed is itself profane. These occupy a rank   4875
above the catechumens, who are last in rank. As I understand it, a person still to be initiated and who has yet to share in the most holy sacraments is not equal to a person who has already taken part in some of these sacraments but has fallen—due to weakness or an excess of emotion—into a state at odds with the effect of the sacraments. These also, like the catechumens, are not to gaze upon the holy mysteries and share in them. [. . .] This is why I believe—or rather why I clearly know—that in their perfectly sound judgment the members of the hierarchy are in no way unaware that those who fail to conform their lives to the divine example and instead adopt the feelings and actions of the detested demons are exposed to the most miserable of conditions. [. . .] The deacon in charge of excluding the people separates these first and foremost rather than the others, for it would be sacrilegious for the former to be present for any other part of the sacrifice other than when the Scriptures are read, the Scriptures whose purpose is to convert them to better things.

The divine liturgy, which transcends the present world, rejects even the   4876
penitents, those who were formerly present for the mysteries. It allows only those who are completely holy to participate in them. In its perfect purity it proclaims, "I am invisible to those who have any imperfection that impedes them from reaching the highest summit of divine conformity, and I reject them from my communion." This saying, totally pure, rejects those who are not united to those who are worthy to share in the divine sacraments. And so there is all the more reason why the crowd of the possessed, who are slaves to their passions, is considered as profane and is excluded from every vision of and participation in the holy mysteries.

The first to be sent forth from the church and excluded from the sa-   4877
cred celebration for which they are unworthy are those who are not yet

---

5. Job 21:14, LXX.

initiated or have not yet been sacramentally consecrated. Then there are those who refuse to lead a holy life. Finally there are those who feebly submit to the enemy's terrors and fantasies. Unable to be firm and constant, they have not attained a conformity with the things of God that would allow them to attain a stable and lasting divinization. Next to be excluded are those who have renounced a sinful life but still remain to be set free from evil imaginations, for they have not yet acquired as permanent a tender and pure desire for God. The last to be excluded are those who have not totally succeeded in making themselves as one, those who, to use the words of the Law,[6] are neither totally blameless nor totally sinful.

4878   In this way the ministers and godly assistants, the holy ones among those who are holy, with eyes reverently upraised toward the most sacred of the sacraments, sing the universal song of praise in honor of that source who is the origin and giver of all that is good and who has instituted for us the life-giving sacraments that purify all who take part in them. At times this chant is called a song of praise, a symbol of adoration, or in a way I believe to be more accurate, the hierarchic thanksgiving since it summarizes all the gifts bestowed on us by God. In fact, it seems to me that this song praises all that God has done for us. First, it recalls that we owe our very being and life to God's goodness, that God has fashioned us in his image by using the eternal model of Beauty, that God has given us a share in the divine condition so that we are capable of being raised up spiritually. It then recalls that we through our own imprudence were once deprived of the gifts we received from God, who then took care to lead us by the gift of Redemption to our original state, granting us, by assuming for himself the fullness of our own nature, the most perfect participation in his own. In this way he allows us to enter into communion with God and with the things of God.

4879   III.3.8. Once God's love for us has been praised in such a holy fashion, the divine bread and the cup of blessing, with a veil covering them, are placed on the altar. The kiss of peace is exchanged, this being followed by the mystical proclamation from the holy tablets, a proclamation not of this world. It is impossible to be gathered in the One God and to share in the peaceful union with God if we remain divided among ourselves. But if, thanks to the light that comes to us from contemplating and knowing the One God, we gather together and attain unity in a truly divine manner, no longer will we succumb to the various covetous desires that bring about corporeal and impassioned dissension among equals. [. . .]

4880   III.3.9. By reading from the holy tablets—this reading follows the kiss of peace—we announce the names of those who lived holy lives and whose constant effort won for them the perfect completion of a virtuous life. In this way we are exhorted and motivated to follow their example and to adopt a manner of life that will ensure us greater happiness, one that

---

6. See Exod 29:1; Lev 1:3; 3:1; Num 6:14.

results from conforming to God. The reading of the tablets proclaims them as if they are living, as those who are not dead but have, as theology instructs us, passed from death to a perfect divine life. [. . .]

III.3.10. Once these rites have been carried out, the hierarch, standing before the holy symbols, washes his hands with water; the venerable priests do likewise. According to Scripture "those who have already bathed need wash only the head and the feet."[7] Thanks to the purification of the feet they retain their pure perfection of conforming to God and will be able to generously proceed to secondary tasks while remaining safe from any attacks of impurity. They do this because they are now completely united to God. [. . .]

III.3.11. I must now explain as best I can the divine actions that pertain to us. To be sure, I am unable to praise all of them, even to understand them clearly and to explain them to others. Having implored the inspiration of the hierarchy to assist us, we can at least explain what the hierarchs—namely, those men of God—carry out in their liturgy according to the Scriptures. [. . .]

III.3.12. [. . .] The hierarch, a man of God, stands before the altar and praises the holy works that have just been recalled, the works that Jesus divinely carried out while exercising for us his holy Providence. Jesus did this for our salvation and with the assent of the holy Father and in the Holy Spirit, as the Scriptures tell us.[8]

Having thus praised the mysteries and knowing intellectually and seeing with the eyes of the spirit their holy contemplation, the hierarch then proceeds to the symbolic holy action according to the rules instituted by God himself. This is why just as he praised God's deeds so he modestly apologizes as is fitting for a hierarch who is performing a liturgy that transcends him. He reverently cries out, "It is you who said, 'Do this in memory of me.'"[9]

The hierarch then prays that he, imitating God, might be worthy to carry out this divine work. He prays that he be made worthy of the divine mysteries and like Christ to reverently distribute them. He likewise prays for all who will share in the mysteries, that they may do so without sacrilege. Next he consecrates the divine mysteries and shows to all the mysteries that he has just praised under the species that are symbolically present. The bread that was veiled and undivided he uncovers and divides into numerous parts; likewise he divides the one cup among all the assistants, thus multiplying and symbolically distributing the One God. This is the holiest part of the whole liturgy. [. . .]

III.3.14. Having himself partaken of and having distributed Communion, the hierarch concludes the ceremony with a holy thanksgiving, which he sings with the whole sacred assembly. Just as it is fitting to receive before

4881

4882

4883

4884

4885

4886

---

7. John 13:10.   8. See Matt 3:17; Mark 1:11; Luke 3:22.   9. 1 Cor 11:24ff.; Luke 22:19.

giving, so participating in the mysteries always precedes their mystical distribution. Such is the universal rule and harmonious disposition fitting to divine things. The holy leader begins by himself receiving the fullness of the holy gifts that God has commissioned him to distribute to others. [. . .]

4887   III.3.15. Once all those in holy orders have come together according to their rank, and after having received the divine mysteries, they conclude the liturgy by giving thanks, each doing so as best he can, for the graces given by the divine action. Those who in no way received the divine mysteries and who in no way confessed them are quite naturally not to give thanks even though the very nature of God's infinite gifts merits that thanks be given. [. . .]

Chapter IV
1. What the holy oils effect and the consecrations for which they are used

4888   IV.1. Such, then, is the greatness of the holy synaxis. Such are the beautiful visions by which, as I have often recalled, elevate our understanding to the One God, doing so through the hierarchic rites which have us enter into community and communion with God. There is, however, another rite that belongs to the same order; our teachers call it the sacrament of the anointing. [. . .]

2. Mystery of the sacrament of the anointing

4889   As is true for the synaxis, those in less perfect orders are to be sent out as soon as the members of the hierarchy have spread the holy perfume throughout the whole sacred place, and after all have reverently sung the psalms and after the most Holy Scriptures have been read. The hierarch then takes the holy oil, covered by a cloth having a dozen folds, and places it upon the altar. Meanwhile, the whole assembly enthusiastically sings the holy hymn which God himself inspired in the prophets.q Having consecrated the oil by means of a very holy prayer, he uses the ointment for the liturgical consecrations during almost all the hierarchic ceremonies.

3. Contemplation

4890   IV.3.1. I believe that the spiritual teaching given by this rite of the blessing of oils instructs us to show that godly people secretly preserve the good odor of holiness in their souls. God himself forbids his holy ones to display, by some vain care for glory, the beauty and good odor of the virtuous effort by which they strive to become like the hidden God. [. . .]

4891   IV.3.2. [. . .] Those standing around the hierarch rightfully assist at the consecration of the holy oil since they are not forbidden to partake of it or to look upon it. This sacrament is celebrated in their presence because they can view what the people in general cannot view. These ministers, however, are to conceal this consecration from the people. They are to eject the multitude [from the church] as determined by the hierarchy. [. . .]

---

q. The "Alleluia"?

iv.3.3. As already said, the holy liturgical rite, which we presently   4892
praise, possesses such great power that it is used for the hierarchic consecrations. In that its dignity is equal to and its power identical to those
of the holy mysteries of the synaxes, our holy leaders have used almost
the same imagery for it, the same mystical ceremonies, and the same
sacramental prayers. It is thus that we likewise see the hierarch depart
from the sanctuary, spread the pleasing fragrance to the least holy areas of
the building, and then return to his point of departure, doing so to teach
that the divine gifts are communicated to all the holy ones according to
their proper merits without undergoing any diminution or change. In
this way they retain the fullness of their characteristics within the divine
immutability.

Likewise, the singing and the scriptural reading bring about in the souls   4893
of the imperfect the life-giving Sonship. In a holy way they convert sinners who have succumbed to evil, delivering from the adversary's evil
curses those who sin due to human weakness, showing each how, according to that person's strength, to live a life that is pleasing to God. [. . .]

iv.3.4. [. . .] The oil, a mixture of aromatic substances, has a multi-   4894
tude of pleasant aromas that perfume those who experience it, doing
so according to the strength of the fragrance that descends upon those
present. Thus we learn that the transcendent aroma of Jesus spreads its
gifts of the mind over our own intellectual strength, filling us with divine pleasure. [. . .]

iv.3.5. [. . .] The twelve folds represent the order of the seraphim. These   4895
enjoy a very high rank at the head of the heavenly beings who surpass us
in their joy. They stand around Jesus, looking at him as intently as possible without being guilty of sacrilege so as to contemplate him with joy,
to receive in the infinitely pure receptacles of their souls the fullness of his
spiritual gifts, and to repeat—to use language drawn from the world of
the senses—with one voice, never silent, the well-known hymn of divine
praise. [. . .]

iv.3.10. [. . .] The holy oil is used for all liturgical consecrations, thus   4896
clearly showing that according to Scripture he who consecrates what is
consecrated[10] remains forever the same throughout all the activities of his
divine goodness. For this reason the divine consecration of the holy oil
completes in us the freely-given and sanctifying gift of our holy birth in
God. It is in such a way, I believe, that we are to explain the rite when in
the sanctifying baptistery the hierarch pours the holy oil so that it forms a
cross. This shows to all who are able to understand this that Jesus, in his
greatest and most divine descent, consented to die on the cross so that we
might become like God. Jesus graciously snatches from the ancient abyss
of destructive death those who, according to the mystical expression of
Scripture, have been "baptized into his death."[11]

---

10. See Heb 2:11; 13:8; John 17:19.   11. Rom 6:3; John 1:17.

4897   IV.3.11. Let us add that we, being initiated into that sacrament whereby God is born in us, receive God's Spirit through the sanctifying anointing with the holy oil. This holy symbol signifies, I believe, that he who in human form was consecrated by the divine Spirit, while conserving unchanged the essence of his divinity, now sees to it that we receive the outpouring of the same Holy Spirit.

4898   IV.3.12. Also notice that the regulations of the hierarchy prescribe that the altar be consecrated with the holy oil. The meaning here is revealed to us as being beyond heaven, beyond that source, that essence, that sanctifying power wrought by God in us. It is, in fact, on Jesus himself, as on the altar of our sacrifices, that the consecration of rational beings takes place. According to the Scriptures it is through Jesus that we have gained access[12] to the consecration and are mystically offered as a sacrifice. This is why we with eyes that are not of this world are to look upon the altar of divine sacrifice, for it is there that the holy victim is sacrificed and consecrated. Let us learn how this sacred oil consecrates this altar. Indeed it is the most holy Jesus who offers himself for us, who distributes to us the fullness of his own consecration, and who offers to us, as to God's children, the fruits of his sacrifice.

4899   In my opinion the divine leaders of the human hierarchy have received from God himself an understanding of the hierarchic symbol. They call this liturgical rite of anointing the "perfecter" since it makes perfect. It is called the sacrament of God and in a double way we praise its perfecting action. We do so first because God, having become human, was sacrificed for us; also because this divine action is the source of all perfection and sanctification.

4900   As to the sacred song God revealed to the prophets, who were inspired when God visited them, those who know Hebrew translate it as "Praise to God" or "Praise the Lord."[r] Almost all holy apparitions and all God's activities can be portrayed symbolically. It is fitting to recall here the hymn that God himself revealed to the prophets; it teaches us in a clear and holy fashion that God's gracious gifts merit being praised in a holy way.

Chapter v
2. Mystery of priestly ordinations

4901   v.2. Before receiving episcopal ordination the future hierarch kneels on both knees before the altar. On his head rest the Scriptures, which have been revealed by God himself. Also placed on his head is the hand of the ordaining hierarch, who carries out the ordination ceremony by saying three prayers.

4902   The future priest likewise kneels on both knees before the altar. The hierarch lays his right hand upon the candidate's head, in this way ordaining him by a sanctifying prayer.

---

r. The "Alleluia"?
12. See Rom 5:2; Eph 2:18; 3:12.

The candidate for the diaconate kneels on only one knee, doing so at   4903
the foot of the altar. The hierarch places his right hand on the candidate's
head and in this way ordains him by means of a prayer that speaks of the
diaconal functions.

The hierarch traces the sign of the cross upon the head of the person   4904
who is ordained. For each of these he makes an announcement and proceeds to the kiss of ordination, which is extended to all the clergy present
at the ceremony. These share it with the man who has been ordained into
one of the clerical orders mentioned above.

3. Contemplation

v.3.1. The rites common to the ordination of a hierarch, a priest, and a   4905
deacon are the presentation before the altar, the kneeling, the hierarch's
imposition of hands, the sign of the cross, the announcement, and the kiss.
The particular and distinctive rite for the ordination of the hierarch is the
imposition of the holy Scriptures—something not done for the lower orders;
for priests it is the kneeling on both knees, something not done during the
diaconal ordination, for, as already said, the deacon kneels on one knee only.

v.3.2. The presentation and the kneeling before the altar teach all who   4906
receive clerical orders to submit their lives completely to God, who is the
source of every sacrament. These rites teach them to offer God minds that
are completely holy and pure, souls that are akin to his, souls that are as
worthy as possible of this holy and sacred altar, an altar where those who
are akin to God are ordained to the priesthood.

v.3.3. The hierarch's imposition of hands indicates that it is under the   4907
protection of the source of every sacrament that the ordained, like pious
infants subject to their father, receive the strength and power of the priesthood at the same time they are being freed from the snares of the enemy.
This rite also teaches them to perform all priestly tasks as if having been
ordered by God himself to do so and in all their undertakings to act with
God as their leader.

v.3.4. The sign of the cross indicates the renunciation of all bodily de-   4908
sires. It symbolizes a life that imitates God, a life constantly turned toward
the divine life of Jesus incarnate, of Jesus who, sinless in that he is God,
humbled himself so to be crucified and to undergo death, Jesus who
marks with the sign of his own sinlessness all who imitate him.

v.3.5. The hierarch's holy proclamation concerning the rites of ordination   4909
and those to be mystically ordained signifies that the person who ordains,
in his love for God, manifests what God has chosen; it is not of the hierarch's own accord that he summons the candidates to ordination, rather, it
is God himself who inspires him in all hierarchic ordinations. [. . .]

v.3.6. The kiss at the conclusion of priestly ordination also has a spiritual   4910
meaning. Not only do all the assistants, garbed with sacred dignity, extend
the kiss to the one ordained, but the ordaining hierarch also does so. [. . .]
The kiss symbolizes both the holy community constituted by like souls

when these people gather as well as the joy of the mutual love which fully ensures for the whole hierarchy the glory of conforming to God.

4911   v.3.7. These rites are common to all sacerdotal ordinations. But only the hierarch reverently bears the holy Scriptures on his head. Since, in fact, the perfecting power and understanding of the whole priesthood were by God's goodness, which is the foundation of every sacrament, granted to the hierarchs, these being men of God, it is right that the Scriptures be place on the hierarch's head. The Scriptures contain the words of God himself, and they reveal to us all that we can know about God, all God's works, manifestations, all his sacred words and holy actions, in brief, all that the Divinity desired to pass on to the human hierarchy, everything that God made and said. The hierarch, living in conformity to God and fully and totally participating in God's power, is not merely content to receive by divine illumination an authentic understanding of all the ritual words and of all the hierarchic sacraments; he is to pass this on to others according to their hierarchic rank. Because the hierarch is endowed with the most divine knowledge and with the highest power for uplifting someone spiritually, it is he who performs ordinations within the hierarchy.

4912   As to the priests, what characterizes their ordination rite is that they kneel on both knees; the deacons, however, kneel on only one knee when being ordained by the hierarch.

4913   v.3.8. Kneeling shows that the candidate is approaching the sacrament with humility and is calling upon God to protect this undertaking. [. . .] It is natural that the deacons, whose function is only one of purification, should be content to reverently escort in and station at the foot of the altar those who have been purified. It is at the altar that we are stripped of all stain and made holy in a way that surpasses this world.

4914   Priests kneel on both knees because their role is not limited to purifying those whom they reverently present for consecration. After having spiritually elevated souls thanks to the sacred rites that they perform and after having purified these from all sin, the priests sacramentally perfect them so that they may continue to contemplate.

4915   The hierarch, having knelt on both knees, receives on his head the book of the Scriptures which have been transmitted by God. It is the hierarch who instructs those whom, according to their respective powers, the deacons have purified and whom the priests have enlightened, doing so according to each one's abilities and understanding of the mysteries into which each has been initiated. Finally, it is the hierarch who, thanks to this understanding, perfects those who are initiated. In this way the sanctification they have received may become as complete as possible.

Chapter VI

1. The orders of those being initiated

4916   VI.1.1. [. . .] We must now say something about the three orders of the initiates who are subordinate to the clergy.

The order of those being purified includes all who are excluded from   4917
holy ministry and from the sacramental actions we have previously mentioned. First, there are those whom the deacons have not yet finished
instructing and forming so that the teaching of the holy Scriptures, like a
mid-wife, might produce life in them. Then there are those who continue
to receive excellent formation in the Scriptures, this being intended to lead
them to the holy life they rejected. Next are the faint-hearted, those who
are still afflicted by the terrors of the enemy and whom the power of the
holy Scriptures is still strengthening. After these come those who are still
on a journey, moving from sin to holiness. Finally, there are those who,
even though converted, are not yet completely following a holy and permanent way of life. [. . .]

vi.1.3. Of the baptized the highest order is that of the holy monks, who   4918
have been completely purified of all sin. [. . .] The holy institutions have
given them a grace that perfects them and sees them as worthy of a certain
consecratory prayer. This prayer is not said by the hierarch, whose role is
to confer priestly ordination; it is the priest who is entrusted with this secondary rite of the hierarchic liturgy.

2. Mystery of monastic profession

The priest stands in front of the holy altar and recites the prayer that   4919
consecrates a monk. Behind the priest is the candidate, who does not
kneel, whether on two knees or on one knee. The Scriptures, containing
the deposit of divine Revelation, are not placed upon his head. The candidate stands before the priest, who pronounces the words that mystically
join the candidate to the monastic life. Finishing this prayer, the priest
approaches him and asks whether he renounces not only actions but also
any thoughts that might introduce discord into his way of life. Then the
priest reminds him of the rules that govern a completely perfect life, stat-
ing aloud that the candidate must exceed all the virtues so characteristic
of a mediocre way of life. Once the candidate has formally promised to do
so, the priest marks him with the sign of the cross and cuts his hair while
invoking the three persons of the divine Goodness. Removing the candidate's clothing, the priest gives him a new garb. Next, the priest, followed
by all the other priests present at the ceremony, gives him the kiss of peace
and grants him the power to take part in the divine mysteries.

3. Contemplation

vi.3.1. During these rites the candidate does not kneel. The Scriptures   4920
containing the deposit of divine Revelation are not placed on his head,
and he remains standing while the priest says the words of consecration.
All this signifies that monks do not have the task of directing others. Remaining firm in holy unity, monks obey the priestly commands and follow
them like faithful companions on a voyage that leads them to a divine
understanding of the mysteries permitted to them.

4921   vi.3.2. The candidate is obliged to renounce all actions and even thoughts that can disturb his life, and so this rite signifies the perfect understanding whereby the monk truly knows the precepts that give unity to life. [. . .]

4922   vi.3.3. As we have already said, the sign of the cross signifies the death of all bodily desires. The cutting of the hair stands for a pure and completely unsullied life, one free from ugly appearances brought about by the mind, a life that freely improves thanks to beauties that exceed what is human, beauties that unify the soul and are suitable to the monastic state whereby there is complete conformity to God.

4923   vi.3.4. The removal of the old garments and the donning of new clothing represent the passage from a life of lukewarm holiness to one of greater perfection. We have already seen that the ceremony by which God is born in souls also entails a change of apparel. Here the change of clothing signifies a spiritual ascent from a state of purification to the higher state of contemplation and illumination. As to the kiss given by the priest who consecrates him and by all the other priests who are present, it is a sign of the holy community composed of those who conform to God by joyful bonds and wherein all share in mutual love and support.

4924   vi.3.5. Once these ceremonies have concluded, the priest calls the new monk to share in the divine Communion. When done in a reverent manner, this shows that the new monk, provided he reaches spiritual unity by following the law of the monastic state, will not only contemplate the holy mysteries shown to him and share with those in the middle order in the very holy symbols, but, thanks to the divine knowledge of the mysteries in which he will share, he will be admitted to divine Communion in a way that differs from that of the holy people.

4925   It is for the same reason that, at the time of their ordination and as the high point of their ordination, those in priestly orders receive Communion from the hands of the hierarch who has just ordained them. This is not only because the reception of God's mysteries is the crown of all hierarchic participation but because all those in holy orders, as they spiritually ascend and are ordained, become, as it were, godlike, each proportionally sharing in the divine gift of this same Communion.

4926   Summing up, the holy sacraments bring about purification, illumination, and perfection. Deacons form the order that purifies; priests, the order that gives light; hierarchs, living in conformity with God, the order that makes perfect. [. . .]

Chapter vii
1. The funeral rites

4927   vii.1.3. [. . .] When the just come to the end of their earthly struggle, they are full of joy, and it is with much happiness that they proceed further on the path of holy rebirth. Those who were close to the deceased, those who were the deceased's neighbors in God and whose manner of life resembled that of the deceased, greet them—no matter who they might be—for having gained victory since they have obtained all that they desired. Songs of thanksgiving are sung in honor of the author of this victory, requesting that the deceased and all the people be granted the grace of such a repose. Then the body is taken and, as if the crown [of victory] being laid upon it, it is brought to the hierarch. Joyfully he receives the body and, following what is required, performs the holy rites to honor those who have died a holy death.

2. The mysteries for those who have died a holy death

Having gathered the holy assembly, the hierarch proceeds as follows. If   4928
the deceased was a priest, his body is placed at the foot of the altar. Then the hierarch begins a prayer of thanksgiving to God. But if the deceased was a holy monk or a member of the faithful, the hierarch places the body in front of the sanctuary at the door to the holy place which is reserved for the priests; it is here that the hierarch says the prayer of thanksgiving. The deacons then read the text of the true promises contained in the divine Scriptures regarding our resurrection. They also sing psalms pertaining to the same subject. The principal deacon then dismisses the catechumens and announces the names of those who have died previously, adding that the person who has just completed life on this earth is worthy to be commemorated with them. He exhorts all to pray that the deceased might obtain divine happiness in Christ. The hierarch, a man of God, says a prayer over the body. Once this is concluded, he kisses the remains of the deceased; those assisting do likewise. When all have exchanged the kiss of peace, the hierarch anoints the body with holy oil. He then prays for all the deceased and places the remains in the earth next to those of others belonging to the same order.

3. Contemplation

vii.3.1. [. . .] Should those who lead a holy life fall short of the highest   4929
conformity with God, they will be rewarded according to each person's merits. It is to acclaim this divine justice that the hierarch says the prayers of thanksgiving and praises the venerable Deity who will deliver all of us from the oppression of the unjust tyrant in order to subject us to the perfect equity of his own just judgments.

vii.3.2. The songs and the readings of the divine promises first inform   4930
us as to the extent that happiness and peace always play in the lives of those who attain divine perfection. Those who die in holiness are an example to the living, encouraging, as they do, the living to strive after the same perfection.

vii.3.3. Notice this. Rather than all in the purified orders being dis-   4931
missed, in this ceremony only the catechumens are sent forth from the assembly. These, in fact, have not yet celebrated any of the sacraments, and so they should not assist at any liturgical ceremony. The God who is the

source and maker of the stars has not yet been born within them. Thus in no way are the catechumens to behold the mysteries. On the other hand, the purified have already been initiated into the reception of the sacred gifts. It is true that in their foolishness they are eager to return to sin rather than uplifting themselves, as they should, to higher perfection. This is why it is not wrong to exclude them from initiation and from Communion, manifested under the sacramental symbols. If they were to participate unworthily in such holy ceremonies, they would be the first victims [of their own foolishness], and they would increase their disrespect for divine realities and for themselves. However, it is still quite proper to admit them to the funeral rite since this ceremony clearly instructs us regarding the unpredictability of the time of death, the rewards promised the holy ones by the unerring Scriptures, and the continual punishment promised to the impious. This is why it is useful that they be present for the solemn proclamation whereby the deacon affirms that those who die in God are indeed admitted into the community of the saints. Perhaps they will then experience such a desire. By listening to the deacon may they learn that the blessed are truly those who die in the peace of Christ.

4932   VII.3.4. The hierarch, coming forward, prays over the deceased. He then kisses the body as do all the others. This prayer is addressed to the gracious God, asking divine pardon for all the deceased's sins, sins for which human weakness is responsible, and to situate the deceased in the light and in the place of the living,[13] in the bosom of Abraham,[14] Isaac, and Jacob, "a place where sorrow, sadness, and lamentation are unknown."[15]

4933   VII.3.8. Let us now return to the rites that follow the prayer concerning which we have just spoken. When this prayer has been concluded, the hierarch, followed by all assisting, gives the kiss of peace to the dead person. It is permissible and reasonable that all living a life in conformity to God do this for someone who has led a godly life. After the kiss the hierarch pours holy oil upon the remains of the deceased. Let us recall that in the ceremony through which God is born in the soul—before the most divine baptism—it is by the anointing with holy oil that the candidate is permitted to participate for the first time in the holy symbols immediately after the old garments have been exchanged for new apparel. Now, on the other hand, it is at the end of the ceremony that the holy oil is applied to the mortal remains. Formerly the holy anointing called the initiate to holy combat; now the anointing with the oil signifies that the deceased has actually been victorious in this struggle.

4934   VII.3.10. As to the consecratory prayers, it would be sacrilegious to explain them in writing, thus revealing to all their mystical meaning and the power given them by God. As our holy tradition teaches, it is by learning them in private, by uplifting ourselves spiritually, by living a more

---

13. See Ps 56:13; 116:9.   14. See Luke 16:22; 13:28; Matt 8:11.   15. See Isa 35:10; 51:11.

holy life, by increasing our love for God and God's holy works, that we, enlightened by the source of every sacrament, will gain the highest understanding of the divine mysteries.

VII.3.11. What seems to merit the derision of the ungodly is that infants,   4935
even though incapable of understanding the divine mysteries, are admitted to a sacrament that brings about a divine birth in the soul and are admitted to the very sacred symbols of divine Communion. [. . .] In this regard we say what is said by those who initiated us—those who themselves were initiated according to the most ancient traditions.

They say, in fact—and it is true—that if infants are raised according to   4936
holy prescriptions, they will act in a holy way and be free from all error and from all temptation to lead a sinful life. Knowing this truth, our teachers judged it fitting to admit infants to the sacraments on condition that the parents of such children entrust them to upright instructors who themselves have been initiated to the sacred mysteries, who can impart religious instruction as spiritual parents, as sponsors. Speaking to those who undertake to instruct a child on how to lead a holy life, the hierarch requests that they themselves assent to the rite's renunciations and that they themselves make the holy promises. It is false, as those who mock [infant baptism] pretend, that the sponsors take the place of the infants in the initiation to the divine secrets, for the sponsors do not say that they abjure or that they are bound rather than the infants. Indeed, it is the infants themselves who abjure and promise. This is to say, "I promise that when these infants can understand the holy truths, we will form them and uplift them by our instruction in such a fashion that they will renounce all the enemy's seductions, that they will make the divine promises, and that they will in fact keep these promises."

In my opinion there is nothing absurd if infants are admitted to the sac-   4937
raments that spiritually benefit them provided that teachers or sponsors instruct them on how to lead a godly life and caution them against the snares of the enemy. If the hierarch allows the infants to participate in the holy symbols, it is to feed them so that thanks to this nourishment their whole lives may pass in continually contemplating the divine mysteries, in entering into communion with these mysteries as they progress in holiness, in acquiring saintly and lasting habits, all leading to holiness under the direction of holy sponsors who themselves live in a way that is pleasing to God. [. . .]

186. EVAGRIUS SCHOLASTICUS

Born ca. 536 in Epiphania in Syria and educated at Apamea, Evagrius Scholasticus (*Scholasticus* being a surname applied at that time to a lawyer) was a highly regarded citizen in Antioch, where he held several public offices. As a friend and advisor of Bishop Gregory of Antioch (d. 592/593), Evagrius accompanied Gregory to Constantinople, where the bishop was summoned to defend his good name. The only surviving work of Evagrius (d. after 594) is his *Church History*.

CPG 3: no. 7500 * Altaner (1961) 277 * Altaner (1966) 229 * Bardenhewer (1908) 554 * Bardenhewer (1910) 479 * Bardenhewer (1913) 5:119–21 * Bautz 1:1576 * Steidle 256 * Tixeront 302–3 * CATH 4:747–48 * CE 5:639–40 * DCB 2:423–24 * DHGE 16:1495–98 * DPAC 1:1311–12 * DTC 5.2:1612–13 * EC 5:878–79 * EEC 1:305–6 * EEChr 1:406 * LTK 3:1028 * NCE 5:645 * NCES 5:465–66 * ODCC 578

186-A. Church History†

Covering the years 431 (the Council of Ephesus) to 594 (the twelfth year of the emperor Maurice [582–610]), this work, in six books, was intended to continue previously written histories. Using a wide variety of sources and preserving several documents that otherwise would have been lost, the author provides valuable information on the controversies of the time, especially the Nestorian (two persons in Christ) and Monophysite (only one nature in Christ) heresies. Not a theologian, Evagrius was a historian, yet one not afraid to reveal his love for pious legends.

4938   I.XIII.When this man [Dommus, the bishop of Antioch] came to him [Symeonª], he was astounded by the [latter's] stance and lifestyle and yearned for what was more mystical. And so the two came together and after consecrating the unbroken body they gave a share of the life-giving Communion to each other. [. . .]

4939   IV.XXXVI. [. . .] According to ancient custom in the imperial city, when a substantial quantity of the holy parts of the immaculate of Christ our God remain, uncorrupted boys are sent for from among those who are pupils of an elementary teacher, and they consume these. [. . .]

187. PSEUDO-EUSEBIUS OF ALEXANDRIA

A collection of homilies on various topics has come down to us under the name of Eusebius of Alexandria. There is, however, no record of a Eusebius being the bishop of this city previous to the eleventh century. The pieces appear to be from the same hand, and yet the name of their author remains unknown. Scholars believe that these homilies date from the late fifth or early sixth century, perhaps originating in Syria or Palestine.

CPG 3: nos. 5510ff. * Altaner (1966) 473 * Bardenhewer (1908) 370 * Bardenhewer (1913) 4:588–89 * CATH 4:708 * DHGE 15:1434 * DictSp 4.2:1686–87 * DTC 5.2:1526–27 * EEC 1:298–99 * LTK 3:1006 * ODCC 575

---

† Translation (modified) from *The Ecclesiastical History of Evagrius Scholasticus*, trans. M. Whitby (Liverpool, 2000) 34, 241.

a. Symeon, namely, Simeon Stylites (ca. 390–459).

G. Lafontaine, "Le sermon 'sur le dimanche' d'Eusèbe d'Alexandrie," Mus 87 (1974) 23–44.

187-A. Homily 16. On the Lord's Day[†]

1. After the Church's gathering on a certain Sunday and when the holy   4940
bishop Eusebius was seated, Alexander said to him, "I ask you, my lord,
why must we observe the Lord's Day, a day when we are to refrain from
labor?" The holy man rose and said, "Listen attentively, my son, for I will
explain to you what tradition has handed down in regard to observing the
Lord's Day and refraining from work."

When the Lord gave the mystery to his disciples, he took bread,   4941
blessed and broke it, and gave it to them, saying, "'Take, eat, this is my
Body which is broken for you unto the forgiveness of sins.'[1] Likewise he
gave them the cup saying, 'This is my Blood of the new covenant which
is poured out for you unto the forgiveness of sins. Do this in memory
of me.'"[2] And so this holy day commemorates our Lord. It is called the
Lord's as if it were the lord of days. Yet it was not called the Lord's before his passion; rather, it was known as the "first day." On this day the
Lord began the fruits of the resurrection and of the world's creation. On
this day he gave the world the first fruits of his resurrection. As we said,
he commanded that the holy mysteries be celebrated on this day. This
day, therefore, gives you the beginning of all grace, the beginning of the
world's creation, the beginning of the resurrection, the beginning of the
week. This day, embracing three beginnings, fully shows forth the preemi-
nence of the most holy Trinity.

2. The week has seven days, six of these being given by God as days for   4942
labor, one day for prayer, for rest, and for expiating our sins so that if we
have committed sins for six days, we are reconciled to God on the extra
day, namely, on the Lord's Day. Therefore in the morning gather in the
church of God, hasten to the Lord, confess your sins to him, do penance
with prayers and a contrite heart, continue doing what is divine and holy,
be faithful to your prayers, and never depart before the assembly is dismissed. Contemplate your Lord who is distributed, handed over, and yet
never used up. If your soul is pure, then come forth to receive the Lord's
Body and Blood. But if your conscience condemns you as being guilty of
forbidden and evil actions, you are to refrain from Communion till you
have been healed through penance; yet assist at the prayers and do not
leave the church till dismissed. [. . .]

3. There is no reason for observing the Lord's Day other than to inter-   4943
rupt our labors and to be free for prayer. But if you cease working and
fail to go to church, you gain nothing, even harming yourself to no small

---

[†] Translated from PG 86:415–22.
1. 1 Cor 11:24.   2. Luke 22:20.

degree. Many look forward to the Lord's Day but not all for the same reason. Those who fear God look forward to this day so that they may pour forth their prayers and refresh themselves with the Lord's Body and Blood. The lazy and the negligent, ceasing work, look forward to the Lord's Day so that they might indulge in evil works. The facts themselves attest the truth of what I say. Just go out at any time and on any other day and there is nothing to be seen. Go out on the Lord's Day and you can find lute players, noisemakers, dancers; some people sitting and jesting; some reviling their neighbors; others wrestling; some fighting among themselves; others with a nod calling one another to evil deeds. And if anywhere there is the lute or the dance, all immediately hasten to it. The herald summons all to the church; all plead sleep or infirmity. Heard is the sound of the lute, that of the flute, or that of the dance. All, as if carried by the wind, hasten to see and hear this. But entering the church, what do they see? I tell you: Christ the Lord upon the holy table; the seraphim thrice singing their holy hymn; the coming and the presence of the Holy Spirit; the sound of David, prophet and king; Paul the blessed apostle impressing his teaching upon the ears of all; the hymn of the angels; the continuous Alleluia; the voices of the evangelists; the Lord's admonitions; the instruction and exhortation given by the venerable bishops and presbyters; all types of spiritual and heavenly things; whatever gives us salvation and the kingdom of God. Whoever enters the church hears these things, sees these things. What is seen upon entering a theater? Whores, diabolical songs, voices full of baseness and perversity, female dancers, indeed those taking pleasure in what is evil. [. . .]

4944   4. [. . .] Woe to any priest who does not offer prayers to God at the appointed hour. If any lay person takes food before the liturgy, he or she is to be judged seriously and punished. If after taking food one also shares in the Mysteries, that person's fate will be that of the traitor Judas. I know that many take food on the holy paschal day and receive Communion. Woe to their souls, especially if they are of a mature age! Rather than expiating sins, they increase sins. No less condemned is the practice whereby a person, conscious of being an evildoer and before washing away one's sins through penance, receives the Eucharist. The greater the day, the greater the sin. But those who are free from sin are to fast till the time of the liturgy during which they receive Communion. But woe to those who on the Lord's Day play the lute or dance. Or institute and execute legal proceedings. Or work in the fields or give or demand oaths. Doomed as they are to an unquenchable fire, their fate will be that of the hypocrites.[3] This day is given to us for prayer and the expiation of sins, for penance and deliverance, for giving our servants and paid employees a time to rest.

4945   5. "This is the day the Lord has made. Let us rejoice and be glad in it."[4] Let us not rejoice out of drunkenness and intoxication but by meditating,

---

3. See Matt 24:57.   4. Ps 118:24.

seeking the delights of the divine Scriptures. God gave us this day on which he began to create the world, on which he broke the power of death, and he called it the Lord's Day so that, influenced by reverence for his name, we might keep the Lord's precepts. The paid employee enters your house, carrying out the tasks you assign; for six days this person hardly dares to raise his or her eyes and see in which direction the sun rises or sets. Fatigued, he or she is worn out by the work you have assigned. Such pitiable people weep loudly. Sweaty and dirty, they are incapable of breathing deeply or of resting. All they can do is to look forward to the Lord's Day when at last they might wash away the dirt from their bodies. And often enough you do not even grant them this. What, I ask, will be your excuse? There are those who, for the sake of kindness, say on Sunday, "Come now, let us today help the poor with their work." These people fail to realize that what they could have done well becomes for them even more of a sin. Do you wish to assist the poor? Then do not steal the day consecrated to God. [. . .] Do not transgress the Lord's command; do not steal his day; do not take away the day of rest given to your servants and employees; do not forget to pray; do not hinder others from attending church. [. . .]

6. [. . .] Do you wish to avoid evil? Then do not profane the Lord's Day;   4946
refrain from evil deeds; devote yourselves to prayer; forgo bad words; gather with religious people and join them in giving thanks to God and in proclaiming his praise. [. . .]

PERSIA

188. *CANONS OF MAR IŠO'YAHB I*[†]

These canons are contained in a letter written in 585 and sent as a reply to certain questions previously asked by James, bishop of Darai, an island in the Persian Gulf near present-day Bahrain. Išo'yahb I was elected metropolitan of Nisibis ca. 582; he died in 594/595.

Canon 2. The priest who is designated as the minister of the awesome   4947
offering of the sacrifice should receive Communion before the bishop and before all the gathered priests, for this is required by ecclesiastical law. It is to be done for two reasons. First, as is written, "it belongs to those who toil to nourish themselves with the first fruits."[1] There is another reason. Even though this priest is the intermediary of the sacrament, it does not follow that he has no need of this sacrament; on the contrary, he has greater need of this gift, of the reconciliation brought by the mysteries. Accordingly, he more than all the faithful, more than all the other priests, should be eager to receive. He is like the poor person who desires to receive assistance.

[†] Translated from *Synodicon Orientale*, trans. and ed. J.B. Chabot (Paris, 1902) 429–30, 445.

1. 2 Tim 2:6.

4948   The bishop, if present, gives Communion to him. But if the bishop is
not present, the senior priest in order of precedence does so. And then the
consecrating priest gives Communion to the priest who gave it to him.
The same is true for the Lord's cup. The consecrating priest gives Communion to the priests and deacons who are within the sanctuary. Standing
on the steps and after those who will distribute the mysteries come to the
bottom of the stairs, he blesses the people and recites these words from
the apostle: "May the grace of our Lord Jesus Christ be with you always.
Amen."[2] Then the priests distribute Communion. If the consecrating priest
does not go down to distribute Communion, he turns, adores, greets the
altar, and then stands to its right, facing south. But if a small number
of priests requires it, he also distributes Communion while a priest or a
deacon carries a flat plate [with the consecrated bread] before him. If he
does not distribute, he goes up and sits by the entrance into the *diaconicon*[a]
where the people, gathering around him receive the peace.

4949   The priest who will consecrate is not appointed beforehand for this
task; only when the bishop and the priests receive the peace from the altar
and exchange it among themselves does the archdeacon designate which
priest will consecrate. If the archdeacon is not present, then his replace-
ment or whoever is officiating at the *bema*[b] will, with the bishop's permission, designate which priest will consecrate.

4950   Canon 3. The divine and synodal canons have decreed that a deacon is
not to give Communion to a priest.[c] They give the reason for this. If there
is no other priest to give Communion other than the priest who desires
to receive it, and if a deacon is present, then all should be done according
to the praiseworthy custom that is current among those who have been
instructed. The priest takes a portion from the altar and gives it to the
deacon; he then comes forward, prostrates, and adores the Body of the
[Divine] Majesty. Next the priest himself takes the portion with his right
hand, raises it on high with his left hand, and holds it with his right hand
while the deacon says, "May the Body of Christ . . ." Once the priest has
consumed [the consecrated bread], he turns, bows his head, takes the cup
from the altar and gives it to the deacon. The priest adores, takes the cup
from the deacon; he consumes some [of the consecrated wine], turns, and
gives the cup back to the deacon who returns it to the altar.

4951   If no deacon is present, the priest takes Communion from the altar in
the same way he would take it from a deacon in the case of necessity.
This is to be done if there is a shortage of ministers. Otherwise, it is not

---

a. *Diaconicon*: a room in the church and under the supervision of a deacon containing the vessels and garments used for worship.

b. *Bema*: in the church a raised platform from which, for example, the Scriptures
are proclaimed.

c. See Council of Nicaea I (325), can. 18 (WEC 2:1455).

2. Rom 16:24.

permitted for the priest to consecrate by himself, doing so without the participation of a deacon or another priest. How, in fact, would it be permissible to consecrate without the presence of him who receives the offerings [from the people?], who is the herald of the Church, who stirs up the attention of the people by his words, and who invites them to pray?

Canon 4. Remember, my lord, you did not request that I write you concerning all the rules governing the ordination of those who are to be ordained. You asked only this: "Is the gospel book to be placed on the altar during ordinations?" Earlier I instructed you that divine [functions] are to take place with the gospel book being present. This is true not only at ordinations but also when the divine sacrifice is offered and when the baptismal oil is consecrated. When the bishop or the priest prepares himself to consecrate the baptismal waters, the archdeacon holds the large book, and a priest does likewise for the vessel containing the oil. They stand around the water with the priest or bishop who will consecrate it.   4952

During ordinations when the gospel book is placed on the altar, the bishop speaks to the ordinands on the greatness and dignity of the ministry to which they will be called. He speaks to them on the chaste and pure life to be led by those ministers of divine things who stand around the holy altar. Immediately the candidates wash their hands as a sign that their spirit is pure and free from all evil. [. . .]   4953

Canon 5. Christ, who gives us life, brings an end to our death by means of his death; by his cross he has slain human enmity. He has come to announce peace both to those who are afar and to those who are near.[3] [. . .] Some of the faithful are afflicted by the evil of anger and are at odds with their neighbors. This is even true when they are in church at the time of reconciliation; they refuse to share the peace and to be healed from the evil of the hatred afflicting them. [. . .] At the moment when the Church's herald cries out, "Share the peace with one another," they either scorn this notice and depart like strangers who in no way share in the mysteries, or they are so bold as to stay and trample underfoot the Lord's law of peace. [. . .]   4954

Canon 17. According to universal tradition the holy oil used for the anointing is reserved in the church. It mystically symbolizes the garment of adoption as children and of indestructibility as well as the promise of the Holy Spirit's anointing which those worthy of baptism receive and by which they through divine power are reborn unto immortality. This is why it has been determined and established that this oil will be used for no other purpose other than for divine baptism, for which this oil is and should be preserved. Those who give it or receive it for any purpose other than baptism will be excommunicated till they have done penance and have been absolved. Just as it is forbidden to use for other purposes the sacred cup, plates, and other vessels employed by the holy minister, the same is forbidden in regard to the oil for the anointing according to   4955

---

3. See Eph 2:17.

the prohibition which has always existed and which shall continue to exist forever.

PALESTINE

189. JOHN MOSCHUS

Born ca. 550 John Moschus (John Eukratas, son of Moschus) was a monk of the monastery of Saint Theodosius near Jerusalem. After spending twenty-five years in Palestine, John with his disciple and good friend Sophronius (later to become archbishop of Jerusalem) engaged upon a life of travel, visiting and often residing at various monastic establishments, e.g., Egypt, Mount Sinai, Antioch, Cyprus. Eventually John and his companion reached Rome in 614, where he died in 619/634.

CPG 3: nos. 7376ff. * Altaner (1961) 258–59 * Altaner (1966) 241–42 * Bardenhewer (1908) 559–61 * Bardenhewer (1910) 483–84 * Bardenhewer (1913) 5:131–35 * Steidle 263 * Tixeront 305 * CATH 6:614 * CE 10:591 * DACL 7.2:2190–96 * DCB 3:406–8 * DHGE 27:321 * DictSp 8:632–40 * DPAC 2:1572–73 * DTC 10.2:2510–13 * EC 8:1468–69 * EEC 1:443–44 * EEChr 1:624 * LTK 5:938 * NCE 10:7 * NCES 10:6 * ODCC 1117–18 * PEA (1894) 9.2:1810 * PEA (1991) 5:1067–68 * TRE 17:140–44

189-A. The Spiritual Meadow[†]

The Spiritual Meadow (*Pratum Spirituale*) is a collection, written at Rome, of more than three hundred sayings and anecdotes either experienced by or told to John Moschus during his monastic wanderings. Its purpose is one of edification.

4956   xxx. In Cyprus there is a market town called Tadai where there is a monastery known as the monastery of Philoxenos. Arriving there, we met a monk by the name of Isidore, a native of Melitene.[a] We noticed that he was constantly weeping and lamenting. When any person attempted to have him lessen his mourning, he stood fast and said to all, "No sinner has been greater than I from the time of Adam till the present day." We said to him, "To be sure, your Reverence, only God is without sin." He replied, "Believe me, my dear brothers, I have not encountered on earth any sin that I have not committed, whether it be written or not. If you think that I am wrong in thus accusing myself, listen to me so that you might pray for me."

4957   "When I was in the world, I had a wife. Both of us were Severans.[b] One day upon returning home I was unable to find her, and I learned that she

---

[†] Translated from *Le pré spirituel*, ed. M.-J. Journel, SChr 12 (Paris, 1946) 70–71.

a. Melitene: a city in Cappadocia.

b. Severans: followers of Severus (ca. 465–538), bishop of Antioch and a prominent Monophysite theologian.

had gone to a neighbor in order to receive Communion. Since my neighbor was in communion with the holy Catholic Church, I immediately ran to stop her. Immediately upon entering my neighbor's house, I found my wife who had just received a portion of the holy Communion. Grabbing her by the throat, I had her spit out the holy portion which I then took and threw down into the mud. Immediately I saw something shining at the very place where the holy Communion fell."

190. JOHN OF SCYTHOPOLIS

Little has come down to us regarding the life of this writer (bishop?) who lived in the early sixth century. A strong defender of the Council of Chalcedon (WEC 3:**137**), he was a fearless adversary of Monophysitism.

CPG 3: nos. 6850ff. * Altaner (1961) 614–15 * Altaner (1966) 508–9 * Bardenhewer (1913) 5:16 * Tixeront 290 * DCB 3:427 * DHGE 27:617–19 * DPAC 2:1577 * EEC 1:446 * EEChr 1:627 * LTK 5:969 * NCE 7:1074 * NCES 7:986 * PEA (1991) 5:1061

190-A. Scholion on Pseudo-Dionysius[†]

Although most of John's works have been lost, there survives his *Scholion on Pseudo-Dionysius*, a series of explanatory notes written after 532 on the works of Dionysius the Pseudo-Areopagite (WEC 4:**185**). In collected form these notes acquired great popularity during the Middle Ages.

III.2. This custom flourishes in Rome[a] where only seven deacons serve at the altar. These, I believe, are called *"selecti"*; others carry out other ministries, this indicating the old age of the bishop; the priests present the bread with the deacons. Such is done wherever deacons are few in number. I believe that this is especially true for Rome where only seven deacons are selected to serve at the altar. Perhaps, however, these seven are selected from among the others by reason of their lives.

4958

EGYPT

191. COSMAS INDICOPLEUSTES

Cosmas Indicopleustes, namely, Comas the "Indian navigator," was an Egyptian merchant, probably from Alexandria, who for business reasons sailed many waters (the Mediterranean, the Red Sea, the Persian Gulf) and visited countries like India and Ceylon. There is reason to believe that Cosmas eventually embraced the monastic life.

[†] Translated from PG 4:135–36.

a. The practice referred to here is that of placing the bread and cup on the altar before the consecratory invocation by the bishop as mentioned in Dionysius's *The Ecclesiastical Hierarchy* (WEC 4:4879).

CPG 3: no. 7468 * Altaner (1961) 624 * Altaner (1966) 517 * Bardenhewer (1908) 555–56 * Bardenhewer (1910) 480–81 * Bardenhewer (1913) 5:95–98 * Steidle 224 * Tixeront 303–4 * CATH 3:226 * CE 4:404–5 * DACL 8:820–49 * DCB 1:692–94 * DPAC 1:793–94 * DTC 3.2:1916–17 * EC 4:684–85 * EEC 1:203 * EEChr 1:295 * LTK 6:393 * NCE 4:359–60 * ODCC 421

E.O. Winstedt, "A Note on Cosmas and the 'Chronicum Paschale,'" JThSt 8 (1906–7) 101–3. * E. Peterson, "Die alexandrinische Liturgie bei Kosmas Indicopleustes," EphL 40 (1932) 56–74.

191-A. Christian Topography[†]

Apparently written over the course of several years and the only work of Cosmas to survive, the twelve books constituting this opus intend to show that the universe is not spherical but rather cuboid, namely, having the same form as the tabernacle of Moses. Those opposing such a view were, in the thinking of Cosmas, nothing less than heretics. Although reflecting the scientific errors of its time, the work provides much geographical data, some obtained from the author's personal experience, others the result of secondhand accounts given by various merchants he met along the way.

4959   V.10. [. . .] Those in Jerusalem apparently rely on what blessed Luke said, namely that the Lord, beginning his work, "was baptized when he was about thirty years old."[1] And so they celebrate his nativity on the Epiphany. What the evangelist and those in Jerusalem say is correct. However, they are not accurate. Certainly the Lord was baptized on his birthday; something both Luke and those in Jerusalem affirm.

4960   V.11. But already in ancient times the Church ordered that twelve days be placed between these two feasts, twelve being the number of the apostles. It did this so that neither feast would be overlooked by celebrating both of them on the same day; thus was instituted the feast of the Epiphany. In like manner the Church ordered that at the time of the Lord's Resurrection a forty day fast is to be observed, a fast akin to that kept by the Lord as he was preparing to struggle against the devil. The Church did this so that we, following the Lord's example, might struggle and imitate him as best we can, thereby sharing in his passion and resurrection although Christ did not fast on the days when these occurred. And so the Church ordained that the Lord's Epiphany should take place twelve days after his nativity.

4961   V.12. Only Christians in Jerusalem, guided by similar yet inexact calculations, celebrate [Christ's birth] on the day of the Epiphany. On the other hand, on Christ's birthday they commemorate David and the apostle

---

[†] Translated from *Cosmas Indicopleustès. Topographie chrétienne*, vol. 2, trans. and ed. W. Wolska-Conus (Paris, 1970) 22–24.
1. Luke 3:23.

James, doing so not because these two illustrious men died on this very day but, as I believe, so that they may not continue to exclude the rest of Christ's kinsmen, whose memory all observe, thereby glorifying God in all things. Amen.

192. *LOUVAIN PAPYRUS*[†]

Located in the Louvain Library (no. 27), this papyrus contains remnants of a sixth-century eucharistic prayer used in the Coptic Church.

L.Th. Lefort, "Coptica lovanensia," Mus 53 (1940) 22–24. * P. Devos, "Un témoin copte de la plus ancienne anaphore en grec," AB 104 (1986) 126. * Jasper 81.

[*Sanctus*]

. . . earth your glory.   4962

[Epiclesis I]

Heaven and earth are full of the glory by which you glorified us   4963
through Jesus Christ, your only-begotten Son, the first-born of all creatures, sitting at the right hand of your majesty in heaven, who will come to judge the living and the dead, whose death we recall as we offer to you this bread and this cup, your creatures. We ask and implore you to send upon them from heaven your Holy Spirit, the Paraclete . . . [to change?] the bread into the Body of Christ, the cup into Christ's Blood of the new covenant.

[Institution Narrative]

And so the Lord, about to be handed over, took bread, gave thanks over   4964
it, blessed it, broke it, and gave it to his disciples and said to them, "Take, eat, for this is my Body, which will be given for you."

Likewise, after the meal he also took the cup, gave thanks over it, and   4965
gave it to them, saying, "Take, drink, for this is my Blood, which will be poured out for many unto the remission [of sins]." [. . .]

193. *MANCHESTER PAPYRUS*[††]

This fragment, dating from the sixth century, comes from an early version of the Alexandrian Anaphora of Saint Mark the Evangelist. The papyrus (no. 465) is found in the John Rylands Library in Manchester, England.

H. Engberding, "Zum Papyrus 465 der John Rylands Library zu Manchester," OC 42 (1958) 68–76.

[†] Translated from Hänggi 140. Text in brackets is added from other sources.
[††] Translated from Hänggi 120–23.

[After the *Sanctus*]

4966   Truly heaven and earth are filled with your glory through Jesus Christ, our Lord, God, and Savior.

[Epiclesis I]

4967   O God, also fill this sacrifice with the blessing that comes from you through your Holy Spirit.

[Institution Narrative]

4968   Because Jesus Christ, our Lord, God, Savior, and highest King, on the night when he handed himself over for our sins and died for all, took bread into his holy, immaculate, and undefiled hands, looked up to you in heaven, up to you, his divine Father. He blessed, sanctified, broke, and gave it to his holy disciples and apostles, saying, "All of you, take and eat from this. This is my Body of the New Testament which is given for many unto the forgiveness of sins. Do this in memory of me." Likewise, after eating he took the cup, gave thanks, and shared it with his disciples and apostles, saying, "All of you, drink from this. This is my Blood which is shed for you and for many and is given for the forgiveness of sins. Do this in memory of me. For as often as you eat this bread and drink this cup, you proclaim my death and resurrection."

[Anamnesis]

4969   O God, all-powerful Father, announcing the death and resurrection of your only begotten Son, our Lord, God, and Savior, and his ascension into heaven and his sitting at your right hand and looking forward to his glorious second coming when he will judge the earth with justice and reward each according to one's merits, whether good or evil, we proclaim your gifts before you.

[Epiclesis II]

4970   We ask and beseech you to send your Holy Spirit upon these gifts which are seen by our eyes, upon this bread and upon this cup, and may the Spirit truly make this bread the Body of Jesus Christ and the cup of the Blood of the new covenant, and of our Lord God and Savior Jesus Christ, our highest king. Amen.

4971   So that they be for all of us who share in them for faith, for moderation, for healing, for joy, for sanctification, for renewal of soul, body and spirit, for fellowship in eternal life, for wisdom and immortality, for [. . .]

[Doxology]

4972   So that in this your holy and honored name may also be glorified, celebrated, and sanctified everywhere . . . for the forgiveness of sins.

Index to Volume Four

Numbers in bold and within parentheses are subhead numbers, which indicate particular authors/documents in this volume. All other numbers refer to marginal paragraph numbers.

Comprehensive Index

The numbers preceding colons refer to volume numbers. Numbers in bold and within parentheses are subhead numbers, which indicate particular authors/documents in the volumes. All other numbers refer to marginal paragraph numbers.

Commodian (3rd century), 1:609–13 (**30**)

Communion, 2:1349 (**67-E-2**)
to apostates, 2:1224
bad Christians receiving, 3:2689
to children, 2:1786, 2293. * 3:2833
not consuming what is received, 2:1296. * 3:3171
as "daily bread," 2:1120–22. * 3:2658
deceased, not given to the, 2:883
dismissal of those not receiving, 2:2470. * 4:4271
dying/Viaticum, to the, 2:1197, 1212, 1224, 1284, 1290, 1435, 1597, 2032–36, 2441. * 3:2770, 2779–80, 2844, 2959, 3125, 3149. * 4:4216, 4237, 4552, 4587, 4609, 4699, 4722, 4732
fasting before, 1:475, 483, 714. * 2:2295, 2312. * 3:2616–17, 3853, 3855, 3876. * 4:4642, 4655, 4694, 4762, 4850, 4944
fruits of, 2:1003, 1157, 1510
the "holy may approach." *See* Communion rite: invitation to receive
layman having a nocturnal emission, 2:2473
married persons and, 1:484. * 2:2466. * 3:3955–56. * 4:4355, 4357, 4363. *See also* married couple: refraining from intercourse
miracles associated with. *See* Eucharist: miracles associated with
monastic order for receiving, 4:4149
monks receiving on Saturday and Sunday, 3:3892
pagans, those who lived with, and were baptized as children, 3:2861
Paschal Vigil and, 3:3181, 3947
prayer after, 2:1650, 1789–90. * 3:3491. * 4:4870
preparation for receiving, 1:766. * 2:1587, 1614, 2145, 2150, 2418. * 3:2654, 3062, 3215, 3492, 3824–25. * 4:4544
prostrating before receiving, 4:4532
receive, not being forced to, 4:4532
receive, obligatory times to, 4:4554

receive, those not to, 2:1270–74, 1281, 1352, 1650. * 3:2734, 3695
received by a catechumen, 2:2462
received outside the liturgy, 4:4957
receiving in the hand, 1:512. * 2:2045, 2159. * 3:3598–3600, 3991
reverence toward. *See* Eucharist, reverence toward
sick, to the, 3:3857. * 4:4350, 4362, 4367, 4732
union with Christ, 2:1484. * 3:2658, 3485
unity of hearts, 3:2693, 3485. * 4:4871
water or bread afterwards, taking, 3:3212
worthy/unworthy, reception of, 1:308. * 2:1236, 1241, 1501, 1518–20. * 3:2612, 2693, 2978. * 4:4157, 4448, 4871, 4942
See also Eucharist: frequency of reception/celebration

Communion rite, 1:244, 300
blessing of the people, 2:2370–71
bread sent to catechumens, 2:2298
cantor singing during, 2:2158
clerics failing to receive, 2:1863–64
cup, misusing, 1:256. * 3:3823
cup of blessing, 2:1489
cup, receiving from, 1:511, 548–65 (**27-E-13**). * 2:1493, 1563, 1589, 1604, 2088, 2160, 2293, 2402. * 3:2691, 2721, 2775, 2933, 2935, 3698, 3823. * 4:4496. *See also* wine, at Eucharist
cup, taking contents to those who are absent, 1:244, 246
disposal of what remains, 2:2454. * 3:3883–88. * 4:4655, 4939
failure to receive, 4:4498
formulas, 1:303, 687, 795. * 2:999, 1092, 1521, 1784–85, 1787–88, 2157. * 3:2712, 2900, 3488–90, 3585–87, 3593–94, 3599, 3697–98, 3822, 3963. * 4:4519, 4622, 4855, 4885, 4950
fraction/breaking of bread, 1:687, 690. * 2:2369, 2439. * 3:3474–80, 3584, 3640. * 4:4519, 4855, 4885
hymns during, 3:2596

hands imposed upon, 2:2396
ordinations and, 2:884. * 4:4206
sharing in decisions, 2:1500
See also faithful
lamps, 2:1386, 2166, 2429. * 3:3567, 3651
lighting of, 2:1284. *See also* Evening
Prayer (*lucernarium*; Vespers)
under Office, Daily (cathedral)—
east; Office, Daily (cathedral)—
west; Office, Daily
(monastic)—east; Office, Daily
(monastic)—west; Office, Daily
(private/early beginnings of)
removed from monastery on Good
Friday, 4:4078
Laodicea, Synod of (between 343 and
381). *See* councils/synods: Laodicea
(between 343 and 381)
lapsed
catechumens as, 2:1454
Cathars and, 2:1449
certificates of reconciliation, 1:530,
533, 537
penance/reconciliation and,
1:528–30 (**27-E-4**), 531 (**27-E-5**), 532
(**27-E-6**), 536 (**27-E-10**), 537–44 (**27-
E-11**), 595–98 (**28**). * 2:1225,
1422–29, 1451, 2221–24, 2228,
2231, 2232. * 3:2959, 3141–42,
3221–22. * 4:4584
reconciliation at time of death, 1:534,
536
Last Supper. *See* Eucharist, Liturgy of:
Last Supper, relationship to
Lateran Baptistery, inscription in,
3:2960 (**117**)
latria, 3:2506
Lawrence, deacon and martyr,
3:2719–22
laying on of hands. *See* hand(s), impo-
sition/laying on of
lectionary, 1:637. * 3:3068, 3115. *
4:4901, 4911, 4915. *See also* gospel
book
lectors. *See* reader(s)/lector(s)
Lent (*Quadragesima*), 3:2881–92,
2905–6 (**114-A-4**), 2913–15 (**114-A-7**),
2920–22 (**114-A-11**). * 4:4295–97,
4439–41 (**168-B-29**)

anniversaries of martyrs during,
4:4683
assemblies during, 2:1933
celebrated once a year, 2:1529
chastity during, observing, 4:4420,
4448
church, those absent from during,
2:1295
church tradition, commended by,
3:2624
churches to observe in same manner, 4:4616
Communion, receiving during,
2:1501
Daily Offices during, 4:4440
date when it begins, 3:2961
Eucharist offered only on Saturdays
and Sundays during, 2:1995
fasting during. *See* fasting: before
the Pasch
feasts during, major, 3:2886
forty days, 4:4296
forty-two days, 3:2921. * 4:4297
length of, 3:3920. * 4:4616
looking forward to, 3:2504
marriages not celebrated during,
2:1998. * 4:4683
monastic practices during, 4:4073,
4075, 4141
Montanists and, 3:3953
as observed in Jerusalem, 2:2182,
2185, 2187
observed in Jerusalem, eight weeks,
2:2178–88
ordinations during, 3:2930
prayer between monastic offices
during, 4:4071–72
prayer during, 3:2905, 3801. * 4:4448
priest not to go to a bath during,
2:2437. * 3:2613
reading of synodal minutes during,
3:2652
representing a toilsome life, 3:2698
scriptural types, 3:2818–21, 2906,
2913–15, 2920–22. * 4:4295
tasks of the people during, 3:3801
tribulation and, present, 3:2567, 2702
washing of feet during, 3:2625
See also "Great Week"

Leo I, Pope (440–61), 3:2823–2900 (**113**). * 4:4020, 4222

Lerida, Synod of (546). *See* councils/synods: Lerida (546)

Lérins, 4:4325

"Let us pray," 2:1499

Letter of Barnabas, 1:421–40 (**24**)

Letter to Diognetus, 1:738–39 (**34**)

levite(s). *See* deacon(s)

Lex supplicandi, lex credendi, 3:3047

Liber diurnus, 4:4196–97 (**162**)

Liber pontificalis, 4:4198–4225 (**163**)

Liberius, Pope (352–66), 2:1193

Libya, 1:255. * 2:1356, 1458. * 3:3920

Licinius, 2:1313, 2072, 2075

Linus, Pope (ca. 70), 4:4198

litania septiformis, 4:4268, 4502–3

litaniae majores. See Rogation Days

litaniae minores. See Rogation Days

liturgy and good order, 1:196

Liturgy of the Eucharist. *See* Eucharist, Liturgy of

Liturgy of the Hours. *See* Office, Daily (cathedral)—east; Office, Daily (cathedral)—west; Office, Daily (monastic)—east; Office, Daily (monastic)—west; Office, Daily (private/early beginnings of)

Liturgy of the Word. *See* Word, Liturgy of

Lord's Day. *See* Sunday/Lord's Day

Lord's Prayer. *See* Our Father

Louvain Papyrus, 4:4962–65 (**192**)

lucernarium, lighting of lamps, 2:2307, 2326. * 3:3831–32. *See also* Evening Prayer (*lucernarium*; Vespers) *under* Office, Daily (cathedral)—east; Office, Daily (cathedral)—west; Office, Daily (monastic)—east; Office, Daily (monastic)—west; Office, Daily (private/early beginnings of)

Lucis conditor, 4:4474

Lupercalia, 3:2935

Lyons II, Synod of (between 518 and 523). *See* councils/synods: Lyons II (between 518 and 523)

Lyons III, Synod of (between 567 and 570). *See* councils/synods: Lyons III (between 567 and 570)

Lyons IV, Synod of (583). *See* councils/synods: Lyons IV (583)

Macedonians, 2:1460. * 3:3244. * 4:4854

Mâcon I, Synod of (581/583). *See* councils/synods: Mâcon I (581/583)

Mâcon II, Synod of (585). *See* councils/synods: Mâcon II (585)

Macrina, 2:1389–93 (**69-B**)

Magi, 2:1186, 1492. * 3:2830

Magna et mirabilia, 4:4474

Magnus Felix Ennodius. *See* Ennodius, Magnus Felix

Mainz Baptistery, inscription in, 4:4661 (**177**)

Mamertus, bishop of Vienne, 4:4313–15, 4495

Manchester Papyrus, 4:4966–72 (**193**)

Manichaeans, 2:1350, 2400. * 3:2605, 2628, 3961. * 4:4196, 4214, 4216, 4230, 4692

manna, 2:993, 1068, 1076, 1091. * 3:2915

mantile, 3:3112

mantle, 3:2808

manutergium, 3:3112

Mark the Deacon (after 420), 3:3975–80 (**146**)

marriage/wedding
adulterous woman, to an, 4:4716
bishop and, 1:223. * 2:1387. * 3:2806
Christians attending celebrations of, 2:1999
cleric attending an illicit, 2:2472
clerics not to attend, 3:3162. * 4:4559
couple spending first night as virgins, 3:3120
doorkeepers and, 4:4716
Eustathius, prohibited by, 3:3219
father crowning couple, 2:1387
hands extended at, 3:2806
heretic, not to a, 2:1963, 1981
Lent, not during, 2:1998
person engaged to another, to a, 2:1196
poem celebrating, 3:2805–6
presbyter and, 2:1439. * 3:3120
readers and, 4:4716
relative, not to a, 4:4360
sacraments, 3:2543

times for prayer, 4:4042, 4105, 4195, 4489

Office, Daily (private/early beginnings of)

Evening Prayer (*lucernarium*), 1:521, 726, 821. * 2:903, 1619, 1821–30. * 3:3831, 3870, 3966

Morning Prayer, 1:482, 521, 713, 719, 821, 844. * 2:903, 906, 1619, 1821, 1831–38. * 3:3872

nocturnal prayer (vigils), 1:482–83, 498, 522, 726, 845. * 2:903. * 3:3871

prayer at cockcrow, 1:728. * 2:1821. * 3:3866

prayer at ninth hour, 1:478, 520, 725, 843. * 2:1821. * 3:3869

prayer at sixth hour, 1:478, 520, 724, 821, 843. * 2:1821. * 3:3868

prayer at third hour, 1:478, 520, 723, 843. * 2:1821. * 3:3867

times for prayer, 1:478, 520–22, 821, 842–43. * 2:903, 936, 1137, 1619, 1821

oil

blessing of, 1:576, 627, 674, 847. * 2:1324, 1396, 2118, 2127, 2243, 2287, 2356, 2372, 2383–84. * 3:3620, 3702–3, 3809, 3931. * 4:4162, 4889–91, 4952

bringing as a gift, 2:1858

drinking of, 2:2471

offering at a pagan sanctuary or a Jewish temple, 2:1901

stealing, 2:1902

symbolism/meaning of, 2:1627, 1811, 2118. * 3:3622. * 4:4894, 4955

See also chrism/myron

Optatus of Milevis (d. ca. 400), 2:868–73 (**49**)

Orange I, Synod of (441). *See* councils/synods: Orange I (441)

orarion, 2:1974–75. * 4:4744

oratory, 3:2598. * 4:4145, 4556. *See also* church(es): place for prayer

orders

distinctions among, 2:1853–55

imposition of hands. *See* hand(s), imposition/laying on of

seven in Church, 2:2426. * 3:3038–46 (**119**)

stages of, 2:1198–99, 1214, 1421. * 3:2794, 2826. * 4:4212, 4215, 4753

ordinations

an adulterous wife, of a man with, 2:1440

age of candidates, 2:2257. * 4:4605

approval by bishop, 2:1179. * 3:2823. * 4:4909

approval by clergy and people, 4:4774

approval by copresbyters and people, 3:3072. * 4:4215

bishop not to receive anything for, 4:4597

of clergy only, 1:636. * 3:3043

confessors and, 2:1805, 2251

day(s) for, 3:2826–27, 2930, 3664. * 4:4192–93, 4196

delay required for the recently baptized, 2:1957. * 4:4678

examination, after an, 2:884

faithful and clergy to be present at, 4:4206

by false bishops, 3:2848

of farmers, 4:4610

fasting before, 3:2827. * 4:4774

gift of healing, of those with, 2:2259

gospel book on altar during, 4:4952–53

hearers, not to be present at, 2:1958

heretical, 1:451. * 4:4196

impediments to, 2:1867–69, 1922, 1931. * 4:4605, 4722

kiss of peace during, 4:4904

obtained by money, 2:1874. * 3:3378. * 4:4756, 4772

ordain, those not to, 4:4230

penitents and, 4:4560, 4605

prayers of the people, requesting, 2:1500

of priests and deacons returning to the Church, 1:581

signing with cross, 4:4904

who sinned before baptism, of those, 2:1430

sinners present at, 4:4931

slaves and, 2:2253. * 3:2823. * 4:4610

poor
  care for, 1:246, 447. * 2:1479–80, 1812.
    * 3:2890, 3829. * 4:4435
  Christ in, recognizing, 3:2865
  Eucharist and, 2:1493. * 4:4435
  Eucharist, present at, 2:1618
  goods of the deceased given to,
    2:1848–49
  meals to assist, 2:2083, 2326
  portion of gifts given to, 4:4196,
    4242, 4568, 4849
  served by deacons, 2:1629, 2248
  wine given to, 2:2436
  See also almsgiving; fasting/fasts:
    almsgiving and
pope(s)
  funerals of, 4:4227
  name mentioned at Eucharist,
    4:4017, 4191, 4193, 4595
Possidius (ca. 370–ca. 440), 3:2735 (**99**)
Postumius Eutenion, Epigraph of,
  2:1215 (**57-D**)
praesidentes, 2:1964
prayer(s)
  adding Alleluia to, 1:480
  almsgiving and fasting, related to,
    3:2813, 2866, 2869, 2871
  angels sharing in, 1:820
  "at the genuflection," 2:2393
  authorized forms of, 2:885. * 3:2748,
    2750
  bishop, improvised by, 1:635. *
    2:2254
  catechumens, heretics, or the unbap-
    tized, not with, 2:1821
  Christ and, 2:885. * 3:2675, 3514
  Christians and, 2:899
  Church, for the, 2:2391–92
  in church, special rooms for, 3:2800.
    * 4:4524
  churches, in town's, 3:2795
  communal, 2:1539–40
  connected in proper order, 4:4728
  Constantine and, 2:2080
  deceased, for the. *See* deceased:
    praying for
  deposed cleric, not with a, 2:1866
  diversity in, 3:3241
  energumens, not with, 2:1907

excommunicated, not with the,
  2:1865
Father and, 2:885. * 3:2675
forgiveness of sins and, 3:2594–95,
  2651
for fruitfulness, 2:2390
heretics, not with, 2:1881, 1897, 1983.
  * 3:3105
at home, 1:479. * 2:903, 936, 1475,
  1511, 1539, 1821, 2307, 2309–10. *
  3:3211
Jewish times for, 2:1915
Jews, not with, 2:1897
law of, 3:3047
at marriage, 3:2806
married, not in houses of the, 3:3219
martyrs, not for the, 3:2668
meals, at. *See* meal(s): prayer at
for others, 2:1929
parts of, 1:829. * 2:1148–51
people, for all, 1:516
people, for the, 2:2394
places for, 1:826. * 2:1137–43, 1821. *
  3:2811. *See also* oratory
priest and, 2:1596. * 3:2626, 3047–48,
  3730, 3733
private, 3:3205
in public, 2:1475
for rulers, 1:202, 446–47. * 2:1509,
  1537, 1615
schismatics, not with, 2:1983
seven times a day, 4:4195
of supplication, 3:3047–48
in synagogue, 2:1915
three times a day, 2:1649
types of, 3:2636–40
unity in, 2:1539–40
widows and, 3:3763, 3768–70
without ceasing, 2:2415
women and, 2:1147
See also orientation for prayer
preaching. *See* Word, Liturgy of:
  preaching
preface. *See* Eucharistic Prayer/
  anaphora: preface
presbyter(s)/priest(s)
  acolytes, not to make, 3:2926
  anointing, assisting at, 3:2583
  apostles, representing the, 1:757, 759